The CAR Book

1997 Edition

The Definitive Buyer's Guide to Car Safety, Fuel Economy, Maintenance, and Much More

by Jack Gillis

with
Scott Beatty
and
Karen Fierst

foreword by
Clarence M. Ditlow
Center for Auto Safety

HarperPerennial
A Division of HarperCollins Publishers

ents

Each year, cars get more complex and so does collecting and analyzing the information you need to make a smart and safe choice. Nevertheless, this 17th edition of *The Car Book* was the smoothest ever thanks to the organizational abilities of coauthor Scott Beatty and computer graphics maven Amy Burch. These two professionals, under tight deadlines and a dynamically changing auto marketplace, were able to collect, analyze, and package more information than we've ever before presented. Scott's ability to manage and come to closure on a variety of complex projects and Amy's ability to make graphical sense out of it all are the main ingredients in successfully providing this important information to the American car buyer. They were able to accomplish this increasingly complex feat with the able and competent assistance of Ashley Cheng, researcher/writer extraordinaire. As has been the case for 12 years, the experience and institutional knowledge of *Car Book* veteran Karen Fierst was the icing on the cake.

Many, many talented professionals enabled Scott, Amy, and Ashley to successfully accomplish this effort. Ailis Aaron (University of North Carolina) and Michael Kott (Goucher College) were truly amazing interns whose performance was both competent and professional. Amy Shock and Kaz Hickock, as always, unselfishly contributed their considerable organizational and proofing skills.

This year's edition would not have been possible without essential contributions from many other talented individuals. Most significant was Clarence Ditlow and the staff of the Center for Auto Safety. In addition, John Noettl, president of Vehicle Support Systems; legal expert Phil Nowicki; Carolyn Gorman of the Insurance Information Institute; Martha Casey, U.S. EPA; Pete Packer, Runzheimer International; Kim Hazelbaker, Highway Loss Data Institute; Debbie Bindeman, Insurance Services Organization; and Susan Cole, design maven, all had a part in our being able to complete this project. Very special thanks go to my friend and terrific literary agent, Stuart Krichevsky.

As always, the most important factor in being able to bring this information to the American car buyer for 17 years is the encouragement, support, and love from my brilliant and beautiful wife, Marilyn Mohrman–Gillis.

J.G.

As Always,

for Marilyn &
Katie, John, Brian, and Brennan

ISSN: 0893-1208
ISBN: 0-06-273436-9
97 98 99 CW 5 4 3 2

Cover design © Gillis and Associates.
Photo credits: Acura; Ford Motor Company; General Motors Corporation; General Motors Corporation, Chevrolet Division; Hyundai.
Cover Photo of Jack Gillis: Donna Cantor-MacLean

Contents

Foreword

by Clarence M. Ditlow, Executive Director, Center for Auto Safety

The 1997 edition of *The Car Book* comes out in an historic year. As we celebrate the 30th anniversary of the passage of the National Traffic and Motor Vehicle Safety Act, we also mourn the three millionth traffic fatality. But without the passage of the Vehicle Highway Safety Acts in 1966, an additional 1.2 million people would have died in crashes. Instead, the highway death rate per 100 million vehicle miles traveled dropped from 5.5 in 1965 to 1.7 in 1996. Every American today who rides in safer cars on safer highways has Ralph Nader to thank. His courage not only brought about passage of these acts, but also led to a personal apology from GM for putting detectives on his trail to find out why a young lawyer from Connecticut was more interested in saving lives than in making money.

Consumers cannot take safer cars or highways for granted. The auto companies are no more interested in saving lives than they were before Ralph Nader wrote *Unsafe At Any Speed* in 1965. Auto companies always have and always will put profits ahead of lives. Major safety improvements come because the government requires them, not because the auto companies volunteer them. In his latest work, *Driving In Reverse*, Mr. Nader points out traffic deaths reached a low of 39,250 in 1992, but reversed their 30-year downward trend and climbed back to 41,465 in 1995 as a result of needed safety measures being blocked or rolled back.

Washington is under the influence of industry lobbyists with fat expense accounts who are paid to stop new safety standards and keep the public unaware of hazards in their cars and on the road. Among their corporate victories and consumer losses in 1996 were the killing of standards needed to control vehicle rollover, which results in 9,000 deaths each year, and exemptions for up to 4.75 million commercial trucks weighing between 10,000 and 26,000 pounds from most current safety regulations, including safety inspections. The next delivery truck that hits you due to bad brakes may be courtesy of your U.S. representative, who voted for this exemption without any public hearings. Auto company lobbyists and lawyers block recall after recall because they come out of corporate profits.

The worst example of an auto company putting corporate profits ahead of human lives is General Motors in its refusal to recall its 1973–87 C/K pickups which have killed over 1,400 people in fire crashes — 20 times as many as the infamous Ford Pinto. Tragically, many victims of GM's pickups are people in other cars who have the misfortune of striking a GM pickup at speeds as low as 20 mph. In 1984, a GM vice president called a $23 safety shield for the pickups "a probable easy fix," but GM refused to install it even though the company made $13 billion in profits on these trucks. Even today, GM's pickups are the most lethal weapon on the road with over 100 more people killed in fire crashes since December 1994, when U.S. Transportation Secretary Federico Pena let GM off the hook without a recall. Upset by this decision, families of GM pickup victims have launched a national petition campaign to recall the trucks, which will be on the road crashing and burning into the 21st century.

Citizen action is often the last barrier against auto abuses. When the car companies successfully lobbied in 1981 to force the government to stop publishing *The Car Book*, the Center for Auto Safety (CAS) helped Jack Gillis rescue it. When auto companies started to launder repurchased lemons and resell them to unsuspecting buyers as low-mileage cream puffs, Consumers for Auto Reliability and Safety led a drive to expose this fraud and to get the Federal Trade Commission to take action.

The Car Book is needed now more than ever to help consumers make sound buying decisions that can save their lives and protect their pocketbooks. Everyone can tell whether there are airbags in cars, but not all airbags are created equal. Some can injure children in low-speed impacts while others protect them—but there is no way for consumers to tell the difference. You can't tell whether a car has 5-mph bumpers or low rollover rates just by looking at the car or asking the dealer. Who would have thought the passenger in a luxurious 1997 Olds Aurora would be 3 times more likely to be seriously injured in a 35-mph frontal barrier crash than the passenger in the less expensive 1997 Ford Crown Victoria. What you learn from *The Car Book 1997* can save your life. That's why we work hard to get such vital information to consumers—CAS cares about you and your family.

Editor's Note: For more information on the state of auto safety today, you may order Ralph Nader's *Driving In Reverse*. Send a check for $10 payable to: Center for Study of Responsive Law, Box 19367, Washington DC 20036.

Safety sells. For 17 years, this has been *The Car Book*'s message to the auto companies and they are finally coming around. Dual airbags can now be found on every single vehicle in *The '97 Car Book* except the Ford Aerostar. Anti-lock brakes are touted as a standard feature on many vehicles and side airbags are now available on several 1997 models. Also, the National Highway Traffic Safety Administration will start performing new crash tests to determine occupant protection in side crashes. You can be assured these results will be found in future editions of *The Car Book*.

In short, cars are now safer and built better than ever before! By making a smart choice, there is no reason why your car shouldn't last over 100,000 miles. These improvements are not limited to quality and safety. As you go car shopping, you'll notice changes in the showroom as well. Dealerships are learning that if they want your business, you need to be treated with respect. The smarter dealers are replacing sleazy sales techniques with informed personnel and fixed prices. By taking the time to use the charts and tips in *The Car Book*, you can easily maintain the "upper hand" in the showroom and leave with a smart, safe, and economical choice.

Safety and sales techniques aren't the only frontier to be broken for 1997. The future of travel has arrived with the introduction of GM's EV1, the first-ever electric car to be available on the market. The EV1 represents a dramatic change in direction for auto companies towards more efficient and environment-friendly automotive technology.

With all of these changes, it is more important than ever to be able to sift through advertising claims to find out what is *truly* the safest and most eco-

nomical new car. To make it easy to do, we've completely updated the 17th edition of *The Car Book* with more data and information than ever!

Your continued use of the information in *The Car Book* dramatically influences how car companies build their cars. In fact, in the last 25 years, even though the number of vehicles on the road has more than doubled, the fatality rate has dropped by an astonishing 66 percent! Now, however, with increased speed limits, we may see that decline slow down. Buying for safety is one way to protect you and your loved ones.

And the new technologies work! Most of us have heard about in-

credible accidents where the *passengers* simply walked away—all because of a simple bag that inflated to cushion the impact.

Clearly, car makers are listening more carefully to consumers. Our buying habits have the ability to continue to change the practices of one of the nation's most powerful industries.

How does today's consumer buy safety? Many consumers mistakenly believe that handling and performance are the key elements in the safety of a car. While an extremely unresponsive car could cause an accident, most new cars meet basic handling requirements. In fact, many people actually feel uncomfortable driving high performance cars be-

---

Missing Safety: Minivans

Minivans, pickups, and sport utility vehicles are the fastest growing vehicle types. Minivans are convenient because few station wagons are large enough to hold growing families. If you are interested in one of these vehicles, be warned: They do not have to meet all of the safety standards applied to passenger cars. Even though thousands of Americans buy these vehicles for family and non-commercial use, the National Highway Traffic Safety Administration has been slow to require safety improvements.

Minivans, pickups and sport utility vehicles were finally required to provide roofs strong enough to support the vehicle's weight if it rolls over and contain reinforcement beams in the doors to protect occupants in side crashes in 1995. By 1999, these vehicles must meet the same side impact standards as passenger cars. However, these vehicles are not yet required to have bumpers that meet any kind of strength requirements. Most importantly, these vehicles are not yet required to provide any automatic crash protection, in the form of either automatic belts or airbags. Automatic crash protection requirements are currently being phased in, but will not become standard until 1998.

Because of their popularity with car buyers, we've included minivans in *The Car Book*. We also compile *The Truck, Van and 4x4 Book*, which provides hundreds of facts about these popular vehicles, including sport utility vehicles.

cause the highly responsive steering, acceleration, and suspension systems can be difficult to get used to. But the main reason handling is over-rated as a safety measure is that automobile collisions are, by nature, accidents. Once they've begun, they are beyond human capacity to prevent, no matter how well your car handles. So the key to protecting yourself is to purchase a car that offers a high degree of crash protection.

As our concern for safety has influenced car makers' attitudes, so have our demands for quality. The result—U.S. cars in the '90s continue to be better built than those of the '80s. And, because we're demanding that companies stand behind their products, we're seeing better warranties, too. Since *The Car Book* began comparing warranties in 1986, a number of car makers have told us that they've been forced to improve their warranties now that consumers can tell the difference.

Consumers are learning that they can get better-performing and safer cars by buying the ones with good safety records, low maintenance costs, long warranties, and insurance discounts. Use "The Buying Guide" to compare cars, and read the chapters to learn more about each model. This year "The Buying Guide" is loaded with new and important information. You'll find everything from crash test results to an ease-of-parking rating.

The "safety" chapter rates crash safety, describes your options for protection, and is where you'll find the detailed crash test results, tips on avoiding unsafe child seats, and a review of safety belt and child seat laws.

The "fuel economy" chapter uncovers the money-saving gas misers and offers advice on some products to avoid.

The "maintenance" chapter allows you to compare those inevitable repair costs *before* you buy. You'll also find advice on dealing with mechanics and how to make your car last longer.

The "warranties" chapter offers a critical comparison of the new warranties and lets you know the best and worst before you get into trouble down the road. If you do have trouble, we'll let you know which companies offer roadside assistance and we'll tip you off to secret warranties.

The "insurance" chapter will help you save money on an expense that is often forgotten in the showroom.

Because most of us can't tell one tire from another, we've included the "tire" chapter to help you select the best.

The "complaint" chapter provides a road map to resolving inevitable problems quickly and efficiently. We provide consumers with their only access to the hundreds of thousands of car complaints on file with the U.S. government. Thanks to the efforts of the Center for Auto Safety,

we continue to include this otherwise unavailable information.

Review the "showroom strategies" chapter for tips on getting the best price—for many of us one of the hardest and most distasteful aspects of car buying.

Finally, our "ratings" chapter provides a detailed review of each of the 1997 cars. These pages provide, at a glance, an overview of all the criteria you need to make a good choice. Here, you'll be able to quickly assess key features and see how the car you're interested in stacks up against its competition so you can make sure your selection is the best car for you. Car prices have more than doubled since 1980, so we've also included the percent of *dealer* markup to help you negotiate the very best price.

The information in *The Car Book* is based on data collected and developed by our staff, the U.S. Department of Transportation, and the Center for Auto Safety. With all of this data in hand, you'll find some great choices for 1997. *The Car Book* will guide you through the trade-offs, promises, facts, and myths to the car that will best meet your needs.

—Jack Gillis

Questions, Comments

If you have any suggestions, questions, or comments, you may e-mail us at JAGillis@aol.com

BUYING GUIDE

The Buying Guide provides an overall comparison of the 1997 cars in terms of safety, fuel economy, maintenance, insurance costs, warranty, complaint ratings, and other key items. The cars are arranged by size class based on weight.

Based on these comparisons, we have developed *The Car Book*'s Best Bets for 1997—these vehicles rated tops when all of these categories were considered. In general, there are five key steps to buying a car.

1 Narrow your choice down to a particular class of car–sports, station wagon, minivan, sedan, large luxury, or economy car. These are general classifications and some cars may fit into more than one category. In most cases, *The Car Book* presents the vehicles by size class.

2 Determine what features are really important to you. Most buyers consider safety on the top of their list, which is why "The Safety Chapter" is right up front in *The Car Book*. Airbags, power options, ABS, and the number of passengers, as well as "hidden" elements such as maintenance and insurance costs, should be considered at this stage in your selection process.

3 Find 3 or 4 cars that meet the needs you outlined above *and* your pocketbook. It's important not to narrow your choice down to one car because then you lose all your bargaining power in the showroom. In fact, because cars today are more similar than dissimilar, it's not hard to keep three or four choices in mind. On the car rating pages in the back of the book, we suggest some competitive choices for your consideration. For example, if you are interested in the Honda Accord, you should also consider the Toyota Camry and Ford Taurus.

4 Make sure you take a good, long test drive. The biggest car buying mistake most of us make is to overlook those nagging problems that seem to surface only after we've brought the car home. Spend at least an hour driving the car without a dealer in the car. If a dealership won't allow you to test drive a car without a dealer, go somewhere else. This includes time on the highway, parking, taking the car in and out of your driveway or garage, sitting in the back seat, and using the trunk or storage area. Whatever you do, *don't talk price until you're ready to buy!*

5 This is the stage most of us dread–negotiating the price. While price negotiation is a car buying tradition, a few car makers and dealers are trying to break tradition by offering so called "no-haggle pricing." Since they're still in the minority and, because it's almost impossible to establish true competition between dealers as individuals, we offer a new means to avoid negotiating altogether by using the non-profit CarBargains pricing service.

Now that you have a quick guide to the steps necessary in making a good choice, use the tables that follow to quickly review the new cars and the pages in the back for a detailed critique of each model. See the "showroom strategies" chapter for more details on getting the best price.

The "Buying Guide" will allow you to quickly compare the 1997 models.

To fully understand these summary charts, it is important to read the appropriate section of the book. You will note that here and throughout the book, some of the charts contain empty boxes. This indicates that data were unavailable at the time of printing.

Here's how to understand what's included in "The Buying Guide."

Page Reference: The page in the back of the book where you'll find all the details for this car.

Overall Rating: This is the "bottom line." It shows how well this car stacks up on a scale of 1 to 10 when compared to all others on the market. The overall rating considers safety, maintenance, fuel economy, warranty, insurance costs and complaints. Due to the importance of crash tests, cars with no results as of our publication date cannot be given an overall rating. More recent results may be available from the Auto Safety Hotline at 1-800-424-9393 (see page 75).

Car Book Crash Test Rating: This indicates how well the car performed in the U.S. Government's 35-mph frontal crash test program. We have analyzed and compared all of the crash test results to date and have given them a rating from *very good* to *very poor*. These ratings allow you to compare the test results of one car with another. A car with a poor rating may have done well according to government injury ratings, but still be among the worst performers of cars being offered in 1997.

Airbags: Hidden in the steering wheel hub and the passenger side of the dashboard, airbags inflate instantly in frontal crashes to prevent the occupant from violently hitting the dashboard, windshield, or steering wheel.

Daytime Running Lights: Daytime running lights are a low-cost method of reducing your chances of being in a crash by increasing the visibility of your vehicle. Studies have shown that daytime running lights can reduce crashes by up to 40 percent. Here we indicate if daytime running lights are *standard*, *optional* or *none*.

Fuel Economy: This is the EPA-rated fuel economy for city and highway driving measured in miles per gallon. A single model may have a number of fuel economy ratings because of different engine and transmission options. We have included the figure for what is expected to be the most popular model.

Repair Rating: This rating is based on nine typical repairs after the warranty expires and the cost of following the manufacturer's preventive maintenance schedule during the warranty period.

Warranty Rating: This is an overall assessment of the car's war-

---

TIP

Best Bets for 1997

Based on information in the *Buying Guide*, this list shows the highest-rated cars in each of the size categories. Ratings are based on expected performance in seven important categories (crash tests, safety features, fuel economy, repair costs, warranties, insurance costs, and complaints), with the heaviest emphasis on crash test performance.

Subcompact
Nissan Sentra (9)
Suzuki Swift (8)
Subaru Impreza (8)

Compact
Buick Skylark (10)
Oldsmobile Achieva (10)
Pontiac Grand Am (9)
Geo Prizm (8)
Mazda MX-6 (8)
Toyota Corolla (8)

Intermediate
Audi A4 (10)
Volkswagen Passat (10)
Ford Taurus (9)
Mercury Sable (9)
Olds Cutlass Supreme (9)
Volvo 850 (9)

Large
Audi A6 (10)
Infiniti J30 (10)
Cadillac Seville (10)
Lincoln Mark VII (10)
Lincoln Town Car (10)
Oldsmobile 88 (9)

Minivan
Honda Odyssey (7)
Nissan Quest (7)
Isuzu Oasis (6)
Chrys. Town and Country (5)
Dodge Caravan (5)
Plymouth Voyager (5)

ranty when compared to all other warranties. The rating considers the important features of each warranty, with emphasis on the length of the basic and powertrain warranties.

Complaint Index: This rating is based on the number of complaints about that car on file at the U.S. Department of Transportation. The complaint index will give you a general idea of experiences others have had with models which are essentially unchanged for this model year. All-new vehicles for 1997 are given an *average* complaint rating as it is unknown how many complaints they will receive.

Insurance Cost: Many automobile insurance companies use ratings based on the car's accident and occupant injury history to determine whether or not the insurance premium of a car should be *discounted* or *surcharged*. (Your insurance company may or may not participate in a rating program.) If the car is likely to receive neither, we label it *regular*.

Parking Index: This rating of *very easy* to *very hard* is an indicator of how much difficulty you will typically have parking. If you regularly parallel park, or find yourself maneuvering in and out of tight spaces, this can be an important factor in your choice of a car. This rating is based on the car's wheelbase, length, and turning circle.

Typical Price: This price range will give you a general idea of the "sticker," or asking price of a car. It is based on the lowest to highest retail price of the various models, and it does not include options or the discount that you should be able to negotiate using a service such as CarBargains (see pg. 90).

Typical Operating Costs

As you can probably guess, buying a 1997 luxury car rather than an economy model will cost considerably more—not only due to higher initial cost, but also higher fuel, maintenance, tire replacement, insurance and finance costs. Also, higher priced cars often decrease faster in value.

The table below shows the *annual* operating costs for fifteen popular cars. Costs include operating expenses (fuel, oil, maintenance and tires) and ownership expenses (insurance, depreciation, financing, taxes, and licensing) and are based on keeping the car for 3 years, driving 20,000 miles per year.

Vehicle	Operating	Ownership	Total
Mercedes 320	$2,340	$15,872	$18,212
Cadillac DeVille	$2,790	$11,806	$14,596
Olds Aurora	$2,490	$10,776	$13,266
Buick Riviera	$2,410	$9,535	$11,945
Ford Crown Victoria LX	$2,420	$8,278	$10,698
Buick LeSabre Ltd.	$2,250	$8,330	$10,580
Nissan Maxima GXE	$2,260	$7,469	$9,729
Dodge Intrepid	$2,390	$6,782	$9,172
Ford Taurus	$2,170	$6,705	$8,875
Chevy Lumina	$2,170	$6,255	$8,425
Toyota Camry DX	$2,050	$6,255	$8,305
Honda Accord DX	$2,090	$6,427	$7,517
Dodge/Plymouth Neon	$1,800	$5,552	$7,352
Saturn SC/SL/SW	$1,790	$5,389	$7,179
Geo Metro	$1,560	$5,265	$6,825

Annual Costs*

Source: Runzheimer International, Rochester, Wisconsin.
*Costs are based on four-door models, with automatic transmission, power steering, power disc brakes, air conditioning, tinted glass, AM-FM stereo, body side molding, cruise control, left-hand remote control mirror, rear window defogger, pulse windshield wipers, ABS, dual air bags and tilt-steering.

Car	See Pg.	Overall Rating[1] Poor ⇔ Good	Crash Test	Airbags	Daytime Running Lights	Fuel Economy	Repair Rating
Subcompact							
Dodge/Plym. Neon	132		Average	Dual	None	29/39	Very Good
Ford Aspire	136		Average	Dual	None	34/42	Average
Ford Escort	139		No Test	Dual	None	26/37	Good
GM EV1	145		No Test	Dual	Standard		
Geo Metro	146		Good	Dual	None	44/49	Poor
Honda Civic	149		Very Good	Dual	None	29/35	Average
Honda del Sol	150		No Test	Dual	None	28/35	Poor
Hyundai Accent	153		Average	Dual	None	28/37	Very Good
Kia Sephia	161		No Test	Dual	None	28/34	Average
Mazda Miata	170		Average	Dual	None	23/29	Average
Mazda Protege	174		No Test	Dual	None	30/37	Average
Mercury Tracer	181		No Test	Dual	None	28/37	Good
Mitsubishi Mirage	186		No Test	Dual	None	33/40	Poor
Nissan Sentra	191		Good	Dual	None	29/39	Average
Saturn SC	207		No Test	Dual	Standard	28/40	Good
Saturn SL/SW	208		No Test	Dual	Standard	28/40	Good
Subaru Impreza	209		Good	Dual	None	23/30	Good
Suzuki Esteem	212		No Test	Dual	Standard	31/37	Poor
Suzuki Swift	213		Good	Dual	Standard	39/43	Poor
Toyota Paseo	218		No Test	Dual	None	31/37	Poor
Toyota Tercel	220		Average	Dual	None	32/39	Poor
Compact							
Acura Integra	101		Average	Dual	None	25/31	Very Poor
BMW 3-Series	106		Good	Dual	None	23/31	Very Poor
BMW Z3	107		No Test	Dual	None	23/31	Very Poor
Buick Skylark	113		Good	Dual	None	22/32	Good
Chevrolet Cavalier	120		Average	Dual	Standard	25/37	Average
Chrysler Sebring	128		Very Good	Dual	None	22/31	Very Good
Eagle Talon	133		Good	Dual	None	22/33	Good
Ford Contour	137		Good	Dual	None	24/33	Good
Ford Probe	141		Very Good	Dual	None	26/33	Poor
Geo Prizm	147		Good	Dual	None	30/34	Poor
Honda Prelude	152		No Test	Dual	None	22/26	Poor

[1]Due to the importance of crash tests, cars with no crash test results as of publication date cannot be given an overall rating.

The CAR Book

Warranty	Complaint Rating	Insurance Rating	Parking Index	Typical Price $	Overall Rating* Poor ⇔ Good	See Pg.	Car
							Subcompact
Very Poor	Very Poor	Regular	Easy	$10-13,000		132	Dodge/Plym. Neon
Very Poor	Average	Surcharge	Very Easy	$9-10,500		136	Ford Aspire
Very Poor	Average	Regular	Very Easy	$11-13,000		139	Ford Escort
	Average	Regular	Very Easy	$33-37,000		145	GM EV1
Very Poor	Poor	Surcharge	Very Easy	$8-10,000		146	Geo Metro
Very Poor	Average	Surcharge	Very Easy	$10-15,000		149	Honda Civic
Very Poor	Average	Surcharge	Very Easy	$15-20,000		150	Honda del Sol
Poor	Poor	Surcharge	Very Easy	$8-10,500		153	Hyundai Accent
Average	Poor	Surcharge	Very Easy	$9-10,000		161	Kia Sephia
Poor	Good	Regular	Very Easy	$18-19,000[2]		170	Mazda Miata
Poor	Poor	Surcharge	Very Easy	$12-15,000[2]		174	Mazda Protege
Very Poor	Average	Regular	Very Easy	$11-13,000		181	Mercury Tracer
Average	Average	Regular	Very Easy	$10-12,500		186	Mitsubishi Mirage
Poor	Good	Surcharge	Very Easy	$11-16,000		191	Nissan Sentra
Poor	Average	Regular	Easy	$12-14,000		207	Saturn SC
Poor	Average	Discount	Easy	$10-13,000		208	Saturn SL/SW
Poor	Good	Regular	Very Easy	$13-14,000		209	Subaru Impreza
Very Poor	Average	Regular	Very Easy	$11-14,500[2]		212	Suzuki Esteem
Very Poor	Very Good	Surcharge	Very Easy	$8-9,000[2]		213	Suzuki Swift
Very Poor	Very Good	Surcharge	Very Easy	$13-17,000		218	Toyota Paseo
Very Poor	Very Good	Surcharge	Very Easy	$11-12,500		220	Toyota Tercel
							Compact
Average	Average	Surcharge	Easy	$16-17,000[2]		101	Acura Integra
Good	Average	Surcharge	Easy	$21-22,000		106	BMW 3-Series
Good	Average	Regular	Very Easy	$29-30,000		107	BMW Z3
Very Poor	Very Good	Discount	Easy	$16-17,000		113	Buick Skylark
Very Poor	Good	Regular	Easy	$10-15,000		120	Chevrolet Cavalier
Very Poor	Poor	Regular	Average	$15-22,000		128	Chrysler Sebring
Very Poor	Very Poor	Surcharge	Average	$14-20,000		133	Eagle Talon
Very Poor	Poor	Regular	Easy	$13-17,000		137	Ford Contour
Very Poor	Good	Surcharge	Easy	$14-17,000		141	Ford Probe
Very Poor	Good	Surcharge	Very Easy	$12-13,500		147	Geo Prizm
Subry Poor	Average	Regular	Easy	$19-24,000[2]		152	Honda Prelude

[1]Due to the importance of crash tests, cars with no crash test results as of publication date cannot be given an overall rating.
[2]Based on 1996 prices.

Car	See Pg.	Overall Rating[1] (Poor ⇔ Good)	Crash Test	Airbags	Daytime Running Lights	Fuel Economy	Repair Rating
Compact (cont.)							
Hyundai Elantra	154		Average	Dual	None	24/32	Very Good
Hyundai Tiburon	156		No Test	Dual	None	22/30	Very Good
Mazda 626	169		Good	Dual	None	26/34	Average
Mazda MX-6	173		Very Good	Dual	None	26/34	Average
Mercury Mystique	179		Good	Dual	None	24/33	Good
Mitsubishi Eclipse	184		Good	Dual	None	23/31	Good
Mitsubishi Galant	185		No Test	Dual	None	23/30	Average
Oldsmobile Achieva	193		Good	Dual	Standard	23/33	Good
Pontiac Grand Am	201		Good	Dual	Standard	23/33	Good
Pontiac Sunfire	203		Average	Dual	Standard	25/37	Average
Subaru Legacy	210		Very Good	Dual	None	23/30	Good
Toyota Celica	216		No Test	Dual	None	29/35	Poor
Toyota Corolla	217		Good	Dual	None	31/35	Poor
VW Golf/Jetta	221		Average	Dual	Standard	40/49	Good
Intermediate							
Audi A4	104		Very Good	Dual	None	20/29	Average
Buick Century	108		No Test	Dual	Standard	20/29	Good
Buick Regal	111		No Test	Dual	None	20/29	Good
Cadillac Catera	114		No Test	Dual	Standard	18/25	Average
Chevrolet Camaro	119		Very Good	Dual	Standard	19/30	Good
Chrysler Cirrus	125		No Test	Dual	None	20/30	Good
Chrysler Concorde	126		Very Good	Dual	None	17/26	Very Good
Dodge Intrepid	131		Very Good	Dual	None	19/27	Very Good
Eagle Vision	134		Very Good	Dual	None	19/27	Very Good
Ford Mustang	140		Good[2]	Dual	None	20/30	Average
Ford Taurus	142		Very Good	Dual	Optional	20/28	Very Good
Honda Accord	148		Average	Dual	None	25/31	Poor
Hyundai Sonata	155		Average	Dual	None	21/28	Very Good
Mazda Millenia	171		Very Good	Dual	None	20/28	Poor
Merc.-Benz C-Class	175		Good	Dual	None	23/30	Poor
Mercury Sable	180		Very Good	Dual	None	20/28	Very Good
Nissan 240SX	187		Average	Dual	None	22/28	Average
Nissan Altima	188		Average	Dual	None	24/30	Good

[1] Due to the importance of crash tests, cars with no crash test results as of publication date cannot be given an overall rating.
[2] Data given for coupe; convertible overall is 2, Crash test is Very Good.

The **CAR** Book

Warranty	Complaint Rating	Insurance Rating	Parking Index	Typical Price $	Overall Rating[1] Poor ⇔ Good	See Pg.	Car
							Compact (cont.)
Poor	Average	Surcharge	Very Easy	$11-14,000	(mark left, ~2/10)	154	Hyundai Elantra
Poor	Average	Regular	Very Easy	$13-16,000	(no rating)	156	Hyundai Tiburon
Poor	Average	Surcharge	Easy	$15-23,000[2]	(mark ~5/10)	169	Mazda 626
Poor	Average	Surcharge	Easy	$18-19,000[2]	(mark ~5/10)	173	Mazda MX-6
Very Poor	Very Poor	Regular	Easy	$14-17,000	(mark ~3/10)	179	Mercury Mystique
Average	Very Poor	Surcharge	Easy	$13-14,000	(mark left, ~2/10)	184	Mitsubishi Eclipse
Average	Very Poor	Surcharge	Easy	$15-16,000	(no rating)	185	Mitsubishi Galant
Poor	Very Good	Regular	Easy	$15-17,500[2]	(mark ~8/10)	193	Oldsmobile Achieva
Very Poor	Good	Regular	Easy	$15-16,000	(mark ~3/10)	201	Pontiac Grand Am
Very Poor	Good	Regular	Average	$12-13,000	(mark ~5/10)	203	Pontiac Sunfire
Poor	Poor	Regular	Easy	$16-17,000	(mark ~6/10)	210	Subaru Legacy
Very Poor	Good	Surcharge	Very Easy	$17-21,000	(no rating)	216	Toyota Celica
Very Poor	Very Good	Surcharge	Very Easy	$13-15,000	(mark ~7/10)	217	Toyota Corolla
Very Good	Poor	Regular	Very Easy	$13-17,000	(mark ~8/10)	221	VW Golf/Jetta
							Intermediate
Very Good	Average	Regular	Easy	$23-28,000	(mark far right, ~9/10)	104	Audi A4
Very Poor	Average	Regular	Average	$16-19,500[2]	(no rating)	108	Buick Century
Very Poor	Average	Regular	Average	$20-26,000	(no rating)	111	Buick Regal
Good	Average	Regular	Easy	$29-30,000	(no rating)	114	Cadillac Catera
Very Poor	Poor	Surcharge	Hard	$16-23,000	(mark left, ~2/10)	119	Chevrolet Camaro
Very Poor	Very Poor	Regular	Average	$18-19,000	(no rating)	125	Chrysler Cirrus
Very Poor	Very Poor	Discount	Average	$20-21,000	(mark ~4/10)	126	Chrysler Concorde
Very Poor	Poor	Discount	Average	$19-23,000	(mark ~5/10)	131	Dodge Intrepid
Very Poor	Poor	Discount	Average	$20-24,500	(mark ~5/10)	134	Eagle Vision
Very Poor	Poor	Surcharge	Average	$15-24,500	(mark far left, ~1/10)	140	Ford Mustang
Very Poor	Average	Discount	Average	$18-23,500	(mark ~9/10)	142	Ford Taurus
Very Poor	Good	Discount	Easy	$15-21,000	(mark left, ~2/10)	148	Honda Accord
Poor	Very Poor	Surcharge	Easy	$14-18,500	(mark far left, ~1/10)	155	Hyundai Sonata
Poor	Average	Regular	Average	$26-32,000[2]	(mark ~5/10)	171	Mazda Millenia
Average	Average	Discount	Easy	$30-35,500	(mark ~5/10)	175	Merc.-Benz C-Class
Very Poor	Average	Discount	Average	$20-23,000	(mark ~8/10)	180	Mercury Sable
Poor	Very Poor	Surcharge	Very Easy	$18-24,500	(mark far left, ~1/10)	187	Nissan 240SX
Poor	Very Good	Regular	Average	$15-21,000	(mark ~8/10)	188	Nissan Altima

[1] Due to the importance of crash tests, cars with no crash test results as of publication date cannot be given an overall rating.
[2] Based on 1996 prices.

Car	See Pg.	Overall Rating[1] Poor ⇔ Good	Crash Test	Airbags	Daytime Running Lights	Fuel Economy	Repair Rating
Intermediate (cont.)							
Nissan Maxima	189	(bar ~2/10)	Average	Dual	None	22/27	Poor
Olds. Cut. Supreme	196	(bar ~8/10)	Average	Dual	Standard	17/26	Average
Oldsmobile Cutlass	195	(no bar)	No Test	Dual	Standard	20/29	Good
Pontiac Firebird	200	(bar ~1/10)	Very Good	Dual	Standard	19/30	Average
Pontiac Grand Prix	202	(no bar)	No Test	Dual	Standard	20/29	Average
Saab 900	205	(bar ~5/10)	Good	Dual	Standard	21/29	Average
Saab 9000	206	(bar ~6/10)	Good	Dual	Standard	20/29	Average
Toyota Avalon	214	(bar ~2/10)	Very Good	Dual	None	21/31	Poor
Toyota Camry	215	(no bar)	No Test	Dual	None	23/31	Poor
Volkswagen Passat	222	(bar ~8/10)	Good	Dual	Standard	38/47	Average
Volvo 850	223	(bar ~7/10)	Good	Dual	Standard	20/29	Poor
Large							
Acura CL	100	(no bar)	No Test	Dual	None	23/29	Very Poor
Acura RL	102	(no bar)	No Test	Dual	None	19/25	Very Poor
Acura TL	103	(bar ~1/10)	Good	Dual	None	20/25	Very Poor
Audi A6	105	(no bar)	Very Good	Dual	None	19/25	Average
Buick LeSabre	109	(bar ~5/10)	Good	Dual	Standard	19/30	Good
Buick Park Avenue	110	(no bar)	No Test	Dual	Standard	19/28	Average
Buick Riviera	112	(no bar)	No Test	Dual	Standard	19/28	Average
Cadillac DeVille	115	(no bar)	No Test	Dual	Standard	17/26	Average
Cadillac Eldorado	116	(no bar)	No Test	Dual	Standard	17/26	Average
Cadillac Seville	117	(bar ~8/10)	Good	Dual	Standard	17/26	Average
Chevrolet Lumina	121	(bar ~2/10)	Very Good	Dual	Standard	20/29	Good
Chevrolet Malibu	122	(no bar)	No Test	Dual	Standard	20/29	Good
Chevrolet Monte Carlo	123	(bar ~1/10)	Good	Dual	Standard	20/29	Good
Chrysler LHS	127	(bar ~1/10)	Good	Dual	None	17/26	Very Good
Ford Crown Victoria	138	(bar ~5/10)	Very Good	Dual	None	17/25	Average
Ford Thunderbird	143	(bar ~4/10)	Very Good	Dual	None	18/26	Average
Infiniti I30	157	(bar ~5/10)	Average	Dual	None	21/28	Poor
Infiniti J30	158	(bar ~8/10)	Good	Dual	None	18/23	Average
Infiniti Q45	159	(no bar)	No Test	Dual	None	18/24	Poor
Lexus ES300	162	(no bar)	No Test	Dual	None	19/26	Average
Lexus GS300	163	(bar ~7/10)	Average	Dual	None	18/24	Average

[1] Due to the importance of crash tests, cars with no crash test results as of publication date cannot be given an overall rating.

The CAR Book

Warranty	Complaint Rating	Insurance Rating	Parking Index	Typical Price $	Overall Rating[1] Poor ⇔ Good	See Pg.	Car
							Intermediate (cont.)
Poor	Good	Regular	Easy	$21-27,000		189	Nissan Maxima
Poor	Very Good	Discount	Average	$19-21,500		196	Olds. Cut. Supreme
Poor	Average	Regular	Average	$16-18,000		195	Oldsmobile Cutlass
Very Poor	Poor	Surcharge	Average	$17-18,000		200	Pontiac Firebird
Very Poor	Average	Regular	Average	$18-19,000		202	Pontiac Grand Prix
Good	Very Poor	Discount	Easy	$24-35,000		205	Saab 900
Good	Poor	Regular	Easy	$31-41,500		206	Saab 9000
Very Poor	Average	Regular	Average	$23-27,500		214	Toyota Avalon
Very Poor	Average	Regular	Easy	$16-22,500		215	Toyota Camry
Very Good	Average	Surcharge	Easy	$19-22,500		222	Volkswagen Passat
Very Good	Average	Discount	Easy	$26-29,000		223	Volvo 850
							Large
Average	Average	Regular	Very Easy	$22-24,000		100	Acura CL
Average	Average	Regular	Average	$40-41,000[2]		102	Acura RL
Average	Average	Regular	Average	$27-28,000[2]		103	Acura TL
Very Good	Very Good	Regular	Easy	$33-35,000		105	Audi A6
Very Poor	Good	Discount	Hard	$22-26,000		109	Buick LeSabre
Very Poor	Average	Regular	Hard	$30-36,000		110	Buick Park Avenue
Very Poor	Very Poor	Discount	Hard	$30-31,000		112	Buick Riviera
Good	Very Good	Discount	Hard	$36-37,000		115	Cadillac DeVille
Good	Average	Discount	Hard	$37-42,000		116	Cadillac Eldorado
Good	Good	Discount	Hard	$40-46,000		117	Cadillac Seville
Very Poor	Very Poor	Discount	Average	$17-19,000		121	Chevrolet Lumina
Very Poor	Average	Regular	Average	$16-18,000		122	Chevrolet Malibu
Very Poor	Poor	Regular	Average	$17-20,000		123	Chevrolet Monte Carlo
Very Poor	Poor	Discount	Average	$30-31,000		127	Chrysler LHS
Very Poor	Poor	Discount	Hard	$22-24,000		138	Ford Crown Victoria
Very Poor	Average	Discount	Average	$18-19,000		143	Ford Thunderbird
Very Good	Average	Regular	Easy	$28-32,500		157	Infiniti I30
Very Good	Very Good	Regular	Average	$35-36,000		158	Infiniti J30
Very Good	Average	Regular	Average	$47-50,000		159	Infiniti Q45
Good	Average	Regular	Average	$30-31,000		162	Lexus ES300
Good	Very Good	Regular	Average	$46-47,000		163	Lexus GS300

[1]Due to the importance of crash tests, cars with no crash test results as of publication date cannot be given an overall rating.
[2]Based on 1996 prices.

Car	See Pg.	Overall Rating[1] Poor ⇔ Good	Crash Test	Airbags	Daytime Running Lights	Fuel Economy	Repair Rating
Large (cont.)							
Lexus LS400	164		No Test	Dual	None	19/25	Poor
Lexus SC300/400	165		No Test	Dual	None	18/24	Average
Lincoln Continental	166		No Test	Dual	None	17/25	Average
Lincoln Mark VIII	167		Very Good	Dual	None	18/26	Average
Lincoln Town Car	168		Very Good	Dual	None	17/25	Good
Merc.-Benz E-Class	176		No Test	Dual	None	26/33	Very Poor
Mercury Cougar	177		Very Good	Dual	None	18/26	Average
Merc. Grand Marquis	178		Very Good	Dual	None	17/25	Good
Mitsubishi Diamante	183		No Test	Dual	None	18/26	Very Poor
Oldsmobile 88	192		Good	Dual	Standard	19/29	Good
Oldsmobile Aurora	194		Average	Dual	Standard	17/26	Average
Pontiac Bonneville	199		Good	Dual	Standard	19/28	Good
Subaru SVX	211		No Test	Dual	None	17/24	Good
Volvo 900 Series	224		No Test	Dual	Standard	18/26	Poor
Minivan							
Chevrolet Astro	118		Poor	Dual	Standard	16/21	Good
Chevrolet Venture	124		No Test	Dual	Standard	18/25	Very Good
Chrysler T&C	129		Average	Dual	None	17/24	Very Good
Dodge Caravan	130		Average	Dual	None	20/25	Very Good
Ford Aerostar	135		Average	Driver	None	17/23	Good
Ford Windstar	144		Very Good	Dual	None	17/25	Good
Honda Odyssey	151		Good	Dual	None	21/26	Poor
Isuzu Oasis	160		Good	Dual	None	21/26	Poor
Mazda MPV	172		Very Good	Dual	None	16/21	Poor
Mercury Villager	182		Good	Dual	None	17/23	Good
Nissan Quest	190		Good	Dual	None	17/23	Good
Olds. Silhouette	197		No Test	Dual	Standard	18/25	Very Good
Plymouth Voyager	198		Average	Dual	None	20/25	Very Good
Pontiac Trans Sport	204		No Test	Dual	Standard	18/25	Very Good
Toyota Previa	219		Average	Dual	None	18/22	Poor

[1]Due to the importance of crash tests, cars with no crash test results as of publication date cannot be given an overall rating.

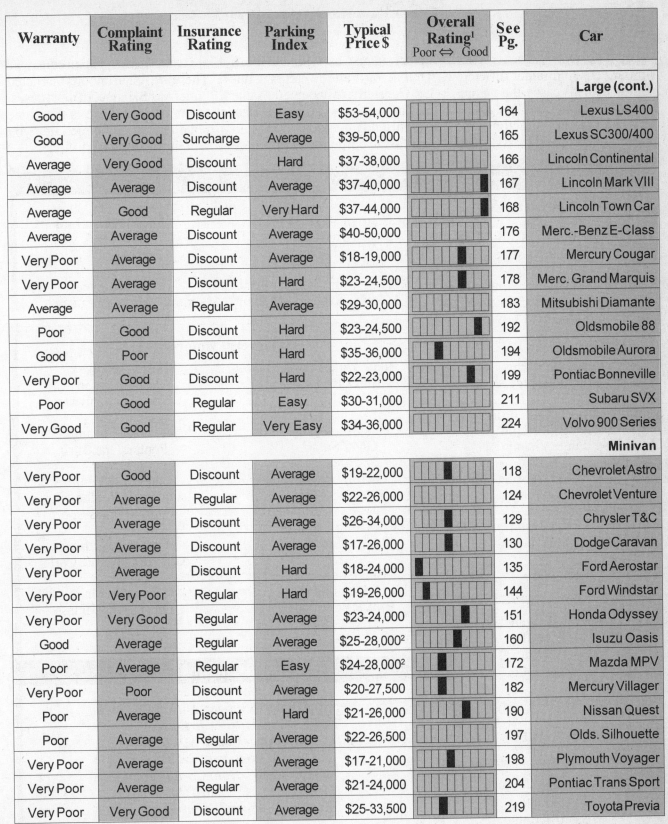

Warranty	Complaint Rating	Insurance Rating	Parking Index	Typical Price $	Overall Rating[1] Poor ⇔ Good	See Pg.	Car
							Large (cont.)
Good	Very Good	Discount	Easy	$53-54,000		164	Lexus LS400
Good	Very Good	Surcharge	Average	$39-50,000		165	Lexus SC300/400
Average	Very Good	Discount	Hard	$37-38,000		166	Lincoln Continental
Average	Average	Discount	Average	$37-40,000		167	Lincoln Mark VIII
Average	Good	Regular	Very Hard	$37-44,000		168	Lincoln Town Car
Average	Average	Discount	Average	$40-50,000		176	Merc.-Benz E-Class
Very Poor	Average	Discount	Average	$18-19,000		177	Mercury Cougar
Very Poor	Average	Discount	Hard	$23-24,500		178	Merc. Grand Marquis
Average	Average	Regular	Average	$29-30,000		183	Mitsubishi Diamante
Poor	Good	Discount	Hard	$23-24,500		192	Oldsmobile 88
Good	Poor	Discount	Hard	$35-36,000		194	Oldsmobile Aurora
Very Poor	Good	Discount	Hard	$22-23,000		199	Pontiac Bonneville
Poor	Good	Regular	Easy	$30-31,000		211	Subaru SVX
Very Good	Good	Regular	Very Easy	$34-36,000		224	Volvo 900 Series
							Minivan
Very Poor	Good	Discount	Average	$19-22,000		118	Chevrolet Astro
Very Poor	Average	Regular	Average	$22-26,000		124	Chevrolet Venture
Very Poor	Average	Discount	Average	$26-34,000		129	Chrysler T&C
Very Poor	Average	Discount	Average	$17-26,000		130	Dodge Caravan
Very Poor	Average	Discount	Hard	$18-24,000		135	Ford Aerostar
Very Poor	Very Poor	Regular	Hard	$19-26,000		144	Ford Windstar
Very Poor	Very Good	Regular	Average	$23-24,000		151	Honda Odyssey
Good	Average	Regular	Average	$25-28,000[2]		160	Isuzu Oasis
Poor	Average	Regular	Easy	$24-28,000[2]		172	Mazda MPV
Very Poor	Poor	Discount	Average	$20-27,500		182	Mercury Villager
Poor	Average	Discount	Hard	$21-26,000		190	Nissan Quest
Poor	Average	Regular	Average	$22-26,500		197	Olds. Silhouette
Very Poor	Average	Discount	Average	$17-21,000		198	Plymouth Voyager
Very Poor	Average	Regular	Average	$21-24,000		204	Pontiac Trans Sport
Very Poor	Very Good	Discount	Average	$25-33,500		219	Toyota Previa

[1]Due to the importance of crash tests, cars with no crash test results as of publication date cannot be given an overall rating.
[2]Based on 1996 prices.

Corporate Twins

"Corporate twin" is a term for similar cars sold under different names. In many cases, the cars are identical, such as the Dodge and Plymouth Neon. Sometimes the difference is in body style and luxury items, as with the Ford Thunderbird and Mercury Cougar. Generally, twins have the same mechanics, engine, drive train, size, weight, and internal workings. In addition to corporate twins, there are what we call "Asian cousins." These are Asian imports marketed under a U.S. name. In most cases, the main difference is the name plate and price; sometimes you will find differences in style.

Twins

Chrysler

Dodge Caravan
Plymouth Voyager

Chrysler Town & Country
Dodge Grand Caravan
Plymouth Grand Voyager

Chrysler Cirrus
Dodge Stratus
Plymouth Breeze

Chrysler Concorde
Dodge Intrepid
Eagle Vision

Chrysler Sebring
Dodge Avenger

Dodge Neon
Plymouth Neon

Volkswagen
VW Golf
VW Jetta

Toyota
Lexus ES 300
Toyota Camry

Nissan
Infiniti I30
Nissan Maxima

Ford

Ford Crown Victoria
Lincoln Town Car
Mercury Grand Marquis

Ford Thunderbird
Lincoln Mark VIII
Mercury Cougar

Ford Taurus
Mercury Sable

Ford Contour
Mercury Mystique

Ford Escort
Mercury Tracer

General Motors

Buick Park Avenue
Buick Riviera
Oldsmobile Aurora

Buick Skylark
Oldsmobile Achieva
Pontiac Grand Am

Chevrolet Astro
GMC Safari

Buick Century
Pontiac Grand Prix

Chevrolet Cavalier
Pontiac Sunfire

Chevrolet Venture
Oldsmobile Silhouette
Pontiac Trans Sport

Chevrolet Camaro
Pontiac Firebird

Chevrolet Lumina
Chevrolet Monte Carlo

Buick LeSabre
Oldsmobile 88
Pontiac Bonneville

Chevrolet Malibu
Oldsmobile Cutlass

Asian Cousins

Chry. Sebring/Dodge Avenger-*Mitsubishi Galant*
Eagle Talon-*Mitsubishi Eclipse*
Ford Probe-*Mazda MX-6*
Geo Metro-*Suzuki Swift*
Geo Prizm-*Toyota Corolla*
Honda Odyssey-*Isuzu Oasis*
Mercury Villager-*Nissan Quest*

SAFETY

For most of us, safety is one of the most important factors in choosing a new car, yet it is also one of the most difficult items to evaluate. To give the greatest possible occupant protection, a car should offer a wide variety of safety features including dual airbags and 4-wheel anti-lock brakes (ABS). Dual airbags are now fairly common, but 4-wheel ABS is still not standard on all models.

Another key factor in occupant protection is how well the car performs in a crash test. In order for you to use the U. S. Department of Transportation crash tests to evaluate your new car choices, we have analyzed and presented the results in this chapter. The crash tests measure how well each vehicle protects the driver and front-seat passenger in a frontal crash.

Also described in this chapter are current options and safety features available in this year's models. In addition, we've included a state-by-state list of the safety belt laws and a detailed discussion of an important, and too often over-looked, safety feature—the child safety seat.

Crash Test Program: In 1979, the U.S. Department of Transportation began a crash test program to compare the occupant protection of cars. These crash tests show significant differences in the abilities of various automobiles to protect belted occupants in frontal crashes.

In the test, an automobile is sent into a concrete barrier at 35-mph, causing an impact which is similar to that of two identical cars crashing head on at 35-mph. The car contains electronically monitored dummies in the driver and passenger seats. This electronic data is analyzed to measure the impact of such a collision on a human being.

The government releases this data in an incomplete and confusing array of numbers that are difficult to understand and use in comparing cars.

We have analyzed the data and presented the results using *The Car Book* Crash Test Index. This Index provides an overall means of comparing the results.

The following tables allow you to compare the crash test performances of today's cars.

It is best to compare the results within weight class, such as compacts to compacts. Do not compare cars with differing weights. For example, a subcompact that is rated "Good" may not be as safe as a large car with the same rating.

The results evaluate performance in frontal crashes only, which account for about 50 percent of auto-related deaths and serious injuries. Even though the tested car may have airbags, the dummies are also belted.

We rate the crash test results of each car relative to all of the cars ever crash tested. This method of rating gives you a better idea of the true top performers among the '97 models and identifies those cars which have substantial room to improve their occupant protection.

The Car Book wants to stimulate competition and that's what this new rating program is intended to do. You, the buyer, now know which are the truly best performers. Manufacturers who have chosen to build better performing cars will likely be rewarded with your decision to purchase their models.

1997 cars missing from this list have not been tested at the time of printing or may not have been selected by the government for testing.

Crash Tests: How the Cars Are Rated

A car's ability to protect you in a crash depends on its ability to absorb the force of impact rather than transfer it to you, the occupant. This is a function of the car's size, weight and, most importantly, design. Crash tests measure how much of the crash force is transferred to the head, chest, and thighs of the occupants in a 35-mph crash into a barrier.

The cars on the following pages are listed by weight class, then alphabetically by manufacturer. The first column provides *The Car Book's* overall Crash Test Index, a number which describes all the forces measured by the test. Lower index numbers are better. The Index is best used to compare cars within the same size and weight class.

The second column provides an overall rating of *Very Good*, *Good*, *Average*, *Poor*, or *Very Poor*. These results reflect the car's performance in relation to all other models ever tested. These ratings let you compare, at a glance, the overall performance of the cars you'll find in the showroom this year.

The next two columns indicate the likelihood of each occupant sustaining a life-threatening injury, based on the dummies' head and chest scores. Lower percentages mean a lower likelihood of being seriously injured. This information is taken directly from government analysis of the crash test results.

The last two columns indicate how the dummies' legs fared. Legs labeled *Poor* did not meet the government's standards. Those that did meet the standards are rated *Average*, *Good*, and *Very Good*, reflecting performance relative to all other cars ever tested.

The leg injury ratings are not weighted as heavily in determining overall performance.

The following pages indicate how this year's cars can be expected to perform in the tests. They are included here only when the automobile design has not changed enough to dramatically alter results. Cars that were tested with less crash protection than is standard on the 1997 model are noted. It is expected that with more crash protection, the current version of these models should produce similar or better results.

"Corporate twins" that are structurally the same, such as the Dodge Caravan and Plymouth Voyager, can be expected to perform similarly.

Crash test results may vary due to differences in the way cars are manufactured, in how models are equipped, and in test conditions. There is no absolute guarantee that a car which passed the test will adequately protect you in an accident. Keep in mind that some two-door models may not perform exactly like their four-door counterparts.

Crash Test Performance: The Best

Here is a list of the best crash test performers among the 1997 cars for which crash test information is available. Lower Crash Test Index numbers indicate better performance. See the following tables for more results.

Subcompact
Honda Civic 4 dr. (2113)
Honda Civic 2 dr. (2344)
Nissan Sentra 4 dr. (2842)
Subaru Impreza 4 dr. (2931)
Geo Metro 4 dr. (3080)
Suzuki Swift 4 dr. (3080)

Large
Ford Thunderbird (1632)
Lincoln Mark VIII (1632)
Mercury Cougar (1632)
Ford Crown Victoria (1678)
Mercury Grand Marquis (1678)
Lincoln Town Car (2103)
Audi A6 (2143)
Chevrolet Lumina (2173)

Compact
Chrysler Sebring (1760)
Dodge Avenger (1760)
Ford Probe (2026)
Mazda MX-6 (2026)
Subaru Legacy (2526)

Minivans
Ford Windstar (1911)
Mazda MPV (2405)
Honda Odyssey (2889)
Isuzu Oasis (2889)
Mercury Villager (3248)
Nissan Quest (3248)

Intermediate
Chev. Camaro (1705)
Pontiac Firebird (1705)
Ford Mustang (1916)
Mazda Millenia (2085)
Toyota Avalon (2196)
Ford Taurus (2294)

Mercury Sable (2294)
Chrysler Concorde (2323)
Dodge Intrepid (2323)
Eagle Vision (2323)
Audi A4 (2385)

Crash Test Performance	Injury Index	Car Book Rating	Likelihood of Life Threatening Injury		Leg Injury Rating	
			Driver	Passenger	Driver	Passenger
Subcompact						
Dodge/Plymouth Neon 4dr.*	3461	Average	19%	18%	Moderate	Moderate
Ford Aspire 4dr.	3473	Average	16%	19%	Moderate	Moderate
Geo Metro 4dr.	3080	Good	15%	16%	Moderate	Good
Honda Civic 2dr.	2344	Vry. Gd.	11%	12%	Good	Moderate
Honda Civic 4dr.	2113	Vry. Gd.	12%	10%	Good	Vry. Gd.
Hyundai Accent 4dr.	4145	Average	29%	19%	Good	Good
Mazda Miata 2dr. Convertible	4053	Average	20%	23%	Moderate	Moderate
Mazda Protégé 4dr.	—	—	29%	—	Good	Moderate
Nissan Sentra 4dr.	2842	Good	16%	16%	Vry. Gd.	Good
Subaru Impreza 4dr.	2931	Good	15%	17%	Vry. Gd.	Good
Suzuki Swift (Metro) 4dr.	3080	Good	15%	16%	Moderate	Good
Toyota Tercel 4dr.	3705	Average	24%	17%	Good	Moderate
Compact						
Acura Integra 4dr.	3543	Average	16%	21%	Moderate	Good
BMW 3-Series 4dr.	3366	Good	19%	17%	Moderate	Good
Buick Skylark (Gr. Am) 4dr.*	2949	Good	14%	15%	Moderate	Moderate
Chevrolet Cavalier 4dr.*	3841	Average	22%	21%	Moderate	Good
Chrys. Sebring (Avenger) 2dr.*	1760	Vry. Gd.	9%	6%	Moderate	Moderate
Dodge Avenger 2dr.*	1760	Vry. Gd.	9%	6%	Moderate	Moderate
Eagle Talon (Eclipse) 2dr.	3013	Good	18%	13%	Moderate	Moderate
Ford Contour 4dr.	2940	Good	10%	20%	Good	Moderate
Ford Probe 2dr.	2026	Vry. Gd.	5%	12%	Moderate	Moderate
Geo Prizm (Corolla) 4dr.	2846	Good	16%	13%	Moderate	Good
Hyundai Elantra 4dr.	4467	Average	21%	29%	Moderate	Moderate

*A version of this vehicle is scheduled to be tested later this year. Results are expected to be equal or better.

HOW TO READ THE CHARTS:

| 1234 | **Injury Index**

The overall numerical injury rating for front seat occupants in a frontal crash. *Lower numbers mean better performance.*

| Very Good | **Car Book Rating**

How the vehicle compares among all government test results to date. The range includes very good, good, average, poor and very poor.

| 00% | **Likelihood of Life Threatening Injury**

The chance of life threatening injury to the driver/passenger in a frontal 35 mph crash. *Lower percentages mean better performance.*

| Good | **Leg Injury Rating**

Injury rating for driver and passenger legs in a frontal crash, when compared to all government test results to date.

Crash Test Performance	Injury Index	Car Book Rating	Likelihood of Life Threatening Injury		Leg Injury Rating	
			Driver	Passenger	Driver	Passenger
Compact (cont.)						
Mazda 626 4dr.	2728	Good	17%	9%	Moderate	Moderate
Mazda MX-6 (Probe) 2dr.	2026	Vry. Gd.	5%	12%	Moderate	Moderate
Mercury Mystique (Contour) 4dr.	2940	Good	10%	20%	Good	Moderate
Mitsubishi Eclipse 2dr.	3013	Good	18%	13%	Moderate	Moderate
Mitsubishi Galant 4dr.	—	—	—	16%	Moderate	Good
Olds Achieva (Grand Am) 4dr.*	2949	Good	14%	15%	Moderate	Moderate
Pontiac Grand Am 4dr.*	2949	Good	14%	15%	Moderate	Moderate
Pontiac Sunfire (Cavalier) 4dr.*	3841	Average	22%	21%	Moderate	Good
Subaru Legacy 4dr.	2526	Vry. Gd.	12%	15%	Good	Vry. Gd.
Toyota Corolla 4dr.	2846	Good	16%	13%	Moderate	Good
Volkswagen Golf/Jetta 4dr.*	3940	Average	21%	22%	Moderate	Moderate
Intermediate						
Audi A4 4dr.	2385	Vry. Gd.	14%	9%	Moderate	Moderate
Chevrolet Camaro 2dr.	1705	Vry. Gd.	8%	9%	Good	Vry. Gd.
Chrysler Cirrus (Stratus) 4dr.	—	—	30%	—	Moderate	Moderate
Chrysler Concorde (Intrepid) 4dr.[2]	2323	Vry. Gd.	9%	12%	Moderate	Moderate
Dodge Intrepid 4dr.[2]	2323	Vry. Gd.	9%	12%	Moderate	Moderate
Dodge Stratus 4dr.	—	—	30%	—	Moderate	Moderate
Eagle Vision (Intrepid) 4dr.[2]	2323	Vry. Gd.	9%	12%	Moderate	Moderate
Ford Mustang Convertible	1916	Vry. Gd.	9%	8%	Moderate	Moderate
Ford Mustang 2dr.	2758	Good	12%	15%	Moderate	Moderate
Ford Taurus 4dr.	2294	Vry. Gd.	12%	11%	Good	Good
Honda Accord 4dr.*	3832	Average	18%	26%	Moderate	Vry. Gd.
Hyundai Sonata 4dr.*	4034	Average	25%	20%	Moderate	Good

*A version of this vehicle is scheduled to be tested later this year. Results are expected to be equal or better.

HOW TO READ THE CHARTS:

1234 **Injury Index**
The overall numerical injury rating for front seat occupants in a frontal crash. *Lower numbers mean better performance.*

Very Good **Car Book Rating**
How the vehicle compares among all government test results to date. The range includes very good, good, average, poor and very poor.

00% **Likelihood of Life Threatening Injury**
The chance of life threatening injury to the driver/passenger in a frontal 35 mph crash. *Lower percentages mean better performance.*

Good **Leg Injury Rating**
Injury rating for driver and passenger legs in a frontal crash, when compared to all government test results to date.

Crash Test Performance	Injury Index	Car Book Rating	Likelihood of Life Threatening Injury		Leg Injury Rating	
			Driver	Passenger	Driver	Passenger
Intermediate (cont.)						
Mazda Millenia 4dr.	2085	Vry. Gd.	11%	8%	Moderate	Moderate
Mercedes-Benz C-Class 4dr.	3420	Good	18%	19%	Moderate	Good
Mercury Sable (Taurus) 4dr.	2294	Vry. Gd.	11%	11%	Good	Good
Nissan 240SX 2dr.	3669	Average	28%	15%	Vry. Gd.	Vry. Gd.
Nissan Altima 4dr.	3444	Average	18%	21%	Good	Good
Nissan Maxima 4dr.	3741	Average	18%	25%	Good	Good
Olds Cut. Supr. (Gr. Prix) 2dr.	3481	Average	15%	22%	Moderate	Moderate
Plymouth Breeze (Stratus) 4dr	—	—	30%	—	Moderate	Moderate
Pontiac Firebird (Camaro)	1705	Vry. Gd.	8%	9%	Good	Vry. Gd.
Saab 900 4dr.	2868	Good	15%	15%	Moderate	Good
Saab 9000 4dr.[1]	2736	Good	12%	17%	Good	Vry. Gd.
Toyota Avalon 4dr.	2196	Vry. Gd.	13%	11%	Vry. Gd.	Good
Volkswagen Passat 4dr.	3232	Good	19%	18%	Vry. Gd.	Good
Volvo 850 4dr.	2939	Good	10%	20%	Moderate	Good
Large						
Acura TL 4dr.	3017	Good	17%	15%	Moderate	Vry. Gd.
Audi A6 4dr.	2143	Vry. Gd.	11%	10%	Moderate	Good
Buick LeSabre (Bonneville) 4dr.*	3334	Good	10%	24%	Moderate	Moderate
Cadillac Seville 4dr.[1]	3031	Good	13%	19%	Good	Good
Chevrolet Lumina 4dr.	2173	Vry. Gd.	9%	13%	Good	Good
Chevrolet Monte Carlo 2dr.	3049	Good	16%	17%	Good	Good
Chrysler LHS (New Yorker) 4dr.	3107	Good	20%	13%	Good	Good
Ford Crown Victoria 4dr.	1678	Vry. Gd.	8%	8%	Good	Good
Ford Thunderbird 2dr.	1632	Vry. Gd.	8%	7%	Moderate	Good
Infiniti (Maxima) I30 4dr.	3741	Average	18%	25%	Good	Good
Infiniti J30 4dr.	3361	Good	18%	17%	Moderate	Moderate
Lexus GS300 4dr.	4025	Average	23%	23%	Good	Moderate
Lincoln Mark VIII (T-Bird) 2dr.	1632	Vry. Gd.	8%	7%	Moderate	Good
Lincoln Town Car 4dr.	2103	Vry. Gd.	12%	8%	Moderate	Good
Mercury Cougar (T-Bird) 2dr.	1632	Vry. Gd.	8%	7%	Moderate	Good
Merc. Gr. Marquis (Cr. Vic.) 4dr.	1678	Vry. Gd.	8%	8%	Good	Good

*A version of this vehicle is scheduled to be tested later this year. Results are expected to be equal or better.

Crash Test Performance	Injury Index	Car Book Rating	Likelihood of Life Threatening Injury		Leg Injury Rating	
			Driver	Passenger	Driver	Passenger
Large (cont.)						
Oldsmobile 88 (Bonneville) 4dr.*	3334	Good	10%	24%	Moderate	Moderate
Oldsmobile Aurora 4dr.	4380	Average	23%	26%	Moderate	Moderate
Pontiac Bonneville 4dr.*	3334	Good	10%	24%	Moderate	Moderate
Minivan						
Chevrolet Astro	5091	**Poor**	25%	34%	Moderate	Moderate
Chrys. T & Cntry (Gr. Caravan)*	3436	Average	25%	11%	Good	Moderate
Dodge Caravan*	3436	Average	25%	11%	Good	Moderate
Ford Aerostar	3544	Average	15%	23%	Moderate	Good
Ford Windstar*	1911	*Vry. Gd.*	10%	8%	Good	Good
GMC Safari (Astro)	5091	**Poor**	25%	34%	Moderate	Moderate
Honda Odyssey	2889	Good	16%	15%	Moderate	Vry. Gd.
Isuzu Oasis (Odyssey)	2889	Good	16%	15%	Moderate	Vry. Gd.
Mazda MPV	2405	*Vry. Gd.*	13%	11%	Good	Moderate
Mercury Villager	3248	Good	11%	22%	Good	Moderate
Nissan Quest (Villager)	3248	Good	11%	22%	Good	Moderate
Plymouth Voyager (Caravan)*	3436	Average	25%	11%	Good	Moderate
Toyota Previa	3858	Average	20%	23%	Moderate	Good

Parentheses indicate actual model tested.

*A version of this vehicle is scheduled to be tested later this year. Results are expected to be equal or better.

[1] Vehicle tested with fewer airbags than now available. Similar or better results should occur with 1997 airbag offering.

[2] *The Car Book*/Center for Auto Safety test results.

HOW TO READ THE CHARTS:

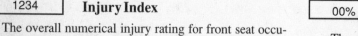

| 1234 | **Injury Index**

The overall numerical injury rating for front seat occupants in a frontal crash. *Lower numbers mean better performance.*

| Very Good | **Car Book Rating**

How the vehicle compares among all government test results to date. The range includes very good, good, average, poor and very poor.

| 00% | **Likelihood of Life Threatening Injury**

The chance of life threatening injury to the driver/passenger in a frontal 35 mph crash. *Lower percentages mean better performance.*

| Good | **Leg Injury Rating**

Injury rating for driver and passenger legs in a frontal crash, when compared to all government test results to date.

Automatic Crash Protection

The concept of automatic protection is not new—automatic fire sprinklers in public buildings, automatic release of oxygen masks in airplanes, purification of drinking water, and pasteurization of milk are all commonly accepted forms of automatic safety protection. Ironically, of all the products we buy, the one most likely to kill us has only recently been equipped with automatic safety protection. As consumer advocates are ready to point out, we incorporate better technology in safely transporting electronic equipment, eggs, and china than we do in packaging humans in automobiles.

Over twenty years ago, in cooperation with the federal government, the automobile industry developed two basic forms of automatic crash protection: airbags and automatic safety belts. These devices will not prevent all deaths, but they will cut in half your chances of being killed or seriously injured in a car accident.

The idea behind automatic crash protection is to protect people from what is called the "second collision" when the occupant comes forward and collides with the interior of his or her own car. Because the "second collision" occurs within milliseconds, and because so many people do not use seat belts, providing automatic rather than manual protection dramatically improves the chances of escaping injury.

Federal law now requires all new cars to be equipped with some form of automatic crash protection that will protect the driver and front seat passenger in a 30-mph collision into a fixed barrier. To meet the standard, auto makers may use airbags or automatic seat belts.

Automatic Belts: Automatic safety belts are supposed to offer protection with little or no effort. As their name implies, they move automatically into place when you enter the car and are released automatically when you leave.

There are two main types of automatic belts—those with an automatic lap and shoulder belt connected to the door, and motorized versions which move out of the way when you open and close the door.

The easiest automatic belt systems to use are the motorized belts where the shoulder belt moves forward, out of your way, when you open the door. When you close the door, the belt moves back, secure over your chest. Unfortunately, these belts only do half the job automatically. You must manually attach a separate lap belt, in this so-called automatic system, which is easy to forget. Forgetting to use the manual lap belt can cause severe injury in an accident.

Non-motorized belts are generally attached to the door. When the door is opened, the attached belt also pulls away to let you in. The problem with all door-mounted belts is that if the door pops open in an accident, you lose the protection of the belt.

Cars with automatic belts often have extra padding under the dash to protect the occupant's knees and lower body. Generally, automatic belts are less expensive than airbags. Airbags, however, offer better protection in a high-speed frontal collision.

Airbags: Hidden in the steering wheel hub and the right side of the dashboard, airbags provide unobtrusive and effective protection in frontal crashes. When needed, they inflate instantly to cushion the driver, and in most cars, the front seat passenger. By spreading crash forces over the head and chest, airbags protect the body from violent contact with the hard surfaces of the car. Cars with airbags also provide manual seat belts to protect occupants in nonfrontal crashes. However, airbags offer protection in frontal crashes even if the safety belt is not fastened.

Consumers with questions about airbags often find that dealers do not know the facts about these safety devices. The following answers to typical airbag questions are pre-

A Note for Pregnant Women:

TIP

The American College of Obstetricians and Gynecologists strongly urges pregnant women to always wear a safety belt, including on the ride to the hospital to deliver the baby! In a car crash, the most serious risk to an unborn baby is that the mother may be injured. Obstetricians recommend that the lap and shoulder belts be used, with the lap belt as low as possible on the hips, under the baby.

When packing your things for the hospital, make sure you include an infant car safety seat to bring your baby home. As the American Academy of Pediatrics says, "Make the first ride a safe ride!"

pared by the Insurance Institute for Highway Safety.

Is the gas that inflates airbags dangerous? Nitrogen, which makes up 79.8 percent of the air we breathe, is the gas that inflates the bags. A solid chemical, sodium azide, generates this nitrogen gas. Sodium azide does not present a safety hazard in normal driving, in crashes, or in disposal. In fact, occupants of the car will never even come in contact with the sodium azide.

Will airbags inflate by mistake? Airbags will inflate only in frontal impacts equivalent to hitting a solid wall at about 10-mph or higher. They will not inflate when you go over bumps or potholes or when you hit something at low speed. Even slamming on your brakes will not cause the airbags to inflate unless you hit something.

In the unlikely event of an inadvertent airbag deployment, you would not lose control of the car. Airbags are designed to inflate and deflate in fractions of a second. GM tested driver reaction by inflating airbags without warning at speeds of up to 45-mph. GM reported that "without exception, the drivers retained control of the automobile."

Will airbag systems last very long? Airbags are reliable and require no maintenance. Only one part moves, the device that senses the impact, so there is nothing to wear out. They work throughout the life of the car although some manufacturers suggest inspections at anywhere from two to ten years.

In a study of 228 cars in which airbags were deployed, 40 had traveled more than 40,000 miles. One car had traveled almost 115,000 miles at the time of the crash. In every case, the airbags worked as they were designed to.

Are airbags reliable? According to the U.S. Department of Transportation, airbags have saved over 1,500 lives since they were introduced in the early 1980's. General Motors installed airbags in over 10,000 cars from 1974 to 1976. These cars traveled over 600 million miles, and the death and injury rate of the occupants was 50 percent lower than the rate for non-airbag cars. Studies of the operation of the airbags reported no cases of failure to deploy or malfunction of the inflator. This reliability rate (99.995 percent) is far higher than that of such safety features as brakes, tires, steering, and lights, which show failure rates of up to 10 percent.

Will airbags protect occupants without seat belts? Airbags are designed to protect unbelted front-seat occupant in 30-mph frontal crashes into a wall. Equipping cars with airbags reduced the average injury severity in serious frontal crashes by 64 percent, even though over 80 percent of the occupants were unbelted. The best protection, however, is provided by a combination of airbags and lap and shoulder safety belts. With airbags and seat belts, you'll be protected in the event of side impact and roll-over crashes, as well as in frontal crashes.

 1997 Models WITHOUT Dual Airbags

Only one manufacturer in the car/minivan category decided to deprive the passenger of airbag protection: **Ford Aerostar.**

Children and Airbags

Will airbags protect children? Studies of actual crashes indicate that children are protected by airbags. However, if not properly buckled up in seat belts, airbags can be deadly. Properly buckling your child has never been more important now that the majority of cars now offer airbags on the passenger's side where children often sit.

While airbags have saved the lives of over 1,500 people, at least 22 children have been killed by the deployment of airbags. The National Highway Traffic Safety Administration estimates about one child per month is killed by airbag deployment and, if certain measures are not implemented, the number could increase to one per week.

Remember — *most children killed by airbags are not properly belted*. To protect the occupant, an airbag must inflate in a fraction of a second before the occupant hits the dashboard. For an adult, the result is coming forward into a cushion of air. For a child who isn't properly buckled, it can be deadly, especially if the child is standing up or leaning on the dashboard.

Never place a rear-facing child seat in front of a passenger side airbag. The best spot for your children is the back seat, preferably in the middle. If you do not have a back seat, here are some tips for keeping your child safe while seated in an airbag seat:

☑ Push seat as far back as it will go.
☑ Make sure your child is sitting up straight and not leaning forward against the dash.
☑ Do not let your child play with any sharp objects like toys or lollipops.

Tip: A child shouldn't have any hard or sharp objects in their mouths while in a vehicle. A sudden stop and the object could be forced down the child's throat.

For tips on how to use a child seat, how to buckle up your child and when a child is ready to use a seat belt, see pages 32-38.

Future Technologies: There are ways to make airbags safer for children. An airbag cutoff switch is available on certain trucks like the Ford F-Series and GM's C/K Pickups. The cutoff switch is only allowed on vehicles without a back seat. However, the cutoff switch has it's own danger— it only takes that one time to forget to turn the airbag back on when an adult sits in the seat.

Automakers are experimenting with sensor switches and smart airbags. For sale in early 1997, the only vehicle which uses a sensor system is the Mercedes Benz SLK sports car (1998 model), which requires a specially-made child seat. The SLK emits an electronic signal which will be reflected back by a sensor in the child seat. When the signal is reflected back, the airbag is turned off. It will even inform you if you've installed the seat improperly. When the seat is removed, the airbag turns back on.

Other solutions include: infrared sensors which detect the passenger's position; an electric field which senses the presence of a child seat; and, ultrasonic sensors which use sound waves to differentiate between an empty seat, a child seat, a child or an adult. The best of the smart airbags will probably use a combination of all these systems. When will these new technologies be available? It is hard to say. However, until such time as this new technology is in place, the government will require very prominent stickers warning of the danger of airbags to unbelted children on the dash, on both sides of the sun visor and the door.

Young Drivers

In 1995, teenagers accounted for 14 percent of highway deaths. According to the Insurance Institute for Highway Safety (IIHS), the highest driver death rate per 100,000 people is among 18-year-olds. Clearly, parents need to make sure their children are fully prepared to be competent, safe drivers before letting them out on the road. All states, except Connecticut and New Hampshire, issue learner's permits. However, only 29 states and the District of Columbia *require* permits before getting a driver's license. It isn't difficult for teenagers to get a license and only nine states prohibit teenagers from driving during night and early morning. Call your MVA for your state's young driver laws.

After airbags, one of the best safety features available is an anti-lock braking system (ABS). ABS shortens stopping distance on dry, wet, and even icy roads by preventing wheel lock-up and keeps you from skidding out of control when you "slam" on the brakes.

The ABS works by sensing the speed of each wheel. If one or more of the wheels begins to lock up or skid, it releases that wheel's brakes, allowing the wheel to roll normally again, thus stopping the skid. When the wheel stops skidding, the hydraulic pressure is reapplied instantly. This cycle can be repeated several times per second, keeping each wheel at its optimum braking performance even while your foot keeps pushing on the brake pedal. Although ABS is typically connected to all four wheels, in some light trucks and vans it is connected to only the rear wheels.

The ABS is only active when it senses that the wheels are about to lock up. When an ABS is active, you may notice that the brake pedal pulsates slightly. This pulsation is normal, and it indicates that the brakes are being released and reapplied. *Don't pump your brakes*—the ABS is doing it for you. If there is a failure in the ABS, the vehicle reverts to its conventional braking system and a warning light indicates that the ABS needs repair.

Note: Using tires other than the ones originally on the vehicle may affect the anti-lock braking system. If you are planning to change the size of the tires on your vehicle, first consult your owner's manual.

You'll find ABS on all 1997 models, but mostly as an option.

Don't Buy Add-On ABS Brakes

Adding "so-called" ABS brakes to your car can be dangerous. These products use a variety of deceptive names that incorporate the letters ABS, such as ABS-Trax (Automotive Breakthrough Science—the company's name) and Brake-Guard ABS (Advanced Braking System). These add-on systems "have virtually no effect on stopping distances, vehicle stability or control," according to government tests. You should *not* purchase or install these systems. Only *electronic* ABS systems are capable of preventing wheel skid in panic braking situations. Currently, true electronic anti-lock brakes are only available as factory installed systems.

What Happens in a Collision

A car crash typically involves two collisions. First, the car hits another object and second, the occupant collides with the inside of the car. Injuries result from this *second collision*. The key to surviving an auto accident is protecting yourself from the second collision. Always wearing your safety belt is the most important defense while having an airbag is a very close second. The whole purpose of the airbag is to protect you in this second collision.

Upon impact, in a typical 35-mph crash, the car begins to crush and slow down. Within 1/10 of a second, the car comes to a stop, but the person keeps moving forward at 35-mph. 1/50 of a second after the car has stopped, the unbelted person slams into the dashboard or windshield.

According to government reports prepared before the widespread use of belts and airbags, these were the major causes of injury in the *second collision*:

Steering wheel	27%
Instrument panel	11%
Side (doors)	10%
Windshield	5%
Front roof pillar	4%
Glove box area	3%
Roof edges	3%
Roof	2%

About 60 percent of occupants killed or injured in auto crashes would have been saved from serious harm had they been wearing safety belts. Yet many Americans do not use these life-saving devices.

Safety belts are particularly important in minivans, 4x4s and pickups because there is a greater chance of being killed or seriously injured in a rollover accident. The simple precaution of wearing your belt greatly improves your odds of survival.

Why don't people wear their belts? They simply don't know the facts. Once you know the facts, you should be willing to buckle up.

While most safety advocates welcome the passage of safety belt usage laws, the ones passed to date are weak and generally unenforced. In addition, most of the laws are based on "secondary" enforcement—meaning that you cannot be stopped for failing to wear your belt. If you are stopped for another reason and the officer notices you don't have your belt on by the time he or she reaches the vehicle, you may be fined. In states with "primary" enforcement, you can be stopped for not wearing a safety belt. Yet, in many cases the fines are less than a parking ticket. In Arkansas, however, you can get a $10 credit toward a primary violation if you are wearing a seat belt and in Wyoming, a $5 credit.

Another unusual feature of these laws is that most of them allow drivers to avoid buckling up if they have a doctor's permission. This loophole was inserted to appease those who were not really in favor of the law. However, many doctors are wondering if they will be held responsible for the injuries of unbuckled patients. In fact, the State of

New York Medical Society cautions doctors never to give medical dispensation from the law because "no medical condition has yet been found to warrant a medical exemption for seat belt use."

Even though most state laws are weak, they have heightened awareness and raised the level of usage. Belt use in states that have passed a safety belt law tends to rise sharply after the law is enacted. However,

after the law has been on the books a few months, safety belt use drops.

The tables on the following pages describe the current safety belt laws. In some cases, the driver is responsible for all or some of the passengers as noted; otherwise, occupants are responsible for themselves. All states are listed, even those that do not yet have safety belt laws. We hope that the blank following New Hampshire will soon be filled with new laws.

Safety Belt Myths and Facts

Myth: *"I don't want to be trapped by a seat belt. It's better to be thrown free in an accident."*

Fact: The chance of being killed is 25 times greater if you're ejected. A safety belt will keep you from plunging through the windshield, smashing into trees, rocks, or other cars, scraping along the ground, or getting run over by your own or another's vehicle. If you are wearing your belt, you're far more likely to be conscious after an accident to free yourself and other passengers.

Myth: *"Pregnant women should not wear safety belts."*

Fact: According to the American Medical Association, "Both the pregnant mother and the fetus are safer, provided the lap belt is worn as low on the pelvis as possible."

Myth: *"I don't need it. In case of an accident, I can brace myself with my hands."*

Fact: At 35 mph, the impact of a crash on you and your passengers is brutal. There's no way your arms and legs can brace you against that kind of collision; the speed and force are just too great. The force of impact at only 10 mph is roughly equivalent to the force of catching a 200-pound bag of cement dropped from a first floor window.

Myth: *"I just don't bellieve it will ever happen to me."*

Fact: Every one of us can expect to be in a crash once every 10 years. For one out of 20 of us, it will be a serious crash. For one out of 60 born today, it will be fatal.

Safety Belt Laws

	Law Applies To:	Driver Fined For:	Enforcement	Max. Fine 1st Offense
Alabama	Front seat only	Self only	Secondary	$25
Alaska*	All occupants	0 to 15 year olds	Secondary	$15
Arizona	Front seat only	5 to 16 year olds	Secondary	$10
Arkansas	Front seat only	Self only	Secondary	$25[1]
California*	All occupants	Over 15 years old	Primary	$20
Colorado	All occupants	4 to 16 year olds	Secondary	$15
Connecticut	All occupants	4 to 16 year olds	Primary	$15
Delaware	Front seat only	All occupants	Secondary	$20
Dist. of Columbia	Front seat only	Self only	Secondary	$15
Florida	Front seat only	0 to 15 year olds	Secondary	$27
Georgia	All occupants	4 to 18 year olds	Primary	$15[2]
Hawaii	Front seat only	4 to 15 year olds	Primary	$20
Idaho	Front seat only	Self only	Secondary	$5
Illinois	Front seat only	6 to 16 year olds	Secondary	$25
Indiana	Front seat only	Self only	Secondary	$25
Iowa	Front seat only	Self only	Primary	$10
Kansas	Front seat only	Self only	Secondary	$10
Kentucky*	All occupants	Over 40 inches	Secondary	$25
Louisiana	Front seat only	Self only	Primary	$25[1]
Maine	All occupants	Over 4 years old	Secondary	$50
Maryland	All occupants	0 to 15 year olds	Secondary	$25
Massachusetts*	All occupants	12 to 16 year olds	Secondary	$25
Michigan	All occupants	4 to 16 year olds	Secondary	$25
Minnesota	All occupants	4 to 11 year olds[3]	Secondary	$25
Mississippi	Front seat only	Self only	Secondary	$25
Missouri	Front seat only	4 to 16 year olds	Secondary	$10

* In these states driver can be held liable in court for *all* passengers.
  See next page for footnotes.

Safety Belt Laws

	Law Applies To:	Driver Fined For:	Enforcement	Max. Fine 1st Offense
Montana*	All occupants	Over 4 years old	Secondary	$20
Nebraska	Front seat	Over 5 years old	Secondary	$25
Nevada*	All occupants	5 to 18 year olds	Secondary	$25
New Hampshire	No law			
New Jersey	Front seat only	5 to 18 year olds	Secondary	$20
New Mexico	Front seat only	Self only	Primary	$25
New York	Front seat[4]	4 to 16 year olds	Primary	$50
North Carolina	Front seat only	6 to 16 year olds	Primary	$25
North Dakota	Front seat	Over 10 years old	Secondary	$20
Ohio	Front seat only	Over 4 years old	Secondary	$25
Oklahoma	Front seat only	Self only	Secondary	$25
Oregon*	All Occupants	0 to 15 year olds	Primary	$95
Pennsylvania	Front seat only	4 to 18 year olds	Secondary	$10
Rhode Island*	All Occupants	Over 11 years old	Secondary	None
South Carolina	All Occupants[5]	6 to 17 year olds	Secondary	$10
South Dakota	Front seat	5 to 18 year olds	Secondary	$20
Tennessee	Front seat only	Over 3 years old	Secondary	$10
Texas	Front seat only	4 to 15 year olds	Primary	$50
Utah	Front seat only	2 to 18 year olds	Secondary	$10
Vermont*	All occupants	Over 13 years old	Secondary	$10
Virginia	Front seat only	4 to 16 year olds	Secondary	$25
Washington*	All occupants	0 to 15 year olds	Secondary	$47
West Virginia	Front seat[6]	All occupants	Secondary	$25
Wisconsin	All occupants[5]	4 to 15 year olds	Secondary	$10
Wyoming	Front seat only	Over 3 years old	Secondary	None[1]

* In these states driver can be held liable in court for *all* passengers.
[1] In Arkansas, reward for buckling up is a $10 reduction in primary violation fine; in Wyoming, a $5 reduction. In Louisiana, 10% reduction in fine for moving violation.
[2] $25 fine if driver is a minor.
[3] Parent driver is responsible for 11 to 15 year olds in front seat.
[4] Driver responsible for 4 to 10 year olds riding in rear seat.
[5] Covers rear seat occupants where shoulder belts are available.
[6] Driver responsible for occupants 0 to 17 years old in rear seat.

Child Safety Seats

How many times have you gone out of your way to prevent your children from being injured by keeping household poisons out of reach, watching carefully as they swam, or keeping a good grip on their hand while crossing a street or parking lot? Probably quite often. Yet, parents ignore the biggest danger of all when they allow their children to lay down in the back of a minivan or roam unrestrained in their car. Ironically, it's your automobile that poses the greatest threat to your child's health.

Child safety seats are the best and only reliable way to protect your child in a vehicle. Automobiles crashes remain the leading cause of death in children over one year old. Sadly, over 100,000 children are injured unnecessarily each year. If used correctly, child safety seats reduce your child's chances of injury by over 50 percent.

Never place a child in your lap. At 30 mph, a crash or sudden stop will wrench a ten pound child from your arms with a force of nearly 300 pounds! If you aren't wearing a seat belt, then your own body will be thrown forward with enough force to crush your child against the dashboard or the back of the front seat.

Hand-Me-Down Seats: To insure that a second hand child seat will adequately protect your child, see if its identification stickers, belt instructions and date of manufacture are still visible. Only use seats less than 5 years old. Make sure no parts or instructions are missing. Most importantly, know the history of the child seat — never use seats that have been in crashes, no matter how perfect they look.

Buying Tips: Purchasing a new child seat for your child is always money well spent. Many vehicles now have built-in child seats which are an excellent option. Child seats with an automatic retracting harness and a shield are typically the easiest to use. Here are some additional tips when shopping for a child safety seat:

☑ Try before you buy. Your car's seat belts and the shape of its seats will determine which child seats fit your car so make sure it can be properly installed.

☑ Determine how many straps or buckles must be fastened to use a child seat. The less complicated the seat, the less chance for misuse. The easiest seats require only one strap or buckle after fastening the seat belt around the child seat.

☑ Make sure the seat is wide enough for growth and bulky winter clothes. If possible, let your child sit in the seat to measure for fit.

☑ Is your child comfortable? Can your child move his or her arms freely, sleep in the seat, or see out a window?

TIP — Locking Clips

Locking clips come with most child safety seats and are needed if the latch plate on the car's seat belt slides freely along the belt. If you don't properly install the locking clip, the child seat can move or tip over. Look for *heavy-duty locking clips*, available at Ford, Toyota and Nissan dealers. The safest way to use a heavy-duty locking clip is to pull the seat belt entirely out and attach the clip so the child seat is secure with no retracting involved. For more information, contact Safety Belt Safe at 800-745-SAFE.

Register Your Child Seat

Last year, the U.S. Department of Transportation recalled millions of child safety seats for serious safety defects. Tragically, most parents never heard about these recalls and the majority of these problem seats are still being used. You can do two things to protect your children—first, call the Auto Safety Hotline at 800-424-9393 and find out if your seat has been recalled. If so, they will tell you how to contact the manufacturer for a resolution. Second, make sure you fill out the registration card that must come with all new seats. This will enable the company to contact you should there be a recall. If you currently own a seat, ask the Hotline for the address of your seat's manufacturer and send them your name, address and seat model, asking them to keep it on file for recall notices.

Child Safety Seat Types

There are six types of child seats: *infant-only, convertible, toddler-only, child/booster, booster* and *built-in.*

Infant-Only Seats: Infant-only seats can be used from birth until your baby reaches a weight of 17-20 pounds. This type of seat must be installed facing the rear in a semi-reclined position. In a collision, the crash forces are spread over the baby's back, the strongest body surface. The seat's harness should come from below the child's shoulders in the rear-facing position.

One benefit of an infant-only seat is that you can easily install and remove the seat with the baby in place. Most infant car seats can also be used as household baby seats. Caution: Some household baby seats look remarkably similar to infant safety seats. These are not crash worthy and should *never* be used as car safety seats.

Convertible Seats: Buying a convertible seat can save you the expense of buying both an infant and a toddler seat. Most convertible seats can be used from birth until the child reaches four years and 40 pounds. When used for an infant, the seat faces rearward in a semi-reclined position. When the child is at least a year old and 20 pounds or more, the frame can be adjusted upright and the seat turned to face forward.

As with any safety seat, it is extremely important that the straps fit snugly over the child's shoulders. A good way to ensure that the straps are adjusted correctly is to buy a seat with an automatically adjusting harness. Like a car safety belt, these models automatically adjust to fit snugly on your child.

Convertible seats come in three basic types:

The *five-point harness* consists of two shoulder and two lap straps that converge at a buckle connected to a crotch strap. These straps are adjustable, allowing for growth and comfort.

The *T-shield* has a small pad joining the shoulder belts. With only one buckle, many parents find this the simplest and easiest-to-use type of convertible seat; but, it will not fit newborns properly.

The *tray shield* is another convenient model, since the safety harness is attached to the shield. As the shield comes down in front of the child, the harness comes over the child's shoulders. The shield is an important part of the restraint system, but like the T-shield, it will not fit small infants.

Toddler-Only Seats: These are really booster child seats and they may take the place of convertible seats when a child is between 20 and 30 pounds. Weight and size limits vary greatly among seats.

Child/Booster Seats: Some manufacturers are now making a variety of combination child/booster seats. For example, one model can be converted from a 5-point harness to a high-backed, belt-positioning booster seat. They can be used for children ranging from 20 to 40 pounds, making them a very economical choice.

Booster Seats: Booster seats are used when your child is too big for a convertible seat, but too small to use safety belts. Most car lap/shoulder belts do not adequately fit children with a seating height less than 28". Booster seats can be used for children over 30 pounds and come in three types:

Belt-positioning booster seats raise the child for a better fit with the car's safety belts. If your child is under 3 years old, do not use belt-positioning booster seats because your child may be able to unbuckle him or herself.

The *removable-shield booster seat* can be used with a lap/shoulder belt with the shield removed, or with a lap belt with the shield on. This seat can be adapted to different cars and seating positions, making it a good choice.

The *shield-type booster seat* has a small plastic shield with no straps and can be used only with lap belts. Typically, the safety belt fastens in front of the shield, anchoring it to the car. Most safety experts recommend using these seats until a child is 4 years old and 40 pounds.

Built-in Seats: Chrysler, Ford, GM, Volvo and other auto companies offer the option of a fold-out toddler seat on some of their models. These seats are only for children older than one and come as either a five-point harness or a booster with 3-point belt; however, the 3-point booster is not recommended for children under 3 years old. This built-in seat is an excellent feature because it is always in the car and does not pose the problem of compatability that often occurs with separate child seats.

Name of Seat	Price	Comments
Infant Safety Seats		
Century 565	$39-49	3-pt.; tilt-indicator
Century 590	$49-59	3-pt.; tilt indicator; separate base stays in car; can be used without base
Cosco Arriva	$35-55	3-pt.; up to 22 lbs.; detachable base with some models
Cosco Dream Ride	$59	3-pt.; up to 17-20 lbs. (depending on mfg date); use as car seat rear facing
Cosco TLC	$20-25	3-pt.
Evenflo Dyn-O-Mite	$25	3-pt.; must use lap/shoulder belt in the most reclined position
Evenflo Joy Ride	$25-45	3-pt.; harness adjuster located in compartment behind seat.
Evenflo On My Way	$55-65	3-pt.; detachable base; can use without base
Evenflo Travel Tandem	$45-55	3-pt.; separate base stays in car; can be used without base; harness adjuster behind seat.
Gerry Guard with Glide	$50-55	3-pt.; use as glider in house; must be converted to in-car position
Gerry Secure Ride	$40	3-pt.; tilt-indicator
Kolcraft Going Places	$55-65	3-pt.; detachable base; can use without base
Kolcraft Infant Rider	$50-60	3-pt.
Kolcraft Rock 'N Ride	$30-35	3-pt.; no harness height adjustment
Convertible Safety Seats		
Babyhood Baby Sitter	$89-99	5-pt.
Century 1000 STE	$49-75	5-pt.; adjustable crotch strap positions
Century 2000 STE	$59-85	T-shield; adjustable crotch strap positions
Century 3000 STE	$69-89	Tray shield; 5-position adjustable shield
Century 5500 Prestige	$89-99	Tray shield; adjustable crotch strap positions
Century Smart Move	$119-129	5-pt./ Tray shield; adjustable shield grows with child
Cosco Hugger	$70-90	Tray shield; use rear-facing up to 22 lbs.; adjustable shield
Cosco Regal Ride	$65-85	5-pt./ T-shield/ Tray shield; use rear-facing up to 22 lbs.
Cosco Touriva 5-pt.	$40-60	5-pt./ T-Shield/ Tray shield; use rear facing up to 22 lbs.
Guardian Comfort	$90-120	5-pt./ T-shield/ Tray shield; harness designed like vehicle seat belts; lock upon impact.

Based on data collected by the American Academy of Pediatrics.

Name of Seat	Price	Comments
Convertible Seats (cont.)		
Evenflo Champion	$50-70	Tray shield; optional tether available
Evenflo Scout	$39-60	5-pt./ T-shield; optional tether available
Evenflo Trooper	$60-70	5-pt./ Tray shield; adjustable shield; optional tether available
Evenflo Ultara I, Premier	$60-110	Tray shield; adjustable shield; optional tether available
Evenflo Ultara V, Premier	$65-110	5-pt.; optional tether available
Gerry One-Click	$80-90	Tray shield; automatic harness adjustment; optional tether available
Gerry Pro-Tech	$60-65	5-pt.; optional tether available
Kolcraft Auto-Mate	$50-60	5-pt.; requires 2-handed operation
Safeline Sit 'N Stroll	$150-169	5-pt.; converts to stroller
Toddler-Only Vests and Built-In Seats		
Chrysler Built-In Seat	$100-200	5-pt. (20-65 lbs.); 2 built in option in minivans; one seat available in sedans and Jeep Grand Cherokee
E-Z-On Vest	$74-90	4-pt. (25+ lbs.); tether strap must be installed in vehicle
Ford Built-In	$135-240	5 pt. (20-60 lbs.); two seats optional in minivans; one seat optional in Explorer, Escort, and Tracer
GM Built-In	$125-225	5-pt. (20-40 lbs., Booster 40-60 lbs.); seats optional in minivans and some sedans.
Little Cargo Travel Vest	$39-49	5-pt.; (25-40 lbs.); simplified strap-buckle system; auto lap belt attached through padded stress plate
Booster		
Century Breverra Premiere	$59-69	High-backed; use 5-point shield with lap belt only; remove shield when using vehicle lap/shoulder belt
Cosco Grand Explorer/ Adventurer	$20-35	Must use shield if vehicle has lap belts only; use as a belt-positioning booster with lap/shoulder belt
Evenflo Sidekick	$20-30	Must use shield if vehicle has lap belts only; use as a belt-positioning booster with lap/shoulder belt
Gerry Evolution	$54-60	High-backed; optional tether available
Gerry Pro Ride	$25	Base only unit; belt-positioning booster; must use with vehicle lap/shoulder belt.

Based on data collected by the American Academy of Pediatrics.

Tips for Using Your Child Safety Seat

The incorrect use of child safety seats has reached epidemic proportions. A stunning 90% of parents misuse their child's safety seat. Problems fall into two categories: incorrect installation of the seat and incorrect use of the seat's straps to secure the child. In most cases, the car's safety belt was improperly routed through the seat.

Incorrect use of a child safety seat prevents lifesaving protection and may even contribute to further injury. In addition to following your seat's installation instructions, here are some important usage tips:

☑ The safest place for the seat is the center of the back seat.

☑ Use a locking clip when needed. Check the instructions that come with your seat and those in your car owner's manual.

☑ Keep your child rear-facing for at least a year.

☑ Regularly check the seat's safety harness and the car's seat belt for a tight, secure fit because the straps will stretch on impact.

☑ Don't leave sharp or heavy objects or groceries loose in the car. Anything loose can be deadly in a crash.

☑ In the winter, dress your baby in a legged suit to allow proper attachment of the harness. If necessary, drape an extra blanket over the seat after your baby is buckled.

☑ Be sure all doors are locked.

☑ Do not give your child lollipops or ice cream on a stick while riding. A bump or swerve could jam the stick into his or her throat.

Seat Belts for Kids: How long should children use car seats? For school age children, a car seat is *twice* as effective in preventing injury than an adult lap and shoulder harness — use a booster as long as possible. Most children can start using seat belts at 65 pounds and when tall enough for the shoulder belt to cross the chest, not the neck. The lap section of the belt should be snug and as low on the hips as possible. If the shoulder belt does cross the face or neck, use a booster.

Never:

☒ Use the same belt on two children.

☒ Move a shoulder belt behind a child's back or under an arm.

☒ Buckle in a pet or any large toys with the child.

☒ Recline a seat with a seat-belted child.

☒ Use a twisted seat belt. The belt must be straight and flat.

☒ Use pillows or cushions to boost your child.

☒ Place a belt around you with a child in your lap. In an accident or sudden stop, your child would absorb most of the crash force.

Buckled Up=Better Behavior

Medical researchers have concluded that belted children are better behaved. When not buckled up, children squirm, stand up, complain, fight, and pull at the steering wheel. When buckled into safety seats, however, they displayed 95 percent fewer incidents of bad behavior.

When buckled up, children feel secure. In addition, being in a seat can be more fun because most safety seats are high enough to allow children to see out the window. Also, children are less likely to feel carsick and more likely to fall asleep in a car seat.

Make the car seat your child's own special place, so he or she will enjoy being in it. Pick out some special soft toys or books that can be used only in the car seat to make using the seat a positive experience.

Set a good example for your child by using your own safety belt every time you get in the car.

Rear-Facing Child Safety Seats

Never use a rear-facing child safety seat in a seating position that has an airbag. To deploy fast enough to protect adult occupants, an airbag inflates with enough force to potentially cause serious head and chest injuries to a child in a rear-facing safety seat. And remember, airbags do not take the place of child safety seats.

Child Restraint Laws

Every state now requires children to be in safety seats or buckled up when riding in automobiles. The following table provides an overview of the requirements and penalties in each state. Note that most states use the child's age to define the law, although some states have height or weight requirements as well. Also, in most states, the laws are not limited to children riding with their parents, but require that any driver with child passengers makes sure those children are buckled up.

	Law Applies To:	Children Covered Through:	Max. Fine 1st Offense	Safety Belt OK:
Alabama	All drivers	5 yrs.	$10	4-5 yrs.
Alaska	All drivers	15 yrs.	$50	4-15 yrs.
Arizona	All drivers	4 yrs. or 40 lbs.	$50	No
Arkansas	All drivers	4 yrs. or 40 lbs.	$25	4 yrs.
California	All drivers	15 yrs.	$100	4-15 yrs.
Colorado	All drivers	15 yrs.	$50	4-15 yrs., over 40 lbs.
Connecticut	All drivers	3 yrs. or 40 lbs.	$90	40 lbs.+
Delaware	All drivers	15 yrs..	$29	4-15 yrs.
Dist. of Columbia	All drivers	15 yrs.	$55	3-15 yrs.
Florida	All drivers	5 yrs.	$155	4-5 yrs.
Georgia	All drivers	4 yrs.	$50	3-4 yrs.
Hawaii	All drivers	3 yrs.	$100	3 yrs. only
Idaho	All drivers	3 yrs. or 40 lbs.	$52	No
Illinois	All drivers	5 yrs.	$25	4-5 yrs.
Indiana	All drivers	4 yrs.	$500	3-4 yrs.
Iowa	All drivers	5 yrs.	$10	3-5 yrs.
Kansas	All drivers	13 yrs.	$20	4-13 yrs.
Kentucky	All drivers	Under 40 inches	$50	No
Louisiana	Resident drivers	4 yrs.	$50	3-4 yrs. in rear
Maine	All drivers	18 yrs.	$55	4-18 yrs.
Maryland	All drivers	15 yrs.	$25	4-15 yrs., over 40 lbs.
Massachusetts	All drivers	11 yrs.	$25	All ages
Michigan	All drivers	3 yrs.	$10	1-3 yrs. in rear
Minnesota	All drivers	3 yrs.	$50	No
Mississippi	All drivers	3 yrs.	$25	No

Child Restraint Laws

	Law Applies To:	Children Covered Through:	Max. Fine 1st Offense	Safety Belt OK:
Missouri	All drivers	3 yrs.	$25	All ages in rear
Montana	Resident Parent/Guardian[1]	3 yrs. or 40 lbs.	$25	2-3 yrs.
Nebraska	Resident drivers	4 yrs.	$25	4 yrs., over 40 lbs.
Nevada	All drivers	4 yrs. or 40 lbs.	$100	No
New Hampshire	All drivers	11 yrs.	$43	4-11 yrs.
New Jersey	All drivers	4 yrs.	$25	1-1/2-4 yrs. in rear
New Mexico	All drivers	10 yrs.	$25	1-4 yrs. in rear[2]
New York	All drivers	15 yrs.[3]	$100	4-10 yrs. in rear
North Carolina	All drivers	11 yrs.	$25	4-11 yrs.
North Dakota	All drivers	10 yrs.	$20	3-10 yrs.
Ohio	All drivers	3 yrs. or 40 lbs.	$100	No
Oklahoma	Resident drivers	5 yrs.	$25	4-5 yrs.
Oregon	All drivers	15 yrs. or 40 lbs.	$95	4-15 yrs.
Pennsylvania	All drivers	3 yrs.	$25	No
Rhode Island	All drivers	12 yrs.	$30	3-12 yrs.
South Carolina	All drivers	5 yrs.	$25	1-5 yrs. in rear[4]
South Dakota	All drivers	4 yrs.	$20	2-4 yrs.
Tennessee	All drivers	12 yrs.	$10	4-12 yrs.
Texas	All drivers	3 yrs.	$50	2-3 yrs.
Utah	All drivers	7 yrs.	$20	2-7 yrs.
Vermont	All drivers	12 yrs.	$25	5-12 yrs.
Virginia	Parent/Guardian	3 yrs.	$50	No
Washington	All drivers	9 yrs.	$47	3-9 yrs.
West Virginia	All drivers	8 yrs.	$20	3-8 yrs.
Wisconsin	All drivers	7 yrs.	$75	4-7 yrs.
Wyoming	Parent/Guardian[1]	2 yrs.[5]	$25	1-2 yrs.

[1] In own car only.
[2] 5-10 year olds in all seats
[3] 9 year olds in rear
[4] 4-5 year olds in front seat
[5] 3 yrs. if less than 40 lbs.

FUEL ECONOMY

A car's fuel efficiency affects both our environment and our wallets—which is why comparative mileage ratings are an important factor to most consumers. To save money and the environment, the first and most obvious step is to select a car that gets high mileage, so we've included the Environmental Protection Agency's fuel economy ratings for all 1997 vehicles. We also discuss numerous factors that affect your car's fuel efficiency, and caution you against the many products that falsely promise more gas mileage.

Using EPA ratings is an excellent way to incorporate fuel efficiency in selecting a new car. By comparing these ratings, even among cars of the same size, you'll find that fuel efficiency varies greatly. One compact car might get 36 miles per gallon (mpg) while another gets only 22 mpg. If you drive 15,000 miles a year and you pay $1.20 per gallon for fuel, the 36 mpg car will save you $319 a year over the "gas guzzler."

Octane Ratings: Once you've purchased your car, you'll be faced with choosing the right gasoline. Oil companies spend millions of dollars trying to get you to buy so-called higher performance or high octane fuels. Because high octane fuel can add considerably to your gas bill, it is important that you know what you're buying.

The octane rating of a gasoline is *not* a measure of power or quality. It is simply a measure of the gas's resistance to engine knock, which is the pinging sound you hear when the air and fuel mixture in your engine ignites prematurely during acceleration.

The octane rating appears on a yellow label on the fuel pump. Octane ratings vary with different types of gas (premium or regular), in different parts of the country (higher altitudes require lower octane ratings), and even between brands (Texaco's gasolines may have a different rating than Exxon's).

Determining the Right Octane Rating for Your Car: Using a lower-rated gasoline saves money. Most cars are designed to run on a posted octane rating of 87. The following procedure can help you select the lowest octane level for your car.

1 Have your engine tuned to exact factory specifications by a competent mechanic, and make sure it is in good working condition.

2 When the gas in your tank is very low, fill it up with your usual gasoline. After driving 10 to 15 miles, find a safe place to come to a complete stop and then accelerate rapidly. If your engine knocks during acceleration, switch to a higher octane rating. If there is no knocking sound, wait until your tank is very low and fill up with a lower rated gasoline. Repeat the test. When you determine the level of octane that causes your engine to knock during the test, use gasoline with the next highest rating.

Note: Your engine may knock when accelerating a heavily loaded car uphill or when the humidity is low. This is normal and does not call for a higher-octane gasoline.

Factors Affecting Fuel Economy

Fuel economy is affected by a number of factors that you can consider before you buy.

Transmission: Manual transmissions are generally more fuel-efficient than automatic transmissions. In fact, a 5-speed manual transmission can add up to 6.5 miles per gallon over a three-speed automatic. However, the incorrect use of a manual transmission wastes gas, so choose a transmission that matches your preference. Many transmissions now feature an overdrive gear, which can improve a vehicle's fuel economy by as much as 9 percent for an automatic transmission and 3 percent for a manual transmission.

Engine: The size of your car's engine greatly affects your fuel economy. The smaller your engine, the better your fuel efficiency. A 10-percent increase in the size of an engine can increase fuel consumption by 6 percent.

Cruise Control: Cruise control can save fuel because driving at a constant speed uses less fuel than changing speeds frequently.

Air Conditioning: Auto air conditioners add weight and require additional horsepower to operate. They can cost up to 3 miles per gallon in city driving. At highway speeds, however, an air conditioner has about the same effect on fuel economy as the air resistance created by opening the windows.

Trim Package: Upgrading a car's trim, installing soundproofing, and adding undercoating can increase the weight of a typical car by 150 pounds. For each 10 percent increase in weight, fuel economy drops 4 percent.

Power Options: Power steering, brakes, seats, windows, and roofs reduce your mileage by adding weight. Power steering alone can cause a 1-percent drop in fuel economy.

Here are some tips for after you buy:

Tune-Up: If you have a 2- to 3-mpg drop over several fill-ups that is not due to a change of driving pattern or vehicle load, first check tire pressure, then consider a tune-up. A properly tuned engine is a definite fuel saver.

Tire Inflation: For maximum fuel efficiency, tires should be inflated to the top of the pressure range stamped on the sidewall. Check tire pressure when the tires are cold—before you've driven a long distance.

Short Trips: Short trips can be expensive because they usually involve a "cold" vehicle. For the first mile or two, a cold vehicle gets 30 to 40 percent of the mileage it gets when fully warm.

TIP

Using Oxyfuels

Today's gasoline contains a bewildering array of ingredients touted as octane boosters or pollution fighters. Some urban areas with carbon monoxide pollution problems are requiring the use of oxygen-containing components (called oxyfuels) such as ethanol and MTBE (methyl-tertiary-butylether). The use of these compounds is controversial. Some auto companies recommend their use; others caution against them. Most companies approve the use of gasoline with up to 10-percent ethanol, and all approve the use of MTBE up to 15 percent. Many companies recommend against using gasoline with methanol, alleging that it will cause poorer driveability, deterioration of fuel system parts, and reduced fuel economy. These companies may not cover the cost of warranty repairs if these additives are used, so check your owner's manual and warranty to determine what additives are covered. Also check the gas pump, as many states now require the pump to display the percentage of methanol and ethanol in the gasoline.

Products That Don't Work

Hundreds of products on the market claim to improve fuel economy. Not only are most of these products ineffective, some may even damage your engine.

Sometimes the name or promotional material associated with these products implies they were endorsed by the federal government. *In fact, no government agency endorses any gas saving products.* Many of the products, however, *have* been tested by the U. S. EPA.

Of the hundreds of so-called gas saving devices on the market, only five tested by the EPA have been shown to *slightly* improve your fuel economy without increasing harmful emissions. Even these, however, offer limited savings because of their cost. They are the Pass Master Vehicle Air Conditioner P.A.S.S. Kit, Idalert, Morse Constant Speed Accessory Drive, Autotherm, and Kamei Spoilers. We don't recommend these products because the increase in fuel economy is not worth the investment in the product.

Do NOT Buy These Devices

Purported gas-saving devices come in many forms. Listed below are the types of products on the market. Under each category are the names of devices actually reviewed or tested by the EPA for which there was *no evidence of any improvement in fuel economy.*

AIR BLEED DEVICES
ADAKS Vacuum Breaker Air Bleed
Air-Jet Air Bleed
Aquablast Wyman Valve Air Bleed
Auto Miser
Ball-Matic Air Bleed
Berg Air Bleed
Brisko PCV
Cyclone - Z
Econo Needle Air Bleed
Econo-Jet Air Bleed Idle Screws
Fuel Max
Gas Saving Device
Grancor Air Computer
Hot Tip
Landrum Mini-Carb
Landrum Retrofit Air Bleed
Mini Turbocharger Air Bleed*
Monocar HC Control Air Bleed
Peterman Air Bleed*
Pollution Master Air Bleed
Ram-Jet
Turbo-Dyne G.R. Valve

DRIVING HABIT MODIFIERS
Fuel Conservation Device
Gastell

FUEL LINE DEVICES
Fuel Xpander

Gas Meiser I
Greer Fuel Preheater
Jacona Fuel System
Malpassi Filter King
Moleculetor
Optimizer
Petro-Mizer
Polarion X
Russell Fuelmiser
Super-Mag Fuel Extender
Wickliff Polarizer

FUELS AND FUEL ADDITIVES
Bycosin*
EI-5 Fuel Additive*
Fuelon Power Gasoline Fuel Additive
Johnson Fuel Additive*
NRG #1 Fuel Additive
QEI 400 Fuel Additive*
Rolfite Upgrade Fuel Additive
Sta-Power Fuel Additive
Stargas Fuel Additive
SYNeRGy-1
Technol G Fuel Additive
ULX-15/ULX-15D
Vareb 10 Fuel Additive*
XRG #1 Fuel Additive

IGNITION DEVICES
Autosaver
Baur Condenser*
BIAP Electronic Ignition Unit

Fuel Economizer
Magna Flash Ignition Ctrl. Sys.
Paser Magnum/Paser 500/ Paser 500 HEI
Special Formula Ignition Advance Springs*

INTERNAL ENGINE MODIFICATIONS
ACDS Auto. Cyl. Deactivation Sys.
Dresser Economizer*
MSU Cylinder Deactivation*

LIQUID INJECTION
Goodman Engine Sys. Model 1800*
Waag-Injection System*

MIXTURE ENHANCERS
Basko Enginecoat
Dresser Economizer
Electro-Dyne Superchoke*
Energy Gas Saver*
Environmental Fuel Saver*
Filtron Urethane Foam Filter*
Gas Saving and Emission Control Improvement Device
Glynn-50*
Hydro-Catalyst Pre-Combustion System
Lamkin Fuel Metering Device

Petromizer System
Sav-A-Mile
Smith Power and Deceleration Governor Spritzer*
Spritzer
Turbo-Carb
Turbocarb

OILS AND OIL ADDITIVES
Analube Synthetic Lubricant
Tephguard*

VAPOR BLEED DEVICES
Atomized Vapor Injector
Econo-Mist Vacuum Vapor Injection System
Frantz Vapor Injection System*
Hydro-Vac
Mark II Vapor Injection System*
Platinum Gasaver
POWER FUeL
Scatpac Vacuum Vapor Induction System
Turbo Vapor Injection System*
V-70 Vapor Injector

MISCELLANEOUS
Brake-Ez*
Dynamix
Fuel Maximiser
Gyroscopic Wheel Cover
Kat's Engine Heater
Lee Exhaust and Fuel Gasification EGR*
Mesco Moisture Extraction Sys.
P.S.C.U. 01 Device
Treis Emulsifier

---

* For copies of reports on these products, write Test and Evaluation Branch, U.S. EPA, 2565 Plymouth Rd., Ann Arbor, MI 48105. For the other products, contact the National Technical Information Service, Springfield, VA 22161. (703-487-4650).

Fuel Economy Ratings

Every year the Department of Energy publishes the results of the Environmental Protection Agency's fuel economy tests in a comparative guide. In the past, millions of these booklets have been distributed to consumers who are eager to purchase fuel-efficient automobiles. However, the government has recently limited the availability of the guide. Because the success of the EPA program depends on consumers' ability to compare the fuel economy ratings easily, we have reprinted the EPA mileage figures for this year's misers and guzzlers.

1997 Fuel Economy Winners and Losers

The Misers	MPG City/Highway	Annual Fuel Cost[1]
Geo Metro (1.0L/3/M5)	44/49	$391
Volkswagen Golf (1.9L/4/M5)	40/49	$409
Volkswagen Jetta (1.9L/4/M5)	40/49	$409
Volkswagen Passat (1.9L/4/M5)	38/47	$428
Volkswagen Passat wagon (1.9L/4/M5)	38/47	$428
Geo Metro (1.3L/4/M5)	39/43	$439
Suzuki Swift (1.3L/4/M5)	39/43	$439
Honda Civic (1.6L/4/M5)	37/44	$450
Ford Aspire (1.3L/4/M5)	34/42	$486

The Guzzlers[2]	MPG City/Highway	Annual Fuel Cost[1]
Ford Aerostar (4.0L/6/L5)	14/19	$1125
Mazda MPV (3.0L/6/L4)	15/19	$1125
Pontiac Firebird (5.7L/8/M6)	16/26	$1105
Chevrolet Astro (4.3L/6/L4)	15/19	$1058
Audi A8 (3.7L/8/L5)	17/26	$1050
Audi A8 (4.2L/8/L5)	17/25	$1050
Cadillac DeVille (4.6L/8/L4)	17/26	$1050
Cadillac Eldorado (4.6L/8/L4)	17/26	$1050
Cadillac Seville (4.6L/8/L4)	17/26	$1050
Chevrolet Camaro (5.7L/8/L4)	17/25	$1050
Chevrolet Camaro (5.7L/8/M6)	16/27	$1050
Ford Taurus (3.4L/8/L4)	17/26	$1050
Infiniti J30 (3.0L/6/L4)	18/23	$1050
Infiniti Q45 (4.1L/8/L4)	18/24	$1050
Lexus GS300 (3.0L/6/L5)	18/24	$1050
Lexus SC300/400 (3.0L/6/L4)	18/24	$1050
Lexus SC300/400 (4.0L/8/L4)	18/23	$1050
Lincoln Continental (4.6L/8/L4)	17/25	$1050
Mercedes-Benz C-Class (3.6L/6/A5)	18/24	$1050
Mercedes-Benz E-Class 420 (4.2L/8/A5)	18/25	$1050
Oldsmobile Aurora (4.0L/8/L4)	17/26	$1050
Pontiac Firebird (5.7L/8/L4)	17/25	$1050
Subaru SVX Awd (3.3L/6/L4)	17/24	$1050

Based on 1997 EPA figures. (Engine size/number of cylinders/transmission type)

[1] Based on driving 15,000 miles per year.

[2] Based on popular models.

1997 EPA Figures

The following pages contain the EPA mileage ratings and the average annual fuel cost for most of the cars and many popular trucks sold in the United States. We have arranged the list in alphabetical order. After the car name, we have listed the engine size in liters, the number of cylinders, and some other identifiers: A = automatic transmission; L = lockup transmission; M = manual transmission.

The table includes the EPA city (first) and highway (second) fuel economy ratings. The city numbers will most closely resemble your expected mileage for everyday driving. The third column presents your average annual fuel cost. Reviewing this number will give you a better idea of how differences in fuel economy can affect your pocketbook. The amount is based on driving 15,000 miles per year.

Car (eng./trans.)	City	Hwy	Cost
Acura CL (2.2L/4/L4)	23	29	$ 720
Acura CL (2.2L/4/M5)	25	31	$ 666
Acura CL (3.0L/6/L4)	20	28	$ 783
Acura Integra (1.8L/4/L4)	24	31	$ 666
Acura Integra (1.8L/4/M5)	25	31	$ 643
Acura RL (3.5L/6/L4)	19	25	$1000
Acura TL (2.5L/5/L4)	20	25	$ 956
Acura TL (3.2L/6/L4)	19	24	$1000
Audi A4 (1.8L/4/L5)	21	30	$ 876
Audi A4 (2.8L/6/L5)	18	28	$ 956
Audi A4 (2.8L/6/M5)	19	27	$ 956
Audi A4 Quattro (1.8L/4/L5)	20	29	$ 914
Audi A4 Quattro (2.8L/6/L5)	18	27	$1000
Audi A4 Quattro (2.8L/6/M5)	19	26	$1000
Audi A6 (2.8L/6/L4)	19	25	$1000
Audi A6 Quattro (2.8L/6/L4)	19	24	$1000
Audi A6 Quattro Wagon (2.8L/6/L4)	19	24	$1000
Audi A6 Wagon (2.8L/6/L4)	19	25	$1000
Audi A8 (3.7L/8/L5)	17	26	$1050
Audi A8 (4.2L/8/L5)	17	25	$1050
BMW 318i (1.9L/4/L4)	22	31	$ 840
BMW 318i (1.9L/4/M5)	23	31	$ 808
BMW 318i Convertible (1.9L/4/L4)	22	31	$ 840
BMW 318i Convertible (1.9L/4/M5)	23	31	$ 808
BMW 318ti (1.9L/4/L4)	23	31	$ 808
BMW 318ti (1.9L/4/M5)	23	31	$ 808
BMW 328i (2.8L/6/L4)	19	26	$1000
BMW 328i (2.8L/6/M5)	20	29	$ 914
BMW 328ic (2.8L/6/L4)	19	26	$1000
BMW 328ic (2.8L/6/M5)	20	29	$ 914
BMW Z3 (1.9L/4/L4)	23	31	$ 808
BMW Z3 (1.9L/4/M5)	23	31	$ 808
BMW Z3 (3.2L/6/L5)	19	28	$ 956
BMW Z3 (3.2L/6/M5)	20	28	$ 914
Buick LeSabre (3.8L/6/L4)	19	30	$ 783
Buick Park Avenue (3.8L/6/L4)	19	28	$ 819
Buick Regal (3.1L/6/L4)	20	29	$ 783
Buick Regal (3.8L/6/L4)	19	30	$ 783
Buick Riviera (3.8L/6/L4)	18	27	$1000
Buick Skylark (2.4L/4/L4)	22	32	$ 693
Buick Skylark (3.1L/6/L4)	20	29	$ 783
Cadillac Catera (3.0L/6/L4)	18	25	$1000
Cadillac DeVille (4.6L/8/L4)	17	26	$1050
Cadillac Eldorado (4.6L/8/L4)	17	26	$1050
Cadillac Seville (4.6L/8/L4)	17	26	$1050
Chevrolet Astro (4.3L/6/L4)	17	23	$ 947
Chevrolet Camaro (3.8L/6/L4)	19	29	$ 819
Chevrolet Camaro (3.8L/6/M5)	19	30	$ 783
Chevrolet Camaro (5.7L/8/L4)	17	25	$1050
Chevrolet Camaro (5.7L/8/M6)	16	27	$1050
Chevrolet Cavalier (2.2L/4/L3)	24	31	$ 666
Chevrolet Cavalier (2.2L/4/L4)	25	34	$ 643
Chevrolet Cavalier (2.2L/4/M5)	25	37	$ 621
Chevrolet Cavalier (2.4L/4/L4)	22	32	$ 693
Chevrolet Cavalier (2.4L/4/M5)	23	33	$ 693
Chevrolet Lumina (3.1L/6/L4)	20	29	$ 783
Chevrolet Lumina (3.4L/6/L4)	17	26	$ 900
Chevrolet Malibu (3.1L/6/L4)	20	29	$ 783
Chevrolet Venture (3.4L/6/L4)	18	25	$ 857
Chrysler Cirrus (2.4L/4/L4)	20	30	$ 751
Chrysler Cirrus (2.5L/6/L4)	20	29	$ 783
Chrysler Concorde (3.3L/6/L4)	19	27	$ 819
Chrysler Concorde (3.5L/6/L4)	17	26	$ 857
Chrysler LHS (3.5L/6/L4)	17	26	$ 857
Chrysler Sebring (2.0L/4/L4)	21	30	$ 751
Chrysler Sebring (2.0L/4/M5)	22	31	$ 720
Chrysler Sebring (2.5L/6/L4)	20	27	$ 819
Chrysler Sebring Conv. (2.4L/4/L4)	20	28	$ 783
Chrysler Sebring Conv. (2.5L/6/L4)	18	28	$ 819
Chrys. Town and Country (3.3L/6/L4)	17	24	$ 900
Chrys. Town and Country (3.8L/6/L4)	17	24	$ 900
Dodge Avenger (2.0L/4/L4)	21	30	$ 751
Dodge Avenger (2.0L/4/M5)	22	32	$ 720
Dodge Avenger (2.5L/6/L4)	20	27	$ 819

Car (eng./trans.)	City	Hwy	Cost
Dodge Caravan 2wd (2.4L/4/L3)	20	25	$ 819
Dodge Caravan 2wd (2.4L/4/L4)	18	25	$ 857
Dodge Caravan 2wd (3.0L/6/L3)	19	24	$ 857
Dodge Caravan 2wd (3.3L/6/L4)	18	24	$ 900
Dodge Caravan 2wd (3.8L/6/L4)	17	24	$ 900
Dodge Caravan 4wd (3.8L/6/L4)	15	22	$1001
Dodge Intrepid (3.3L/6/L4)	19	27	$ 819
Dodge Intrepid (3.5L/6/L4)	17	26	$ 857
Dodge/Plymouth Neon (2.0L/4/L3)	25	34	$ 643
Dodge/Plymouth Neon (2.0L/4/M5)	29	39	$ 562
Dodge Stratus (2.0L/4/L4)	22	32	$ 720
Dodge Stratus (2.0L/4/M5)	26	37	$ 599
Dodge Stratus (2.4L/4/L4)	20	30	$ 751
Dodge Stratus (2.5L/6/L4)	20	29	$ 783
Eagle Talon (2.0L/4/L4)	21	31	$ 720
Eagle Talon (2.0L/4/M5)	22	33	$ 693
Eagle Vision (3.3L/6/L4)	19	27	$ 819
Eagle Vision (3.5L/6/L4)	17	26	$ 857
Ford Aerostar (3.0L/6/L4)	17	23	$ 947
Ford Aerostar (4.0L/6/L5)	16	22	$ 947
Ford Aspire (1.3L/4/L3)	28	31	$ 621
Ford Aspire (1.3L/4/M5)	34	42	$ 486
Ford Contour (2.0L/4/L4)	23	32	$ 693
Ford Contour (2.0L/4/M5)	24	33	$ 666
Ford Contour (2.5L/6/L4)	21	30	$ 751
Ford Contour (2.5L/6/M5)	20	30	$ 751
Ford Crown Victoria (4.6L/8/L4)	17	25	$ 900
Ford Escort (2.0L/4/L4)	26	34	$ 621
Ford Escort (2.0L/4/M5)	28	37	$ 581
Ford Escort Wagon (2.0L/4/L4)	26	34	$ 621
Ford Escort Wagon (2.0L/4/M5)	28	37	$ 581
Ford Mustang (3.8L/6/L4)	20	30	$ 783
Ford Mustang (3.8L/6/M5)	20	30	$ 751
Ford Mustang (4.6L/8/L4)	17	24	$ 947
Ford Mustang (4.6L/8/M5)	17	26	$ 900
Ford Probe (2.0L/4/L4)	23	31	$ 693
Ford Probe (2.0L/4/M5)	26	33	$ 621
Ford Probe (2.5L/6/L4)	20	26	$ 914
Ford Probe (2.5L/6/M5)	21	27	$ 914
Ford Taurus (3.0L/6/L4)	20	28	$ 783
Ford Taurus (3.0L/6/L4)	19	28	$ 819
Ford Taurus Wagon (3.0L/6/L4)	19	27	$ 819
Ford Thunderbird (3.8L/6/L4)	18	26	$ 857
Ford Thunderbird (4.6L/8/L4)	17	25	$ 900
Ford Windstar Van (3.0L/6/L4)	17	25	$ 900
Ford Windstar Van (3.8L/6/L4)	17	23	$ 947
Ford Windstar Wagon (3.0L/6/L4)	17	25	$ 900
Ford Windstar Wagon (3.8L/6/L4)	17	23	$ 947
Geo Metro (1.0L/3/M5)	44	49	$ 391
Geo Metro (1.3L/4/A3)	30	34	$ 562
Geo Metro (1.3L/4/M5)	39	43	$ 439
Geo Prizm (1.6L/4/L3)	25	29	$ 666
Geo Prizm (1.6L/4/M5)	30	34	$ 562
Geo Prizm (1.8L/4/L4)	27	34	$ 599
Geo Prizm (1.8L/4/M5)	29	35	$ 562
Honda Accord (2.2L/4/L4)	23	30	$ 693
Honda Accord (2.2L/4/M5)	25	31	$ 666
Honda Accord (2.7L/6/L4)	19	25	$ 857
Honda Accord Wagon (2.2L/4/L4)	23	29	$ 720
Honda Accord Wagon (2.2L/4/M5)	23	28	$ 720
Honda Civic (1.6L/4/L4)	29	35	$ 581
Honda Civic (1.6L/4/M5)	37	44	$ 450
Honda del Sol (1.6L/4/L4)	28	35	$ 581
Honda del Sol (1.6L/4/M5)	33	39	$ 515
Honda Odyssey (2.2L/4/L4)	21	26	$ 783
Hyundai Accent (1.5L/4/L4)	27	36	$ 599
Hyundai Accent (1.5L/4/M5)	28	37	$ 562
Hyundai Elantra (1.8L/4/L4)	23	31	$ 693
Hyundai Elantra (1.8L/4/M5)	24	32	$ 666
Hyundai Sonata (2.0L/4/L4)	20	27	$ 783
Hyundai Sonata (2.0L/4/M5)	21	28	$ 751
Hyundai Sonata (3.0L/6/L4)	18	24	$ 900
Hyundai Tiburon (1.8L/4/L4)	23	31	$ 693
Hyundai Tiburon (1.8L/4/M5)	22	30	$ 720
Hyundai Tiburon (2.0L/4/L4)	21	28	$ 783
Hyundai Tiburon (2.0L/4/M5)	22	29	$ 720
Infiniti I30 (3.0L/6/L4)	21	28	$ 914
Infiniti I30 (3.0L/6/M5)	21	26	$ 914
Infiniti J30 (3.0L/6/L4)	18	23	$1050
Infiniti Q45 (4.1L/8/L4)	18	24	$1050
Isuzu Oasis (2.2L/4/L4)	21	26	$ 783
Kia Sephia (1.6L/4/L4)	24	31	$ 666
Kia Sephia (1.6L/4/M5)	28	34	$ 599
Kia Sephia (1.8L/4/L4)	23	30	$ 693
Kia Sephia (1.8L/4/M5)	24	32	$ 666
Lexus ES300 (3.0L/6/L4)	19	26	$ 819
Lexus GS300 (3.0L/6/L5)	18	24	$1050
Lexus LS400 (4.0L/8/L4)	19	25	$ 956
Lexus SC300/400 (3.0L/6/L4)	18	24	$1050
Lexus SC300/400 (3.0L/6/M5)	19	24	$1000
Lexus SC300/400 (4.0L/8/L4)	18	23	$1050
Lincoln Continental (4.6L/8/L4)	17	25	$1050
Lincoln Mark VIII (4.6L/8/L4)	18	26	$1000
Lincoln Town Car (4.6L/8/L4)	17	25	$ 900
Mazda 626 (2.0L/4/L4)	23	31	$ 693
Mazda 626 (2.0L/4/M5)	26	34	$ 621
Mazda 626 (2.5L/6/L4)	20	26	$ 956
Mazda 626 (2.5L/6/M5)	21	26	$ 914

Car (eng./trans.)	City	Hwy	Cost
Mazda Miata (1.8L/4/L4)	22	28	$ 751
Mazda Miata (1.8L/4/M5)	23	29	$ 720
Mazda Millenia (2.3L/6/L4)	20	28	$ 956
Mazda Millenia (2.5L/6/L4)	20	27	$ 956
Mazda MPV (3.0L/6/L4)	16	21	$1001
Mazda MX-6 (2.0L/4/L4)	23	31	$ 693
Mazda MX-6 (2.0L/4/M5)	26	34	$ 621
Mazda MX-6 (2.5L/6/L4)	20	26	$ 956
Mazda MX-6 (2.5L/6/M5)	21	26	$ 914
Mazda Protege (1.5L/4/L4)	25	33	$ 643
Mazda Protege (1.5L/4/M5)	30	37	$ 545
Mazda Protege (1.8L/4/L4)	23	30	$ 693
Mazda Protege (1.8L/4/M5)	26	32	$ 621
Merc.-Bz C-Class 230 (2.3L/4/A5)	23	30	$ 808
Merc.-Bz C-Class 280 (2.8L/6/A5)	20	27	$ 914
Merc.-Bz E-Class 300Dies. (3.0L/6/L5)	26	33	$ 621
Merc.-Bz E-Class 320 (3.2L/6/L5)	20	27	$ 956
Merc.-Bz E-Class 420 (4.2L/8/A5)	18	25	$1050
Mercury Cougar (3.8L/6/L4)	18	26	$ 857
Mercury Cougar (4.6L/8/L4)	17	25	$ 900
Mercury Grand Marquis (4.6L/8/L4)	17	25	$ 900
Mercury Mystique (2.0L/4/L4)	23	32	$ 693
Mercury Mystique (2.0L/4/M5)	24	33	$ 666
Mercury Mystique (2.5L/6/L4)	21	30	$ 751
Mercury Mystique (2.5L/6/M5)	20	29	$ 783
Mercury Sable (3.0L/6/L4)	20	28	$ 783
Mercury Sable Wagon (3.0L/6/L4)	19	27	$ 819
Mercury Tracer (2.0L/4/L4)	26	34	$ 621
Mercury Tracer (2.0L/4/M5)	28	37	$ 581
Mercury Tracer Wagon (2.0L/4/L4)	26	34	$ 621
Mercury Tracer Wagon (2.0L/4/M5)	28	37	$ 581
Mercury Villager Van (3.0L/6/L4)	17	23	$ 900
Mercury Villager Wagon (3.0L/6/L4)	17	23	$ 900
Mitsubishi Diamante (3.5L/6/L4)	18	26	$1000
Mitsubishi Eclipse (2.0L/4/L4)	21	31	$ 720
Mitsubishi Eclipse (2.0L/4/M5)	22	33	$ 693
Mitsubishi Eclipse Conv. (2.0L/4/L4)	20	26	$ 956
Mitsubishi Eclipse Conv. (2.0L/4/M5)	23	31	$ 808
Mitsubishi Eclipse Conv. (2.4L/4/L4)	20	28	$ 783
Mitsubishi Eclipse Conv. (2.4L/4/M5)	22	30	$ 720
Mitsubishi Galant (2.4L/4/L4)	22	28	$ 751
Mitsubishi Galant (2.4L/4/M5)	23	30	$ 693
Mitsubishi Galant (2.5L/6/L4)	20	27	$ 819
Mitsubishi Mirage (1.5L/4/L4)	29	36	$ 581
Mitsubishi Mirage (1.5L/4/M5)	33	40	$ 500
Mitsubishi Mirage (1.8L/4/L4)	27	33	$ 621
Mitsubishi Mirage (1.8L/4/M5)	29	37	$ 562
Nissan 240SX (2.4L/4/L4)	21	27	$ 914
Nissan 240SX (2.4L/4/M5)	22	28	$ 876

Car (eng./trans.)	City	Hwy	Cost
Nissan Altima (2.4L/4/L4)	21	29	$ 751
Nissan Altima (2.4L/4/M5)	24	30	$ 693
Nissan Maxima (3.0L/6/L4)	21	28	$ 914
Nissan Maxima (3.0L/6/M5)	22	27	$ 876
Nissan Quest (3.0L/6/L4)	17	23	$ 900
Nissan Sentra (1.6L/4/L4)	27	36	$ 599
Nissan Sentra (1.6L/4/M5)	29	39	$ 545
Nissan Sentra (2.0L/4/L4)	23	30	$ 693
Nissan Sentra (2.0L/4/M5)	23	31	$ 693
Oldsmobile 88 (3.8L/6/L4)	19	29	$ 783
Olds Achieva (2.4L/4/L4)	22	32	$ 693
Olds Achieva (2.4L/4/M5)	23	33	$ 693
Olds Achieva (3.1L/6/L4)	20	29	$ 751
Olds Aurora (4.0L/8/L4)	17	26	$1050
Olds Cutlass (3.1L/6/L4)	20	29	$ 783
Olds Cutlass Supreme (3.1L/6/L4)	20	29	$ 783
Olds Cutlass Supreme (3.4L/6/L4)	17	26	$ 900
Olds Silhouette 2wd (3.4L/6/L4)	18	25	$ 857
Plymouth Breeze (2.0L/4/L4)	22	32	$ 720
Plymouth Breeze (2.0L/4/M5)	26	37	$ 599
Plymouth Voyager 2wd (2.4L/4/L3)	20	25	$ 819
Plymouth Voyager 2wd (2.4L/4/L4)	18	25	$ 857
Plymouth Voyager 2wd (3.0L/6/L3)	19	24	$ 857
Plymouth Voyager 2wd (3.3L/6/L4)	18	24	$ 900
Pontiac Bonneville (3.8L/6/L4)	19	28	$ 819
Pontiac Firebird (3.8L/6/L4)	19	29	$ 819
Pontiac Firebird (3.8L/6/M5)	19	30	$ 783
Pontiac Firebird (5.7L/8/L4)	17	25	$1050
Pontiac Firebird (5.7L/8/M6)	16	26	$1105
Pontiac Grand Am (2.4L/4/L4)	22	32	$ 693
Pontiac Grand Am (2.4L/4/M5)	23	33	$ 693
Pontiac Grand Am (3.1L/6/L4)	20	29	$ 783
Pontiac Grand Prix (3.1L/6/L4)	20	29	$ 783
Pontiac Grand Prix (3.8L/6/L4)	19	30	$ 783
Pontiac Sunfire (2.2L/4/L3)	24	31	$ 666
Pontiac Sunfire (2.2L/4/L4)	25	34	$ 643
Pontiac Sunfire (2.2L/4/M5)	25	37	$ 621
Pontiac Sunfire (2.4L/4/L4)	22	32	$ 720
Pontiac Sunfire (2.4L/4/M5)	23	33	$ 693
Pontiac Trans Sport 2wd (3.4L/6/L4)	18	25	$ 857
Saab 900 (2.0L/4/L4)	18	26	$ 857
Saab 900 (2.0L/4/M5)	20	27	$ 783
Saab 900 (2.3L/4/L4)	19	27	$ 819
Saab 900 (2.3L/4/M5)	21	29	$ 751
Saab 900 (2.5L/6/L4)	19	25	$ 857
Saab 900 Conv. (2.0L/4/L4)	18	26	$ 857
Saab 9000 (2.3L/4/A4)	17	26	$ 900
Saab 9000 (2.3L/4/M5)	20	29	$ 783
Saab 9000 (3.0L/6/A4)	18	26	$ 857

Car (eng./trans.)	City	Hwy	Cost
Saturn SC (1.9L/4/L4)	27	37	$ 581
Saturn SC (1.9L/4/M5)	28	40	$ 545
Saturn SL (1.9L/4/L4)	27	37	$ 581
Saturn SL (1.9L/4/M5)	28	40	$ 545
Saturn SW (1.9L/4/L4)	27	34	$ 599
Saturn SW (1.9L/4/M5)	28	37	$ 562
Subaru Impreza Awd (1.8L/4/M5)	24	30	$ 693
Subaru Impreza Awd (2.2L/4/L4)	23	30	$ 693
Subaru Impreza Awd (2.2L/4/M5)	23	30	$ 720
Subaru Impreza Wgn Awd (2.2L/4/L4)	23	30	$ 693
Subaru Impreza Wgn Awd (2.2L/4/M5)	23	30	$ 720
Subaru Legacy (2.2L/4/L4)	24	31	$ 666
Subaru Legacy Awd (2.2L/4/L4)	23	30	$ 693
Subaru Legacy Awd (2.2L/4/M5)	23	30	$ 720
Subaru Legacy Awd (2.5L/4/L4)	21	27	$ 783
Subaru Legacy Awd (2.5L/4/M5)	21	27	$ 783
Subaru Legacy Wgn (2.2L/4/L4)	24	31	$ 666
Subaru Legacy Wgn Awd (2.2L/4/L4)	23	30	$ 720
Subaru Legacy Wgn Awd (2.2L/4/M5)	23	30	$ 720
Subaru Legacy Wgn Awd (2.5L/4/L4)	21	27	$ 783
Subaru Legacy Wgn Awd (2.5L/4/M5)	21	27	$ 783
Subaru SVX Awd (3.3L/6/L4)	17	24	$1050
Suzuki Esteem (1.6L/4/L4)	27	34	$ 599
Suzuki Esteem (1.6L/4/M5)	31	37	$ 545
Suzuki Swift (1.3L/4/A3)	30	34	$ 562
Suzuki Swift (1.3L/4/M5)	39	43	$ 439
Toyota Avalon (3.0L/6/L4)	21	31	$ 751
Toyota Camry (2.2L/4/L4)	23	30	$ 720
Toyota Camry (2.2L/4/M5)	23	31	$ 693
Toyota Camry (3.0L/6/L4)	19	26	$ 819
Toyota Camry (3.0L/6/M5)	20	28	$ 783
Toyota Celica (1.8L/4/L4)	27	34	$ 599
Toyota Celica (1.8L/4/M5)	29	35	$ 562
Toyota Celica (2.2L/4/L4)	22	29	$ 751
Toyota Celica (2.2L/4/M5)	22	28	$ 751

Car (eng./trans.)	City	Hwy	Cost
Toyota Celica Conv. (2.2L/4/L4)	22	30	$ 720
Toyota Celica Conv. (2.2L/4/M5)	22	28	$ 751
Toyota Corolla (1.6L/4/L3)	25	29	$ 666
Toyota Corolla (1.6L/4/M5)	31	35	$ 562
Toyota Corolla (1.8L/4/L4)	27	34	$ 599
Toyota Corolla (1.8L/4/M5)	29	35	$ 562
Toyota Paseo (1.5L/4/L4)	27	32	$ 621
Toyota Paseo (1.5L/4/M5)	31	37	$ 545
Toyota Paseo Conv. (1.5L/4/L4)	27	32	$ 621
Toyota Paseo Conv. (1.5L/4/M5)	29	35	$ 562
Toyota Previa (2.4L/4/L4)	18	22	$ 947
Toyota Previa All-trac (2.4L/4/L4)	17	20	$1001
Toyota Tercel (1.5L/4/L3)	29	34	$ 581
Toyota Tercel (1.5L/4/L4)	30	37	$ 545
Toyota Tercel (1.5L/4/M5)	32	39	$ 515
Volkswagen Golf/Jetta (1.9L/4/M5)	40	49	$ 409
Volkswagen Golf/Jetta (2.0L/4/L4)	22	29	$ 751
Volkswagen Golf/Jetta (2.0L/4/M5)	24	31	$ 693
Volkswagen Golf/Jetta (2.8L/6/L4)	18	24	$ 857
Volkswagen Golf/Jetta (2.8L/6/M5)	19	25	$ 857
Volkswagen Passat (1.9L/4/M5)	38	47	$ 428
Volkswagen Passat (2.8L/6/L4)	18	25	$ 900
Volkswagen Passat (2.8L/6/M5)	19	26	$ 857
Volkswagen Passat Wgn (1.9L/4/M5)	38	47	$ 428
Volkswagen Passat Wgn (2.8L/6/L4)	18	25	$ 900
Volkswagen Passat Wgn (2.8L/6/M5)	19	26	$ 857
Volvo 850 (2.3L/5/L4)	19	26	$ 956
Volvo 850 (2.4L/5/L4)	20	29	$ 914
Volvo 850 (2.4L/5/M5)	20	29	$ 914
Volvo 850 Wagon (2.3L/5/L4)	19	26	$ 956
Volvo 850 Wagon (2.4L/5/L4)	20	29	$ 914
Volvo 850 Wagon (2.4L/5/M5)	20	29	$ 914
Volvo 900 Series (2.9L/6/L4)	18	26	$1000
Volvo 900 Series Wagon (2.9L/6/L4)	18	26	$1000

MAINTENANCE

After you buy a car, maintenance costs will be a significant portion of your operating expenses. This chapter allows you to consider and compare some of these costs *before* deciding which car to purchase. These costs include preventive maintenance servicing—such as changing the oil and filters—as well as the cost of repairs after your warranty expires. On the following pages, we compared the costs of preventive maintenance and nine likely repairs for the 1997 models. Since the cost of a repair also depends on the shop and the mechanic, this chapter includes tips for finding a good shop, communicating effectively with a mechanic, and extending the life of your car.

Preventive maintenance is the periodic servicing, specified by the manufacturer, that keeps your car running properly. For example, regularly changing the oil and oil filter. Every owner's manual specifies a schedule of recommended servicing for at least the first 50,000 miles, and the tables on the following pages estimate the cost of following this preventive maintenance schedule.

If for some reason you do not have an owner's manual with the preventive maintenance schedule, contact the manufacturer to obtain one.

Note: Some dealers and repair shops create their own maintenance schedules which call for more frequent (and thus more expensive) servicing than the manufacturer's recommendations. If the servicing recommended by your dealer or repair shop doesn't match what the car maker recommends, make sure you understand and agree to the extra items.

The tables also list the costs for nine repairs that typically occur during the first 100,000 miles. There is no precise way to predict exactly when a repair will be needed. But if you keep a car for 75,000 to 100,000 miles, it is likely that you will experience most of these repairs at least once. The last column provides a relative indication of how expensive these nine repairs are for many cars. Repair cost is rated as *Very Good* if the total for nine repairs is in the bottom fifth of all the cars rated, and *Very Poor* if the total is in the top fifth.

Most repair shops use "flat-rate manuals" to estimate repair costs. These manuals list the approximate time required for repairing many items. Each automobile manufacturer publishes its own manual and there are several independent manuals as well. For many repairs, the time varies from one manual to another. Some repair shops even use different manuals for different repairs. To determine a repair bill, a shop multiplies the time listed in its manual by its hourly labor rate and then adds the cost of parts.

Our cost estimates are based on flat-rate manual repair times multiplied by a nationwide average labor rate of $50 per hour. All estimates also include the cost of replaced parts and related adjustments, which are based on 1996 figures.

Prices in the following tables may not predict the exact costs of these repairs. For example, the labor rate for your area may be more or less than the national average. However, the prices will provide you with a relative comparison of maintenance costs for various automobiles.

	PM Costs to 50,000 Miles	Water Pump	Alternator	Front Brake Pads	Starter	Fuel Injection	Fuel Pump	Struts	Timing Belt	Power Steering Pump	Relative Maint. Cost
Subcompact											
Dodge/Plymouth Neon	719	207	295	132	209	131	288	200	167	234	Vry. Gd.
Ford Aspire	676	302	836	104	481	325	424	335	133	648	Vry. Pr.
Ford Escort	676	217	359	108	337	260	182	305	191	552	Average
Geo Metro	805	259	488	118	441	298	498	343	127	811	Vry. Pr.
Honda Civic	906	185	318	108	305	154	280	321	170	541	Average
Honda del Sol	906	185	350	108	294	143	511	330	185	659	Poor
Hyundai Accent	364	195	310	79	273	92	351	249	177	485	Good
Kia Sephia	721	248	425	118	289	325	437	353	192	400	Poor
Mazda Miata	808	234	249	108	179	303	394	321	174	638	Average
Mazda Protege	808	250	275	121	181	330	357	305	169	746	Poor
Mercury Tracer	676	217	359	106	280	141	182	300	140	450	Good
Mitsubishi Mirage	1069	253	302	128	264	236	387	361	186	606	Poor
Nissan Sentra	741	190	335	104	316	170	153	291	588	241	Average
Saturn SC	901	137	248	93	171	150	260	232	286	288	Vry. Gd.
Saturn SL/SW	901	137	248	93	171	140	260	232	271	273	Vry. Gd.
Subaru Impreza	602	217	417	107	407	136	279	418	184	397	Average
Suzuki Esteem	805	207	759	129	332	271	455	427	195	624	Vry. Pr.
Suzuki Swift	805	271	344	129	317	267	417	417	177	646	Poor
Toyota Paseo	962	170	449	84	268	204	322	398	158	579	Average
Toyota Tercel	962	160	390	115	252	219	317	405	153	584	Average
Compact											
Acura Integra	1121	284	391	113	383	164	413	380	229	639	Poor
BMW 3-Series	1144	180	514	135	428	225	187	654	436	628	Vry. Pr.
BMW Z-3	1144	170	450	123	242	235	325	518	376	707	Vry. Pr.
Buick Skylark	724	288	232	112	363	173	212	378	242	346	Good
Chevrolet Cavalier	719	213	262	111	299	198	570	371	302	353	Average
Chrysler Sebring	702	212	232	135	207	125	228	261	202	310	Vry. Gd.
Dodge Avenger	702	212	232	135	207	130	228	261	202	310	Vry. Gd.
Eagle Talon	719	247	222	118	327	145	263	282	217	325	Good
Ford Contour	676	232	456	121	374	106	214	303	177	214	Good
Average	769	229	368	125	332	197	323	320	284	453	

	PM Costs to 50,000 Miles	Water Pump	Alternator	Front Brake Pads	Starter	Fuel Injection	Fuel Pump	Struts	Timing Belt	Power Steering Pump	Relative Maint. Cost
Compact (cont.)											
Ford Probe	742	270	462	139	775	300	222	355	181	448	Vry. Pr.
Geo Prizm	873	203	579	123	474	186	331	405	160	598	Poor
Honda Prelude	908	223	381	108	453	145	515	345	213	666	Poor
Hyundai Elantra	364	202	307	71	254	92	277	206	194	490	Good
Hyundai Tiburon	364	202	307	71	254	92	277	206	194	490	Good
Mazda 626	808	225	260	105	235	295	350	342	158	298	Good
Mazda MX-6	808	225	260	105	235	295	350	362	158	298	Good
Mercury Mystique	687	232	456	104	388	82	219	303	177	214	Good
Mitsubishi Eclipse	719	262	220	128	225	162	318	264	229	305	Good
Mitsubishi Galant	1022	263	339	128	231	186	206	223	234	347	Good
Oldsmobile Achieva	724	248	242	111	373	176	207	373	201	356	Good
Pontiac Grand Am	724	211	218	111	309	219	217	399	383	378	Average
Pontiac Sunfire	724	213	262	111	299	188	585	371	302	349	Average
Subaru Legacy	583	217	387	122	410	135	274	379	176	341	Average
Toyota Celica	945	246	403	94	348	221	392	425	156	664	Poor
Toyota Corolla	873	204	460	108	281	211	337	345	136	655	Poor
Volkswagen Golf/Jetta	401	291	525	130	464	168	370	329	88	291	Average
Intermediate											
Audi A4	0	301	699	196	540	152	262	350	195	450	Vry. Pr.
Buick Century	730	198	199	99	299	213	281	291	332	291	Good
Buick Regal	730	126	239	113	304	234	263	626	394	235	Average
Cadillac Catera	559	220	364	97	320	325	347	586	331	557	Vry. Pr.
Chevrolet Camaro	730	209	212	122	336	169	532	289	234	373	Average
Chrysler Cirrus	702	366	300	179	218	226	226	214	186	337	Good
Chrysler Concorde	702	88	185	137	200	117	240	232	221	275	Vry. Gd.
Dodge Intrepid	702	88	185	142	200	117	240	262	241	255	Vry. Gd.
Dodge Stratus	702	217	305	179	214	155	226	209	187	322	Vry. Gd.
Eagle Vision	702	88	195	137	200	117	240	237	246	255	Vry. Gd.
Ford Mustang	742	219	422	177	366	152	237	287	341	377	Average
Ford Taurus	659	184	360	137	314	115	225	319	262	273	Good
Average	769	229	368	125	332	197	323	320	284	453	

	PM Costs to 50,000 Miles	Water Pump	Alternator	Front Brake Pads	Starter	Fuel Injection	Fuel Pump	Struts	Timing Belt	Power Steering Pump	Relative Maint. Cost
Intermediate (cont.)											
Honda Accord	908	278	386	108	332	145	311	304	263	727	Poor
Hyundai Sonata	364	252	332	78	215	95	211	254	257	525	Good
Mazda Millenia	806	279	768	126	255	371	481	430	248	901	Vry. Pr.
Mercedes-Benz C-Class	1019	356	225	116	199	160	294	366	472	861	Poor
Mercury Sable	659	182	311	137	286	123	222	319	202	268	Vry. Gd.
Nissan 240SX	724	157	298	112	214	204	348	532	716	389	Poor
Nissan Altima	719	157	303	112	259	189	195	297	781	227	Average
Nissan Maxima	748	257	425	110	318	248	318	680	771	534	Vry. Pr.
Olds Cutlass	730	198	194	99	304	223	271	285	302	291	Good
Olds Cutlass Supreme	730	126	242	113	304	235	247	608	413	353	Average
Plymouth Breeze	702	302	310	179	218	154	224	179	186	322	Good
Pontiac Firebird	730	370	247	127	336	176	538	289	299	423	Poor
Pontiac Grand Prix	730	126	247	113	304	235	263	626	393	294	Average
Saab 900	642	222	677	128	300	153	328	492	165	662	Vry. Pr.
Saab 9000	692	207	665	117	459	205	302	297	440	778	Vry. Pr.
Toyota Avalon	945	252	436	117	296	266	349	426	173	573	Poor
Toyota Camry	945	271	471	112	286	256	314	405	172	619	Poor
Volkswagen Passat	412	280	590	128	537	182	381	273	185	661	Vry. Pr.
Volvo 850	1125	238	606	106	391	132	296	314	158	492	Poor
Large											
Acura CL	1120	328	366	113	369	125	370	312	244	721	Poor
Acura RL	1120	328	366	113	369	125	370	307	244	721	Poor
Acura TL	1120	267	1145	114	389	136	417	451	214	669	Vry. Pr.
Audi A6	0	302	683	143	510	165	249	825	198	452	Vry. Pr.
Buick LeSabre	736	234	261	128	263	154	289	406	259	358	Good
Buick Park Avenue	736	234	317	123	303	154	276	401	259	355	Average
Buick Riviera	736	229	281	120	321	157	520	334	254	358	Average
Cadillac DeVille	559	183	354	119	442	194	557	1179	753	341	Vry. Pr.
Cadillac Eldorado	559	163	383	119	458	160	547	1169	745	351	Vry. Pr.
Cadillac Seville	559	163	369	119	442	179	547	1169	745	341	Vry. Pr.
Average	769	229	368	125	332	197	323	320	284	453	

Maintenance Costs

	PM Costs to 50,000 Miles	Water Pump	Alternator	Front Brake Pads	Starter	Fuel Injection	Fuel Pump	Struts	Timing Belt	Power Steering Pump	Relative Maint. Cost
Large (cont.)											
Chevrolet Lumina	736	126	247	113	304	234	263	428	393	230	Good
Chevrolet Malibu	730	126	247	113	304	234	263	428	393	230	Good
Chevrolet Monte Carlo	736	126	247	113	304	239	263	428	393	230	Good
Chrysler LHS	719	195	190	137	200	139	240	242	224	260	Vry. Gd.
Ford Crown Victoria	742	200	382	130	301	223	282	143	336	382	Average
Ford Thunderbird	742	214	437	149	348	199	269	283	351	390	Average
Infiniti I30	730	279	461	110	361	258	333	779	625	544	Vry. Pr.
Infiniti J30	730	272	615	117	195	342	345	746	264	464	Vry. Pr.
Infiniti Q45	730	209	419	116	315	345	368	444	1200	535	Vry. Pr.
Lexus ES300	730	260	467	113	307	266	356	415	530	662	Vry. Pr.
Lexus GS300	730	285	536	116	307	321	390	219	186	682	Poor
Lexus LS400	730	365	535	128	704	344	410	178	256	750	Vry. Pr.
Lexus SC300/400	730	280	624	110	302	325	344	299	186	682	Vry. Pr.
Lincoln Continental	730	223	497	180	329	149	269	1035	266	352	Vry. Pr.
Lincoln Mark VIII	730	150	475	194	423	160	367	213	456	387	Poor
Lincoln Town Car	730	190	397	130	361	132	362	137	326	387	Average
Mercedes-Benz E-Class	1227	476	351	139	539	172	322	454	565	606	Vry. Pr.
Mercury Cougar	742	213	437	149	348	178	269	289	361	395	Average
Mercury Grand Marquis	742	200	376	130	332	207	280	100	346	382	Good
Mitsubishi Diamante	1093	318	389	147	262	219	479	345	315	635	Vry. Pr.
Oldsmobile 88	724	234	261	128	258	157	283	406	259	368	Good
Oldsmobile Aurora	745	153	376	123	438	174	514	202	480	373	Poor
Pontiac Bonneville	724	234	249	128	295	164	276	406	259	363	Average
Subaru SVX	602	258	417	138	415	135	347	423	221	499	Poor
Volvo 900 Series	1125	226	431	97	439	176	236	328	94	540	Average
Minivan											
Chevrolet Astro	680	257	263	116	259	199	212	165	245	373	Good
Chevrolet Venture	680	132	225	130	285	183	185	260	322	305	Vry. Gd.
Chrys. Town and Country	626	114	313	146	200	90	268	269	260	315	Vry. Gd.
Dodge Caravan	626	233	293	146	225	129	268	209	220	285	Vry. Gd.
Average	769	229	368	125	332	197	323	320	284	453	

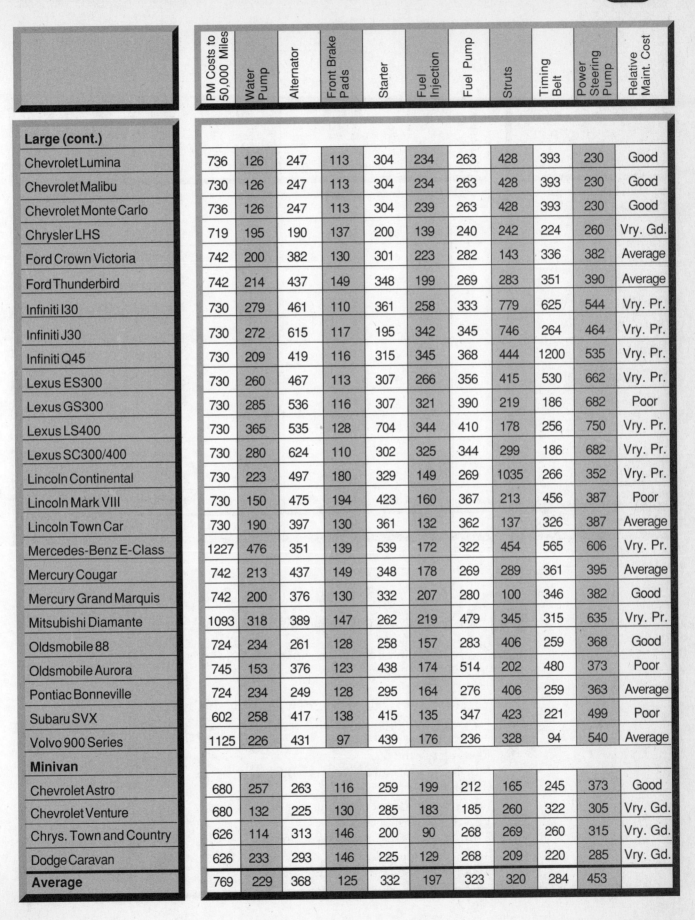

	PM Costs to 50,000 Miles	Water Pump	Alternator	Front Brake Pads	Starter	Fuel Injection	Fuel Pump	Struts	Timing Belt	Power Steering Pump	Relative Maint. Cost
Minivan (cont.)											
Ford Aerostar	605	249	362	154	347	162	203	166	367	367	Average
Ford Windstar	605	301	431	156	276	208	273	349	607	263	Poor
GMC Safari	680	237	263	116	259	164	212	163	245	388	Vry. Gd.
Honda Odyssey	906	257	353	109	530	130	397	304	218	731	Poor
Isuzu Oasis	906	277	355	109	384	131	409	346	218	740	Poor
Mazda MPV	851	241	253	138	243	317	240	370	236	829	Poor
Mercury Villager	631	233	413	153	298	315	344	265	169	482	Average
Nissan Quest	631	247	320	129	209	331	236	273	227	489	Average
Oldsmobile Silhouette	680	132	229	130	303	208	185	205	323	185	Vry. Gd.
Plymouth Voyager	626	263	303	146	225	132	263	192	205	256	Vry. Gd.
Pontiac Trans Sport	680	132	217	130	303	208	172	209	333	190	Vry. Gd.
Toyota Previa	812	144	398	112	361	216	375	455	583	678	Vry. Pr.
Average	769	229	368	125	332	197	323	320	284	453	

Top Ten Things to Do on a Test Drive

The biggest mistake most of us make when buying a new car is not taking a good, long test drive. Plan on spending at least an hour to an hour and a half with the car, and include the following:

1. Take the car on a highway to review handling, acceleration, braking and wind noise.
2. Take the car on the bumpiest road you know.
3. Parallel park the car.
4. Pull the car in and out of your driveway and garage.
5. Sit in the passenger and back seats.
6. Put things in and out of the trunk or cargo space.
7. Look for blind spots.
8. Try the driver's seat in various positions.
9. Take a ride with other members of your family.
10. Make sure everyone tries on the seat belts.

Each year nearly 50 percent of new car buyers buy "service contracts." Ranging from $400 to $1500 in price, a service contract is one of the most expensive options you can buy. In fact, service contracts are a major profit source for many dealers.

A service contract is not a warranty. It is more like an insurance plan that, in theory, covers repairs that are not covered by your warranty or that occur after the warranty runs out.

Service contracts are generally a very poor value. The companies who sell contracts are very sure that, on average, your repairs will cost considerably less than what you pay for the contract—if not, they wouldn't be in business.

Tip: One alternative to buying a service contract is to deposit the cost of the contract into a savings account. If the car needs a major repair not covered by your warranty, the money in your account will cover the cost. Most likely, you'll be building up your down payment for your next car!

If you believe that you really need a service contract, contact an insurance company, such as GEICO. You can save up to 50-percent by buying from an insurance company.

Here are some important questions to ask before buying a service contract:

How reputable is the company responsible for the contract? If the company offering the contract goes out of business, you will be out of luck. Recently, a number of independent service contract companies have gone under, so be very careful about who you buy from. Check with your Better Business Bureau or office of consumer affairs if you are not sure of a company's reputation. Service contracts from car and insurance companies are more likely to remain in effect than those from independent companies.

Exactly what does the contract cover and for how long? Service contracts vary considerably—different items are covered and different time limits are offered. This is true even among service contracts offered by the same company. For example, Ford's plans range from 3 years/50,000 miles maximum coverage to 6 years/ 100,000 miles maximum coverage, with other options for only powertrain coverage.

If you plan to resell your car in a few years, you won't want to purchase a long-running service contract. Some service contracts automatically cancel when you resell the car, while others require a hefty transfer fee before extending privileges to the new owner.

Some automakers offer a "menu" format which lets you pick the items you want covered in your service contract. Find out if the contract pays for preventive maintenance, towing, and rental car expenses. If not written into the contract, assume they are not covered.

Finally, think twice before purchasing travel services offered in the contract. Such amenities are offered by auto clubs, and you should compare prices before adding them into your contract cost.

How will the repair bills be paid? It is best to have the service contractor pay bills directly. Some contracts require you to pay the repair bill, and reimburse you later.

Where can the car be serviced? Can you take the car to any mechanic if you have trouble on the road? What if you move?

What other costs can be expected? Most service contracts will have a deductible expense. Compare deductibles on various plans. Also, some companies charge the deductible for each individual repair while other companies charge per visit, regardless of the number of repairs made.

Turbocharging

A turbocharger is an air pump that forces more air into the engine for combustion. Most turbo chargers consist of an air compressor driven by a small turbine wheel that is powered by the engine's exhaust. The turbine takes advantage of energy otherwise lost and forces increased efficiency from the engine. Turbochargers are often used to increase the power and sometimes the fuel efficiency of small engines. Engines equipped with turbochargers are more expensive than standard engines. The extra power may not be necessary when you consider the added expense and the fact that turbocharging adds to the complexity of the engine.

Tips for Dealing with a Mechanic

Call around. Don't choose a shop simply because it's nearby. Calling a few shops may turn up estimates cheaper by half.

Don't necessarily go for the lowest price. A good rule is to eliminate the highest and lowest estimates; the mechanic with the highest estimate is probably charging too much, and the lowest may be cutting too many corners.

Check the shop's reputation. Call your local consumer affairs agency and the Better Business Bureau. They don't have records on every shop, but if their reports on a shop aren't favorable, you can disqualify it.

Look for certification. Mechanics can be certified by the National Institute for Automotive Service Excellence, an industry-wide yardstick for competence. Certification is offered in eight areas of repair and shops with certified mechanics are allowed to advertise this fact. However, make sure the mechanic working on your car is certified for the repair.

Take a look around. A well-kept shop reflects pride in workmanship. A skilled and efficient mechanic would probably not work in a messy shop.

Don't sign a blank check. The service order you sign should have specific instructions or describe your vehicle's symptoms. Signing a vague work order could make you liable to pay for work you didn't want. Be sure you are called for final approval before the shop does extra work.

Show interest. Ask about the repair. A mechanic may become more helpful just knowing that you're interested. But don't act like an expert if you don't really understand what's wrong. Demonstrating your ignorance, on the other hand, may set you up to be taken by a dishonest mechanic, so strike a balance.

Express your satisfaction. If you're happy with the work, compliment the mechanic and ask for him or her the next time you come in. You will get to know each other and the mechanic will get to know your vehicle.

Develop a "sider." If you know a mechanic, ask about work on the side—evenings or weekends. The labor will be cheaper.

Test drive, then pay! Before you pay for a major repair, you should take the car for a test drive. The few extra minutes you spend checking out the repair could save you a trip back to the mechanic. If you find that the problem still exists, there will be no question that the repair wasn't properly completed. It is more difficult to prove the repair wasn't properly made after you've left the shop.

Repair Protection By Credit Card

Paying your auto repair bills by credit card can provide a much-needed recourse if you are having problems with an auto mechanic. According to federal law, you have the right to withhold payment for sloppy or incorrect repairs. Of course, you may withhold no more than the amount of the repair in dispute.

In order to use this right, you must first try to work out the problem with the mechanic. Also, unless the credit card company owns the repair shop (this might be the case with gasoline credit cards used at gas stations), two other conditions must be met. First, the repair shop must be in your home state (or within 100 miles of your current address), and second, the cost of repairs must be over $50. Until the problem is settled or resolved in court, the credit card company cannot charge you interest or penalties on the amount in dispute.

If you decide to take action, send a letter to the credit card company and a copy to the repair shop, explaining the details of the problem and what you want as settlement. Send the letter by certified mail with a return receipt requested.

Sometimes the credit card company or repair shop will attempt to put a "bad mark" on your credit record if you use this tactic. Legally, you can't be reported as delinquent if you've given the credit card company notice of your dispute, but a creditor can report that you are disputing your bill, which goes in your record. However, you have the right to challenge any incorrect information and add your side of the story to your file.

For more information, write to the Federal Trade Commission, Credit Practices Division, 601 Pennsylvania Avenue, NW, Washington, DC 20580.

With the popularity of self-service gasoline stations, many of us overlook the simplest and most vital maintenance task of all: checking various items to prevent serious problems down the road. In about fifteen minutes a month, you can make the following checks yourself. *Warning:* Many new vehicles have electric cooling fans that operate when the engine is off. Be sure to keep your hands away from the fan if the engine is warm.

Coolant: We'll start with the easiest fluid to check. Most vehicles have a plastic reservoir next to the radiator. This bottle will have "full hot" and "full cold" marks on it. If coolant is below "full cold" mark, add water to bring it up to that mark. (Anti-freeze should be used if you want extra protection in cold weather.) *Caution:* If vehicle is hot, do not open the radiator cap. Pressure and heat that can cause a severe burn may be released.

Brakes: The most important safety item on the vehicle is the most ignored. A simple test will signal problems. (With power brakes, turn on engine to test.) Push the brake pedal down and hold it down. It should stop firmly and stay about halfway to the floor. If the stop is mushy or the pedal keeps moving to the floor, you should have your brakes checked. Checking the brake fluid on most vehicles is also easy. Your owner's manual tells you where to find the fluid reservoir, which indicates minimum and maximum fluid levels. If you add your own brake fluid, buy it in small cans and keep them tightly sealed. Brake fluid absorbs moisture, and excess moisture can damage your brake system. Have the brakes checked if you need to replace brake fluid regularly.

Oil: A few years ago, the phrase "fill it up and check the oil" was so common that it seemed like one word. Today, checking the oil often is the responsibility of the driver. To check your oil, first turn off the engine. Find the dip-stick (look for a loop made of flat wire located on the side of the engine). If the engine has been running, be careful, because the dipstick and surrounding engine parts will be hot. Grab the loop, pull out the dipstick, clean it off, and reinsert it into the engine. Pull it out again and observe the oil level. "Full" and "add" are marked at the end of the stick. If the level is between "add" and "full," you are OK. If it is below "add," you should add enough oil until it reaches the "full" line. To add oil, remove the cap at the top of the engine. You may have to add more than one quart. Changing your oil regularly (every 3000-5000 miles based on your driving habits) is the single most important way to protect your engine. Many owner's manuals also contain directions for doing so. Change the oil filter whenever you change the oil.

Transmission Fluid: An automatic transmission is a complicated and expensive item. Checking your transmission fluid level is easy and can prevent a costly repair job. As in the oil check, you must first find the transmission fluid dipstick. Usually it is at the rear of the engine and looks like a smaller version of the oil dipstick. To get an accurate reading, the engine should be warmed up and running. If fluid is below the "add" line, pour in one pint at a time, but do not overfill the reservoir.

While you check the fluid, also note its color. It should be a bright, cherry red. If it is a darker, reddish brown, the fluid needs changing. If it is very dark, nearly black, and has a burnt smell (like varnish), your transmission may be damaged. You should take it to a specialist.

Automatic transmission fluid is available at most department stores; check your owner's manual for the correct type for your vehicle.

Power Steering: The power steering fluid reservoir is usually connected by a belt to the engine. To check it, unscrew the cap and look in the reservoir. There will be markings inside; some vehicles have a little dipstick built in to the cap.

Belts: You may have one or more belts connected to your engine. A loose belt in the engine can lead to electrical, cooling, or even air conditioning problems. To check, simply push down on the middle of each belt. It should feel tight. If you can push down more than half an inch, the belt needs tightening.

Battery: If your battery has caps on the top, lift off the caps and check that fluid comes up to the bottom of the filler neck. If it doesn't, add water (preferably distilled). If it is very cold outside, add water only if you are planning to drive the vehicle immediately. Otherwise the newly added water can freeze and damage your battery.

Also, look for corrosion around the battery connections. It can prevent electrical circuits from being completed, leading you to assume your perfectly good battery is "dead." If cables are corroded, remove and clean with fine sandpaper or steel wool. The inside of the connection and the battery posts should be shiny when you put the cables back on. *Caution:* Do not smoke or use any flame when checking the battery.

Tires: Improperly inflated tires are a major cause of premature tire failure. Check for proper inflation at least once a month. The most fuel-efficient inflation level is the maximum pressure listed on the side of the tire. Because many gas station pumps do not have gauges, and those that do are generally inaccurate, you should invest in your own tire gauge.

Air Filter: Probably the easiest item to maintain is your air filter. You can usually check the filter by just looking at it. If it appears dirty, change it—it's a simple task. If you are not sure how clean your filter is, try the following: Once the engine warms up, put the vehicle in park or neutral and, with the emergency brake on, let the vehicle idle. Open the filter lid and remove the filter. If the engine begins to run faster, change the filter.

Battery Safety

Almost all motorists have had to jump start a vehicle because of a dead battery. But that innocent-looking battery can cause some serious injuries.

Batteries produce hydrogen gas when they discharge or undergo heavy use (such as cranking the engine for a long period of time). A lit cigarette or a spark can cause this gas to explode. Whenever you work with the battery, always remove the negative (or ground) cable first and reconnect it last; it is usually marked with a minus sign. This precaution will greatly reduce the chance of causing a spark that could ignite any hydrogen gas present.

For a safe jump start:

1 Connect each end of the red cable to the positive (+) terminal on each battery.

2 Connect one end of the black cable to the negative (-) terminal of the *good* battery.

3 Connect the other end of the black cable to exposed metal away from the battery of the vehicle being started.

4 To avoid damaging electrical parts, make sure the engine is idling before disconnecting the cables.

Saving Gasoline

A cold-running engine dramatically reduces fuel economy. Most engines operate efficiently at 180 degrees, and an engine running at 125 degrees can waste one out of every ten gallons of gas. Your engine temperature is controlled by a thermostat valve. A faulty thermostat can be a major cause of poor fuel economy. If you feel that your vehicle should be getting better mileage, have your thermostat checked. They are inexpensive and easy to replace.

WARRANTIES

Along with your new car comes a warranty, which is a promise from the manufacturer that the car will perform as it should. Most of us never read the warranty—until it is too late. In fact, because warranties are often difficult to read and understand, most of us don't really know what our warranties offer. This chapter will help you understand what to look for in a new car warranty, tip you off to secret warranties, and provide you with the best and worst among the 1997 warranties.

There are two types of warranties: one provided by the manufacturer and one implied by law.

Manufacturers' warranties are either "full" or "limited." The best warranty you can get is a full warranty because, by law, it must cover all aspects of the product's performance. Any other guarantee is called a limited warranty, which is what most car manufacturers offer. Limited warranties must be clearly marked as such, and you must be told exactly what is covered.

Warranties implied by law are warranties of merchantability and fitness. The "warranty of merchantability" ensures that your new car will be fit for the purpose for which it is used—that means safe, efficient, and trouble-free transportation. The "warranty of fitness" guarantees that if the dealer says a car can be used for a specific purpose, it will perform that purpose.

Any claims made by the salesperson are also considered warranties. They are called expressed warranties and you should have them put in writing if you consider them to be important. If the car does not live up to promises made to you in the showroom, you may have a case against the seller.

The manufacturer can restrict the amount of time the limited warranty is in effect. And in most states, the manufacturer can also limit the time that the warranty implied by law is in effect.

Through the warranty, the manufacturer is promising that the way the car was made and the materials used are free from defects, provided that the car is used in a normal fashion for a certain period after you buy it. This period of time is usually measured in both months and miles— whichever comes first is the limit.

While the warranty is in effect, the manufacturer will perform, at no charge to the owner, repairs that are necessary because of defects in materials or in the way the car was manufactured.

The warranty does not cover parts that have to be replaced because of normal wear, such as filters, fuses, light bulbs, wiper blades, clutch linings, brake pads, or the addition of oil, fluids, coolants, and lubricants. Tires, batteries, and the emission control system are covered by separate warranties. Options, such as a stereo system, should have their own warranties as well. Service should be provided through the dealer. A separate rust (corrosion) warranty is also included.

The costs for the required maintenance listed in the owner's manual are not covered by the warranty. Problems resulting from misuse, negligence, changes you make in the car, accidents, or lack of required maintenance are also not covered.

Any implied warranties, including the warranties of merchantability and fitness, are limited to 12 months or 12,000 miles. Also, the manufacturer is not responsible for other problems caused by repairs, such as the loss of time or use of your car, or any expenses they might cause.

In addition to the rights granted to you in the warranty, you may have other rights under your state laws.

To keep your warranty in effect, you must operate and maintain your car according to the instructions in your owner's manual. Remember, it is important to keep a record of all maintenance performed on your car.

To have your car repaired under the warranty, take it to an authorized dealer or service center. The work should be done in a reasonable amount of time during normal business hours.

Be careful not to confuse your warranty with a service contract. The *service contract* must be purchased separately while the warranty is yours at no extra cost when you buy the car. (See page 55 for more on service contracts.)

Corrosion Warranty: All manufacturers warrant against corrosion. The typical corrosion warranty lasts for six years or 100,000 miles, whichever comes first.

Some dealers offer extra rust protection at an additional cost. Before you purchase this option, compare the extra protection offered to the corrosion warranty already included in the price of the car—it probably already provides sufficient protection against rust. (See page 95 for more important information on rustproofing.)

Emission System Warranty: The emission system is warranted by federal law. Any repairs required during the first two years or 24,000 miles will be paid for by the manufacturer if an original engine part fails because of a defect in materials or workmanship, and the failure causes your car to exceed federal emissions standards. Major components, such as an onboard computer emissions control unit, are covered for eight years or up to 80,000 miles.

Using leaded fuel in a car designed for unleaded fuel will void your emission system warranty and may prevent the car from passing your state's inspection. Because an increasing number of states are requiring an emissions test before a car can pass inspection, you may have to pay to fix the system if you used the wrong type of fuel. Repairs to emission systems are usually very expensive.

Dealer Options & Your Warranty

Make sure that "dealer-added" options will not void your warranty. For example, some consumers who have purchased cruise control as an option to be installed by the dealer have found that their warranty is void when they take the car in for engine repairs. Also, some manufacturers warn that dealer-supplied rustproofing will void your corrosion warranty. If you are in doubt, contact the manufacturer before you authorize the installation of dealer-supplied options. If the manufacturer says that adding the option will not void your warranty, get it in writing.

Getting Warranty Service

Ford dealers are finally offering better warranty service to their customers! Now, most Ford dealers will perform warranty work on all Ford vehicles, regardless of where the vehicle was purchased. Previously, only the selling dealer was required to perform repairs under warranty. Individual Ford dealers can still set their own policy, however, so it is best to call and ask before taking your vehicle in for warranty service. GM, Japanese, and European car dealers also provide this service to their customers, and Chrysler "recommends" that dealers follow this policy.

Secret Warranties

If dealers report a number of complaints about a certain part and the manufacturer determines that the problem is due to faulty design or assembly, the manufacturer may permit dealers to repair the problem at no charge to the customer even though the warranty is expired. In the past, this practice was often reserved for customers who made a big fuss. The availability of the free repair was never publicized, which is why we call these *secret* warranties.

Manufacturers deny the existence of secret warranties. They call these free repairs "policy adjustments" or "goodwill service." Whatever they are called, most consumers never hear about them.

Many secret warranties are disclosed in service bulletins that the manufacturers send to dealers. These bulletins outline free repair or reimbursement programs, as well as other problems and their possible causes and solutions.

Service bulletins from many manufacturers may be on file at the National Highway Traffic Safety Administration. For copies of the bulletins on file, send a letter with the make, model and year of the car, and the year you believe the service bulletin was issued, to the NHTSA's Technical Reference Library, Room 5108, NHTSA, Washington, DC 20590. If you write to the government, ask for "service bulletins" rather than "secret warranties."

If you find that a secret warranty is in effect and repairs are being made at no charge after the warranty has expired, contact the Center for Auto Safety, 2001 S Street, NW, Washington, DC 20009. They will publish the information so others can benefit.

Disclosure Laws: Spurred by the proliferation of secret warranties and the failure of the FTC to take action, California, Connecticut, Virginia, and Wisconsin have passed legislation that requires consumers to be notified of secret warranties on their cars. Several other states have introduced similar warranty bills.

Typically, the laws require the following: Direct notice to consumers within a specified time after the adoption of a warranty adjustment policy; notice of the disclosure law to new car buyers; reimbursement, within a number of years after payment, to owners who paid for covered repairs before they learned of the extended warranty service; and dealers must inform consumers who complain about a covered defect that it is eligible for repair under warranty.

New York's bill has another requirement—the establishment of a toll-free number for consumer questions, despite opposition from Ford, GM, Toyota, and other auto manufacturers.

If you live in a state with a secret warranty law already in effect, write your state attorney general's office (in care of your state capitol) for information. To encourage passage of such a bill, contact your state representative (in care of your state capitol).

Secret Warranties Made Public

Due to past secret warranty problems, three auto companies are required to make their service bulletins public.

Ford: Information on goodwill adjustments is available through Ford's "defect line" at 800-241-3673.

General Motors: Bulletins are available from the past three years for a charge and free indexes to bulletins are available through GM dealers or call 800-551-4123.

Volkswagen: An index of all service bulletins can be ordered by calling 800-544-8021.

Uncovering Secret Warranties

Every auto company makes mistakes building cars. When they do, they often issue a technical service bulletins telling dealers how to fix the problem. Rarely do they publicize these fixes, many of which are offered for free, called secret warranties. The Center for Auto Safety has published a new book called *Little Secrets of the Auto Industry*, a consumer guide to secret warranties. This book explains how to find out about secret warranties, offers tips for going to small claims court and getting federal and state assistance, and lists information on state secret warranty laws. To order a copy, send $16.50 to: Center for Auto Safety, Pub. Dept., 2001 S Street, NW, Washington, DC 20009.

Warranties are difficult to compare because they contain lots of fine print and confusing language. The following table will help you understand this year's new car warranties. Because the table does not contain all the details about each warranty, you should review the actual warranty to make sure you understand its fine points. Remember, you have the right to inspect a warranty before you buy—it's the law.

The table provides information on five areas covered by a typical warranty:

The **Basic Warranty** covers most parts of the car against manufacturer's defects. The tires, batteries, and items you may add to the car are covered under separate warranties. The table describes coverage in terms of months and miles; for example, 36/36,000 means the warranty is good for 36 months or 36,000 miles, whichever comes first. This is the most important part of your warranty.

The **Powertrain Warranty** usually lasts longer than the basic warranty. Because each manufacturer's definition of the powertrain is different, it is important to find out exactly what your warranty will cover. Powertrain coverage should include parts of the engine, transmission, and drivetrain. The warranty on some luxury cars will often cover some additional systems such as steering, suspension, and electrical systems.

The **Corrosion Warranty** usually applies only to actual holes due to rust. Read this section carefully, because many corrosion warranties *do not* apply to what the manufacturer may describe as cosmetic rust or bad paint.

The **Roadside Assistance** column indicates whether or not the warranty includes a program for helping with problems on the road. Typically, these programs cover such things as lock outs, jump starts, flat tires, running out of gas and towing. Most of these are offered for the length of the basic warranty. Some have special limitations or added features, which we have pointed out. Because each one is different, check yours out carefully.

The last column contains the **Warranty Rating Index,** which provides an overall assessment of this year's warranties. The higher the Index number, the better the warranty. The Index number incorporates the important features of each warranty. In developing the Index, we gave the most weight to the basic and powertrain components of the warranties. The corrosion warranty was weighted somewhat less, and the roadside assistance features received the least weight. We also considered special features such as whether you had to bring the car in for corrosion inspections, or if rental cars were offered when warranty repairs were being done.

After evaluating all the features of the new warranties, here are this year's best and worst ratings.

1997 Warranties: The Best and The Worst

The Best		The Worst	
Audi	1591	Suzuki	670
Infiniti	1518	Honda	834
Volkswagen	1470	Chrysler	932
Volvo	1411	Dodge	932
Cadillac	1377	Eagle	932
Lexus	1367	Jeep	932
Saab	1279	Plymouth	932

The higher the index number, the better the warranty. See the table on the following pages for complete details.

Manufacturer	Basic Warranty	Powertrain Warranty	Corrosion Warranty	Roadside Assistance	Index	Warranty Rating
Acura	48/50,000	48/50,000	60/unlimited	48/50,000	1163	Average
Audi	36/50,000[1]	36/50,000	120/unlimited	36/50,000[2]	1591	Very Good
BMW	48/50,000	48/50,000	72/unlimited[3]	48/50,000[2]	1254	Good
Buick	36/36,000	36/36,000	72/100,000	36/36,000	956	Very Poor
Cadillac	48/50,000	48/50,000	72/100,000	Lifetime[4,5]	1377	Good
Chevrolet/Geo	36/36,000	36/36,000	72/100,000	36/36,000	956	Very Poor
Chrysler	36/36,000	36/36,000	60/100,000	36/36,000	932	Very Poor
Dodge	36/36,000	36/36,000	60/100,000	36/36,000	932	Very Poor
Eagle	36/36,000	36/36,000	60/100,000	36/36,000	932	Very Poor
Ford	36/36,000	36/36,000	60/unlimited	36/36,000	942	Very Poor
Honda	36/36,000	36/36,000	60/unlimited	None	834	Very Poor
Hyundai	36/36,000	60/60,000	60/100,000	36/36,000[6]	1022	Poor
Infiniti	48/60,000	72/70,000	84/unlimited	48/unlimited	1518	Very Good
Isuzu	36/50,000	60/60,000	72/100,000	60/60,000	1228	Good
Jeep	36/36,000	36/36,000	60/100,000	36/36,000	932	Very Poor
Kia	36/36,000	60/60,000	60/100,000	36/36,000[2]	1126	Average
Land Rover	36/42,000	36/42,000	72/unlimited	36/42,000	1059	Poor
Lexus	48/50,000	72/72,000	72/unlimited	48/50,000	1367	Good
Lincoln	48/50,000[7]	48/50,000	60/unlimited	48/50,000	1163	Average
Mazda	36/50,000	36/50,000	60/unlimited	36/50,000	1061	Poor
Mercedes-Benz	48/50,000	48/50,000	48/50,000	Lifetime	1179	Average
Mercury	36/36,000	36/36,000	60/unlimited	36/36,000	942	Very Poor
Mitsubishi	36/36,000	60/60,000	84/100,000	36/36,000	1124	Average
Nissan	36/36,000	60/60,000	60/unlimited	36/36,000[6]	1032	Poor
Oldsmobile	36/36,000	36/36,000	72/100,000	36/36,000[2]	1006	Poor

[1] Includes all service, repairs and parts to 36/50,000.
[2] Covers trip interruption expenses.
[3] Inspection required every 2 years.
[4] <48/50,000=Free; >48/50,000=Small Charge.
[5] Covers trip interuption expenses up to 48/50,000 for a warranty failure.
[6] Limited roadside services.
[7] The basic warranty also includes car rental payments of a maximum of $30/day for 5 days (if car kept overnight for servicing).
[8] SVX only.
[9] Suzuki Soft Tops have a 24/24,000 Basic Warranty on the soft top itself.
[10] Includes all service, repairs and parts to 24/24,000.

Manufacturer	Basic Warranty	Powertrain Warranty	Corrosion Warranty	Roadside Assistance	Index	Warranty Rating
Olds Aurora	48/50,000	48/50,000	72/100,000	48/50,000[2]	1227	Good
Plymouth	36/36,000	36/36,000	60/100,000	36/36,000	932	Very Poor
Pontiac	36/36,000	36/36,000	72/100,000	36/36,000	956	Very Poor
Saab	48/50,000	48/50,000	72/unlimited	48/50,000[2]	1279	Good
Saturn	36/36,000	36/36,000	72/100,000	36/36,000[2]	1006	Poor
Subaru	36/36,000	60/60,000	60/unlimited	36/36,000[8]	1050	Poor
Suzuki[9]	36/36,000	36/36,000	36/unlimited	None	670	Very Poor
Toyota	36/36,000	60/60,000	60/unlimited	Optional	978	Very Poor
Volkswagen	24/24,000[10]	120/100,000	72/unlimited	24/24,000[2]	1470	Very Good
Volvo	48/50,000	48/50,000	96/unlimited	48/50,000[2]	1411	Very Good

[1] Includes all service, repairs and parts to 36/50,000.
[2] Covers trip interruption expenses.
[3] Inspection required every 2 years.
[4] <48/50,000=Free; >48/50,000=Small Charge.
[5] Covers trip interuption expenses up to 48/50,000 for a warranty failure.
[6] Limited roadside services.
[7] The basic warranty also includes car rental payments of a maximum of $30/day for 5 days (if car kept overnight for servicing).
[8] SVX only.
[9] Suzuki Soft Tops have a 24/24,000 Basic Warranty on the soft top itself.
[10] Includes all service, repairs and parts to 24/24,000.

INSURANCE

Insurance is a big part of ownership expenses, yet it's often forgotten in the showroom. As you shop, remember that the car's design and accident history may affect your insurance rates. Some cars cost less to insure because experience has shown that they are damaged less, less expensive to fix after a collision, or stolen less.

This chapter provides you with the information you need to make a wise insurance purchase. We discuss the different types of insurance, offer special tips on reducing this cost, and include information on occupant injury, theft, and bumper ratings—all factors that can affect your insurance.

More and more consumers are saving hundreds of dollars by shopping around for insurance. In order to be a good comparison shopper, you need to know a few things about automobile insurance. First, there are six basic types of coverage:

Collision Insurance: This pays for the damage to your car after an accident.

Comprehensive Physical Damage Insurance: This pays for damages when your car is stolen or damaged by fire, floods, or other perils.

Property Damage Liability: This pays claims and defense costs if your car damages someone else's property.

Medical Payments Insurance: This pays for your car's occupants' medical expenses resulting from an accident.

Bodily Injury Liability: This provides money to pay claims against you and to pay for the cost of your legal defense if your car injures or kills someone.

Uninsured Motorists Protection: This pays for injuries caused by an uninsured or a hit-and-run driver.

A number of factors determine what these coverages will cost you. A car's design can affect both the chances and severity of an accident. A car with a well-designed bumper may escape damage altogether in a low-speed crash. Some cars are easier to repair than others or may have less expensive parts.

Cars with four doors tend to be damaged less than cars with two doors.

The reason one car may get a discount on insurance while another receives a surcharge also depends upon the way it is traditionally driven. Sports cars, for example, are usually surcharged due, in part, to the typical driving habits of their owners. Four-door sedans and station wagons generally merit discounts.

Insurance companies use this and other information to determine whether to offer a *discount* on insurance premiums for a particular car, or whether to levy a *surcharge*.

Not all companies offer discounts or surcharges, and many cars receive neither. Some companies offer a discount or impose a surcharge on collision premiums only. Others apply discounts and surcharges on both collision and comprehensive coverage. Discounts and surcharges usually range from 10 to 30 percent. Allstate offers discounts of up to 35 percent on certain cars. Remember that one company may offer a discount on a particular car while another may not.

Check with your insurance agent to find out whether your company has a rating program. The "ratings" pages at the end of the book indicate the expected insurance rates for each of the 1997 models.

No-Fault Insurance

One of the major expenses of vehicular accidents has been the cost of determining who is "at fault." Often, both parties hire lawyers and wait for court decisions, which can take a long time. Another problem with this system is that some victims receive considerably less than others for equivalent losses.

To resolve this, many states have instituted "no-fault" vehicle insurance. The concept is that each person's losses are covered by his or her personal insurance protection, regardless of who is at fault. Lawsuits are permitted only under certain conditions, usually restricted by the severity of the injuries.

While the idea is the same from state to state, the details of the no-fault laws vary. These variations include the amounts paid in similar situations, conditions of the right to sue, and the inclusion or exclusion of property damage.

Ironically, some no-fault states still permit lawsuits to determine who is at fault. Although the laws in each state may vary, here is a list of states with and without no-fault laws.

No-Fault States

Colorado	Massachusetts	New York
Florida	Michigan	North Dakota
Hawaii	Minnesota	Pennsylvania*
Kansas	New Jersey*	Utah
Kentucky*		

States Without No-Fault

Alabama	Louisiana	Oregon
Alaska	Maine	Rhode Island
Arizona	Maryland	South Carolina
Arkansas	Mississippi	South Dakota
California	Missouri	Tennessee
Connecticut	Montana	Texas
Delaware	Nebraska	Vermont
District of Columbia	Nevada	Virginia
Georgia	New Hampshire	Washington
Idaho	New Mexico	West Virginia
Illinois	North Carolina	Wisconsin
Indiana	Ohio	Wyoming
Iowa	Oklahoma	

*NJ, KY, PA have a policy option for choosing no-fault.

Insurance Injury Statistics

The insurance industry regularly publishes information about the accident history of cars currently on the road. The most reliable source of this rating information is the Highway Loss Data Institute (HLDI). These ratings, which range from very good to very poor, are based on the frequency of medical claims under personal injury protection coverages. A few companies will charge you more to insure a car rated poor than for one rated good.

A car's accident history may not match its crash test performance. Such discrepancies arise because the accident history includes driver performance. A sports car, for example, may have good crash test results but a poor accident history because its owners tend to drive relatively recklessly.

If you want more information about the injury history, bumper performance, and theft rating of today's cars, write to HLDI, 1005 North Glebe Road, Arlington, VA 22201.

Reducing Insurance Costs

After you have shopped around and found the best deal by comparing the costs of different coverages, consider other factors that will affect your final insurance bill.

Your Annual Mileage: The more you drive, the more your vehicle will be "exposed" to a potential accident. The insurance cost for a car rarely used will be less than the cost for a frequently used car.

Where You Drive: If you regularly drive and park in the city, you will most likely pay more than if you drive in rural areas.

Youthful Drivers: Usually the highest premiums are paid by male drivers under the age of 25. Whether or not the under-25-year-old male is married also affects insurance rates. (Married males pay less.) As the driver gets older, rates are lowered.

In addition to shopping around, take advantage of certain discounts to reduce your insurance costs. Most insurance companies offer discounts of 5 to 30 percent on various parts of your insurance bill. The availability of discounts varies among companies and often depends on where you live. Many consumers do not benefit from these discounts simply because they don't ask about them.

To determine whether you are getting all the discounts that you're entitled to, ask your insurance company for a complete list of the discounts that it offers.

Here are some of the most common insurance discounts:

Driver Education/Defensive Driving Courses: Many insurance companies offer (and in some cases mandate) discounts to young people who have successfully completed a state-approved driver education course. Typically, this can mean a $40 reduction in the cost of coverage. Also, a discount of 5-15 percent is available in some states to those who complete a defensive driving course.

Good Student Discounts: Many insurance companies offer discounts of up to 25 percent on insurance to full-time high school or college students who are in the upper 20 percent of their class, on the dean's list, or have a B or better grade point average.

Good Driver Discounts: Many companies will offer discounts to drivers with an accident and violation-free record.

Mature Driver Credit: Drivers ages 50 and older may qualify for up to a 10 percent discount, or a lower price bracket.

Sole Female Driver: Some companies offer discounts of 10 percent for females, ages 30 to 64, who are the only driver in a household, citing favorable claims experience.

Non-Drinkers and Non-Smokers: A limited number of companies offer incentives ranging from 10-25 percent to those who abstain.

Farmer Discounts: Many companies offer farmers either a discount of 10-30 percent or a lower price bracket.

Car Pooling: Commuters sharing driving may qualify for discounts of 5-25 percent or a lower price bracket.

Insuring Driving Children: Children away at school don't drive the family car very often, so it's usually less expensive to insure them on the parents' policy rather than

Don't Speed

Besides endangering the lives of your passengers and other drivers, speeding tickets will increase your insurance premium. It only takes one speeding ticket to lose your "preferred" or "good driver" discount, which requires a clean driving record. Two or more speeding tickets or accidents can increase your premium by 40% to 200%. Some insurers may simply drop your coverage. According to the Insurance Institute for Highway Safety (IIHS), you are 17% more likely to be in an accident if you have just one speeding ticket. Insurance companies know this and will charge you for it.

separately. If you do insure them separately, discounts of 10-40 percent or a lower price bracket are available.

Desirable Cars: Premiums are usually much higher for cars with high collision rates or that are the favorite target of thieves.

Passive Restraints/Anti-Lock Brake Credit: Many companies offer discounts (from 10 to 30 percent) for automatic belts and air bags. Some large companies are now offering a 5 percent discount to owners of vehicles with anti-lock brakes.

Anti-Theft Device Credits: Discounts of 5 to 15 percent are offered in some states for cars equipped with a hood lock and an alarm or a disabling device (active or passive) that prevents the car from being started.

Multi-Car Discount: Consumers insuring more than one car in the household with the same insurer can save up to 20 percent.

Account Credit: Some companies offer discounts of up to 10 percent for insuring your home and auto with the same company.

Long-Term Policy Renewal: Although not available in all states, some companies offer price breaks of 5-20 percent to customers who renew a long-term policy.

First Accident Allowance: Some insurers offer a "first accident allowance," which guarantees that if a customer achieves five accident-free years, his or her rates won't go up after the first at-fault accident.

Deductibles: Opting for the largest reasonable deductible is the obvious first step in reducing premiums. Increasing your deductible to $500 from $200 could cut your collision premium about 20 percent. Raising the deductible to $1,000 from $200 could lower your premium about 45 percent. The discounts may vary by company.

Collision Coverage: The older the car, the less the need for collision insurance. Consider dropping collision insurance entirely on an older car. Regardless of how much coverage you carry, the insurance company will only pay up to the car's "book value." For example, if your car requires $1,000 in repairs, but its "book value" is only $500, the insurance company is required to pay only $500.

Uninsured Motorist Coverage/ Optional Coverage: The necessity of both of these policies depends upon the extent of your health insurance coverage. In states where they are not required, consumers with applicable health insurance may not want uninsured motorist coverage. Also, those with substantial health insurance coverage may not want an optional medical payment policy.

Rental Cars: If you regularly rent cars, special coverage on your personal auto insurance can cover you while renting for far less than rental agencies offer.

Tip: Expensive fender bender repairs can add up for both you and your insurance company. To reduce repairs, look for a car with bumpers that can withstand a 5-mph impact without damage. See page 68 for more information on bumpers.

Beep, Beep

As car instrument panels become more and more sophisticated, there is growing confusion about the location of horn buttons. There are no regulations requiring a standard location so manufacturers put them in various places around the steering wheel. On your test drive, make sure the horn button is easy to locate and use. When renting a car or driving an unfamiliar car, also be sure you know where the horn button is located. Proper use of a car horn can avoid serious accidents. Because of this, the Center for Auto Safety has been urging the government to standardize horn location since 1980. If you have experienced a problem due to a non-standard horn location, we urge you to contact the National Highway Traffic Safety Administration, Rulemaking Division, 400 7th St., SW, Washington, DC 20590 and the Center for Auto Safety, 2001 S Street, NW, Suite 410, Washington, DC 20009.

Auto Theft

The risk of your vehicle being stolen is an important factor in the cost of your insurance. In fact, each year over 1.5 million vehicles are stolen. As a result, the market is flooded with expensive devices designed to prevent theft. Before you spend a lot of money on anti-theft devices, consider this: Of the vehicles stolen, nearly 80 percent were unlocked and 40 percent actually had the keys in the ignition. Most of these thefts are by amateurs. While the most important way to protect your vehicle is to keep it locked and remove the keys, this precaution will not protect you from the pros. If you live or travel in an area susceptible to auto thefts, or have a high-priced vehicle, here are some steps you can take to prevent theft.

Inexpensive Prevention:

☑ Replace door lock buttons with tapered tips. They make it difficult to hook the lock with a wire hanger. (But it will also keep you from breaking into your own vehicle!)

☑ Buy an alarm sticker (even if you don't have an alarm) for one of your windows.

☑ Buy an electric etching tool (about $15) and write your driver's license number in the lower corners of the windows and on unpainted metal items where it can be seen. Many police departments offer this service at no charge. They provide a sticker and enter the number into their records. The purpose of these identifying marks is to deter the professional thief who is planning to take the vehicle apart and sell the components. Since the parts can be traced, your vehicle becomes less attractive.

☑ Remove the distributor wire. This is a rather inconvenient, but effective, means of rendering your vehicle inoperable. If you are parking in a particularly suspect place, or leaving your vehicle for a long time, you may want to try this. On the top of the distributor, there is a short wire running to the coil. Removing the wire makes it impossible to start the vehicle.

A recently popular anti-theft device is a long rod that locks the steering wheel into place. It costs about $50 and requires a separate key to remove. Beware, however, that thieves now use a spray can of freon to freeze the lock, making it brittle enough to be smashed open with a hammer.

More Serious Measures:

☑ Cutting off the fuel to the engine will keep someone from driving very far with your vehicle. For around $125, you can have a fuel cutoff device installed that enables you to open or close the gasoline line to the engine. One drawback is that the thief will be able to drive a few blocks before running out of gas. If your vehicle is missing, you'll have to check your neighborhood first!

☑ Another way to deter a pro is to install a second ignition switch for about $150. To start your vehicle, you activate a hidden switch. The device is wired in such a complicated manner that a thief could spend hours trying to figure it out. Time is the thief's worst enemy, and the longer it takes to start your vehicle, the more likely the thief is to give up.

☑ The most common anti-theft devices on the market are alarms. These cost from $100 to $500 installed. Their complexity ranges from simply sounding your horn when someone opens your door to setting off elaborate sirens when someone merely approaches the vehicle. Alarms usually require a device such as a key or remote control to turn them on or off. Some people buy the switch, mount it on their vehicle, and hope that its presence will intimidate the thief.

The Highway Loss Data Institute regularly compiles statistics on motor vehicle thefts. In rating cars, they consider the frequency of theft and the loss resulting from the theft. The result is an index based on "relative average loss payments per insured vehicle year." The list below includes the most and least stolen cars among the 1997 models.

Auto Theft

Most Stolen		Least Stolen	
Mercedes S-Class LWB	1533	Chevrolet Lumina	11
BMW 3-Series Conv.	1051	Saab 900 Sedan	15
Mercedes S-Class Conv.	972	Buick Skylark Sedan	15
Lexus GS300	620	Subaru Impreza 4WD	19
BMW 3-Series Coupe	555	Buick LeSabre	19
Mercedes S-Class SWB	537	Buick Regal	20
BMW 3-Series Sedan	428	Ford Aerostar 4WD	21
Lexus SC300/400	309	Buick Skylark Coupe	24
Ford Mustang Conv.	303	Oldsmobile Achieva	24

Bumpers

The main purpose of the bumper is to protect your car in low-speed collisions. Despite this intention, most of us have been victims of a $200 to $400 repair bill resulting from a seemingly minor impact. Because most bumpers offered little or no damage protection in low-speed crashes, the federal government *used* to require that auto makers equip cars with bumpers capable of withstanding up to 5-mph crashes with no damage. Unfortunately, this is no longer the case.

In the early eighties, under pressure from car companies, the government rolled back the requirement that bumpers protect cars in collisions up to 5-mph. Now, car companies only build bumpers to protect cars in 2.5-mph collisions—about the speed at which we walk. This rollback has cost consumers millions of dollars in increased insurance premiums and repair costs. While the rollback satisfied car companies, most car owners were unhappy.

To let consumers know that today's bumpers offer widely varying amounts of protection in 5-mph collisions, each year the Insurance Institute for Highway Safety tests bumpers to see how well they prevent damage. Thankfully, some automobile manufacturers are betting that consumers still want better bumpers on at least some of their models. For example, in a 5-mph front test, the Ford Contour withstood $1056 worth of damage while the Ford Windstar withstood only $30 worth of damage.

These results are rather startling when you consider that the sole purpose of a bumper is to protect a car from damage in low-speed collisions. Only about one-third of the cars tested to date have bumpers which actually prevented damage in front and rear 5-mph collisions. As the Institute's figures show, there is no correlation between the price of the car and how well the bumper worked.

Unfortunately, we can't simply look at a bumper and determine how good it will be at doing its job—protecting a car from inevitable bumps. The solution to this problem is quite simple—simply require car makers to tell the consumer the highest speed at which their car could be crashed with no damage to the car. Three states—California, Hawaii, and New York—have passed laws requiring car companies to disclose in the showroom, in various formats, the expected performance of the bumper on the car. These laws are currently being challenged by the car companies and we won't see them implemented for some time.

Following are the results of the IIHS bumper crash tests, listed from the best to the worst performers. We have included some of the cars which we believe will have similiar bumpers in 1997. *Note:* If the bumpers have changed at all since the time it was tested, the result could be drastically different. This should, however, give you a good basis for comparison. When available, additional information is on each car's page.

Bumper Bashing—Some Damage Repair Costs in 5-mph Crash Tests

Car (Year)	Front Crash	Rear Crash	Total Cost
Best			
Saab 900 S (1994)	$0	$0	$0
Ford Windstar GL (1995)	$0	$30	$30
Nissan Quest XE (1994)	$172	$0	$172
Honda Accord LX (1995)	$251	$97	$348
Mazda Millenia (1995)	$75	$311	$386
Worst			
Mazda MPV (1994)	$787	$1597	$2384
Mazda 626 (1993)	$801	$1041	$1842
Toyota Previa LE (1994)	$661	$962	$1623
Ford Contour GL (1995)	$406	$650	$1056
Pontiac Grand Am SE (1993)	$304	$708	$1012

TIRES

For most of us, buying tires has become an infrequent task. The reason—most cars now come with radial tires, which last much longer than the bias and bias-belted tires of the past. However, when we do get around to buying tires, making an informed purchase is not easy. The tire has to perform more functions simultaneously than any other part of the car (steering, bearing the load, cushioning the ride, and stopping). And not only is the tire the hardest-working item on the car, but there are nearly 1,800 tire lines to choose from. With only a few major tire manufacturers selling all those tires, the difference in many tires may only be the brand name.

Because it is so difficult to compare tires, it is easy to understand why many consumers mistakenly use price and brand name to determine quality. One company's definition of "first line" or "premium" may be entirely different from another's. But there is help. The U.S. government now requires tires to be rated according to their safety and expected mileage.

A little-known system grades tires on their *treadwear*, *traction*, and *heat resistance*. The grades are printed on the sidewall and are also attached to the tire on a paper label. In addition, every dealer can provide you with the grades of the tires he or she sells.

Treadwear: The treadwear grade gives you an idea of the mileage you can expect from a tire. It is shown in numbers—300, 310, 320, 330, and so forth. A tire graded 400 should give you 33 percent more mileage than one graded 300. In order to *estimate* the expected actual mileage, multiply the treadwear grade by 200. Under average conditions a tire graded 300 should last 60,000 miles. Because driving habits vary considerably, use the treadwear as a *relative* basis of comparison rather than an absolute predictor of mileage. Tire wear is affected by regional differences in the level of abrasive material used in road surfaces.

Traction: Traction grades of A, B, and C describe the tire's ability to stop on wet surfaces. Tires graded A will stop on a wet road in a shorter distance than tires graded B or C. Tires rated C have poor traction. If you drive frequently on wet roads, buy a tire with a higher traction grade.

Heat Resistance: Heat resistance is also graded A, B, and C. This grading is important because hot-running tires can result in blowouts or tread separation. An A rating means the tire will run cooler than one rated B or C, and it is less likely to fail if driven over long distances at highway speeds. In addition, tires that run cooler tend to be more fuel efficient. If you do a lot of high speed driving, a high heat resistance grade is best.

Speed Ratings: All passenger car tires meet government standards up to 85 mph. Some tires are tested at higher speeds because certain cars require tires that perform at higher speeds. Consult your owner's manual for the right speed rating for your car. See the tire size code: (For example, P215/60 SR15). The 'S' indicates the tire is tested for speeds up to 112 mph. Other letters include: "T" for up to 118 mph; "H" for up to 130 mph; "V" for up to 149 mph; "Z" for over 149 mph.

The tables at the end of this section give you a list of the highest rated tires on the market. For a complete listing of all the tires on the market, you can call the Auto Safety Hotline toll free, at 800-424-9393 or 800-424-9153 (TTY). (In Washington, DC, the number is 202-366-7800.)

In This Chapter...

Tires: Getting the Best Price

There are few consumer products on the market today as price competitive as tires. While this situation provides a buyer's market, it does require some price shopping.

The price of a tire is based on its size, and tires come in as many as nine sizes. For example, the list price of the same Goodyear Arriva tire can range from $74.20 to $134.35, depending on its size. Some manufacturers do not provide list prices, leaving the appropriate markup to the individual retailer. Even when list prices are provided, dealers rarely use them. Instead, they offer tires at what is called an "everyday low price," which can range from 10 to 25 percent below list.

The following tips can help you get the best buy.

1 Check to see which manufacturer makes the least expensive "off brand." Only twelve major manufacturers produce the over 1,800 types of tires sold in the U.S. So you can save money and still get high quality.

2 Remember, generally the wider the tire, the higher the price.

3 Don't forget to inquire about balancing and mounting costs when comparing tire prices. In some stores, the extra charges for balancing, mounting and valve stems can add up to more than $25. Other stores may offer them as a customer service at little or no cost. That good buy in the newspaper may turn into a poor value when coupled with these extra costs. Also, compare warranties; they do vary from company to company.

4 Never pay list price for a tire. A good rule of thumb is to pay at least 30 to 40 percent off the suggested list price.

5 Use the treadwear grade the same way you would the "unit price" in a supermarket. It is the best way to ensure that you are getting the best tire value. The tire with the lowest cost per grade point is the best value.

For example, if tire A costs $100 and has a treadwear grade of 300, and tire B costs $80 and has a treadwear grade of 200:

Tire A:
$100 ÷ 300 = $.33 per point

Tire B:
$80 ÷ 200 = $.40 per point

Since 33 cents is less than 40 cents, tire A is the better buy even though its initial cost is more.

New Tire Registration

You may be missing out on free or low-cost replacement tires or, worse, driving on potentially hazardous ones, if you don't fill out the tire registration form when you buy tires. The law once required all tire sellers to submit buyers' names automatically to the manufacturer, so the company could contact them if the tires were ever recalled. While this is still mandatory for tire dealers and distributors owned by tire manufacturers, it is not required of independent tire dealers. A recent government study found that 70 percent of independent tire dealers had not registered a single tire purchase. Ask for the tire registration card when you buy tires, and remember to fill it out and send it in. This information will allow the company to notify you if the tire is ever recalled.

Do Tires Affect Fuel Economy?

Yes, a tire's *rolling resistance* affects its fuel economy. In the past, fuel efficiency (low rolling resistance) was traded off with traction. Tires with good traction had lower fuel economy. Michelin has introduced a new rubber compound that doesn't sacrifice traction for fuel economy. In order to give consumers better information and to encourage the widespread use of this new compound, we have asked that the government change its heat resistance grade to a fuel efficiency rating.

America's Top-Rated Tires

Brand Name	Model	Description	Grades			Expected Mileage		
			Trac.	Heat	Tred.	High	Medium	Low
Cooper	Grand Classic STE	All	A	B	560	168,000	112,000	84,000
Cordovan	Grand Prix Touring	All	A	B	560	168,000	112,000	84,000
Dean	Touring Edition	All	A	B	560	168,000	112,000	84,000
El Dorado	Legend	All	A	B	560	168,000	112,000	84,000
Falls	Mark VII	All	A	B	560	168,000	112,000	84,000
Hallmark	Ultra Touring GT	All	A	B	560	168,000	112,000	84,000
Kelly	Aqua Tour	All	A	B	560	168,000	112,000	84,000
Lee	Ultra Touring GT	All	A	B	560	168,000	112,000	84,000
Monarch	Ultra Touring GT	All	A	B	560	168,000	112,000	84,000
Sigma	Supreme Touring ST	All	A	B	560	168,000	112,000	84,000
Star	Ultra Touring GT	All	A	B	560	168,000	112,000	84,000
Winston	Signature	All	A	B	560	168,000	112,000	84,000
Dayton	Daytona Premium GT	All	A	B	540	162,000	108,000	81,000
Dunlop	Elite 65	15 & 16	A	B	540	162,000	108,000	81,000
Falken	FK315	All	A	B	540	162,000	108,000	81,000
Hankook	Mileage Plus	All	A	B	540	162,000	108,000	81,000
Ohtsu	HS311	All	A	B	540	162,000	108,000	81,000
Toyo	800+70,75	15	A	B	540	162,000	108,000	81,000
Toyo	800+65	All	A	B	540	162,000	108,000	81,000
Toyo	800+60	15 & 16	A	B	540	162,000	108,000	81,000
Concorde	Touring 9000	All	A	A	520	156,000	104,000	78,000
Cavalier	Precept GT 70/75	15	A	B	520	156,000	104,000	78,000
Centennial	Interceptor	15 & 16	A	B	520	156,000	104,000	78,000
CO-OP	Golden Mark 65/70	All	A	B	520	156,000	104,000	78,000
Dunlop	Elite 65	14	A	B	520	156,000	104,000	78,000
General	Ameri G4S	All	A	B	520	156,000	104,000	78,000
Kleber	CP751,701	15	A	B	520	156,000	104,000	78,000
Michelin	XH4	14 & 15	A	B	520	156,000	104,000	78,000
Pirelli	P400 Aquamile	All	A	B	520	156,000	104,000	78,000
Riken	Classic MR-60	15	A	B	520	156,000	104,000	78,000
Toyo	800+75,70,60	14	A	B	520	156,000	104,000	78,000
Toyo	800+70	175/70R14	B	B	520	156,000	104,000	78,000
Atlas	Pinnacle TE 70/75	14 & 15	A	B	500	150,000	100,000	75,000
Atlas	Pinnacle TE 70	13	A	B	500	150,000	100,000	75,000
Centennial	Interceptor	14	A	B	500	150,000	100,000	75,000
Dayton	Touring 70/75S	All	A	B	500	150,000	100,000	75,000
Dayton	Touring 70	All	A	B	500	150,000	100,000	75,000
Duralon	IV Plus	All	A	B	500	150,000	100,000	75,000
Duralon	Touring Plus IV	All	A	B	500	150,000	100,000	75,000
Gillette	Kodiak LE	All	A	B	500	150,000	100,000	75,000
Sumitomo	SC890 75	15	A	B	500	150,000	100,000	75,000
Toyo	800+75	235/75RL15	A	B	500	150,000	100,000	75,000
CO-OP	Golden Mark 75	All	A	B	480	144,000	96,000	72,000
Concord	Max 6000	All	A	B	480	144,000	96,000	72,000
Cooper	Lifeliner	All	A	B	480	144,000	96,000	72,000
Cordovan	Classic	All	A	B	480	144,000	96,000	72,000
Cordovan	Gran Prix SE70	All	A	B	480	144,000	96,000	72,000
Cordovan	Gran Prix G/T 70RWL	All	A	B	480	144,000	96,000	72,000
Cordovan	Grand Prix STE	All Except	A	B	480	144,000	96,000	72,000
Dean	Quasar	All	A	B	480	144,000	96,000	72,000
Douglas	Premium Plus WTE	All	A	B	480	144,000	96,000	72,000
Dunlop	Elite 65	13	A	B	480	144,000	96,000	72,000
El Dorado	Crusader SR, SRX	All	A	B	480	144,000	96,000	72,000
Falls	P794 SR	All	A	B	480	144,000	96,000	72,000
Goodyear	Aquatred II	All Others	A	B	480	144,000	96,000	72,000
Hallmark	Prestige PWR4	All Others	A	B	480	144,000	96,000	72,000
Hercules	Ultra Plus	All	A	B	480	144,000	96,000	72,000
Kelly	Navigator 800S	All Others	A	B	480	144,000	96,000	72,000
Lee	GT VI Steel Trak	All Others	A	B	480	144,000	96,000	72,000
Michelin	XH4	13	A	B	480	144,000	96,000	72,000

Brand Name	Model	Description	Grades			Expected Mileage		
			Trac.	Heat	Tred.	High	Medium	Low
Monarch	Ultra Trak A/S	All Others	A	B	480	144,000	96,000	72,000
Multi-Mile	Grand Am G/T70RWL	All	A	B	480	144,000	96,000	72,000
Multi-Mile	Grand Am STE	All	A	B	480	144,000	96,000	72,000
Multi-Mile	Grand Am SE70	All	A	B	480	144,000	96,000	72,000
Pacemark	Premium A/S	All Except	A	B	480	144,000	96,000	72,000
Republic	Weather King	All Except	A	B	480	144,000	96,000	72,000
Sigma	Grand Sport 70 RWL	All	A	B	480	144,000	96,000	72,000
Sigma	Supreme STE	All Ecept	A	B	480	144,000	96,000	72,000
Sigma	Supreme SE	All	A	B	480	144,000	96,000	72,000
Star	Imperial PSR	All Others	A	B	480	144,000	96,000	72,000
Starfire	Spectrum SR 70	All	A	B	480	144,000	96,000	72,000
Starfire	Spectrum SR 60/65	15 & 16	A	B	480	144,000	96,000	72,000
Ultra-Tech	Touring A/S	All	A	B	480	144,000	96,000	72,000
Vanderbilt	Turbo Tech Tour A/S	All	A	B	480	144,000	96,000	72,000
Vogue	Premium A/S 70,75	All	A	B	480	144,000	96,000	72,000
Winston	Classic 70	All	A	B	480	144,000	96,000	72,000
Hallmark	Prestige PWR4	235/75R15	A	C	480	144,000	96,000	72,000
Kelly	Navigator 800S	235/75R15	A	C	480	144,000	96,000	72,000
Lee	GT VI Steel Trak	235/75R15	A	C	480	144,000	96,000	72,000
Monarch	Ultra Trak A/S	235/75R15	A	C	480	144,000	96,000	72,000
Multi-Mile	Grand Am STE	XL	A	C	480	144,000	96,000	72,000
Pacemark	Premium A/S	P235/75415XL	A	C	480	144,000	96,000	72,000
Republic	Weather King	P235/75R15	A	C	480	144,000	96,000	72,000
Sigma	Supreme STE	XL	A	C	480	144,000	96,000	72,000
Star	Imperial	235/75R15	A	C	480	144,000	96,000	72,000
Big-O	Legacy Plus 65	P205/65R15	A	B	460	138,000	92,000	69,000
Brigadier	Touring Pro 70/75	15	A	B	460	138,000	92,000	69,000
Brigadier	Touring Pro 65	P205/65R15	A	B	460	138,000	92,000	69,000
Cavalier	Precept GT 70/75	14	A	B	460	138,000	92,000	69,000
Cavalier	SRX 70	14 & 15	A	B	460	138,000	92,000	69,000
Centennial	Interceptor	13	A	B	460	138,000	92,000	69,000
Continental	CS24	15	A	B	460	138,000	92,000	69,000
Firestone	Affinity T-1	All	A	B	460	138,000	92,000	69,000
General	Ameri Tech 4 75	15	A	B	460	138,000	92,000	69,000
General	Ameri Tech ST 70	15	A	B	460	138,000	92,000	69,000
General	Ameri Tech ST	P215,P225/75R15	A	B	460	138,000	92,000	69,000
General	GS	All	A	B	460	138,000	92,000	69,000
Goodyear	Aquatred II	13	A	B	460	138,000	92,000	69,000
Goodyear	Regatta	All Others	A	B	460	138,000	92,000	69,000
Hercules	Mega TR	14 & 15	A	B	460	138,000	92,000	69,000
Kleber	CP751,701	14	A	B	460	138,000	92,000	69,000
Kleber	CPR700S	P225-P235/70R15	A	B	460	138,000	92,000	69,000
Kleber	CPR700S	P215/70R14	A	B	460	138,000	92,000	69,000
Kumho	782	All	A	B	460	138,000	92,000	69,000
Pirelli	P100	All	A	B	460	138,000	92,000	69,000
Remington	Touring	13	A	B	460	138,000	92,000	69,000
Reynolds	Touring Plus 70/75	15	A	B	460	138,000	92,000	69,000
Reynolds	Touring Plus 65	P205/65R15	A	B	460	138,000	92,000	69,000
Riken	Classic MR-GT	P225/70SR15	A	B	460	138,000	92,000	69,000
Riken	Classic MR-60	14	A	B	460	138,000	92,000	69,000
Riken	Classic MR-GT	P215/70SR14	A	B	460	138,000	92,000	69,000
Riken	Classic MR-GT	P235/70SR15	A	B	460	138,000	92,000	69,000
Riken	Classic MR-GT	P255/70SR15	A	B	460	138,000	92,000	69,000
Sonic	Sentinel 65	P205/65R15	A	B	460	138,000	92,000	69,000
Sonic	Sentinel 70/75	15	A	B	460	138,000	92,000	69,000
Touring Supreme	SE 65 Series	P205/65R15	A	B	460	138,000	92,000	69,000
Touring Supreme	SE 70/75 Series	15	A	B	460	138,000	92,000	69,000
Toyo	800+80	All	A	B	460	138,000	92,000	69,000
Toyo	800+70	13	A	B	460	138,000	92,000	69,000

COMPLAINTS

Americans spend billions of dollars on motor vehicle repairs every year. While many of those repairs are satisfactory, there are times when getting your vehicle fixed can be a very difficult process. In fact, vehicle defects and repairs are the number one cause of consumer complaints in the U.S., according to the Federal Trade Commission.

This chapter is designed to help you resolve your complaint, whether it's for a new vehicle still under warranty or for one you've had for years. In addition, we offer a guide to arbitration, the names and addresses of consumer groups, federal agencies and the manufacturers themselves. Finally, we tell you how to take the important step of registering your complaint with the U.S. Department of Transportation.

No matter what your complaint, keep accurate records. Copies of the following items are indispensable in helping to resolve your problems:

☑ your service invoices

☑ bills you have paid

☑ letters you have written to the manufacturer or the repair facility owner

☑ written repair estimates from your independent mechanic.

Resolving Complaints: If you are having trouble, here are some basic steps to help you resolve your problem:

1 First, return your vehicle to the repair facility that did the work. Bring a written list of the problems and make sure that you keep a copy of the list. Give the repair facility a reasonable opportunity to examine your vehicle and attempt to fix it. Speak directly to the service manager (not to the service writer who wrote up your repair order), and ask him or her to test drive the vehicle with you so that you can point out the problem.

2 If that doesn't resolve the problem, take the vehicle to a diagnostic center for an independent examination. This may cost $45 to $60. Get a written statement defining the problem and outlining how it may be fixed. Give your repair shop a copy. If your vehicle is under warranty, do not allow any warranty repair by an independent mechanic; you may not be reimbursed by the manufacturer.

3 If your repair shop does not respond to the independent assessment, present your problem to a mediation panel. These panels hear both sides of the story and try to come to a resolution.

If the problem is with a new vehicle dealer, or if you feel that the manufacturer is responsible, you may be able to use one of the manufacturer's mediation programs discussed on page 76.

If the problem is solely with an independent dealer, a local Better Business Bureau (BBB) may be able to mediate your complaint. It may also offer an arbitration hearing. In any case, the BBB should enter your complaint into its files on that establishment.

When contacting any mediation program, determine how long the process takes, who makes the final decision, whether you are bound by that decision, and whether the program handles all problems or only warranty complaints.

4 If there are no mediation programs in your area, contact private consumer groups, local government agencies, or your local "action line"

newspaper columnist, newspaper editor, or radio or TV broadcaster. A phone call or letter from them may persuade a repair facility to take action. Send a copy of your letter to the repair shop.

5 One of your last resorts is to bring a law suit against the dealer, manufacturer, or repair facility in small claims court. The fee for filing such an action is usually small, and you generally act as your own attorney, saving attorney's fees. There is a monetary limit on the amount you can claim, which varies from state to state. Your local consumer affairs office, state attorney general's office, or the clerk of the court can tell you how to file such a suit.

6 Finally, talk with an attorney. It's best to select an attorney who is familiar with handling automotive problems. If you don't know of one, call the lawyer referral service listed in the telephone directory (or see box) and ask for the names of attorneys who deal with automobile problems. If you can't afford an attorney, contact the Legal Aid Society.

Warranty Complaints: If your vehicle is under warranty or you are having problems with a factory-authorized dealership, here are some special guidelines:

Have the warranty available to show the dealer. Make sure you call the problem to the dealer's attention before the end of the warranty period.

If you are still unsatisfied after giving the dealer a reasonable opportunity to fix your vehicle, contact the manufacturer's representative (also called the zone representa-

tive) in your area. This person can authorize the dealer to make repairs or take other steps to resolve the dispute. Your dealer will have your zone representative's name and telephone number. Explain the problem and ask for a meeting and a personal inspection of your vehicle.

If you can't get satisfaction from the zone representative, call or write the manufacturer's owner relations department. Your owner's manual contains this phone number and address. In each case, as you move up the chain, indicate the steps you have already taken.

Your next option is to present your problem to a complaint-handling panel or to the arbitration program in which the manufac-

turer of your vehicle participates. See page 76 for additional information.

If you complain of a problem during the warranty period, you have a right to have the problem fixed even after the warranty runs out. If your warranty has not been honored, you may be able to "revoke acceptance," which means that you return the vehicle to the dealer. If you are successful, you may be entitled to a replacement vehicle, or to a full refund of the purchase price and reimbursement of legal fees under the Magnuson-Moss Warranty Act. Or, if you are covered by one of the state Lemon Laws (see page 83), you may be able to return the vehicle and receive a refund or replacement from the manufacturer.

Legal Aid

If you need legal assistance with your repair problem, the Center for Auto Safety has a list of lawyers who specialize in helping consumers with auto repair problems. For the names of some attorneys in your area, send a stamped, self-addressed envelope to: Center for Auto Safety, 2001 S Street, NW, Washington, DC 20009-1160.

In addition, the Center has published *The Lemon Book,* a detailed, 368-page guide to resolving automobile complaints. The book is available for $16.50 directly from the Center.

Attorneys Take Note: For information on litigation assistance provided by the Center for Auto Safety, including The Lemon Law Litigation Manual, please contact the Center for Auto Safety at the above address.

Auto Safety Hotline

One of the most valuable but often unused services of the government is the Auto Safety Hotline. By calling the Hotline to report safety problems, your particular concern or problem will become part of the National Highway Traffic Safety Administration's (NHTSA) complaint database. This complaint program is extraordinarily important to government decision makers who often take action based on this information. In addition, it provides consumer groups, like the Center for Auto Safety, with the evidence they need to force the government to act. Unless government engineers or safety advocates have evidence of a wide-scale problem, little can be done to get the manufacturers to correct the defect.

Few government services have the potential to do as much for the consumer as this complaint database, so we encourage you to voice your concerns to the government.

Your letter can be used as the basis of safety defect investigations and recall campaigns. When you file a complaint, be sure to indicate that your name and address can be made public. Without names and addresses, it is more difficult for consumer groups to uncover safety defects.

Hotline Complaints: When you call the Hotline to report a safety problem, you will be mailed a questionnaire asking for information that the agency's technical staff will need to evaluate the problem. This information also gives the government an indication of which vehicles are causing consumers the most problems.

You can also use this questionnaire to report defects in tires and child safety seats. In fact, we strongly encourage you to report problems with child safety seats. Now that they are required by law in all fifty states, we have noticed that numerous design and safety problems have surfaced. If the government knows about these problems, they will be more likely to take action so that modifications are made to these life-saving devices.

After you complete and return the questionnaire, the following things will happen:

1. A copy will go to NHTSA's safety defect investigators.
2. A copy will be sent to the manufacturer of the car or equipment, with a request for help in resolving the problem.
3. You will be notified that your questionnaire has been received.
4. Your problem will be recorded in the complaint database which we use to provide you with complaint ratings.

Hotline Services: Hotline operators can also provide information on recalls. If you want recall information on a particular automobile, simply tell the Hotline operator the make, model, and year of the car, or the type of equipment involved. You will receive any recall information that NHTSA has about that car or item. This information can be very important if you are not sure whether your car has ever been recalled. If you want a printed copy of the recall information, it will be mailed within twenty-four hours at no charge.

If you have other car-related problems, the Hotline operators can refer you to the appropriate federal, state, and local government agencies. If you need information about federal safety standards and regulations, you'll be referred to the appropriate experts.

You may call the Hotline day or night, seven days a week. If you call when no operators are available, a recorded message will ask you to leave your name and address and a description of the information you want. The appropriate materials will be mailed to you.

TIP

Complaints and Safety Information

Auto Safety Hotline
800-424-9393
(in Washington, DC: 202-366-0123)
TTY for hearing impaired:
800-424-9153
(in Washington, DC: 202-366-7800)

The toll-free Auto Safety Hotline can provide information on recalls, record information about safety problems, and refer you to the appropriate government experts on other vehicle related problems. You can even have recall information mailed to you within 24 hours of your call at no charge.

Arbitration

An increasingly popular method of resolving automobile repair problems is through arbitration. This procedure requires that both parties present their cases to an arbitrator or panel that makes a decision based on the merits of the complaint. You can seek repairs, reimbursement of expenses, or a refund or replacement for your car through arbitration.

In theory, arbitration can be an effective means of resolving disputes. It is somewhat informal, relatively speedy, and you do not need a lawyer to present your case. Plus, you avoid the time and expense of going to court.

Almost all manufacturers now offer some form of arbitration, usually for problems that arise during the warranty period. Some companies run their own and others subscribe to programs run by groups like the Better Business Bureau or the National Center for Dispute Settlement. Your owner's manual will identify which programs you can use. Also, contact your state attorney general to find out what programs your state offers.

How it works: Upon receiving your complaint, the arbitration program will attempt to mediate a resolution between you and the manufacturer or dealer. If you are not satisfied with the proposed solution, you have the right to have your case heard at an arbitration hearing.

These hearings vary among the programs. In the BBB program, each party presents its case in person to a volunteer arbitrator. Other programs decide your case based on written submissions from both you and the manufacturer.

If an arbitration program is incorporated into your warranty, you may have to use that program before filing a legal claim. Federal law requires that arbitration programs incorporated into a warranty be nonbinding on the consumer. So, if you do not like the result, you can seek other remedies.

Arbitration programs have different eligibility requirements, so be sure you are eligible for the program you are considering.

Let the Federal Trade Commission, the Center for Auto Safety (their addresses are on pages 80 and 81), and your state attorney general (c/o your state capitol) know of your experience with arbitration. It is particularly important to contact these offices if you have a complaint about how your case was handled.

Ford Dispute Settlement Board: Each case is considered by a four-person panel that includes one dealer. In most cases, no oral presentations are given, although the customer may request to give one. Only cases under warranty are reviewed. For information, call 800-392-3673.

Chrysler Customer Arbitration Board: In 1997, the National Center for Dispute Settlement (NCDS) will start handling cases in some states. Otherwise, the Customer Arbitration Board will handle the dispute. In both programs, decisions will be based on written submissions by each party. Customers who live in AR, KY, MN, and OH and in states where complaints are handled by NCDS have the right to request oral presentation. The

NCDS board consists of a local consumer advocate, an independent, A.S.E. certified technical representative, and a representative from the general public. The Consumer Arbitration Board is a panel whose members have many years of experience in consumer affairs and/or automotive service. Both boards will only hear cases under warranty. For information, call 800-992-1997.

Better Business Bureau (BBB) Arbitration Programs (Auto Line): The BBB always tries to mediate a dispute before recommending arbitration. About 12% of the disputes it handles actually go to arbitration. The arbitrators are selected at random and an impartial technical expert can be present if requested. The consumer can object if conflict exists.

Arbitrators are volunteers from the local community and are not always automobile experts. This can both help and harm your case. As a result, it is important to be well prepared when participating in the BBB program. If you're not, the potential exists for the dealer or manufacturer to appear as the "expert" on automobiles. For more information, contact your local BBB or 800-955-5100.

Automobile Consumer Action Program: AUTOCAP was established by the National Automobile Dealers Association (NADA) to assist consumers in resolving auto sales or service disputes with dealers and manufacturers. The program is sponsored on a voluntary basis by state and local dealer associations. Currently, most AUTOCAPs do not operate under the FTC guidelines required for warranty cases. Sixty-five percent of the cases that AUTOCAP considers are resolved in preliminary mediation. Of those cases that go to arbitration, 45 percent are resolved in favor of the consumer, 22 percent are a compromise, and 33 percent are in favor of the company. For more information and the name of your local panel, contact: AUTOCAP, 8400 Westpark Drive, McLean, Virginia 22102; 703-821-7144.

Arbitration Tips: Arbitration is designed to be easier and less intimidating than going to court. However, the process can still be nerve-racking, especially if you've never been through it before. Here are some tips to help make the process simple and straightforward:

1. Before deciding to go to arbitration, get a written description of how the program works and make sure you understand the details. If you have any questions, contact the local representatives of the program. Remember, the manufacturer or dealer probably has more experience with this process than you do.
2. Make sure the final decision is nonbinding on you. If the decision is binding, you give up your right to appeal.
3. Determine whether the program allows you to appear at the hearing. If not, make sure your written statement is complete and contains all the appropriate receipts and documentation. If you think of something that you want considered after you have sent in your material, send it immediately and specifically request that the additional information be included.
4. Make sure the program follows the required procedures. If the arbitration program is incorporated into the car's warranty, for example, the panel must make a decision on your case within 40 days of receiving your complaint.
5. Contact the manufacturer's zone manager and request copies of any technical service bulletins that apply to your car. (See "Secret Warranties" on page 59 for a description of technical service bulletins and how to get them.) Service bulletins may help you prove that your car is defective.
6. Well before the hearing, ask the program representative to send you copies of all material submitted by the other party. You may want to respond to this information.
7. Make sure all your documents are in chronological order, and include a brief outline of the events. Submit copies of all material associated with your problem and a copy of your warranty.
8. Even though you may be very angry about the situation, try to present your case in a calm, logical manner.
9. If you are asking for a refund or a replacement for your car in accordance with your state's Lemon Law, do not assume that the arbitrator is completely familiar with the law. Be prepared to explain how it entitles you to your request.
10. In most programs, you have to reject the decision in order to go to court to pursue other action. If you accept the decision, you may limit your rights to pursue further action. You will, however, have additional claims if the manufacturer or dealer does not properly follow through on the decision or if your car breaks down again.

State-Run Arbitration

State-run arbitration programs are often more fair to consumers than national programs. The following states have set up programs (or guidelines) which are far better than their national counterparts. If you live in one of these areas, contact your attorney general's office (in care of your state capitol) for information. If your state is not listed below, you should still contact your state attorney general's office for advice on arbitration.

Connecticut	Hawaii	New Hampshire	Texas
Florida	Maine	New Jersey	Vermont
Georgia	Massachusetts	New York	Washington

Complaint Index

Thanks to the efforts of the Center for Auto Safety, we are able to provide you with the vehicle complaints on file with the National Highway Traffic Safety Administration (NHTSA). Each year, thousands of Americans call the government to register complaints about their vehicles. The federal government collects this information but has never released it to the public.

The complaint index is the result of our analysis of these complaints. It is based on a ratio of the number of complaints for each vehicle to the sales of that vehicle. In order to predict the expected complaint performance of the 1997 models, we have examined the complaint history of that car's *series*. The term *series* refers to the fact that when a manufacturer introduces a new model, that vehicle remains essentially unchanged for 4-6 years. For example, the Pontiac Bonneville was introduced in 1992 and remains essentially the same car for 1997. As such, we have compiled the complaint experience for that series in order to give you some additional information to use in deciding which car to buy. For those vehicles just introduced in 1996 or 1997, we do not yet have enough data to develop a complaint index.

The following table presents the complaint indexes for the best and worst 1997 models. Higher index numbers mean the vehicle generated a greater number of complaints. Lower numbers indicate fewer complaints. After calculating the indexes, we compared the results among all 1997 vehicles.

1997 Complaint Ratings

The Best		The Worst	
Vehicle	Index	Vehicle	Index
Audi A6	0	Saab 900	16787
Lexus GS300	0	Mitsubishi Eclipse	15500
Suzuki Swift	0	Dodge/Plymouth Neon	14790
Olds Cutlass Supreme	228	Hyundai Sonata	12988
Lincoln Continental	531	Chrysler Cirrus	10645
Honda Odyssey	1103	Nissan 240SX	10305
Infiniti J30	1126	Ford Windstar	8974
Toyota Paseo	1168	Eagle Talon	8953
Toyota Corolla	1389	Chev. Lumina/Monte Carlo	8847
Cadillac DeVille	1394	Dodge Avenger	8020
Nissan Altima	1406	Mitsubishi Galant	7626
Oldsmobile Achieva	1437	Mercury Mystique	7017
Lexus SC300/400	1478	Chrysler Concorde	6901
Lexus LS400	1518	Acura NSX	6728
Buick Skylark	1670	Buick Riviera	6512
Toyota Tercel	1686	Dodge Stratus	6054
Toyota Previa	1687	Kia Sephia	5826
Mazda Miata	1736	Subaru Legacy	5779
Pontiac Grand Am	1739	Ford Contour	5578
Pontiac Bonneville	1789	Dodge Intrepid	5547
Oldsmobile 88	1888	Geo Metro	5475
Toyota Celica	1902	Eagle Vision	5438
Geo Prizm	2052	Mazda Protege	5403
Nissan Sentra	2067	Dodge Viper	5110
Pontiac Sunfire	2091	Chrys. LHS/New Yorker	5042
Buick LeSabre	2112	Volkswagen Golf/Jetta	4637
Volvo 900 Series	2140	Chevrolet Camaro	4634
Honda Accord	2226	Chrysler Sebring	4311

Every year automobile manufacturers spend millions of dollars making their voices heard in government decision making. For example, General Motors and Ford have large staffs in Detroit and Washington that work solely to influence government activity. But who looks out for the consumer?

For over twenty-five years, the nonprofit Center for Auto Safety (CAS) has told the consumer's story to government agencies, to Congress and to the courts. Its efforts focus on all consumers rather than only those with individual complaints.

The CAS was established in 1970 by Ralph Nader and Consumers Union. As consumer concerns about auto safety issues expanded, so did the work of CAS. It became an independent group in 1972, and the original staff of two has grown to fourteen attorneys and researchers. CAS' activities include:

Initiating Safety Recalls: CAS analyzes over 50,000 consumer complaints each year. By following problems as they develop, CAS requests government investigations and recalls of defective vehicles. CAS was responsible for the Ford Pinto faulty gas tank recall, the Firestone 500 steel-belted radial tire recall, and the record recall of over 3 million Evenflo One Step child seats.

Representing the Consumer in Washington: CAS follows the activities of federal agencies and Congress to ensure that they carry out their responsibilities to the American taxpayer. CAS brings a consumer's point of view to vehicle safety policies and rule-making.

Since 1970, CAS has submitted more than 500 petitions and comments on federal safety standards.

One major effort in this area has been the successful fight for adoption of automatic crash protection in passenger cars. These systems are a more effective and less intrusive alternative to crash protection than mandatory safety belt laws or belts that must be buckled in order to start the car.

In 1992, the Center for Auto Safety uncovered a fire defect that dwarfed the highly publicized flammability of the Ford Pinto. It had to do with the side-saddle gas tanks on full size 1973-87 GM pickups and 1988-90 crew cabs that tend to explode on impact. Over 1,400 people have been killed in fire crashes involving these trucks. After mounting a national campaign to warn consumers to steer clear of these GM fire hazards, the U.S. Department of Transportation (DOT) granted CAS' petition and conducted one of its biggest defect investigations in history. The result—GM was asked to recall its pickups. GM, sadly, denied this request.

Thanks to a petition originally filed by CAS, NHTSA adopted a new registration system to better enable manufacturer notification to parents with defective child seats. This will enable more parents to find out about potentially hazardous safety seats.

Exposing Secret Warranties: CAS played a prominent role in the disclosure of secret warranties, "policy adjustments," as they are called by manufacturers. These occur when an auto maker agrees to pay for repair of certain defects beyond the warranty period but refuses to notify consumers. (See "Se-

cret Warranties" in the Warranty Chapter.)

Improving Rust Warranties: Rust and corrosion cost American car owners up to $14 billion annually. CAS has been successful in its efforts to get domestic and foreign auto companies to lengthen their all-important corrosion warranties.

Lemon Laws: CAS' work on Lemon Laws aided in the enactment of state laws which make it easier to return a defective new automobile and get money back.

Tire Ratings: After a suspension between 1982-84, consumers have reliable treadwear ratings to help them get the most miles for their dollar. CAS' lawsuit overturned DOT's revocation of this valuable new tire information program.

Initiating Legal Action: When CAS has exhausted other means of obtaining relief for consumer problems, it will initiate legal action. For example, in 1978 when the Department of Energy attempted to raise the price of gasoline 4 cents per gallon without notice or comment, CAS succeeded in stopping this illegal move through a lawsuit, thus saving consumers $2 billion for the six month period that the action was delayed.

A CAS lawsuit against the Environmental Protection Agency (EPA) in 1985 forced the EPA to recall polluting cars, rather than let companies promise to make cleaner cars in the future. As part of the settlement, GM (which was responsible for the polluting cars) funded a $7 million methanol bus demonstration program in New York City.

Publications: CAS has many publications on automobiles, motor homes, recreational vehicles, and fuel economy, including a number of free information packets. For each of the packets listed below, or for a complete description of all of the CAS' publications, send a separate stamped, self-addressed, business-sized envelope with 55 cents postage to the address below. Unless otherwise noted, the packets listed below cover all known major problems for the models indicated and explain what to do about them. Requests for information should include make, model, and year of vehicle (with VIN number), as well as the type of problem you are experiencing. (Allow 2 to 3 weeks for delivery.)

Audi (1978-92)
Cadillac (1982-95)
Chrys. Paint/Water Leaks (1983-1995)
Chrys. Ultradrive Trans. (1989-95)
Chrys. Aries Reliant/K-Cars (1981-95)
Chrys. Cirrus/Stratus/Neon (1994-95)
Chrys. LHS/Intrepid/Concorde (1993-95)
Chrys. Minivan (1984-95)
Chrys. Pickups/Big Vans (1981-95)
Ford Aerostar (1986-95)
Ford Bronco II/Explorer/Ranger (1981-96)
Ford Cr. Vic./Gr. Marquis/ Lincolns (1983-95)
Ford Escort/Lynx/Tracer (1981-95)
Ford F-Series Trucks (1981-96)
Ford Taurus/Sable (1986-95)
Ford Tempo/Topaz (1984-95)
Ford Mustang/Capri/Probe (1979-95)
Ford Paint (1985-95)

GM All Geo's/LeMans/Sprint/ Nova (1985-95)
GM Saturn (1991-95)
GM Auto. Trans.: FWD (1981-93)
GM Auto. Trans.: RWD (1981-92)
GM Beretta/Corsica (1987-95)
GM Cut. Supr./Gr. Prix/Lumina/ Regal (1988-95)
GM Celebrity/6000/Century/Cut. Ciera & Cruiser (1982-95)
GM Camaro/Firebird (1982-96)
GM Achieva/Calais/Gr. Am/ Skylark/Somerset Regal (1985-95)
GM Roadmaster/Caprice (1981-95)
GM Cavalier/Cimarron/Firenza/ Skyhawk/Sunbird/J2000 (1982-95)
GM 98/Electra & Park Ave. (1984-96)
GM 88/LeSabre/Bonneville (1985-96)
GM Power Steering Failure (1980-88)
GM C/K Pickup/Suburban & Blazer/Jimmy Utility & Big Vehicle (1984-95)
GM S-Series/Blazer/Jimmy/ Sonoma (1982-96)
GM Big Vans/Astro/Safari/APVs (1980-95)

GM Pontiac Fiero (1984-88)
GM Paint (1985-95)
Honda/Acura (1988-95)
Hyundai (1986-95)
Jeep–all models (1984-95)
Lemon Lawyer References (1995)
Mazda Cars (1988-95)
Mazda Trucks (1988-95)
Mercedes (1980-95)
Mitsubishi (1983-95)
Nissan Cars (1983-95)
Nissan Vans/Trucks (1986-95)
Renault/Eagle (1981-95)
Saab (1985-96)
Subaru (1985-96)
Toyota (1988-95)
Volkswagen (1980-95)
Volvo (1980-95)

CAS depends on the public for its support. Annual consumer membership is $15. All contributions to this nonprofit organization are tax-deductible. Annual membership includes a quarterly newsletter called "LEMON TIMES." To join, send a check to:

Center for Auto Safety
2001 S Street NW
Washington DC 20009-1160

Lemon Aid

The Center for Auto Safety has published *The Lemon Book,* a detailed, 368 page guide to resolving automobile complaints. Co-authored by Ralph Nader and CAS Executive Director, Clarence Ditlow, this handbook is designed to help car buyers avoid lemons and tells you what to do if you wind up with one. To obtain this valuable book, send $16.50 to the Center for Auto Safety, 2001 S St., NW, Washington, DC 20009-1160. CAS is a non-profit consumer group supported, in part, by the sales of its publications.

Here are the names of additional consumer groups which you may find helpful:

Advocates for Highway and Auto Safety
750 First Street, NE, Suite 901
Washington, DC 20002
(202) 408-1711
Focus: An alliance of consumer, health and safety groups, and insurance companies.

Consumer Action San Francisco
116 New Montgomery St., #233
San Francisco, CA 94105
(415) 777-9635
Focus: General problems of California residents.

Consumers for Auto Reliability and Safety Foundation
1500 W. El Camino Ave, #419
Sacramento, CA 95833-1945
(916) 759-9440
Focus: Auto safety, airbags, and lemon laws.

Consumers Education and Protective Association
6048 Ogontz Avenue
Philadelphia, PA 19141
(215) 424-1441
Focus: Pickets on behalf of members to resolve auto purchase and repair problems.

SafetyBelt Safe, U.S.A.
P.O. Box 553
Altadena, CA 91003
(800) 745-SAFE or
(310) 673-2666
Focus: Provides excellent information and training on child safety seats and safety belt usage.

Several federal agencies conduct automobile-related programs. Listed below is each agency with a description of the type of work it performs as well as the address and phone number for its headquarters in Washington, DC. Useful web sites are also listed.

National Highway Traffic Safety Administration
400 7th Street, SW, NOA-40
Washington, DC 20590
(202) 366-9550
www.nhtsa.dot.gov

NHTSA issues safety and fuel economy standards for new motor vehicles; investigates safety defects and enforces recall of defective vehicles and equipment; conducts research and demonstration programs on vehicle safety, fuel economy, driver safety, and automobile inspection and repair; provides grants for state highway safety programs in areas such as police traffic services, driver education and licensing, emergency medical services, pedestrian safety, and alcohol abuse.

Environmental Protection Agency
401 M Street, SW
Washington, DC 20460
(202) 260-2090
www.epa.gov

EPA is responsible for the control and abatement of air, noise, and toxic substance pollution. This includes setting and enforcing air and noise emission standards for motor vehicles and measuring fuel economy in new vehicles (EPA Fuel Economy Guide).

Federal Trade Commission
PA Avenue & 6th Street, NW
Washington, DC 20580
(202) 326-2000
www.ftc.gov

FTC regulates advertising and credit practices, marketing abuses, and professional services and ensures that products are properly labeled (as in fuel economy ratings). The commission covers unfair or deceptive trade practices in motor vehicle sales and repairs, as well as in non-safety defects.

Federal Highway Administration
400 7th Street, SW,
Room 3401, HHS1
Washington, DC 20590
(202) 366-1153

FHA develops standards to ensure highways are constructed to reduce occurrence and severity of accidents.

Department of Justice
Consumer Litigation
Civil Division
1331 Pennsylvania Avenue
National Place Bldg., Suite 950N
Washington, DC 20004
(202) 514-6786

The Department of Justice enforces the federal law that requires manufacturers to label new automobiles and forbids removal or alteration of labels before delivery to consumers. Labels must contain the make, model, vehicle identification number, dealer's name, suggested base price, manufacturer option costs, and manufacturer's suggested retail price.

Automobile Manufacturers

Acura Automobile Division
Mr. Richard B. Thomas
Executive V. P. and General Manager
1919 Torrance Blvd.
Torrance, CA 90501-2746
(310) 783-2000/(310) 783-3900 (fax)

BMW of North America, Inc.
Mr. Victor H. Doolan
President
300 Chestnut Ridge Road
Woodcliff Lake, NJ 07675
(201) 307-4000/(201) 307-4003 (fax)

Chrysler Corporation
Mr. Robert Eaton
Chairman and CEO
1000 Chrysler Drive
Auburn Hills, MI 48326-2766
(810) 512-9300

Ford Motor Company
Mr. Alex Trotman
Chairman and CEO
The American Road
Dearborn, MI 48121
(313) 322-3000/(313) 446-9475 (fax)

General Motors Corporation
Mr. John F. Smith, Jr.
CEO and Chairman
3044 W. Grand Blvd.
Detroit, MI 48202
(313) 556-5000/(313) 556-5108 (fax)

American Honda Motor Co.
Mr. K. Amemiya
President
1919 Torrance Blvd.
Torrance, CA 90501-2746
(310) 783-2000/(310) 783-3900 (fax)

Hyundai Motor America
Mr. Y. I. Lee
President and CEO
10550 Talbert Avenue
Fountain Valley, CA 92728
(714) 965-3939/(714) 965-3816 (fax)

American Isuzu Motors, Inc.
Mr. Yoshito Mochizuki
President
2300 Pellissier Place
Whittier, CA 90601
(310) 699-0500/(310) 692-7135 (fax)

Jaguar Cars Inc.
Mr. Michael H. Dale
President N. American Operations
555 MacArthur Blvd.
Mahwah, NJ 07430-2327
(201) 818-8500/(201) 818-9770 (fax)

Kia Motors America, Inc.
Mr. H.R. Park
President and CEO
2 Cromwell
Irvine, CA 92618
(714) 470-7000/(714) 470-2801 (fax)

Land Rover of America
Mr. Charles R. Hughes
President
4390 Parliament Place, PO Box 1503
Lanham, MD 20706
(301) 731-9040/(301) 731-9054 (fax)

Mazda Motor of America, Inc.
Mr. George Toyama
President
7755 Irvine Center Dr.
Irvine, CA 92718
(714) 727-1990/(714) 727-6529 (fax)

Mercedes-Benz of N.A.
Mr. Michael Bassermann
President and CEO
1 Mercedes Drive
Montvale, NJ 07645-0350
(201) 573-0600/(201) 573-0117 (fax)

Mitsubishi Motor Sales
Mr. Tohei Takeuchi
President and CEO
6400 Katella Ave.
Cypress, CA 90630-0064
(714) 372-6000/(714) 373-1019 (fax)

Nissan Motor Corp. U.S.A.
Mr. Robert Thomas
President and CEO
P.O. Box 191
Gardena, CA 90248-0191
(310) 532-3111/(310) 719-3343 (fax)

Porsche Cars North America, Inc.
Mr. Frederick J. Schwab
President and CEO
P.O. Box 30911
Reno, NV 89520-3911
(702) 348-3000/(702) 348-3770 (fax)

Rolls Royce Motor Cars, Inc.
Mr. Robert R. Wharen
Managing Dir., American Operations
140 E. Ridgewood Ave.
Paramus, NJ 07652
(201) 967-9100/(201) 967-2070 (fax)

Saab Cars USA, Inc.
Mr. Joel Manby
President and CEO
4405-A Saab Drive
Norcross, GA 30091
(770) 279-0100/(770) 279-6499 (fax)

Subaru of America, Inc.
Mr. Yasuo Fujiki
Chairman and CEO
P.O. Box 6000
Cherry Hill, NJ 08034-6000
(609) 488-8500/(609) 488-0485 (fax)

American Suzuki Motor Corp.
Mr. Masao Nagura
President
3251 E. Imperial Hwy.
Brea, CA 92621-6722
(714) 996-7040/(714) 524-2512 (fax)

Toyota Motor Sales, U.S.A., Inc.
Mr. Yoshio Ishizaka
President and CEO
19001 S. Western Avenue
Torrance, CA 90509
(310) 618-4000/(310) 618-7800 (fax)

Volkswagen of America, Inc.
Mr. Clive Warrilow
President
3800 Hamlin Road
Auburn Hills, MI 48326
(810) 340-5000/(810) 340-4643 (fax)

Volvo Cars of North America
Mr. Helge Alten
President and CEO
7 Volvo Drive
Rockleigh, NJ 07647
(201) 767-4710/(201) 784-4535 (fax)

Lemon Laws

Sometimes, despite our best efforts, we buy a vehicle that just doesn't work right. There may be little problem after little problem, or perhaps one big problem that never seems to be fixed. Because of the bad taste that such vehicles leave in the mouths of consumers who buy them, these vehicles are known as "lemons."

In the past, it's been difficult to obtain a refund or replacement if a vehicle was a lemon. The burden of proof was left to the consumer. Because it is hard to define exactly what constitutes a lemon, many lemon owners were unable to win a case against a manufacturer. However, as of 1993, all states have passed "Lemon Laws." Although there are some important state-to-state variations, all of the laws have similarities: They establish a period of coverage, usually one year from delivery or the written warranty period, whichever is shorter; they may require some form of noncourt arbitration; and most importantly they define a lemon. In most states a lemon is a new car, truck, or van that has been taken back to the shop at least four times for the same repair, or is out of service for a total of 30 days during the covered period.

This time does not mean consecutive days. In some states the total time must be for the same repair; in others, it can be based on different repair problems.

Be sure to keep careful records of your repairs since some states now require only one of the three or four repairs to be within the specified time period.

Specific information about laws in your state can be obtained from your state attorney general's office (c/o your state capitol) or your local consumer protection office. The following table offers a general description of the Lemon Law in your state and what you need to do to set it in motion (*Notification/Trigger*). An **L** indicates that the law covers leased vehicles and we indicate where state-run arbitration programs are available. State-run programs are the best type of arbitration.

Alabama	**Qualification:** 3 unsuccessful repairs or 30 calendar days out of service within shorter of 24 months or 24,000 miles, provided 1 repair attempt or 1 day out of service is within shorter of 1 year or 12,000 miles. **Notification/Trigger:** Certified mail notice to manufacturer, who has 14 calendar days to make final repair.
Alaska	**Qualification:** 3 unsuccessful repairs or 30 business days out of service within shorter of 1 year or warranty. **Notification/Trigger:** Certified mail notice to manufacturer and dealer, or agent within 60 days after expiration of warranty or 1 year. Consumer must demand refund or replacement to be delivered within 60 days after mailing the notice. Final repair attempt within 30 days of receipt of notice.
Arizona	**Qualification:** 4 unsuccessful repairs or 30 calendar days out of service within shorter of 2 years or 24,000 miles. **Notification/Trigger:** Written notice to manufacturer and opportunity to repair.
Arkansas	**Qualification:** 3 unsuccessful repairs, or 1 unsuccessful repair of a problem likely to cause death or serious bodily injury within longer of 24 months or 24,000 miles. **Notification/Trigger:** Certified or registered mail notice to manufacturer. Manufacturer has 10 days to notify consumer of repair facility. Facility has 10 days to repair.
California	**Qualification:** 4 unsuccessful repairs or 30 calendar days out of service within shorter of 1 year or 12,000 miles. **Notification/Trigger:** Written notice to manufacturer and delivery of car to repair facility for repair attempt within 30 days. *State has certified guidelines for arbitration.* **L**
Colorado	**Qualification:** 4 unsuccessful repairs or 30 business days out of service within shorter of 1 year or warranty. **Notification/Trigger:** Prior certified mail notice for each defect occurance and opportunity to repair.
Conn.	**Qualification:** 4 unsuccessful repairs or 30 calendar days out of service within shorter of 1 year or warranty. **Notification/Trigger:** Report to manufacturer, agent or dealer. Written notice to manufacturer only if required in owner's manual or warranty. *State-run arbitration program is available.* **L**

Delaware	**Qualification:** 4 unsuccessful repairs or 30 calendar days out of service within shorter of 1 year or warranty. **Notification/Trigger:** Written notice to manufacturer and opportunity to repair. **L**
D. C.	**Qualification:** 4 unsuccessful repairs or 30 calendar days out of service or 1 unsuccessful repair of a safety-related defect, within shorter of 2 years or 18,000 miles. **Notification/Trigger:** Report of each defect occurance to manufacturer, agent or dealer. *State-run arbitration program is available.* Note: Enforcement by D.C. is suspended until October 1, 1998. **L**
Florida	**Qualification:** 3 unsuccessful repairs or 20 calendar days out of service within shorter of 12 months or 12,000 miles. **Notification/Trigger:** Written notice by certified or express mail to manufacturer who has 14 calendar days (10 if vehicle has been out of service 20 cumulative calendar days) for final repair attempt after delivery to designated dealer. *State-run arbitration program is available.* **L**
Georgia*	**Qualification:** 3 unsuccessful repair attempts or 30 calendar days out of service within shorter of 24,000 miles or 24 months, with 1 repair or 15 days out of service within shorter or 1 year or 12,000 miles; or one unsuccessful repair of a serious safety defect in the braking or steering system within shorter of 1 year or 12,000 miles. **Notification/Trigger:** Certified mail notice return receipt requested. Manufacturer has 7 days to notify consumer of repair facility. Facility has 14 days to repair. *State-run arbitration program is available.* **L**
Hawaii	**Qualification:** 3 unsuccessful repairs, or 1 unsuccessful repair of a nonconformity likely to cause death or serious bodily injury, or out of service within shorter of 2 years or 24,000 miles. **Notification/Trigger:** Written notice to manufacturer and opportunity to repair. *State-run arbitration program is available.* **L**
Idaho	**Qualification:** 4 repair attempts or 30 business days out of service within shorter of 12 months or 12,000 miles. **Notification/Trigger:** Written notice to manufacturer or dealer.
Illinois*	**Qualification:** 4 unsuccessful repairs or 30 business days out of service within shorter of 1 year or 12,000 miles. **Notification/Trigger:** Written notice to manufacturer and opportunity to repair.
Indiana	**Qualification:** 4 unsuccessful repairs or 30 business days out of service within the shorter of 18 months or 18,000 miles. **Notification/Trigger:** Written notice to manufacturer only if required in warranty. **L**
Iowa	**Qualification:** 3 unsuccessful repairs, or 1 unsuccessful repair of a nonconformity likely to cause death or serious bodily injury, or 20 calendar days out of service within shorter of 2 years or 24,000 miles. **Notification/Trigger:** Written notice to manufacturer and final opportunity to repair within 10 calendar days of receipt of notice. *State has certified guidelines for arbitration.* **L**
Kansas	**Qualification:** 4 unsuccessful repairs of the same problem or 30 calendar days out of service or 10 total repairs of any problem within shorter of 1 year or warranty. **Notification/Trigger:** Actual notice to manufacturer.
Kentucky	**Qualification:** 4 unsuccessful repairs or 30 calendar days out of service within shorter of 1 year or 12,000 miles. **Notification/Trigger:** Written notice to manufacturer.
Louisiana	**Qualification:** 4 unsuccessful repairs or 30 calendar days out of service within shorter of 1 year or warranty. **Notification/Trigger:** Report to manufacturer or dealer. **L**
Maine	**Qualification:** 3 unsuccessful repairs (when at least 2 times the same agent attempted the repair) or 15 business days out of service within shorter of 2 years or 18,000 miles. **Notification/Trigger:** Written notice to manufacturer or dealer only if required in warranty or owner's manual. Manufacturer has 7 business days after receipt for final repair attempt. *State-run arbitration program is available.* **L**
Maryland	**Qualification:** 4 unsuccessful repairs, 30 calendar days out of service or 1 unsuccessful repair of braking or steering system within shorter of 15 months or 15,000 miles. **Notification/Trigger:** Certified mail notice, return receipt requested to manu. or factory branch and opportunity to repair within 30 calendar days of receipt of notice. **L**
Mass.	**Qualification:** 3 unsuccessful repairs or 15 business days out of service within shorter of 1 year or 15,000 miles. **Notification/Trigger:** Notice to manufacturer or dealer who has 7 business days to attempt a final repair. *State-run arbitration program is available.*
Michigan	**Qualification:** 4 unsuccessful repairs or 30 calendar days out of service within shorter of 1 year or warranty. **Notification/Trigger:** Certified mail notice, return receipt requested, to manufacturer who has 5 business days to repair after delivery.

Minn.	**Qualification:** 4 unsuccessful repairs or 30 business days out of service or 1 unsuccessful repair of total braking or steering loss likely to cause death or serious bodily injury within shorter of 2 years or warranty. **Notification/Trigger:** At least one written notice to manufacturer, agent or dealer and opportunity to repair. **L**
Miss.	**Qualification:** 3 unsuccessful repairs or 15 business days out of service within shorter of 1 year or warranty. **Notification/Trigger:** Written notice to manufacturer who has 10 business days to repair after delivery to designated dealer.
Missouri	**Qualification:** 4 unsuccessful repairs or 30 business days out of service within shorter of 1 year or warranty. **Notification/Trigger:** Written notice to manufacturer who has 10 calendar days to repair after delivery to designated dealer.
Montana	**Qualification:** 4 unsuccessful repairs or 30 business days out of service after notice within shorter of 2 years or 18,000 miles. **Notification/Trigger:** Written notice to manufacturer and opportunity to repair. *State-run arbitration program is available.*
Nebraska	**Qualification:** 4 unsuccessful repairs or 40 calendar days out of service within shorter of 1 year or warranty. **Notification/Trigger:** Certified mail notice to manufacturer and opportunity to repair.
Nevada	**Qualification:** 4 unsuccessful repairs or 30 calendar days out of service within shorter of 1 year or warranty. **Notification/Trigger:** Written notice to manufacturer.
N. H.	**Qualification:** 3 unsuccessful repairs by same dealer or 30 business days out of service within warranty. **Notification/Trigger:** Report to manufacturer, distributor, agent or dealer (on forms provided by manufacturer) and final opportunity to repair before arbitration. *State-run arbitration program is available.* **L**
N. J.	**Qualification:** 3 unsuccessful repairs or 20 calendar days out of service within shorter of 2 years or 18,000 miles. **Notification/Trigger:** Certified mail notice, written notice to manufacturer who has 15 days to repair. *State-run arbitration program is available.* **L**
N. M.	**Qualification:** 4 unsuccessful repairs or 30 business days within shorter of 1 year or warranty. **Notification/Trigger:** Written notice to manufacturer, agent or dealer and opportunity to repair.
N. Y.	**Qualification:** 4 unsuccessful repairs or 30 calendar days out of service within shorter of 2 years or 18,000 miles. **Notification/Trigger:** Certified notice to manufacturer, agent or dealer. *State-run arbitration program is available.* **L**
N. C.	**Qualification:** 4 unsuccessful repairs within the shorter of 24 months, 24,000 miles or warranty or 20 business days out of service during any 12 month period of the warranty. **Notification/Trigger:** Written notice to manufacturer and opportunity to repair within 15 calendar days of receipt only if required in warranty or owner's manual. **L**
N. D.	**Qualification:** 3 unsuccessful repairs or 30 business days out of service within shorter of 1 year or warranty. **Notification/Trigger:** Direct written notice and opportunity to repair to manufacturer. *(Manufacturer's informal arbitration process serves as a prerequisite to consumer refund of replacement.)* **L**
Ohio	**Qualification:** 3 unsuccessful repairs of same nonconformity, 30 calendar days out of service, 8 total repairs of any problem, or 1 unsuccessful repair of problem likely to cause death or serious bodily injury within shorter of 1 year or 18,000 miles. **Notification/Trigger:** Report to manufacturer, its agent or dealer.
Okla.	**Qualification:** 4 unsuccessful repairs or 45 calendar days out of service within shorter of 1 year or warranty. **Notification/Trigger:** Written notice to manufacturer and opportunity to repair.
Oregon	**Qualification:** 4 unsuccessful repairs or 30 business days out of service within shorter of 1 year or 12,000 miles. **Notification/Trigger:** Direct written notice to manufacturer and opportunity to repair. **L**
Penn.	**Qualification:** 3 unsuccessful repairs or 30 calendar days out of service within shorter of 1 year, 12,000 miles, or warranty. **Notification/Trigger:** Delivery to authorized service and repair facility. If delivery impossible, written notice to manufacturer or its repair facility obligates them to pay for delivery.
R. I.	**Qualification:** 4 unsuccessful repairs or 30 calendar days out of service within shorter of 1 year or 15,000 miles. **Notification/Trigger:** Report to dealer or manufacturer who has 7 days for final

R. I. repair opportunity. *(Manufacturer's informal arbitration process serves as a prerequisite to consumer refund of replacement.)* **L**

S. C. **Qualification:** 3 unsuccessful repairs or 30 calendar days out of service within shorter of 1 year or 12,000 miles. **Notification/Trigger:** Written notice to manufacturer by certified mail and oppportunity to repair only if manufacturer informed consumer of such at time of sale. Manufacturer has 10 days to notify consumer of repair facility. Facility has 10 days to repair. *State-run arbitration program is available.* **L**

S. D. **Qualification:** 4 unsuccessful repairs, at least 1 of which occurred during the shorter of 1 year or 12,000 miles, or 30 calendar days out of service during the shorter of 24 months or 24,000 miles. **Notification/Trigger:** Certified mail notice to manufacturer and final opportunity to repair. Manufacturer has 7 calendar days to notify consumer of repair facility. Facility has 14 days to repair. *(Manufacturer's informal arbitration process serves as a prerequisite to consumer refund of replacement.)*

Tenn. **Qualification:** 4 unsuccessful repairs or 30 calendar days out of service within shorter of 1 year or warranty. **Notification/Trigger:** Certified mail notice to manufacturer and final opportunity to repair within 10 calendar days. **L**

Texas **Qualification:** 4 unsuccessful repairs when 2 occured within shorter of 1 year or 12,000 miles, and other 2 occur within shorter of 1 year or 12,000 miles from date of 2nd repair attempt; or 2 unsuccessful repairs of a serious safety defect when 1 occured within shorter of 1 year or 12,000 miles and other occured within shorter of 1 year or 12,000 miles from date of 1st repair; or 30 calendar days out of service within shorter of 2 years or 24,000 miles and at least 2 attempts were made within shorter of 1 year or 12,000 miles. **Notification/Trigger:** Written notice to manufacturer. *State-run arbitration program is available.* **L**

Utah **Qualification:** 4 unsuccessful repairs or 30 business days out of service within shorter of 1 year or warranty. **Notification/Trigger:** Report to manufacturer, agent or dealer. **L**

Vermont **Qualification:** 3 unsuccessful repairs when at least 1st repair was within warranty, or 30 calendar days within warranty **Notification/Trigger:** Written notice to manufacturer (on provided forms) after 3rd repair attempt, or 30 days. Arbitration must be held within 45 days after notice, during which time manufacturer has 1 final repair. *State-run arbitration program is available.* **L**

Virginia **Qualification:** 3 unsuccessful repairs, or 1 repair attempt of a serious safety defect, or 30 calendar days out of service within 18 months. **Notification/Trigger:** Written notice to manufacturer. If 3 unsuccessful repairs or 30 days already exhausted before notice, manufacturer has 1 more repair attempt not to exceed 15 days.

Wash. **Qualification:** 4 unsuccessful repairs, 30 calendar days out of service (15 during warranty period), or 2 repairs of serious safety defects, first reported within shorter of the warranty or 24 months or 24,000 miles. One repair attempt and 15 of the 30 days must fall within manufacturer's express warranty of at least 1 year or 12,000 miles. **Notification/Trigger:** Written notice to manufacturer. *State-run arbitration program is available.* **L** *Note: Consumer should receive replacement or refund within 40 calendar days of request.*

W. V. **Qualification:** 3 unsuccessful repairs or 30 calendar days out of service or 1 unsuccessful repair of problem likely to cause death or serious bodily injury within shorter of 1 year or warranty. **Notification/Trigger:** Prior written notice to manufacturer and at least one opportunity to repair.

Wisc. **Qualification:** 4 unsuccessful repairs or 30 calendar days out of service within shorter of 1 year or warranty. **Notification/Trigger:** Report to manufacturer or dealer. **L** *Note: Consumer should receive replacement or refund within 30 calendar days after offer to return title.*

Wyoming **Qualification:** 3 unsuccessful repairs or 30 business days out of service within 1 year. **Notification/Trigger:** Direct written notice to manufacturer and opportunity to repair.

SHOWROOM STRATEGIES

Buying a car means matching wits with a seasoned professional. But if you know what to expect, you'll have a much better chance of getting a really good deal! This chapter offers practical advice on buying a car, tips on getting the best price and financing, information on buying vs. leasing, and tips on avoiding lemons. We'll also take a peek at some options for the future that will increase driving safety.

For most of us, the auto showroom can be an intimidating environment. We're matching wits with professional negotiators over a very complex product. Being prepared is the best way to turn a potentially intimidating showroom experience into a profitable one. Here's some advice on handling what you'll find in the showroom.

Beware of silence. Silence is often used to intimidate, so be prepared for long periods of time when the salesperson is "talking with the manager." This tactic is designed to make you want to "just get the negotiation over with." Instead of becoming a victim, do something that indicates you are serious about looking elsewhere. Bring the classified section of the newspaper and begin circling other cars or review brochures from other manufacturers. By sending the message that you have other options, you increase your bargaining power and speed up the process.

Don't fall in love with a car. Never look too interested in any particular car. Advise family members who go with you against being too enthusiastic about any one car. *Tip:* Beat the dealers at their own game— bring along a friend who tells you that the price is "too much compared to the *other* deal."

Keep your wallet in your pocket. Don't leave a deposit, even if it's refundable. You'll feel pressure to rush your shopping, and you'll have to return and face the salesperson again before you are ready.

Shop at the end of the month. Salespeople anxious to meet sales goals are more willing to negotiate a lower price at this time.

Buy last year's model. The majority of new cars are the same as the previous year, with minor cosmetic changes. You can save considerably by buying in early fall when dealers are clearing space for "new" models. The important trade-off you make using this technique is that the car maker may have added air bags or anti-lock brakes to an otherwise unchanged vehicle.

Buying from stock. You can often get a better deal on a car that the dealer has on the lot. However, these cars usually have expensive options you may not want or need. Do not hesitate to ask the dealer to remove an option (and its accompanying charge) or sell you the car without charging for the option. The longer the car sits there, the more interest the dealer pays on the car, which increases the dealer's incentive to sell.

Ordering a car. Domestic cars can be ordered from the manufacturer. Simply offering a fixed amount over invoice may be attractive because it's a sure sale and the dealership has not invested in the car. All the salesperson has to do is take your order.

If you do order a car, make sure when it arrives that it includes only the options you requested. Don't fall for the trick where the dealer offers you unordered options at a "special price," because it was their mistake. If you didn't order the option, don't pay for it.

Don't trade in. Although it is more work, you can usually do better by selling your old car yourself than by trading it in. To determine what you'll gain by selling the car yourself, check the NADA "Blue Book" at your credit union or library. The difference between the trade-in price (what the dealer will give you) and the retail price (what you typically can sell it for) is your extra payment for selling the car yourself.

If you do decide to trade your car in at the dealership, *keep the buying and selling separate.* First, negotiate the best price for your new car, then find out how much the dealer will give you for your old car. Keeping the two deals separate ensures that you know what you're paying for your new car and simplifies the entire transaction.

Question everything the dealer writes down. Nothing is etched in stone. Because things are written down, we tend not to question them. This is wrong—always assume that anything written down is negotiable.

Test drive without the salesperson. When you test drive a car, go alone and take a good long test drive. If a dealership will not let you take a car without a salesperson, go to another dealership. Test driving without the distraction of a salesperson is a necessity when trying out a new car. See page 52 for tips on test driving.

Avoiding Lemons

One way to avoid the sour taste of a lemon after you've bought your car is to protect yourself *before* you sign on the dotted line. These tips will help you avoid problems down the road.

1 **Avoid new models.** Any new car in its very first year of production often turns out to have a lot of defects. Sometimes the manufacturer isn't able to remedy the defects until the second, third, or even fourth year of production. If the manufacturer has not worked out problems by the third model year, the car will likely be a lemon forever.

2 **Avoid the first cars off the line.** Most companies close down their assembly lines every year to make annual style changes. In addition to adding hundreds of dollars to the price of a new car, these changes can introduce new defects. It can take a few months to iron out these bugs. Ask the dealer when the vehicle you are interested in was manufactured, or look on the metal tag found on the inside of the driver-side door frame to find the date of manufacture.

3 **Avoid delicate options.** Delicate options have the highest frequency-of-repair records. Power seats, power windows, power antennas, and special roofs are nice conveniences—until they break down. Of all the items on the vehicles, they tend to be the most expensive to repair.

4 **Inspect the dealer's checklist.** Request a copy of the dealer's pre-delivery service and adjustment checklist (also called a "make-ready list") at the time your new vehicle is delivered. Write the request directly on the new vehicle order. This request informs the dealer that you are aware of the dealer's responsibility to check your new car for defects.

5 **Examine the car on delivery.** Most of us are very excited when it comes time to take the vehicle home. This is the time where a few minutes of careful inspection can save hours of aggravation later. Carefully look over the body for any damage, check for the spare tire and jack equipment, make sure all electrical items work, and make sure all the hubcaps and body molding are on. You may want to take a short test drive. Finally, make sure you have the owner's manual, warranty forms, and all the legal documents.

One of the most difficult aspects of buying a new car is getting the best price. Most of us are at a disadvantage negotiating because we don't know how much the car actually cost the dealer. The difference between what the dealer paid and the sticker price represents the negotiable amount.

Until recently, the key to getting the best price was finding out the dealer cost. Many shoppers now ask to see the factory invoice, so some dealers promote their cars by offering to sell at only $49 or $99 over invoice. This sounds like a good deal, but these cars often have options you may not want and most invoice prices do not reveal the extra, hidden profit to the dealer.

Now that most savvy consumers know to check the so-called "dealer invoice," the industry has camouflaged this number. Special incentives, rebates, and kickbacks can account for $500 to $2,000 worth of extra profit to a dealer selling a car at "dealer invoice." The non-profit Center for the Study of Services recently discovered that in 37 percent of cases when dealers are forced to bid against each other for the sale, they offered the buyer a price below the "dealer invoice"—an unlikely event if the dealer was actually losing money. The bottom line is that "dealer invoice" doesn't mean anything anymore.

Because the rules have changed, we believe that most consumers are ill-advised to try and negotiate with a dealer. Introducing competition is the best way to get the lowest price on a new car. What this means is that you have to convince 3 or 4 dealers that you are, in fact, prepared to buy a car; that you have decided on the make, model, and features; and that your decision now rests solely on which dealer will give you the best price. You can try to do this by phone, but often dealers will not give you the best price, or will quote you a price over the phone that they will not honor later. Instead, you should try to do this in person. As anyone knows who has ventured into an auto showroom simply to get the best price, the process can be lengthy and arduous. Nevertheless, if you can convice the dealer that you are serious and are willing to take the time to go to a number of dealers, it will pay off. Otherwise, we suggest you use the CarBargains service listed on the next page.

If you find a big savings at a dealership far from your home, call a local dealer with the price. They may very well match it. If not, pick up the car from the distant dealer, knowing your trip has saved you hundreds of dollars. You can still bring it to your local dealer for warranty work and repairs. Here are some other showroom strategies:

Beware of misleading advertising. New car ads are meant to get you into the showroom. They usually promise low prices, big rebates, high trade-in, and spotless integrity—don't be deceived. Advertised prices are rarely the true selling price. They usually exclude transportation charges, service fees, or document fees. And always look out for the asterisk, both in advertisements and on invoices. It can be a signal that the advertiser has something to hide.

Don't talk price until you're ready to buy. On your first few trips to the showroom, simply look over the cars, decide what options you want, and do your test driving.

Shop the corporate twins. Page 18 contains a list of corporate twins—nearly identical cars that carry different name plates. Check the price and options of the twins of the car you like. A higher priced twin may have more options, so it may be a better deal than the lower priced car without the options you want.

Watch out for dealer preparation overcharges. Before paying the dealer to clean your car, make sure that preparation is not included in the basic price. The price sticker will state: "Manufacturer's suggested retail price of this model includes dealer preparation."

If you must negotiate . . . negotiate up from the "invoice" price rather than down from the sticker price. Simply make an offer close to or at the "invoice" price. If the sales person says that your offer is too low to make a profit, ask to see the factory invoice.

The 180-Degree Turn

If you try to negotiate a car purchase, remember that you have the most important weapon in the bargaining process: *the 180-degree turn*. Be prepared to walk away from a deal, even at the risk of losing the "very best deal" your salesperson has ever offered, and you will be in the best position to get a genuine "best deal." Remember: dealerships need you, the buyer, to survive.

Price Shopping Service

Even with the information that we provide you in this chapter of *The Car Book*, most of us will *not* be well prepared to negotiate a good price for the cars we are considering. In fact, as we indicated on the previous page, we don't believe that you can negotiate the best price with *a* dealer. The key to getting the best price is to get the dealers to compete with each other. This page describes a new and easy way to find the best price by actually getting the dealers to compete.

CarBargains is a service of the non-profit Center for the Study of Services, a Washington, DC, consumer group, set up to provide comparative price information for many products and services.

CarBargains will "shop" the dealerships in your area and obtain at least five price quotes for the make and model of the car that you want to buy. The dealers who submit quotes know that they are competing with other area dealerships and have agreed to honor the prices that they submit. It is important to note that CarBargains is not an auto broker or "car buying" service; they have no affiliation with dealers.

Here's how the service works:

1. You provide CarBargains with the make, model, and style of car you wish to buy (Ford Taurus GL, for example) by phone or mail.

2. Within two weeks, CarBargains will send you dealer quote sheets from at least 5 local dealers who have bid against one another to sell you that car. The offer is actually a commitment to a dollar amount above (or below) "factory invoice cost" for that model.

You will also receive a printout with the exact dealer cost for the car and each available option. Included in the information will be the name of the sales manager responsible for honoring the quote.

3. Use the factory invoice cost printout to add up the invoice cost for the base car and the options you want and then determine which dealer offers the best price using the dealer quote sheets. Contact the sales manager of that dealership and arrange to purchase the car.

If a car with the options you want is not available on the dealer's lot, you can have the dealer order the car from the factory or, in some cases, from another dealer at the agreed price.

When you receive your quotes, you will also get some suggestions on low-cost sources of financing and a valuation of your used car (trade-in).

The price for this service may seem expensive, but when you consider the savings that will result by having dealers bid against each other, as well as the time and effort of trying to get these bids yourself, we believe it's a great value. First of all, the dealers know they have a bona fide buyer (you've paid $150 for the service) and they know they are bidding against 5–7 of their competitors.

To obtain CarBargains' competitive price quotes, send a check for $150 to CarBargains, 733 15th St., NW, Suite 820CB, Washington, DC 20005. Include your complete mailing address, phone number (in case of questions), and the exact make, model, and year of the car you want to buy. You should receive your bids within 2-3 weeks. For faster service, call them at 800-475-7283. They will accept Visa or Mastercard on phone orders.

Auto Brokers

While CarBargains is a non-profit organization created to help you find the best price for the car you want to purchase, auto brokers are typically in the business to make money. As such, whatever price you end up paying for the car will include additional profit for the broker. While many brokers are legitimately trying to get their customers the best price, others have developed special relationships with certain dealers and may not do much shopping for you. As a consumer, it is difficult to tell which are which. If you use a broker, make sure the contract to purchase the car is with the dealer, not the broker. In addition, it is best to pay the broker *after* the service is rendered, not before. There have been cases where the auto broker makes certain promises, takes your money, and you never hear from him or her again. If CarBargains is not for you, then we suggest you consider using a buying service associated with your credit union or auto club, which can arrange for the purchase of a car at some fixed price over "dealer invoice."

Depreciation

Over the past 20 years, new vehicle depreciation costs have steadily increased. A recent study conducted by Runzheimer International shows that depreciation and interest now account for slightly over 50 percent of the costs of owning and operating a vehicle. This number is up from 41 percent in 1976. On the other hand, the relative cost of gasoline has dropped by half, from 35 percent to 17 percent of every dollar spent on the average car. Other costs, including insurance, maintenance, and tires, have remained at relatively steady shares of the automotive dollar.

The high cost of depreciation is largely due to skyrocketing new car prices. While there is no reliable method of predicting retained value, your best bet is to purchase a popular new car. Chances are that it will also be popular as a used car.

Most new cars are traded in within four years and are then available on the used car market. The priciest used cars may not necessarily be the highest quality. Supply and demand, as well as appearance, are extremely important factors in determining used car prices.

1992 Cars with the Best and Worst Resale Value

The following table indicates which of the 100 top-selling 1992 cars held their value the best and which did not.

The Best				The Worst			
Model	1992 Price	1996 Price	Retained Value	Model	1992 Price	1996 Price	Retained Value
Saturn SL/SW/SC	$ 8,995	$ 7,875	88%	Chrys. NY'er 5th Ave.	$22,074	$11,225	51%
Toyota Tercel	$ 8,528	$ 7,325	86%	Cadillac Seville	$34,975	$17,900	51%
VW Golf/Jetta	$ 9,950	$ 8,275	83%	Oldsmobile 98	$24,595	$12,625	51%
Mazda Miata	$14,800	$12,225	83%	Ford Crown Victoria	$19,563	$ 9,975	51%
Toyota Paseo	$10,338	$ 8,525	82%	Cadillac DeVille/Fltwd.	$31,740	$15,725	50%
Acura Integra	$14,240	$11,725	82%	Dodge Dynasty	$14,477	$ 7,050	49%
Mazda MX-3	$11,000	$ 8,750	80%	Chev. Caprice/Impala	$17,300	$ 8,450	49%
Toyota Celica	$13,378	$10,700	80%	Chrys. LeBaron Sedan	$13,160	$ 6,125	47%
Mitsubishi Mirage	$ 8,939	$ 6,950	78%	Lincoln Town Car	$34,252	$15,925	46%
Mitsubishi Eclipse	$12,529	$ 9,800	78%	Lincoln Continental	$32,263	$ 2,325	38%

Prices based on the *N.A.D.A. Official Used Car Guide*, July 1996.

Financing

You've done your test drive, researched prices, studied crash tests, determined the options you want, and haggled to get the best price. Now you have to decide how to pay for the car.

If you have the cash, *pay for the car right away*. You avoid finance charges, you won't have a large debt haunting over you and the full value of the car is yours. You can then make the monthly payments to yourself to save up for your next car.

However, most of us cannot afford to pay cash for a car, which leaves two options: financing or leasing. While leasing *seems* more affordable, financing will actually cost you less. When you finance a car, you own it after you finish your payments. At the end of a lease, you have nothing. We don't recommend leasing, but if you want more information, see page 94.

Here are some tips when financing your car:

Shop around for interest rates. Most banks and credit unions will knock off at least a quarter of a percent for their customers. Have these quotes handy when you talk financing with the dealer.

The higher your down payment, the less you'll have to finance. This will not only reduce your overall interest charges, but often qualifies you for a lower interest rate. Down payments are typically 10-20% of the final price.

Avoid long car loans. The monthly payments are lower, but you'll pay far more in overall interest charges. For example, a two year, $15,000 loan at 9% will cost you $1,446.51 in interest; the same amount at five years will cost you $3,682.52 — over twice as much!

Check out manufacturer promotional rates — the 2.9-3.9% rates you see advertised. These low rates are usually only valid on 2-3 year loans.

Read everything you are asked to sign and ask questions about anything you don't fully understand.

Make sure that an extended warranty has *not* been added to the purchase price. Dealers will sometimes add this cost without informing the consumer. Extended warranties are generally a bad value. See "The Warranties Chapter" for more information.

GAP Insurance: GAP insurance covers the difference between what you owe on a car and its actual value, should the car be "totaled" or stolen. If you finance or lease through a dealer, he or she will likely suggest you purchase GAP insurance, which can cost up to $500. If you think this situation is likely, then your financing plan is probably too long.

Whether you need GAP or not, be wary of how dealers try to sell GAP. Dealers may insist the only way to give you financing is if you purchase GAP insurance — this is untrue. When negotiating finance

Don't Be Tongue-Tied

Beware of high pressure phrases like "I've talked to the manuager and this is really the best we can do...as it is, we're losing money on this deal." It is rare that this is true. Dealers are in the business to make money and most do very well. Don't tolerate a take it or leave it attitude. Simply repeat that you will only buy when you see the deal you want and that you don't appreciate the dealer pressuring you. Threaten to leave if the dealer continues to pressure you to buy today.

Don't let the dealer answer your questions with a question. For instance, if you ask, "Can I get air conditioning with this car?" And the salesperson answers, "If I get you air conditioning in this car, will you buy today?" This response tries to force you to decide to buy before you are ready. Ask the dealer to just answer your question and that you'll buy when you're ready. Remember, its the dealer's job to answer questions, not yours.

If you are having a difficult time getting what you want, ask the dealer: "Why won't you let me buy a car today?" Most salespeople will be thrown off by this phrase as they are often too busy trying to use it on you. If they respond in frustration, "OK, what do you want?" then you can say straightforward answers to simple questions.

Make sure you get a price, don't settle for: "If you're shopping price, go to the other dealers first and then come back." This technique insures that they don't have to truly negotiate. Your best response is: "I only plan to come back if your price is the lowest, so that's what I need today, you're lowest price."

terms, be sure to ask if GAP insurance has been added to the cost, as the dealer may not tell you.

Credit Unions vs. Banks: Credit unions generally charge fewer and lower fees and offer better rates than banks. In addition, credit unions offer counseling services where consumers can find pricing information on cars or compare monthly payments for financing. You can join a credit union either through your employer, an organization or club, or if you have a relative who is part of a credit union.

Low Rate or Cash Back? Sometimes auto manufacturers offer a choice of below market financing or cash back. The following table will tell you if it is better to take the lower rate or the cash back rebate. For example, say you want to finance $18,000. Your credit union or bank offers you 8.5% for an auto loan and the dealer offers either a 6% loan or a $1,500 rebate. Which is better? Find your bank or credit union's rate (8.5%) and the dealer's low rate (6%) on the table. Find where the two intersect on the table and you will find the difference per thousand dollars between the two interest rates (47). When you multiply this number (47) by the number of thousands you're financing (18 for $18,000), you get $846. Since the dealer's $1,500 rebate is more than the breakeven $846, taking your bank's rate (8.5%) and the rebate is a better deal than the dealer's low rate (6%). If the answer had been more than $1,500, then the dealer's rate would have been the better deal. An asterisk (*) means that the bank or credit union's rate is the better deal.

Destination Charges

There once was a time when you could go directly to the factory and buy a car, saving yourself a few hundred dollars in destination and freight charges. Today, destination charges are a non-negotiable part of buying a new car, no matter where you purchase it. They are, however, an important factor when comparing prices. You'll find the destination charges on the price sticker attached to the vehicle. According to automakers, destination charges are the cost of shipping a vehicle from its "final assembly point" to the dealership. The cost of shipping other components for final assembly is sometimes also added.

But, the following table illustrates that there is little correlation between destination charges and where the cars are assembled:

Vehicle	Destination Charge	Assembly Country	Parts from N. America
Acura Integra	$420	Japan	5%
Cadillac DeVille	$640	U.S.	95%
BMW 318i	$570	U.S./Germany	5%
Ford Aspire	$335	South Korea	5%
Chevrolet Lumina	$545	Canada	95%

Based on data from Automotive News 1996 Market Data Book.

Rebate vs. Low Rates (Four Year Loan)

Multiply the number that intersects your dealer's rate with the rate from your credit union or bank by the number of thousands you are financing. If the result is less than the rebate, take the rebate; if it is above the rebate, go for the dealer financing.

Bank/ C.U. Rate	Dealer Rate						
	2%	3%	4%	5%	6%	7%	8%
7.0	94	76	57	38	19	*	*
7.5	103	85	66	48	29	10	*
8.0	111	93	75	57	38	19	*
8.5	120	102	84	66	47	28	10
9.0	128	111	93	75	56	38	19
9.5	136	119	101	83	65	47	28

Based on data from *Everybody's Money*, a publication of the Credit Union National Association.

Leasing vs. Buying

As car prices continue to rise, many car buyers are being seduced by the low monthly lease payments. Don't be deceived—in general, leasing costs more than buying outright or financing. When you pay cash or finance a car, you own an asset; leasing leaves you with nothing except all the headaches and responsibilities of ownership with none of the benefits. In addition, leased cars are often not covered by lemon laws.

When you lease you pay a monthly fee for a predetermined time in exchange for the use of a car. However, you also pay for maintenance, insurance and repairs as if you owned the car. There are two types of leases: *closed-* and *open-ended*. Most are closed-ended where you simply return the car at the end of the lease. Your monthly payments are based on the original cost of the car and what the company thinks the car can be sold for after the lease is up. An open-ended lease is riskier because you pay the difference between the car's expected value and its *actual* resale value when the lease ends. If the lessor underestimated the resale value of your payments, you'll pay a lump sum at the end.

Be careful, leases can vary greatly. For instance, many dealers offer a vehicle purchase option. They will guarantee to sell you the car at the end of the lease for a pre-determined amount called the *residual value*. If the car is worth more than this pre-determined price, you may want to buy it; if not, turn it in.

If the benefit of lower monthly payments outweighs the higher overall costs and you decide leasing is for you, contact your state attorney general's office for the *Reality Checklist*, to help you compare various lease offers. Here are some other questions to ask when shopping for a lease:

Know the make and model of the vehicle you want. Tell the agent exactly how you want the car equipped. You don't have to pay for options you don't request. Decide in advance how long you will keep the car.

Find out the price of the options on which the lease is based. Typically, they will be full retail price. The price can be negotiated (albeit with some difficultly)—before you settle on the monthly payment.

Find out how much you are required to pay at delivery. Most leases require at least the first month's payment. Others have a security deposit, registration fees, or other "hidden" costs. When shopping around, make sure price quotes include security deposit and taxes—sales tax, monthly use tax, or gross receipt tax. Ask how the length of the lease affects your monthly cost.

Find out the annual mileage limit. Don't accept a contract with a lower limit than you need. Most standard contracts allow 15,000 to 18,000 miles per year. If you go under the allowance one year, you can go over it the next.

Avoid "capitalized cost reduction" or "equity leases." Here the lessor offers to lower the monthly payment by asking you for more money up front. This defeats the principal benefit of a lease. By paying more initially, you lose the opportunity to use or earn interest on this money. These opportunity costs are based on the interest rate that you would otherwise earn.

Ask about early termination. Between 30 and 40 percent of two year leases are terminated early, and 40–60 percent of four-year leases terminate early—this means expensive early termination fees. If you terminate the lease before it is up, what are the financial penalties? Ask the dealer *exactly* what you would owe at the end of each year if you wanted out of the lease. Remember, if your car is stolen, the lease will typically be terminated. While your insurance should cover the value of the car, you still may owe additional amounts per your lease contract.

Avoid maintenance contracts. Getting work done privately is cheaper in the long run—and don't forget, this is a new car with a standard warranty.

Arrange for your own insurance. You can generally find less expensive insurance than what's offered by the lessor.

Ask how quickly you can expect delivery. If your agent can't deliver in a reasonable time, maybe he or she can't meet the price quoted.

Find out the service charges at the end of the lease. Usually around $100, they can go up to $250.

Retain your option to buy the car at the end of the lease at a predetermined price. The price should equal the residual value; if it is more, then the lessor is trying to make an additional profit. Regardless of how the end-of-lease value is determined, if you want the car make an offer based on the current "Blue Book" value of the car at the end of the lease.

Find out how the lease price was figured. Lease prices are generally based on the manufacturer's suggested retail price, less the predetermined residual value. The best values are cars with a high expected residual value. To protect themselves, lessors tend to underestimate residual value, but you can do little about this estimate.

Here's what First National Lease Systems' Automotive Lease Guide estimates the residual values for a few 1997 cars will be after four years:

Buick Skylark Sedan (Cust.)	36%
Dodge Intrepid	43%
Ford Taurus GL	41%
Honda Accord DX sdn.	51%
Infiniti Q45	46%
Lexus LS400	46%
Lincoln Mark VIII	41%
Mazda Miata	46%
Mercury Tracer sdn.	42%
Nissan Quest XE	46%
Plymouth Neon sdn.	37%
Toyota Camry DX cpe.	53%

The following table compares the typical costs of leasing vs. buying the same car. Your actual costs may vary, but you can use this format to compare the cars you are considering. Our example assumes that the residual value of a purchased car is 60 percent after two years and 45 percent after four.

Financing vs. Leasing

	2 Years		4 Years	
	Lease	Finance*	Lease	Finance*
Number of Months	24	24	48	48
Manu. Suggested Price	$15,000	$15,000	$15,000	$15,000
Cash Down Payment		$1,500		$1,500
Monthly Payment	$425	$678	$300	$366
Total Amt. of Pymnts**	$10,200	$16,272	$14,400	$17,568
Less Veh. Value at End	$0	$9,000	$0	$6,750
Actual Cost	$10,200	$8,772	$14,400	$12,318

*Based on an annual percentage rate of 8%
**In a lease, this is the total amount paid for the use of the vehicle. When financing, this is the total amount paid to become the owner.

Don't Buy Rustproofing

For years, we've recommended *against* spending the hundreds of dollars dealers charge for rustproofing. Some manufacturers (GM, Nissan, Saturn, Subaru, Suzuki, Toyota, and Volkswagen) now also recommend against aftermarket rustproofing. General Motors' warranty presents one of the clearest arguments against buying this expensive item: *Some after-manufacture rustproofing may create a potential environment which reduces the corrosion resistance designed and built into your vehicle. Depending upon application technique, some after-manufacture rustproofing could result in damage or failure of some electrical or mechanical systems of your vehicle. Repairs to correct damage or malfunctions caused by after-manufacture rustproofing are not covered under any of your GM new vehicle warranties.* Other manufacturers who suggest that rustproofing may void your corrosion warranty include Nissan, Saturn, and Volkswagen.

Options: The Future of Safety

Many car manufacturers claim that cars are safe enough today since airbags, anti-lock brakes and traction control are becoming standard features. The fact is there's lots more that can be done. We continue to pay high prices in personal injury and insurance premiums for accidents that could be less serious if manufacturers would market more advanced safety features.

While these features may increase the car costs, those increases would be minor in relation to the dramatic reduction in the risk of injuries in crashes. Unfortunately, car makers are slow to offer us new technology. Following are a few options that will dramatically increase driving safety—if manufacturers choose to offer them.

Radar Brakes: Using radar to detect objects in front of you, a warning sounds for the need to brake. It could perhaps be used to automatically apply the brakes when a driver falls asleep.

Side Airbags: The newest automatic crash protection technology has found its way into a handful of 1997 models, and one day may become the standard. These airbags ignite out of doors and out of the back of the front seat to protect the driver and passenger in crashes from all directions as well as rollovers.

Air Pads: Air pads are double layers of plastic with multiple compartments which look like ordinary trim in the uninflated condition. When the crash sensors for the airbags detect a crash, the air pads inflate out a few inches over all hard surfaces, such as the area over the windshield.

Glass-Plastic Glazing: This adds a layer of thin, strong, transparent plastic on the inside surface of all windows. When the glass breaks, the plastic layer holds the pieces of glass away from the occupants and provides a "safety net" to reduce the chance of ejection.

Night Vision Enhancement: This device will see through fog, rain, and darkness to provide an image of any obstacles or problems in the road. Infared light cameras project a visible image of what is ahead on a screen located on the car's instrument panel. The system could also detect, through a heat-seeking infrared system, someone lurking in a darkened parking lot.

Navigation Computer: With the use of global-positioning satellites, these on-board computers would eliminate the need for road maps. They could provide instructions on how to get to particular locations, such as hospitals, airports, restaurants and hotels, as well as warn of traffic and construction delays. GM, Volvo and Acura have begun experimenting with these systems in their cars. Using much the same technology, Lincoln's RESCU (Remote Emergency Satellite Cellular Unit) will send a distress signal for help to either a tow truck or an ambulance, depending on which signal you send.

Black Box Monitor: This device would detect whether the driver is driving drunk or irresponsibly. By monitoring the car's behavior and noting irregular actions, it will shut the car down.

Intelligent Brakes: These brakes sense and compensate for over- or under-steering.

Crash Recorder: This would record airbag performance in the event of an accident. (Introduced in 1995 Saturns.)

Toyota's Drowsy Driving Warning Sytem: By monitoring the steering and pulse of the driver, this innovation checks the driver to verify alertness. Once it detects drowsiness, the system will warn the driver with lights and sound to wake up, then shake the seat, and finally automatically stop the car.

Self-Dimming Mirrors: A gel-like material placed between two glass sheets darkens and lightens to reduce the headlight glare from mirrors while driving at night.

Inflatable Curtain: Volvo is developing an inflatable curtain, which deploys like an airbag, to provide increased protection against head injuries during side impact collisions. The curtain covers the sides of the car's interior, cushioning the heads of all the occupants.

Smart Airbags: Several auto makers are devloping smart airbag systems which will differentiate between an adult, a child, a rear-facing child seat or an empty seat, using various heat, ultrasonic sound wave and infrared sensors. Not only will they save lives, smart airbags will prevent the passenger side airbag from deploying when the passenger seat is empty—saving thousands in repair costs.

RATINGS

This chapter provides an overview of the most important features of the new 1997 cars. In this section of *The Car Book,* you can see on each "car page" all the ingredients you need to make a smart choice. In addition to some descriptive text and a photo, the page contains six important information boxes:

THE DESCRIPTION

The vast majority of information in *The Car Book* is purely objective—we research and present the facts so that you can make an informed choice among the models that fit your taste and pocketbook. For the third year we are adding, among other new features, some background details. Specifically, for every car we include some general information to help you round out the hard facts. Much of the information in this section is subjective and you may not share our opinion. Nevertheless, like the photo which gives you a general idea of what the car looks like, the description will give you a snapshot of some of the features we think are worth noting and which may not show up in the statistics.

GENERAL INFORMATION

This is additional information you may want to consider when buying a new car.

Where made: Here we tell you where the car was assembled and where its parts were manufactured. If more than one country is listed, the first is where the majority of parts originate or where the vehicle was assembled.

Year of Production: We generally recommend against buying a car during its first model year of production. Each year the model is made, the production process is usually improved and there are fewer minor design defects. Therefore, the longer a car has been made, the less likely you are to be plagued with manufacturing and design defects. On the other hand, the newer a car is,

the more likely it is to have the latest in engineering.

Parking Index: Using the car's length, wheelbase and turning circle, we have calculated how easy it will be to maneuver this car in tight spots. This rating of *very easy* to *very hard* is an indicator of how much difficulty you may have parking. If you regularly parallel park, or find yourself maneuvering in and out of tight spaces, this can be an important factor in the car you choose.

Bumpers: Here we indicate the damage-resistance of the car's bumpers. *Weak* bumpers meet only the basic government requirements at 2.5-mph. *Strong* bumpers are just as damage-resistant at 5-mph. This information may not be available for some minivans.

Theft Rating: This rating is given by the Insurance Institute for Highway Safety. It predicts the likelihood of the car being stolen or broken into based on its past history. If no information appears, it means that the car is too new to have a rating.

Corporate Twins: Often a car company will make numerous models on the same platform. This is a list of this car's twins.

Drive: This tells if the car comes with front, rear or four wheel drive, or if you have a choice.

In This Chapter...

PRICES

This box contains sample price information. When available, we list the base and the most luxurious version of the car. The difference is often substantial. Usually the more expensive versions have fancy trim, larger engines and lots of automatic equipment. The least expensive versions usually have manual transmission and few extra features. In addition, some manufacturers try to sell popular options as part of a package. For example, to get air conditioning you may have to buy power steering and deluxe seats.

This information provides an idea of the price range and the expected dealer markup. Be prepared for higher retail prices when you get to the showroom. Manufacturers like to load their cars with factory options, and dealers like to add their own items such as fabric protection and paint sealant. Remember, prices and dealer costs can change during the year. Use these figures for general reference and comparisons, not as a precise indication of exactly how much the car you are interested in will cost. See page 90 for a new buying service designed to ensure that you get the very best price.

RATINGS

These are ratings in eight important categories, as well as an overall comparative rating. We have adopted the Olympic rating system with "10" being the best.

Comparative Rating: This is the "bottom line." Using a combination of all of the ratings, this tells how this car stacks up against the other '97's on a scale of 1 to 10. Due to the importance of crash tests, cars with no crash test results as of our publication date cannot be given an overall rating. More recent results may be available from the Auto Safety Hotline at 1-800-424-9393.

Crash Test Performance: This rating compares the 1997 models against all crash test results to date. We give the best performers a 10 and the worst a 1. Remember to compare crash test results relative to other cars in the same size class. For complete details, see "The Safety Chapter."

Safety Features: This is an evaluation of how much extra safety is built into the car. We give credit for airbags, ABS, daytime running lights, belt height adjustors, and built-in child safety seats.

Fuel Economy: Here we compare the EPA mileage ratings of each car. The gas misers get a 10 and the guzzlers get a 1. For more information, see "The Fuel Economy Chapter."

PM Cost: Each manufacturer suggests a preventive maintenance schedule designed to keep the car in good shape and to protect your rights under the warranty. The cost of these schedules varies from car to car—ranging from $0 to $1227 for the first 50,000 miles of driving. Those with the lowest PM costs get a 10 and the highest a 1. See "The Maintenance Chapter" for the actual costs.

Repair Cost: It is virtually impossible to predict exactly what any new car will cost you in repairs. As such, we take nine typical repairs that you are likely to experience *after* your warranty expires and compare those costs among this year's models. Those with the lowest cost get a 10 and the highest a 1. For details, see "The Maintenance Chapter."

Warranty: There are good warranties and not so good warranties. This is an overall assessment of the car's warranty when compared to all 1997 warranties. The rating considers the important features of each warranty, with emphasis on the length of the basic and powertrain warranties. We give the highest rated warranties a 10 and the lowest a 1. See "The Warranty Chapter" for details.

Complaints: This is where you'll find how your car stacks up against hundreds of others on the road, based on the U.S. government complaint data. If the car has not been around long enough to have developed a complaint history, it is given a 5. The least complained about cars get a 10 and the most problematic, a 1.

Insurance Cost: Insurance companies have rated most of the cars on the road to determine how they plan to charge for insurance. Here, you'll find whether you can expect a discount or a surcharge for what we expect to be the most popular model. If the car is likely to receive neither, we label it *regular*. Those receiving a discount get a 10, while cars with a surcharge get a 1; any with neither get a 5.

SAFETY

For most of us, safety is a critical consideration in buying a new car. This box will tell you, at a glance, whether or not the car has the safety features you care about.

Crash Test: Here's where we tell you if its crash test was *very good, good, average, poor,* or *very poor*.

Airbag: Here's where you'll find out which occupants benefit from this invaluable safety feature and who is left unprotected.

Anti-lock Brakes: Find out if this model has the two- or four-wheel version of this safety feature, and whether you'll have to pay extra for it. Two-wheel ABS is of marginal value.

Daytime Running Lights: Daytime runnings lights can help reduce your chances of being in a crash by up to 40 percent by increasing the visibility of your vehicle. Mandatory in Canada and Scandinavia, daytime running lights are now being offered on many 1997 U.S. models. Here we indicate whether daytime running lights are *standard*, *optional* or *none*.

Belt Adjustors: This tells if the car maker offers a safety belt height/comfort adjustor. People often don't wear safety belts because they are uncomfortable. In fact, a belt's effectiveness is due, in part, to how well it fits your body. In order to make sure shoulder belts fit properly (squarely across the front of your chest) some manufacturers have installed devices that let you adjust the height of the belt. This allows for proper fit among drivers and passengers of various heights. In addition to allowing a safer fit, it helps prevent such problems as the belt scraping across the neck of a shorter driver. Availability is indicated for both front seat occupants, unless otherwise noted.

Built-in Child Safety Seats: Some manufacturers are offering "built-in" child safety seats which reduces the chances that your child rides unprotected.

Insurance Injury Claims: This rating reflects the number of injury claims the vehicle gets as presented by the Insurance Institute for Highway Safety, based on actual experience. If the model or style is all new this year, it has no rating. A car may have a good crash test rating, but a poor injury claim rating. This could be due to the way the car is driven. For example, a sporty car may have a good crash test result, but a poor injury claim rating. This may be due to the fact that the car is typically driven by young males who are in accidents more frequently than others.

SPECIFICATIONS

Here are the "nuts and bolts." In this box we have listed seven key specifications which enable you to evaluate how best that car meets your particular needs. We provide the information for what we expect to be the most popular model.

Fuel Economy: This is the EPA-rated fuel economy for city and highway driving measured in miles per gallon. Most models have a number of fuel economy ratings because of different engine and transmission options. For more individual ratings, see "The Fuel Economy Chapter."

Driving Range: Given the car's expected fuel economy and gas tank size, this gives an idea of how far you can go on a full tank.

Seating: This figure represents the maximum number of seating positions equipped with safety belts. When more than one number is listed (for example, 5/6/7) it means that different models have different seat configurations.

Length: This is the overall length of the vehicle from bumper to bumper.

Head/Leg Room: This tells how roomy the front seat is.

Interior Space: This tells how roomy the car is. For minivans, see cargo space.

Cargo Space: This gives you the cubic feet available for cargo. For minivans, it is the back of the two front seats to the rear of the vehicle. In cars, it's the trunk space.

COMPETITION

Here we tell you how the car stacks up with what is expected to be its competition. Use this information to compare the overall rating of similar cars and as a stepping-off point to broaden your choice of new car possibilities. This may help you select a more economical or better performing car than the one you were originally considering. We've added page references so you can easily check out the details on the competition. This list is meant as a guideline, not as an all-inclusive list of every possible competitive choice.

The newest addition to the Acura family is a two-door, U.S.-designed and produced replacement for the Legend called the CL. Its four-door sibling is the RL and, with minor exceptions, is no different. Based on the Accord coupe, the CL comes standard with dual airbags and 4-wheel ABS.

For 1997, you have a choice of two engines. A 2.2-liter, 4-cylinder engine is standard, which produces 145 hp, using the VTEC system first developed for Acura's NSX sports car. The optional 3.0-liter V-6 provides more power at the cost of fuel economy. Like other Acura's, the CL offers a smooth, comfortable ride. Other standard features include a keyless entry system and a theft deterrent system. The CL should be competitive in a crowded luxury coupe market. However, check out a fully-loaded Accord coupe before buying a CL; you could save almost $2,000.

The Ratings

	POOR — GOOD
COMPARATIVE RATING*	(blank)
CRASH TEST	(blank)
SAFETY FEATURES	▮ (right of center)
FUEL ECONOMY	▮ (left of center)
PM COST	▮ (far left)
REPAIR COST	▮ (left)
WARRANTY	▮ (center-right)
COMPLAINTS	▮ (center-right)
INSURANCE COST	▮ (center)

Safety

CRASH TEST	No government results
AIRBAGS	Dual
ABS	4-wheel
DAY. RUNNING LIGHTS	None
BELT ADJUSTORS	None
BUILT-IN CHILD SEAT	None
INSURANCE INJURY CLAIMS	

General Information

WHERE MADE	U.S.
YEAR OF PRODUCTION	First
PARKING INDEX	Very Easy
BUMPERS	Strong
THEFT RATING	
TWINS	
DRIVE	Front

Specifications

FUEL ECONOMY (cty/hwy)	23/29	Average
DRIVING RANGE (miles)	428	Long
SEATING	5	
LENGTH (inches)	190.0	Average
HEAD/LEG ROOM (in.)	37.4/42.9	Cramped
INTERIOR SPACE (cu. ft.)	85	Cramped
CARGO SPACE (cu. ft.)	12	Small

Specifications may vary.

Prices

Model	Retail	Mkup
CL Manual	22,100	15%
CL Automatic	22,910	15%
CL Premium Manual	23,160	15%
CL Premium Auto	23,960	15%

Competition

	POOR — GOOD	Pg.
Acura CL	(blank)	100
BMW 3-Series	▮ (left)	106
Infiniti I30	▮ (right)	157
Merc.-Bz C-Class	▮ (center-right)	175
Saab 900	▮ (center)	205

*Due to the importance of crash tests, cars with no results as of publication date cannot be given an overall rating.

Acura Integra

The Integra is next in line for the chopping block as Acura overhauls its lineup to improve declining sales. This will be the final year for the Civic-based hatchback, which remains the least expensive Acura. For 1998, the Integra is expected to receive a new look and a new name. For '97, dual airbags are still standard; ABS is optional.

The standard engine on the base RS and mid-level LS delivers over 140 hp, more than enough for this fairly light car. The GS-R gets a 170-hp VTEC version of the same engine and doesn't lose a bit in fuel economy. The 5-speed is fun and the handling ranks among the best for small cars. The Integra emphasizes sportiness rather than luxury. Front seats, driver's controls, and instruments are fine, but the rear seat is definitely not for adults on long trips. Look for great deals in the fall.

The Ratings

	POOR — GOOD
COMPARATIVE RATING	▮ (poor)
CRASH TEST	(good side)
SAFETY FEATURES	(good side)
FUEL ECONOMY	(mid)
PM COST	▮ (poor)
REPAIR COST	(low-mid)
WARRANTY	(good side)
COMPLAINTS	(good side)
INSURANCE COST	▮ (poor)

Safety

CRASH TEST	Average
AIRBAGS	Dual
ABS	4-wheel (optional)
DAY. RUNNING LIGHTS	None
BELT ADJUSTORS	Standard (Sdn. Only)
BUILT-IN CHILD SEAT	None
INSURANCE INJURY CLAIMS	Average

General Information

WHERE MADE	Japan
YEAR OF PRODUCTION	Fourth
PARKING INDEX	Easy
BUMPERS	Strong
THEFT RATING	Very High
TWINS	
DRIVE	Front

Specifications

FUEL ECONOMY (cty/hwy)	25/31	Average
DRIVING RANGE (miles)	370	Short
SEATING	5	
LENGTH (inches)	178.1	Short
HEAD/LEG ROOM (in.)	38.9/42.2	Average
INTERIOR SPACE (cu. ft.)	83	Cramped
CARGO SPACE (cu. ft.)	12	Small

Specifications may vary.

Prices**

Model	Retail	Mkup
Integra RS Coupe	15,880	16%
Integra LS Coupe	18,560	16%
Integra LS Sedan	20,360	16%
Integra GS-R Coupe	20,770	16%
Integra GS-R Sedan	21,100	16%

Competition

	POOR — GOOD	Pg.
Acura Integra	▮ (poor)	101
Eagle Talon	▮ (poor)	133
Ford Probe	(good)	141
Mazda MX-6	(good)	173
Mitsubishi Eclipse	▮ (poor)	184

**1997 prices not available at press time. Prices based on 1996 data.

Acura RL

The RL is Acura's third generation replacement for its former luxury flagship, the Legend. The RL stands for "Road Luxury" and the numbers preceding the RL are engine sizes. The new RL is built on the same wheelbase and track width as the previous Legend; however, major improvements have been made in ride and comfort. The RL comes standard with dual airbags and 4-wheel ABS.

Oddly enough, the new V6 found in the RL, a 3.5-liter, is actually less powerful than the old 3.2-liter V6 found in the Legend. However, Acura engineers knew what they were doing; they sacrificed hp for torque and the new engine feels more like a V8 than a V6. Noise, vibration and harshness are all improved due to increased insulation and a beefed-up suspension. The interior is well designed and the ride is good.

The Ratings

	POOR	GOOD
COMPARATIVE RATING*		
CRASH TEST		
SAFETY FEATURES		
FUEL ECONOMY		
PM COST		
REPAIR COST		
WARRANTY		
COMPLAINTS		
INSURANCE COST		

Safety

CRASH TEST	No government results
AIRBAGS	Dual
ABS	4-wheel
DAY. RUNNING LIGHTS	None
BELT ADJUSTORS	Standard
BUILT-IN CHILD SEAT	None
INSURANCE INJURY CLAIMS	

General Information

WHERE MADE	Japan
YEAR OF PRODUCTION	Second
PARKING INDEX	Average
BUMPERS	Strong
THEFT RATING	
TWINS	
DRIVE	Front

Specifications

FUEL ECONOMY (cty/hwy)	19/25	Poor
DRIVING RANGE (miles)	396	Average
SEATING	5	
LENGTH (inches)	195.1	Long
HEAD/LEG ROOM (in.)	38.8/42.1	Average
INTERIOR SPACE (cu. ft.)	96	Average
CARGO SPACE (cu. ft.)	15	Average

Specifications may vary.

Prices**

Model	Retail	Mkup
RL	41,000	15%

Competition

	POOR	GOOD	Pg.
Acura RL			102
Audi A6			105
BMW 3-Series			106
Infiniti I30			157
Mazda Millenia			171

**1997 prices not available at press time. Prices based on 1996 data.

102

*Due to the importance of crash tests, cars with no results as of publication date cannot be given an overall rating.

The TL replaced the Vigor last year and is closely related to its new siblings, the CL and RL. It isn't difficult to mistake the RL and TL for the same car. The TL stands for "Touring Luxury" and Acura is hoping to attract Lexus ES300 buyers. The TL comes standard with dual airbags and 4-wheel ABS; traction control is a great option.

You'll find two models, the 3.2TL or the 2.5TL. Like other Acuras, the 3.2 and 2.5 stand for engine sizes and both engines should provide plenty of power. However, more power from the 3.2 hurts gas mileage. Its speed-sensitive power steering is responsive and light. There are few options to choose from, so be prepared for a high base price. The TL has a conservative look, like the Accord, and the spacious interior and smooth ride are what you expect from a luxury car.

The Ratings

	POOR ... GOOD
COMPARATIVE RATING	▮ (1)
CRASH TEST	(7)
SAFETY FEATURES	(8)
FUEL ECONOMY	(4)
PM COST	(1)
REPAIR COST	(1)
WARRANTY	(7)
COMPLAINTS	(6)
INSURANCE COST	(5)

Safety

CRASH TEST	Good
AIRBAGS	Dual
ABS	4-wheel
DAY. RUNNING LIGHTS	None
BELT ADJUSTORS	Standard
BUILT-IN CHILD SEAT	None
INSURANCE INJURY CLAIMS	

General Information

WHERE MADE	Japan
YEAR OF PRODUCTION	Second
PARKING INDEX	Average
BUMPERS	Strong
THEFT RATING	
TWINS	
DRIVE	Front

Specifications

FUEL ECONOMY (cty/hwy)	20/25	Average
DRIVING RANGE (miles)	378	Short
SEATING	5/6	
LENGTH (inches)	191.5	Long
HEAD/LEG ROOM (in.)	39.1/43.7	Roomy
INTERIOR SPACE (cu. ft.)	92	Average
CARGO SPACE (cu. ft.)	14	Average

Specifications may vary.

Prices**

Model	Retail	Mkup
TL 2.5 Base	27,900	15%
TL 2.5 Premium	29,950	15%
TL 3.2 Base	32,950	15%
TL 3.2 Premium	35,500	15%

Competition

	POOR ... GOOD	Pg.
Acura TL	(1)	103
Cadillac Seville	(9)	117
Infiniti J30	(9)	158
Lexus GS300	(9)	163
Saab 9000	(6)	206

**1997 prices not available at press time. Prices based on 1996 data.

Audi A4

Audi's alpha-numeric naming system is working out well. The A4 has become a solid seller. Previously the 90, the A4 enters 1997 with only minor changes. The A4 is, in some ways, a lower priced version of the Audi A6. ABS and dual airbags are standard.

The base engine, a 1.8-liter four cylinder turbo, will provide ample power, but if you are looking for more power, go for the optional 2.8 liter V6. The A4 is available with either front-wheel drive or all-wheel drive, called Quattro, which improves overall handling and traction on slick roads. The A4 has a decent trunk and cabin and is well equipped to handle 4 passengers. Preventive maintenance costs are minimal; Audi covers the preventive maintenance costs for the first 50,000 miles. Also, the warranty is tops. If you're shopping for a luxury car, the A4 is hard to beat.

The Ratings

	POOR — GOOD
COMPARATIVE RATING	■ (good)
CRASH TEST	■
SAFETY FEATURES	■
FUEL ECONOMY	■
PM COST	■
REPAIR COST	■ (poor)
WARRANTY	■ (good)
COMPLAINTS	■
INSURANCE COST	■

Safety

CRASH TEST	Very Good
AIRBAGS	Dual
ABS	4-wheel
DAY. RUNNING LIGHTS	None
BELT ADJUSTORS	Standard
BUILT-IN CHILD SEAT	None
INSURANCE INJURY CLAIMS	

General Information

WHERE MADE	Germany
YEAR OF PRODUCTION	Second
PARKING INDEX	Easy
BUMPERS	Strong
THEFT RATING	
TWINS	
DRIVE	Front/All

Specifications

FUEL ECONOMY (cty/hwy)	20/29	Average
DRIVING RANGE (miles)	377	Short
SEATING	5	
LENGTH (inches)	178.0	Short
HEAD/LEG ROOM (in.)	38.1/41.3	Cramped
INTERIOR SPACE (cu. ft.)	88	Cramped
CARGO SPACE (cu. ft.)	14	Average

Specifications may vary.

Prices

Model	Retail	Mkup
A4 1.8 Liter Engine	23,490	14%
A4 2.8 Liter Engine	27,930	14%

Competition

	POOR — GOOD	Pg.
Audi A4	■	104
BMW 3-Series	■	106
Nissan Maxima	■	189
Subaru Legacy	■	210
Volvo 850	■	223

The A6, which used to be called the 100, is a slightly larger version of the Audi A4. The alphanumeric names, which Audi will use exclusively in the future, are meant to clear up confusion; the 6 stands for the mid-level size of the cars, while the A is for Audi. Last year's S6 (sport model) has been discontinued for 1997. Dual airbags and 4-wheel ABS are standard.

The 2.8-liter V6 found on the A6, as well as most other Audi's, offers more than enough power for the average driver, plus a little more for those who like more pep in their engines. There is plenty of room for four, but five might be a squeeze. You have many options to choose from on the A6. Both the sedan and wagon A6 offer all-wheel drive, which will improve handling and poor-weather traction. Ride and comfort inside are good and expect a myriad of luxury choices.

The Ratings

	POOR → GOOD
COMPARATIVE RATING	Good
CRASH TEST	Above Average
SAFETY FEATURES	Above Average
FUEL ECONOMY	Poor
PM COST	Good
REPAIR COST	Very Poor
WARRANTY	Good
COMPLAINTS	Good
INSURANCE COST	Below Average

Safety

CRASH TEST	Very Good
AIRBAGS	Dual
ABS	4-wheel
DAY. RUNNING LIGHTS	None
BELT ADJUSTORS	Standard
BUILT-IN CHILD SEAT	None
INSURANCE INJURY CLAIMS	

General Information

WHERE MADE	Germany
YEAR OF PRODUCTION	Third
PARKING INDEX	Easy
BUMPERS	Strong
THEFT RATING	
TWINS	
DRIVE	Front/All

Specifications

FUEL ECONOMY (cty/hwy)	19/25	Poor
DRIVING RANGE (miles)	443	Long
SEATING	5	
LENGTH (inches)	192.6	Long
HEAD/LEG ROOM (in.)	38.3/42.4	Average
INTERIOR SPACE (cu. ft.)	92	Average
CARGO SPACE (cu. ft.)	17	Large

Specifications may vary.

Prices

Model	Retail	Mkup
A6	33,100	14%
A6 Wagon	34,900	14%

Competition

	POOR → GOOD	Pg.
Audi A6	Good	105
BMW 3-Series	Below Average	106
Infiniti I30	Above Average	157
Mazda Millenia	Average	171
Merc.-Bz C-Class	Average	175

A slightly changed fascia this fall is designed to bring the BMW 3-Series into line with the rest of the BMW offerings. You can get either a 318 or 325 in their sedan, coupe and convertible incarnations, or the relatively new 318 hatchback version. The new hatchback is almost a foot shorter and costs nearly $5,000 less. Photo is from '96.

The 1.8-liter engine on the 318 is strong enough. The 2.5-liter on the 325 is better, but less fuel efficient. The optional limited-slip differential will help control the engine's power. Front seats offer good comfort on long trips; however, the back seat is a squeeze for adults. Controls are excellent. One negative is the easily damaged and expensive-to-repair, front bumper. If you enjoy driving a responsive car and don't mind spending $30,000, this BMW is a fine choice, including the cheaper hatchback.

The Ratings

	POOR — GOOD
COMPARATIVE RATING	▮ (3)
CRASH TEST	▮ (7)
SAFETY FEATURES	▮ (8)
FUEL ECONOMY	▮ (5)
PM COST	▮ (1)
REPAIR COST	▮ (2)
WARRANTY	▮ (7)
COMPLAINTS	▮ (7)
INSURANCE COST	▮ (1)

Safety

CRASH TEST	Good
AIRBAGS	Dual
ABS	4-wheel
DAY. RUNNING LIGHTS	None
BELT ADJUSTORS	Standard
BUILT-IN CHILD SEAT	None
INSURANCE INJURY CLAIMS	Average

General Information

WHERE MADE	Germany
YEAR OF PRODUCTION	Sixth
PARKING INDEX	Easy
BUMPERS	Weak
THEFT RATING	Very High
TWINS	
DRIVE	Rear

Specifications

FUEL ECONOMY (cty/hwy)	23/31	Average
DRIVING RANGE (miles)	464	Very Long
SEATING	4	
LENGTH (inches)	174.5	Short
HEAD/LEG ROOM (in.)	38.1/41.2	Cramped
INTERIOR SPACE (cu. ft.)	86	Cramped
CARGO SPACE (cu. ft.)	10	Very Small

Specifications may vary.

Prices

Model	Retail	Mkup
3-Series	21,390	13%

Competition

	POOR — GOOD	Pg.
BMW 3-Series	▮ (3)	106
Infiniti I30	▮ (6)	157
Mazda Millenia	▮ (5)	171
Merc.-Bz C-Class	▮ (6)	175
Saab 900	▮ (4)	205

BMW Z3

This new two-seat roadster will have a familiar look to BMW enthusiasts; the Z-3 is built on the 3-Series hatchback platform. While the Z-3 is aimed towards the Miata crowd, Mazda isn't too worried—the Z-3 will cost $7,000 more than the Miata. Yet, the Z-3 is a touch larger than the Miata and has a more boulevard-quality ride. Dual airbags are standard as is 4-wheel ABS.

Engine choices for the first year are quite limited—the standard 1.8-liter, four cylinder engine is from the 318i, producing only 113 hp. A more powerful version, which cranks out 138 hp, is expected later in the year. The interior offers bins for small luggage, but don't expect to bring much along with you. Noise levels should be tolerable and controls easy to use. With its long-nosed, short-tailed appearance, the Z-3 is designed to appeal to sports car enthusiasts.

The Ratings

	POOR — GOOD
COMPARATIVE RATING*	(no rating)
CRASH TEST	(no rating)
SAFETY FEATURES	▮ (high)
FUEL ECONOMY	▮ (mid)
PM COST	▮ (poor)
REPAIR COST	▮ (low)
WARRANTY	▮ (high)
COMPLAINTS	▮ (mid-high)
INSURANCE COST	▮ (mid)

Safety

CRASH TEST	No government results
AIRBAGS	Dual
ABS	4-wheel
DAY. RUNNING LIGHTS	None
BELT ADJUSTORS	Standard
BUILT-IN CHILD SEAT	None
INSURANCE INJURY CLAIMS	

General Information

WHERE MADE	U.S.
YEAR OF PRODUCTION	Second
PARKING INDEX	Very Easy
BUMPERS	Weak
THEFT RATING	
TWINS	
DRIVE	Rear

Specifications

FUEL ECONOMY (cty/hwy)	23/31	Average
DRIVING RANGE (miles)	365	Short
SEATING	2	
LENGTH (inches)	158.5	Very Short
HEAD/LEG ROOM (in.)	Not Available	
INTERIOR SPACE (cu. ft.)	47	Vry. Cramped
CARGO SPACE (cu. ft.)	5	Very Small

Specifications may vary.

Prices

Model	Retail	Mkup
Z-3	29,000	18%

Competition

	POOR — GOOD	Pg.
BMW Z3	(no rating)	107
Chevrolet Camaro	▮ (low)	119
Ford Mustang	▮ (poor)	140
Nissan 240SX	▮ (poor)	187
Pontiac Firebird	▮ (low)	200

*Due to the importance of crash tests, cars with no results as of publication date cannot be given an overall rating.

Buick Century

After 15 years, Buick has finally given the Century a long overdue changeover. The 1997 Century is a great improvement over past versions and, best of all, it finally comes with standard belts, replacing the dangerous door-mounted belts that can be found in 1996. Its new twins are the Pontiac Grand Prix and the yet-to-be released 1998 Oldsmobile Intrigue. Smoother and sleeker on the outside, this six passenger car is 5.4 inches longer and more attention was paid to interior comfort. Dual airbags and 4-wheel ABS are both standard.

Powering the new Century is last year's optional 3.1-liter V6. There are two trim levels: Custom and Limited. A "can't miss" option for parents is the new built-in child seat. Ride and handling are improved by a new rear suspension, making traveling more enjoyable. The new Century is a vast, much-needed improvement.

The Ratings

	POOR	GOOD
COMPARATIVE RATING*		
CRASH TEST		
SAFETY FEATURES		▮
FUEL ECONOMY	▮	
PM COST		▮
REPAIR COST		▮
WARRANTY	▮	
COMPLAINTS	▮	
INSURANCE COST	▮	

Safety

CRASH TEST	No government results
AIRBAGS	Dual
ABS	4-wheel
DAY. RUNNING LIGHTS	Standard
BELT ADJUSTORS	Standard
BUILT-IN CHILD SEAT	Optional
INSURANCE INJURY CLAIMS	

General Information

WHERE MADE	U.S.
YEAR OF PRODUCTION	First
PARKING INDEX	Average
BUMPERS	Strong
THEFT RATING	
TWINS	Pontiac Grand Prix
DRIVE	Front

Specifications

FUEL ECONOMY (cty/hwy)	20/29	Average
DRIVING RANGE (miles)	425	Long
SEATING	6	
LENGTH (inches)	194.5	Long
HEAD/LEG ROOM (in.)	39.3/42.4	Roomy
INTERIOR SPACE (cu. ft.)	119	Very Roomy
CARGO SPACE (cu. ft.)	17	Large

Specifications may vary.

Prices**

Model	Retail	Mkup
Century Special Sedan	16,720	7%
Century Custom Sedan	18,383	7%
Century Limited Sedan	19,406	7%
Century Special Wagon	18,135	7%

Competition

	POOR	GOOD	Pg.
Buick Century			108
Ford Taurus		▮	142
Honda Accord	▮		148
Mazda 626		▮	169
Pontiac Grand Am		▮	201

**1997 prices not available at press time. Prices based on 1996 data.

*Due to the importance of crash tests, cars with no results as of publication date cannot be given an overall rating.

Buick LeSabre

Each GM division has its niche market and Buick's is the traditional domestic buyer. For many years, Buick has been attracting consumers with conservative automobiles and the refreshed 1997 LeSabre is no exception. The LeSabre comes in two trim levels: a limited or custom sedan, all with standard safety features like dual airbags, ABS and daytime running lights.

Like its twin, the Oldsmobile 88, the LeSabre emphasizes a soft ride. For crisper handling, like that of the Bonneville SSE (another LeSabre twin) without sacrificing ride, order LeSabre's Gran Touring package. Buick offers only one engine with the LeSabre, a 3.8 liter V6 engine that can deliver up to 30 mpg on the highway. Interior room is spacious, especially in back. There are many new options like delayed locking which helps prevent lockouts.

The Ratings

	POOR — GOOD
COMPARATIVE RATING	▮ (good side)
CRASH TEST*	▮ (mid-good)
SAFETY FEATURES	▮ (mid-good)
FUEL ECONOMY	▮ (middle)
PM COST	▮ (mid-good)
REPAIR COST	▮ (good side)
WARRANTY	▮ (poor side)
COMPLAINTS	▮ (good side)
INSURANCE COST	▮ (good end)

Safety

CRASH TEST	Good
AIRBAGS	Dual
ABS	4-wheel
DAY. RUNNING LIGHTS	Standard
BELT ADJUSTORS	Standard
BUILT-IN CHILD SEAT	None
INSURANCE INJURY CLAIMS	Very Low

General Information

WHERE MADE	U.S.
YEAR OF PRODUCTION	Sixth
PARKING INDEX	Hard
BUMPERS	Strong
THEFT RATING	Very Low
TWINS	Olds 88, Pont. Bonneville
DRIVE	Front

Specifications

FUEL ECONOMY (cty/hwy)	19/30	Average
DRIVING RANGE (miles)	414	Average
SEATING	6	
LENGTH (inches)	200.8	Long
HEAD/LEG ROOM (in.)	38.8/42.6	Average
INTERIOR SPACE (cu. ft.)	109	Roomy
CARGO SPACE (cu. ft.)	17	Large

Specifications may vary.

Prices

Model	Retail	Mkup
LeSabre Custom	22,620	9%
LeSabre Limited	26,170	9%

Competition

	POOR — GOOD	Pg.
Buick LeSabre	▮ (good side)	109
Ford Taurus	▮ (mid-good)	142
Mazda 626	▮ (middle)	169
Oldsmobile 88	▮ (mid-good)	192
Pontiac Bonneville	▮ (mid-good)	199

*A version of this vehicle is scheduled to be tested later this year. Results are expected to be equal or better.

Buick Park Avenue

Buick spent lots of time and money improving one of its best-sellers, the Park Avenue. For 1997, Buick's goal was to provide a smooth ride without sacrificing comfort and handling. Now a twin of the Riviera and the Olds Aurora, the Park Avenue is aimed at car buyers looking for an affordable luxury car. It comes standard with dual airbags and 4-wheel ABS.

There are two engine choices available for 1997, both are 3.8 liter V-6's. The standard engine delivers a respectable 19/28 mpg while the turbo charged version sacrifices fuel economy slightly delivering 18/27 mpg. Buick increased the stiffness and rigidity to create a better ride with fewer shakes and rattles. Standard features include keyless entry and delayed locking. The revised Park Avenue should continue to be a best-seller for Buick.

The Ratings

	POOR	GOOD
COMPARATIVE RATING*		
CRASH TEST		
SAFETY FEATURES		
FUEL ECONOMY		
PM COST		
REPAIR COST		
WARRANTY		
COMPLAINTS		
INSURANCE COST		

Safety

CRASH TEST	No government results
AIRBAGS	Dual
ABS	4-wheel
DAY. RUNNING LIGHTS	Standard
BELT ADJUSTORS	None
BUILT-IN CHILD SEAT	None
INSURANCE INJURY CLAIMS	

General Information

WHERE MADE	U.S.
YEAR OF PRODUCTION	First
PARKING INDEX	Hard
BUMPERS	Strong
THEFT RATING	
TWINS	Buick Riviera, Olds Aurora
DRIVE	Front

Specifications

FUEL ECONOMY (cty/hwy)	19/28	Poor
DRIVING RANGE (miles)	396	Average
SEATING	6	
LENGTH (inches)	206.8	Very Long
HEAD/LEG ROOM (in.)	39.8/42.4	Roomy
INTERIOR SPACE (cu. ft.)	111	Very Roomy
CARGO SPACE (cu. ft.)	19	Large

Specifications may vary.

Prices

Model	Retail	Mkup
Park Avenue	30,660	10%
Park Avenue Ultra	35,660	10%

Competition

	POOR	GOOD	Pg.
Buick Park Avenue			110
Chrysler Concorde			126
Ford Crown Victoria			138
Nissan Maxima			189
Toyota Avalon			214

*Due to the importance of crash tests, cars with no results as of publication date cannot be given an overall rating.

The 1996 Regal carries over into 1997 on an extended production run as Buick prepares to release a new version sometime in early 1997. Because of its late release, the 1996 Regal is pictured and the information given for the Regal is based on 1996 specifications. Standard features include dual airbags and 4-wheel ABS.

You have a choice between two V6 engines and both V6's provide ample power, though you get slightly more power from the 3.8-liter with no loss in fuel economy. Typical of Buicks, the Regal provides low-grade handling with a good ride on smooth roads; the Gran Touring package, which is also standard on Gran Sport, should help improve cornering ability. You can choose between a sedan or a coupe, but beware—the 1996 Regal has not been restyled in eight years. You may want to wait for the 1997 edition.

The Ratings

	POOR ... GOOD
COMPARATIVE RATING*	
CRASH TEST	
SAFETY FEATURES	
FUEL ECONOMY	
PM COST	
REPAIR COST	
WARRANTY	
COMPLAINTS	
INSURANCE COST	

Safety

CRASH TEST	No government results
AIRBAGS	Dual
ABS	4-wheel
DAY. RUNNING LIGHTS	None
BELT ADJUSTORS	Standard
BUILT-IN CHILD SEAT	None
INSURANCE INJURY CLAIMS	

General Information

WHERE MADE	U.S./Canada
YEAR OF PRODUCTION	First
PARKING INDEX	Average
BUMPERS	Strong
THEFT RATING	
TWINS	Pontiac Grand Prix
DRIVE	Front

Specifications

FUEL ECONOMY (cty/hwy)	20/29	Average
DRIVING RANGE (miles)	393	Average
SEATING	5	
LENGTH (inches)	194.1	Long
HEAD/LEG ROOM (in.)	38.7/42.4	Average
INTERIOR SPACE (cu. ft.)	102	Roomy
CARGO SPACE (cu. ft.)	17	Large

Specifications may vary.

Prices**

Model	Retail	Mkup
Regal Custom	20,280	9%
Regal Gran Sport	22,340	9%
Regal Limited	26,170	9%

Competition

	POOR ... GOOD	Pg.
Buick Regal		111
Ford Taurus		142
Honda Accord		148
Mazda 626		169
Oldsmobile Achieva		193

**1997 prices not available at press time. Prices based on 1996 data.

*Due to the importance of crash tests, cars with no results as of publication date cannot be given an overall rating.

The Riviera, Buick's sleek luxury sports coupe, is designed to grab your eye and give you a unique driving experience. Buick is in the middle of modernizing itself. The Riviera is a fine example. New for 1997 are additions to standard equipment and interesting options such as parallel parking assistance which pivots the passenger-side outside mirror so that the driver can see the curb better. Traction control is optional, and dual airbags and ABS are standard.

At over 17 feet and almost two tons, the Riviera is big. The standard V6 offers enough power, but the optional 3.8-liter provides more hp in exchange for a couple of mpg. The specially designed seats are very comfortable and interior noise is very low. The Riviera beats out many higher priced luxury cars in terms of ride, interior and style.

The Ratings

	POOR ... GOOD
COMPARATIVE RATING *	(no rating)
CRASH TEST	(no rating)
SAFETY FEATURES	■ (near good)
FUEL ECONOMY	■ (poor side)
PM COST	■ (good side)
REPAIR COST	■ (middle)
WARRANTY	■ (poor)
COMPLAINTS	■ (poor)
INSURANCE COST	■ (good)

Safety

CRASH TEST	No government results
AIRBAGS	Dual
ABS	4-wheel
DAY. RUNNING LIGHTS	Standard
BELT ADJUSTORS	Standard
BUILT-IN CHILD SEAT	None
INSURANCE INJURY CLAIMS	Very Low

General Information

WHERE MADE	U.S.
YEAR OF PRODUCTION	Third
PARKING INDEX	Hard
BUMPERS	Strong
THEFT RATING	Very Low
TWINS	Buick Park Ave., Olds Aurora
DRIVE	Front

Specifications

FUEL ECONOMY (cty/hwy)	19/28	Poor
DRIVING RANGE (miles)	440	Long
SEATING	5	
LENGTH (inches)	207.2	Very Long
HEAD/LEG ROOM (in.)	38.2/42.6	Average
INTERIOR SPACE (cu. ft.)	99	Average
CARGO SPACE (cu. ft.)	17	Large

Specifications may vary.

Prices

Model	Retail	Mkup
Riviera	30,775	11%

Competition

	POOR ... GOOD	Pg.
Buick Riviera	(no rating)	112
Chev. Monte Carlo	■ (poor)	123
Dodge Avenger	■ (middle)	128
Ford Thunderbird	■ (good side)	143
Mercury Cougar	■ (good side)	177

*Due to the importance of crash tests, cars with no results as of publication date cannot be given an overall rating.

Buick Skylark

After receiving significant changes last year, the Skylark enters 1997 with only minor additions. Offered in a Limited, Gran Sport and Custom, the Skylark is designed to transport six with comfort for a low price. The Skylark is Buick's smallest model and is almost identical to its twins, the Oldsmobile Achieva and the Pontiac Grand Am. Dual airbags, ABS and traction control are all standard.

Buyers have a choice of a 2.4-liter, 4-cylinder engine which delivers good power or an optional 3.1-liter V6 which delivers slightly more power, but guzzles considerably more gas (22/32 mpg for the 2.4-liter, 20/29 for the 3.1-liter). Options such as radio controls on the steering wheel make the Skylark driver friendly. Seating for five adults is only adequate; try to squeeze in six and it becomes very snug.

The Ratings

	POOR — GOOD
COMPARATIVE RATING	
CRASH TEST *	
SAFETY FEATURES	
FUEL ECONOMY	
PM COST	
REPAIR COST	
WARRANTY	
COMPLAINTS	
INSURANCE COST	

Safety

CRASH TEST	Good
AIRBAGS	Dual
ABS	4-wheel
DAY. RUNNING LIGHTS	None
BELT ADJUSTORS	Standard
BUILT-IN CHILD SEAT	None
INSURANCE INJURY CLAIMS	Average

General Information

WHERE MADE	U.S.
YEAR OF PRODUCTION	Sixth
PARKING INDEX	Easy
BUMPERS	Strong
THEFT RATING	Very Low
TWINS	Olds Achieva, Pont. Gr. Am
DRIVE	Front

Specifications

FUEL ECONOMY (cty/hwy)	22/32	Average
DRIVING RANGE (miles)	395	Average
SEATING	5	
LENGTH (inches)	188.4	Average
HEAD/LEG ROOM (in.)	37.8/43.1	Average
INTERIOR SPACE (cu. ft.)	87	Cramped
CARGO SPACE (cu. ft.)	13	Small

Specifications may vary.

Prices

Model	Retail	Mkup
Skylark	16,495	6%

Competition

	POOR — GOOD	Pg.
Buick Skylark		113
Mazda 626		169
Olds Achieva		193
Pontiac Grand Am		201
Subaru Legacy		210

*A version of this vehicle is scheduled to be tested later this year. Results are expected to be equal or better.

Cadillac Catera

This is not your grandfather's Caddy. The all-new Catera is designed to appeal to buyers younger than the typical Cadillac. Cadillac hopes to capture one of the fastest growing automotive segments, the affordable luxury sedan. The Catera's chief competitors will be mostly imported models such as the BMW 3-Series and the Infiniti I30. With plenty of interior volume and a large trunk, this car could compete with even larger luxury sedans. The Catera comes standard with dual airbags and 4-wheel ABS.

Instead of the highly promoted Northstar engine, you'll find a 3.0-liter V6 under the hood. Interior comfort and ride are what you have come to expect from a Cadillac—excellent with little noise. Up front, the controls are nicely designed. Look for the Catera to be a hot seller.

The Ratings

	POOR ⬚⬚⬚ GOOD
COMPARATIVE RATING*	⬚⬚⬚⬚⬚⬚⬚⬚⬚⬚
CRASH TEST	⬚⬚⬚⬚⬚⬚⬚⬚⬚⬚
SAFETY FEATURES	⬚⬚⬚⬚⬚⬚⬚⬚■⬚
FUEL ECONOMY	⬚⬚⬚■⬚⬚⬚⬚⬚⬚
PM COST	⬚⬚⬚⬚⬚⬚⬚⬚⬚■
REPAIR COST	■⬚⬚⬚⬚⬚⬚⬚⬚⬚
WARRANTY	⬚⬚⬚⬚⬚⬚⬚⬚■⬚
COMPLAINTS	⬚⬚⬚⬚⬚■⬚⬚⬚⬚
INSURANCE COST	⬚⬚⬚⬚⬚■⬚⬚⬚⬚

Safety

CRASH TEST	No government results
AIRBAGS	Dual
ABS	4-wheel
DAY. RUNNING LIGHTS	Standard
BELT ADJUSTORS	Standard
BUILT-IN CHILD SEAT	None
INSURANCE INJURY CLAIMS	

General Information

WHERE MADE	Germany
YEAR OF PRODUCTION	First
PARKING INDEX	Easy
BUMPERS	Weak
THEFT RATING	
TWINS	
DRIVE	Rear

Specifications

FUEL ECONOMY (cty/hwy)	18/25	Poor
DRIVING RANGE (miles)	378	Short
SEATING	5	
LENGTH (inches)	193.8	Long
HEAD/LEG ROOM (in.)	38.6/42.0	Average
INTERIOR SPACE (cu. ft.)	99	Average
CARGO SPACE (cu. ft.)	14	Average

Specifications may vary.

Prices

Model	Retail	Mkup
Catera	29,995	9%

Competition

	POOR ⬚⬚⬚ GOOD	Pg.
Cadillac Catera	⬚⬚⬚⬚⬚⬚⬚⬚⬚⬚	114
Audi A6	⬚⬚⬚⬚⬚⬚⬚⬚■⬚	105
BMW 3-Series	⬚⬚⬚■⬚⬚⬚⬚⬚⬚	106
Mazda Millenia	⬚⬚⬚⬚⬚⬚■⬚⬚⬚	171
Oldsmobile Aurora	⬚⬚⬚■⬚⬚⬚⬚⬚⬚	194

*Due to the importance of crash tests, cars with no results as of publication date cannot be given an overall rating.

Cadillac decided that creating one new car, the Catera, was not enough to stay competitive in the luxury car market. So, they also refined their #1 seller, the DeVille. The 1997 DeVille has a new five-passenger interior and a restyled exterior along with changes under the hood which improve its handling. Only available as a 4-door sedan, the DeVille comes standard with almost every possible safety feature, including traction control, dual airbags, 4-wheel ABS and even side airbags, too.

Like most other big GM cars, the DeVille emphasizes a soft, quiet ride and lots of room for six adults. The standard Northstar engine provides plenty of horsepower. Speed-sensitive steering and a new chassis control system which includes road texture detection help improve traction and control. This car is good competition with the other luxury models of this size.

The Ratings

	POOR ‹———› GOOD
COMPARATIVE RATING	(no rating shown)
CRASH TEST	(no rating shown)
SAFETY FEATURES	Good
FUEL ECONOMY	Poor
PM COST	Average
REPAIR COST	Poor
WARRANTY	Good
COMPLAINTS	Good
INSURANCE COST	Good

Safety

CRASH TEST	No government results
AIRBAGS	Dual
ABS	4-wheel
DAY. RUNNING LIGHTS	Standard
BELT ADJUSTORS	Standard
BUILT-IN CHILD SEAT	None
INSURANCE INJURY CLAIMS	Very Low

General Information

WHERE MADE	U.S./Canada
YEAR OF PRODUCTION	Fifth
PARKING INDEX	Hard
BUMPERS	Strong
THEFT RATING	Very Low
TWINS	
DRIVE	Front

Specifications

FUEL ECONOMY (cty/hwy)	17/26	Poor
DRIVING RANGE (miles)	400	Average
SEATING	5/6	
LENGTH (inches)	209.7	Very Long
HEAD/LEG ROOM (in.)	38.5/42.6	Average
INTERIOR SPACE (cu. ft.)	117	Very Roomy
CARGO SPACE (cu. ft.)	20	Very Large

Specifications may vary.

Prices

Model	Retail	Mkup
DeVille	36,995	9%

Competition

	POOR ‹———› GOOD	Pg.
Cadillac DeVille	(no rating shown)	115
Acura TL	Poor	103
Cadillac Seville	Good	117
Lexus GS300	Good	163
Lincoln Town Car	Good	168

Cadillac Eldorado

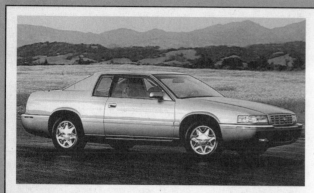

For 1997, Cadillac lowered the price of the Eldorado and its twin, the Seville, due to customer complaints about haggling. Cadillac designed this sports coupe with unique, aggressive styling. Performance and comfort are what Cadillac aims for in both the base level Eldorado and the upscale Touring Coupe. The Eldorado comes standard with 4-wheel ABS and dual airbags.

As with other large Cadillacs, the signature Northstar V8 comes standard with the base model Eldorado. The Touring Coupe comes with an even more powerful engine. Both of these sacrifice fuel economy for performance. Upgrades for 1997 include a new chassis control system which greatly improves traction and stability. The front seat is as comfortable and roomy, but the rear seat is cramped and inaccessible like most sports coupes.

The Ratings

	POOR	GOOD
COMPARATIVE RATING*		
CRASH TEST		
SAFETY FEATURES		■
FUEL ECONOMY	■	
PM COST		■
REPAIR COST	■	
WARRANTY		■
COMPLAINTS		■
INSURANCE COST		■

Safety

CRASH TEST	No government results
AIRBAGS	Dual
ABS	4-wheel
DAY. RUNNING LIGHTS	Standard
BELT ADJUSTORS	Standard
BUILT-IN CHILD SEAT	None
INSURANCE INJURY CLAIMS	Very Low

General Information

WHERE MADE	U.S./Canada
YEAR OF PRODUCTION	Sixth
PARKING INDEX	Hard
BUMPERS	Strong
THEFT RATING	Very High
TWINS	
DRIVE	Front

Specifications

FUEL ECONOMY (cty/hwy)	17/26	Poor
DRIVING RANGE (miles)	400	Average
SEATING	5	
LENGTH (inches)	200.2	Long
HEAD/LEG ROOM (in.)	37.8/42.6	Cramped
INTERIOR SPACE (cu. ft.)	100	Roomy
CARGO SPACE (cu. ft.)	15	Average

Specifications may vary.

Prices

Model	Retail	Mkup
Eldorado	37,995	16%
Eldorado Touring	42,060	16%

Competition

	POOR	GOOD	Pg.
Cadillac Eldorado			116
Audi A6		■	105
Mazda Millenia		■	171
Oldsmobile Aurora		■	194
Saab 9000		■	206

*Due to the importance of crash tests, cars with no results as of publication date cannot be given an overall rating.

Cadillac Seville

The Seville and the Eldorado are very much alike on the insides where they share the same chassis; however, on the outside, they are quite distinct. The Seville is aimed towards BMW and Lexus buyers. Like the Eldorado, the Seville has two trim levels: the Seville Luxury Sedan (SLS) or the Seville Touring Sedan (STS). Options are limited, but most everything you'll want, including traction control, dual airbags and ABS, comes standard.

The base Seville has a smaller version of Cadillac's Northstar V8; the Seville Touring Sedan has an larger version which offers even more power. Don't expect good gas mileage with either model. The handling is better in the Touring Sedan, but it isn't great. Room inside is good for four. You will be hard-pressed to do better, however, if you are looking to save some money, the Bonneville is a good choice also.

The Ratings

	POOR GOOD
COMPARATIVE RATING	■ (near good)
CRASH TEST	■ (middle)
SAFETY FEATURES	■ (good side)
FUEL ECONOMY	■ (poor side)
PM COST	■ (good side)
REPAIR COST	■ (poor end)
WARRANTY	■ (good side)
COMPLAINTS	■ (middle)
INSURANCE COST	■ (good end)

Safety

CRASH TEST	Good
AIRBAGS	Dual
ABS	4-wheel
DAY. RUNNING LIGHTS	Standard
BELT ADJUSTORS	Standard
BUILT-IN CHILD SEAT	None
INSURANCE INJURY CLAIMS	Very Low

General Information

WHERE MADE	U.S./Canada
YEAR OF PRODUCTION	Sixth
PARKING INDEX	Hard
BUMPERS	Strong
THEFT RATING	Average
TWINS	
DRIVE	Front

Specifications

FUEL ECONOMY (cty/hwy)	17/26	Poor
DRIVING RANGE (miles)	400	Average
SEATING	5	
LENGTH (inches)	204.1	Very Long
HEAD/LEG ROOM (in.)	38.0/43.0	Average
INTERIOR SPACE (cu. ft.)	102	Roomy
CARGO SPACE (cu. ft.)	14	Average

Specifications may vary.

Prices

Model	Retail	Mkup
Seville SLS	40,660	16%
Seville STS	45,660	16%

Competition

	POOR GOOD	Pg.
Cadillac Seville	■ (near good)	117
Chrysler LHS	■ (poor side)	127
Infiniti J30	■ (poor end)	158
Lexus GS300	■ (good side)	163
Lincoln Town Car	■ (good end)	168

Chevrolet Astro/GMC Safari

The Astro and Safari are the "old shoe" versions of GM's mini-sized vans that don't seem to die. Unlike the all-new Chevrolet Venture, Olds Silhouette and Pontiac Trans Sport, the Astro and Safari are basic minivans that concentrate on hauling and towing. They offer one of the largest cargo-carrying and towing capacities in the minivan market and they come standard with dual airbags and an optional child safety seat.

The standard 4.3-liter V6 with automatic overdrive provides ample power, but handling is sloppy. Fuel economy is fairly dismal, as well. You have the choice between 2-wheel and 4-wheel drive. The seats are reasonably comfortable, but make sure you have enough leg room in the front. If you are looking to carry cargo, this is a good bet. But if you are looking to move people, this vehicle is greatly outclassed by its younger siblings.

The Ratings

	POOR → GOOD
COMPARATIVE RATING	▮ (middle)
CRASH TEST	▮ (below middle)
SAFETY FEATURES	▮ (good)
FUEL ECONOMY	▮ (poor)
PM COST	▮ (good)
REPAIR COST	▮ (good)
WARRANTY	▮ (poor)
COMPLAINTS	▮ (middle)
INSURANCE COST	▮ (good)

Safety

CRASH TEST	Poor
AIRBAGS	Dual
ABS	4-wheel
DAY. RUNNING LIGHTS	Standard
BELT ADJUSTORS	Standard
BUILT-IN CHILD SEAT	Optional
INSURANCE INJURY CLAIMS	Low (4WD=Very Low)

General Information

WHERE MADE	U.S./Canada
YEAR OF PRODUCTION	Thirteenth
PARKING INDEX	Average
BUMPERS	Strong
THEFT RATING	Very Low
TWINS	GMC Safari
DRIVE	Rear/All

Specifications

FUEL ECONOMY (cty/hwy)	16/21	Poor
DRIVING RANGE (miles)	450	Long
SEATING	5/8	
LENGTH (inches)	189.8	Average
HEAD/LEG ROOM (in.)	39.2/41.6	Average
INTERIOR SPACE (cu. ft.)		
CARGO SPACE (cu. ft.)	170	Very Large

Specifications may vary.

Prices

Model	Retail	Mkup
Astro RWD	19,582	10%
Astro AWD	21,141	10%

Competition

	POOR → GOOD	Pg.
Chevrolet Astro	▮ (middle)	118
Dodge Caravan	▮ (middle)	130
Ford Aerostar	▮ (poor)	135
Honda Odyssey	▮ (good)	151
Toyota Previa	▮ (below middle)	219

Chevrolet Camaro

Now entering its 30th year of production, the Camaro maintains its 'pony car' image while updating its interior with a new instrument panel and seat contours. A strong performer in the crash tests, the Camaro comes standard with dual airbags and 4-wheel ABS.

If you are looking for a car with lots of power, the Camaro is not a bad choice. The standard engine is a 3.8-liter V6 with plenty of hp. If you need even more, look into the Z28 which has a 5.7-liter V8 that is more powerful and only slightly less economical. The standard manual transmission is more fuel efficient compared to the optional automatic, and much more fun to drive. The Camaro is roomy for the driver and front seat passenger, but the rear seat is almost too small for young children—but this is not a typical parent's car!

The Ratings

	POOR GOOD
COMPARATIVE RATING	■ (poor end)
CRASH TEST	■ (good end)
SAFETY FEATURES	■ (good)
FUEL ECONOMY	■ (mid)
PM COST	■ (mid-good)
REPAIR COST	■ (mid-good)
WARRANTY	■ (poor)
COMPLAINTS	■ (poor)
INSURANCE COST	■ (poor)

Safety

CRASH TEST	Very Good
AIRBAGS	Dual
ABS	4-wheel
DAY. RUNNING LIGHTS	Standard
BELT ADJUSTORS	None
BUILT-IN CHILD SEAT	None
INSURANCE INJURY CLAIMS	Average

General Information

WHERE MADE	Canada/U.S.
YEAR OF PRODUCTION	Fifth
PARKING INDEX	Hard
BUMPERS	Strong
THEFT RATING	Average (Conv.=Vr. High)
TWINS	Pontiac Firebird
DRIVE	Rear

Specifications

FUEL ECONOMY (cty/hwy)	19/30	Average
DRIVING RANGE (miles)	357	Short
SEATING	4	
LENGTH (inches)	193.2	Long
HEAD/LEG ROOM (in.)	37.2/42.9	Cramped
INTERIOR SPACE (cu. ft.)	82	Cramped
CARGO SPACE (cu. ft.)	13	Small

Specifications may vary.

Prices

Model	Retail	Mkup
Camaro Coupe	16,215	9%
Camaro RS Coupe	17,970	9%
Camaro Z28 Coupe	20,115	9%
Camaro Convertible	21,770	9%
Camaro RS Convertible	23,170	9%

Competition

	POOR GOOD	Pg.
Chevrolet Camaro	■	119
Eagle Talon	■	133
Ford Mustang	■	140
Mitsubishi Eclipse	■	184
Pontiac Firebird	■	200

In 1995, Chevrolet's redesigned Cavalier was awarded with praise and high sales. For 1997, the Cavalier should remain one of the most popular selling vehicles on the road today. Standard daytime running lamps and optional traction control are new safety features in addition to standard dual airbags and 4-wheel ABS. The Cavalier is one of the safest compact cars on the road.

A stylish RS coupe joins the up-level LS sedan, slick Z24 convertible, and the base model this year. The standard 2.2-liter engine delivers good power; a more powerful 2.4-liter engine is optional on the base sedan and coupe, standard on the LS. Ride is good on smooth roads, but like other compact cars, you will feel the bumps on not-so-smooth roads. The Cavalier easily holds its own against the Civic, Neon and Tercel.

The Ratings

	POOR → GOOD
COMPARATIVE RATING	▮ (middle)
CRASH TEST *	▮ (above middle)
SAFETY FEATURES	▮ (good side)
FUEL ECONOMY	▮ (middle)
PM COST	▮ (above middle)
REPAIR COST	▮ (below middle)
WARRANTY	▮ (poor side)
COMPLAINTS	▮ (above middle)
INSURANCE COST	▮ (below middle)

Safety

CRASH TEST	Average
AIRBAGS	Dual
ABS	4-wheel
DAY. RUNNING LIGHTS	Standard
BELT ADJUSTORS	Standard (Sdn. Only)
BUILT-IN CHILD SEAT	None
INSURANCE INJURY CLAIMS	Average (Coupe=High)

General Information

WHERE MADE	U.S./Canada/Mexico
YEAR OF PRODUCTION	Third
PARKING INDEX	Easy
BUMPERS	Strong
THEFT RATING	Very Low
TWINS	Pontiac Sunfire
DRIVE	Front

Specifications

FUEL ECONOMY (cty/hwy)	25/37	Good
DRIVING RANGE (miles)	441	Long
SEATING	5	
LENGTH (inches)	180.3	Short
HEAD/LEG ROOM (in.)	38.9/42.3	Average
INTERIOR SPACE (cu. ft.)	92	Average
CARGO SPACE (cu. ft.)	14	Average

Specifications may vary.

Prices

Model	Retail	Mkup
Cavalier Coupe	10,980	7%
Cavalier Sedan	11,180	7%
Cavalier RS Coupe	12,225	7%
Cavalier LS Sedan	13,380	7%
Cavalier Z24 Coupe	14,465	7%

Competition

	POOR → GOOD	Pg.
Chevrolet Cavalier	▮ (middle)	120
Dodge Neon	▮ (poor side)	132
Honda Civic	▮ (below middle)	149
Nissan Sentra	▮ (good side)	191
Toyota Tercel	▮ (middle)	220

*A version of this vehicle is scheduled to be tested later this year. Results are expected to be equal or better.

Chevrolet Lumina

This steady seller for Chevrolet continues its popularity in the crowded intermediate market. The Lumina enters 1997 with only one major addition, a sportier trim line called the LTZ. This version will feature new front and rear fascias which are designed to give the car a sportier, sleeker look. After its revision in '95, the Lumina has distanced itself from its near-twin, the Monte Carlo in sales. Standard safety features include dual airbags; ABS is optional on the base Lumina, standard on all other trim levels.

The standard 3.1-liter provides adequate power, though the optional 3.4-liter provides even more power with similar gas mileage. If you like a firmer ride, choose the sport suspension which is optional on the Lumina LS and standard on the new LTZ. Ride is good and controls are logically designed. The Lumina deserves a look.

The Ratings

	POOR GOOD
COMPARATIVE RATING	▓ (low-mid)
CRASH TEST	▓ (high)
SAFETY FEATURES	▓ (high)
FUEL ECONOMY	▓ (mid)
PM COST	▓ (mid-high)
REPAIR COST	▓ (mid-high)
WARRANTY	▓ (low)
COMPLAINTS	▓ (low)
INSURANCE COST	▓ (high)

Safety

CRASH TEST	Very Good
AIRBAGS	Dual
ABS	4-wheel (optional)
DAY. RUNNING LIGHTS	Standard
BELT ADJUSTORS	Standard
BUILT-IN CHILD SEAT	Optional
INSURANCE INJURY CLAIMS	Very Low

General Information

WHERE MADE	Canada/U.S.
YEAR OF PRODUCTION	Third
PARKING INDEX	Average
BUMPERS	Strong
THEFT RATING	Very Low
TWINS	Chevrolet Monte Carlo
DRIVE	Front

Specifications

FUEL ECONOMY (cty/hwy)	20/29	Average
DRIVING RANGE (miles)	382	Average
SEATING	6	
LENGTH (inches)	200.9	Long
HEAD/LEG ROOM (in.)	38.4/42.4	Average
INTERIOR SPACE (cu. ft.)	100	Roomy
CARGO SPACE (cu. ft.)	16	Average

Specifications may vary.

Prices

Model	Retail	Mkup
Lumina Sedan	16,945	10%
Lumina LS Sedan	19,145	10%

Competition

	POOR GOOD	Pg.
Chevrolet Lumina	▓ (low-mid)	121
Dodge Intrepid	▓ (mid-high)	131
Honda Accord	▓ (low-mid)	148
Nissan Altima	▓ (high)	188
Olds Achieva	▓ (mid-high)	193

Don't get Chevrolet's replacement for the Beretta/Corsica confused with the Malibu of the past—this Malibu is all-new and is expected to be a popular model. This new sleek looking mid-sized car will surely steal buyers from the Toyota Camry, Honda Accord and Dodge Stratus. You can choose between the base model or the up-level LS; both come standard with dual airbags and 4-wheel ABS.

Chevrolet has equipped this new car with its powerful 2.4-liter 4-cylinder engine which can deliver 150 hp. You'll find good interior room, nice handling and owner-friendly features such as 100,000 mile coolant and platinum-tip spark plugs. The Malibu was designed from the inside-out in order to ensure that the interior space and controls met the needs of all owners. There are plenty of options, so be careful.

The Ratings

	POOR — GOOD
COMPARATIVE RATING*	(no rating)
CRASH TEST	(no rating)
SAFETY FEATURES	7
FUEL ECONOMY	5
PM COST	7
REPAIR COST	7
WARRANTY	1
COMPLAINTS	6
INSURANCE COST	4

Safety

CRASH TEST	No government results
AIRBAGS	Dual
ABS	4-wheel
DAY. RUNNING LIGHTS	Standard
BELT ADJUSTORS	Standard
BUILT-IN CHILD SEAT	None
INSURANCE INJURY CLAIMS	

General Information

WHERE MADE	U.S.
YEAR OF PRODUCTION	First
PARKING INDEX	Average
BUMPERS	Strong
THEFT RATING	
TWINS	Oldsmobile Cutlass
DRIVE	Front

Specifications

FUEL ECONOMY (cty/hwy)	20/29	Average
DRIVING RANGE (miles)	345	Short
SEATING	5	
LENGTH (inches)	190.4	Average
HEAD/LEG ROOM (in.)	39.4/42.2	Average
INTERIOR SPACE (cu. ft.)	99	Average
CARGO SPACE (cu. ft.)	16	Average

Specifications may vary.

Prices

Model	Retail	Mkup
Prices unavailable at press time.		
Expected range: $16-18,000		

Competition

	POOR — GOOD	Pg.
Chevrolet Malibu	(no rating)	122
Chrysler Concorde	3	126
Eagle Vision	6	134
Ford Crown Victoria	5	138
Merc. Gr. Marquis	7	178

*Due to the importance of crash tests, cars with no results as of publication date cannot be given an overall rating.

Chevrolet Monte Carlo

Like the Malibu, the Monte Carlo nameplate is a carry over from the 70's and 80's. For 1997, Chevrolet is touting the Monte Carlo as an affordable luxury, mid-sized coupe; however, its main competitor is the Ford Thunderbird. There are two trim levels to choose from, an LS or Z34. All models have dual airbags, which help make the Monte Carlo one of the best performers in the government's crash test program. It also has optional 4-wheel ABS.

The standard engine is a 3.1-liter V6 which was enhanced for '97 to produce more power. The optional 3.4-liter V6 delivers much more power and slightly lower gas mileage. The ride is only about average. The Monte Carlo offers many options; get only what you want. This is only a two door model so using the rear seat is difficult.

The Ratings

	POOR → GOOD
COMPARATIVE RATING	▓ (1)
CRASH TEST	(7)
SAFETY FEATURES	(7)
FUEL ECONOMY	(4)
PM COST	(6)
REPAIR COST	(7)
WARRANTY	(1)
COMPLAINTS	(3)
INSURANCE COST	(4)

Safety

CRASH TEST	Good
AIRBAGS	Dual
ABS	4-wheel (optional)
DAY. RUNNING LIGHTS	Standard
BELT ADJUSTORS	Standard
BUILT-IN CHILD SEAT	None
INSURANCE INJURY CLAIMS	Average

General Information

WHERE MADE	Canada/U.S.
YEAR OF PRODUCTION	Third
PARKING INDEX	Average
BUMPERS	Strong
THEFT RATING	Very Low
TWINS	Chevrolet Lumina
DRIVE	Front

Specifications

FUEL ECONOMY (cty/hwy)	20/29	Average
DRIVING RANGE (miles)	415	Long
SEATING	6	
LENGTH (inches)	200.7	Long
HEAD/LEG ROOM (in.)	37.9/42.4	Cramped
INTERIOR SPACE (cu. ft.)	100	Roomy
CARGO SPACE (cu. ft.)	16	Average

Specifications may vary.

Prices

Model	Retail	Mkup
Monte Carlo LS Coupe	17,445	10%
Monte Carlo Z34 Coupe	19,945	10%

Competition

	POOR → GOOD	Pg.
Chev. Monte Carlo	(1)	123
Chrys. Sebring	(7)	128
Ford Thunderbird	(6)	143
Mazda MX-6	(8)	173
Mercury Cougar	(7)	177

Chevrolet Venture

In an effort to catch up with the highly successful Dodge Caravan and Plymouth Voyager, GM has introduced its minivans as all-new for 1997. The Venture was designed with 'global' thinking as both US and European engineers got together to plan this contemporary minivan. Like the Caravan, the Venture has sliding doors on both sides, and you will notice that the Venture does not have a radio antenna—it's built into the windshield. Dual airbags and 4-wheel ABS are standard.

You have only one engine choice, a 3.4-liter V6. The interior is spacious, allowing this minivan to carry some of the largest loads in the industry. You have a choice between standard or extended length versions and the options list is quite long. Seating for seven is average and removal of the seats is relatively easy. Chrysler's minivans may no longer be so far ahead anymore.

The Ratings

	POOR ⟷ GOOD
COMPARATIVE RATING*	(no rating)
CRASH TEST	(no rating)
SAFETY FEATURES	Good
FUEL ECONOMY	Poor
PM COST	Good
REPAIR COST	Good
WARRANTY	Poor
COMPLAINTS	Average
INSURANCE COST	Below average

Safety

CRASH TEST	No government results
AIRBAGS	Dual
ABS	4-wheel
DAY. RUNNING LIGHTS	Standard
BELT ADJUSTORS	None
BUILT-IN CHILD SEAT	Optional (two)
INSURANCE INJURY CLAIMS	

General Information

WHERE MADE	U.S.
YEAR OF PRODUCTION	First
PARKING INDEX	Average
BUMPERS	Strong
THEFT RATING	
TWINS	Trans Sport, Silhouette
DRIVE	Front

Specifications

FUEL ECONOMY (cty/hwy)	18/25	Poor
DRIVING RANGE (miles)	420	Long
SEATING	7	
LENGTH (inches)	186.9	Average
HEAD/LEG ROOM (in.)	39.9/39.9	Cramped
INTERIOR SPACE (cu. ft.)		
CARGO SPACE (cu. ft.)	127	Average

Specifications may vary.

Prices

Model	Retail	Mkup
Venture 3dr	22,245	10%
Venture 3dr Ext.	23,075	10%
Venture GL 3dr Ext.	24,595	10%
Venture GL 4dr Ext.	25,145	10%
Venture GLS 3dr Ext.	26,255	10%

Competition

	POOR ⟷ GOOD	Pg.
Chevrolet Venture	(no rating)	124
Dodge Caravan	Average	130
Ford Windstar	Poor	144
Isuzu Oasis	Good	160
Toyota Previa	Below average	219

*Due to the importance of crash tests, cars with no results as of publication date cannot be given an overall rating.

Chrysler Town and Country

The Town and Country is running away from the competition in the minivan market. An upscale model of the Grand Caravan/Voyager, the Town and Country offers luxuries like leather seats, which are converting luxury sedan buyers into minivan owners. For the extra money, you get lots of power equipment. Dual airbags and ABS are standard; optional built-in child seats are a must for any parents, but not available with leather seats.

The Town and Country offers a 3.8-liter V6 to go with the standard automatic overdrive, but its gas mileage is among the lowest for minivans. All-wheel drive is optional. You can't get the "sport handling" package that's optional on the Grand Voyager, but if you want a firmer suspension, check out the trailer-towing package. The ride is comfortable on smooth roads.

The Ratings

	POOR GOOD
COMPARATIVE RATING	
CRASH TEST *	
SAFETY FEATURES	
FUEL ECONOMY	
PM COST	
REPAIR COST	
WARRANTY	
COMPLAINTS	
INSURANCE COST	

Safety

CRASH TEST	Average
AIRBAGS	Dual
ABS	4-wheel
DAY. RUNNING LIGHTS	None
BELT ADJUSTORS	Standard
BUILT-IN CHILD SEAT	Optional (two)
INSURANCE INJURY CLAIMS	Very Low

General Information

WHERE MADE	U.S.
YEAR OF PRODUCTION	Second
PARKING INDEX	Average
BUMPERS	Strong
THEFT RATING	
TWINS	Gr. Caravan, Gr. Voyager
DRIVE	Front

Specifications

FUEL ECONOMY (cty/hwy)	17/24	Poor
DRIVING RANGE (miles)	400	Average
SEATING	7	
LENGTH (inches)	199.7	Long
HEAD/LEG ROOM (in.)	39.8/41.2	Average
INTERIOR SPACE (cu. ft.)		
CARGO SPACE (cu. ft.)	163	Very Large

Specifications may vary.

Prices

Model	Retail	Mkup
Town and Country SX	26,600	10%
Town and Country LX	26,815	10%
Town and Country LX Awd	29,685	10%
Town and Country LXi	31,465	10%
Town and Country LXi Awd	33,740	10%

Competition

	POOR GOOD	Pg.
Chrys. T & C		129
Ford Windstar		144
Honda Odyssey		151
Mazda MPV		172
Nissan Quest		190

*A version of this vehicle is scheduled to be tested later this year. Results are expected to be equal or better.

Dodge Caravan

Even after its redesign last year, the Caravan continued to rule the minivan market in sales. The redesigned Caravan still maintained much of the original feel, while bringing fresh new styling to a crowded minivan market. Dual airbags are standard as is 4-wheel ABS. The Caravan also meets 1997 side impact standards for cars.

The standard 4-cylinder engine is really not adequate—go for one of the three V6 engines to get more power with only a small sacrifice in fuel efficiency. Order the heavy duty suspension or "sport handling group" for improved cornering. The longer wheelbase and length of the Grand Caravan translates into more cargo room. The built-in child restraints are a great option. Comfort is good for seven and the seats are easy to remove. The Caravan is a best bet for 1997.

The Ratings

	POOR ... GOOD
COMPARATIVE RATING	▮ (middle)
CRASH TEST *	▮ (center-right)
SAFETY FEATURES	▮ (right)
FUEL ECONOMY	▮ (left)
PM COST	▮ (right)
REPAIR COST	▮ (right)
WARRANTY	▮ (far left)
COMPLAINTS	▮ (center)
INSURANCE COST	▮ (far right)

Safety

CRASH TEST	Average
AIRBAGS	Dual
ABS	4-wheel
DAY. RUNNING LIGHTS	None
BELT ADJUSTORS	Standard
BUILT-IN CHILD SEAT	Optional (two)
INSURANCE INJURY CLAIMS	Low (4WD=Very Low)

General Information

WHERE MADE	U.S./Canada
YEAR OF PRODUCTION	Second
PARKING INDEX	Average
BUMPERS	Strong
THEFT RATING	
TWINS	Plymouth Voyager
DRIVE	Front

Specifications

FUEL ECONOMY (cty/hwy)	20/25	Poor
DRIVING RANGE (miles)	440	Long
SEATING	7	
LENGTH (inches)	186.3	Average
HEAD/LEG ROOM (in.)	39.8/41.2	Average
INTERIOR SPACE (cu. ft.)		
CARGO SPACE (cu. ft.)	143	Large

Specifications may vary.

Prices

Model	Retail	Mkup
Caravan	17,235	10%
Grand Caravan	18,580	10%
Caravan SE	19,925	11%
Grand Caravan SE	20,755	11%
Caravan ES	25,825	11%

Competition

	POOR ... GOOD	Pg.
Dodge Caravan	▮ (middle)	130
Ford Windstar	▮ (left)	144
Honda Odyssey	▮ (center-right)	151
Mazda MPV	▮ (center-left)	172
Nissan Quest	▮ (center-right)	190

*A version of this vehicle is scheduled to be tested later this year. Results are expected to be equal or better.

Dodge Intrepid

Now entering its fifth year of production, the cheapest member of Chrysler's cab-forward LH triplets continues to be a good seller. This solid, safe car is gaining the attention of both families and driving enthusiast because of its excellent blend of performance and practicality. Standard dual airbags have helped make the Intrepid a very strong performer in the government's crash test program. Great options include a well-designed, built-in rear child restraint and ABS.

The standard 3.3-liter V6 performs well; the somewhat noisier 3.5-liter V6 offers more power with similar gas mileage. The Intrepid's standard "touring" suspension offers an excellent balance between ride and handling. If you want even better handling and don't mind a stiffer ride, try the "performance" suspension on the ED. A spacious interior allows plenty of room for five.

The Ratings

	POOR — GOOD
COMPARATIVE RATING	▮ (mid)
CRASH TEST	▮ (high)
SAFETY FEATURES	▮ (high)
FUEL ECONOMY	▮ (low)
PM COST	▮ (mid-high)
REPAIR COST	▮ (high)
WARRANTY	▮ (low)
COMPLAINTS	▮ (low)
INSURANCE COST	▮ (high)

Safety

CRASH TEST	Very Good
AIRBAGS	Dual
ABS	4-wheel (optional)
DAY. RUNNING LIGHTS	None
BELT ADJUSTORS	None
BUILT-IN CHILD SEAT	Optional
INSURANCE INJURY CLAIMS	Low

General Information

WHERE MADE	Canada
YEAR OF PRODUCTION	Fifth
PARKING INDEX	Average
BUMPERS	Strong
THEFT RATING	Very Low
TWINS	Chrys. Concorde, Eagle Vision
DRIVE	Front

Specifications

FUEL ECONOMY (cty/hwy)	19/27	Poor
DRIVING RANGE (miles)	396	Average
SEATING	5	
LENGTH (inches)	201.8	Very Long
HEAD/LEG ROOM (in.)	38.3/42.4	Average
INTERIOR SPACE (cu. ft.)	104	Roomy
CARGO SPACE (cu. ft.)	17	Large

Specifications may vary.

Prices

Model	Retail	Mkup
Intrepid	19,405	9%
Intrepid ES	22,910	9%

Competition

	POOR — GOOD	Pg.
Dodge Intrepid	▮ (mid)	131
Chevrolet Lumina	▮ (low)	121
Ford Taurus	▮ (high)	142
Nissan Maxima	▮ (low)	189
Toyota Avalon	▮ (low)	214

Dodge/Plymouth Neon

Sales of this small car have been outstanding and Dodge is hoping they continue for 1997. The Dodge Neon benefits from its cab-forward design, which provides excellent interior space for a small car. The '97 version should be quieter and smoother as Dodge made many adjustment to the body. Dual airbags are standard; ABS is optional.

The single-cam version of the 2-liter engine provides adequate power, but the dual-cam version has even more zing. Not only is the cab longer than its competitors, the Neon is also taller, resulting in more head room. Choose the sedan with options, or get the "sport" coupe package with dual cams and a firmer suspension. A built-in child restraint is an excellent option. While the Neon is an affordable compact, be sure to check out its stiff competitors like the Chevrolet Cavalier and Nissan Sentra.

The Ratings

	POOR — GOOD
COMPARATIVE RATING	■ (poor)
CRASH TEST*	(mid)
SAFETY FEATURES	(good)
FUEL ECONOMY	(good)
PM COST	(mid-good)
REPAIR COST	(good)
WARRANTY	(poor)
COMPLAINTS	■ (poor)
INSURANCE COST	(mid)

Safety

CRASH TEST	Average
AIRBAGS	Dual
ABS	4-wheel (optional)
DAY. RUNNING LIGHTS	None
BELT ADJUSTORS	Standard
BUILT-IN CHILD SEAT	Optional
INSURANCE INJURY CLAIMS	Very High

General Information

WHERE MADE	U.S./Mexico
YEAR OF PRODUCTION	Third
PARKING INDEX	Easy
BUMPERS	Strong
THEFT RATING	Very Low
TWINS	
DRIVE	Front

Specifications

FUEL ECONOMY (cty/hwy)	29/39	Good
DRIVING RANGE (miles)	400	Average
SEATING	5	
LENGTH (inches)	171.8	Very Short
HEAD/LEG ROOM (in.)	39.6/42.5	Roomy
INTERIOR SPACE (cu. ft.)	90	Average
CARGO SPACE (cu. ft.)	12	Small

Specifications may vary.

Prices

Model	Retail	Mkup
Neon 2dr	10,393	6%
Neon 4dr	10,595	6%
Neon 2dr Highline	12,470	9%
Neon 4dr Highline	12,670	9%

Competition

	POOR — GOOD	Pg.
Dodge/Plym. Neon	(poor)	132
Chevrolet Cavalier	(mid-good)	120
Honda Civic	(poor-mid)	149
Nissan Sentra	(good)	191
Toyota Tercel	(mid)	220

*A version of this vehicle is scheduled to be tested later this year. Results are expected to be equal or better.

Eagle Talon

Before you even get in the Eagle Talon, you'll notice a host of refinements, which Eagle hopes will make this already popular sports/performance car even more attractive. A twin of the Mitsubishi Eclipse, the Talon is available in four trim levels: Base, ESi, TSi and TSi AWD (all-wheel drive). New features include a new front fascia, a new sleeker side panel and a redesigned control panel. It has standard dual airbags, but you will still have to pay extra for ABS.

The base and ESi models come with a more-than-adequate 2-liter engine. However, the turbo version found on the up-level TSi is much more powerful and just as efficient. All-wheel drive is an attractive option, but is only available on the pricier TSi. Competitive pricing makes the Talon attractive though it still falls below the competition in the overall ratings.

The Ratings

	POOR GOOD
COMPARATIVE RATING	■
CRASH TEST	■
SAFETY FEATURES	■
FUEL ECONOMY	■
PM COST	■
REPAIR COST	■
WARRANTY	■
COMPLAINTS	■
INSURANCE COST	■

Safety

CRASH TEST	Good
AIRBAGS	Dual
ABS	4-wheel (optional)
DAY. RUNNING LIGHTS	None
BELT ADJUSTORS	Standard
BUILT-IN CHILD SEAT	None
INSURANCE INJURY CLAIMS	

General Information

WHERE MADE	U.S./Japan
YEAR OF PRODUCTION	Third
PARKING INDEX	Average
BUMPERS	Strong
THEFT RATING	Average
TWINS	Mitsubishi Eclipse
DRIVE	Front

Specifications

FUEL ECONOMY (cty/hwy)	22/33	Average
DRIVING RANGE (miles)	439	Long
SEATING	4	
LENGTH (inches)	174.9	Short
HEAD/LEG ROOM (in.)	37.9/43.3	Average
INTERIOR SPACE (cu. ft.)	79	Vry. Cramped
CARGO SPACE (cu. ft.)	15	Average

Specifications may vary.

Prices

Model	Retail	Mkup
Talon	14,059	8%
Talon ESi	14,830	8%
Talon TSi	18,015	8%
Talon TSi Awd	20,271	8%

Competition

	POOR GOOD	Pg.
Eagle Talon	■	133
Acura Integra	■	101
Ford Probe	■	141
Mazda MX-6	■	173
Mitsubishi Eclipse	■	184

Eagle Vision

If you are looking for a stylish, sporty and performance-oriented sedan, you can't go wrong with the Eagle Vision. Like its LH twins, the Chrysler Concorde and the Dodge Intrepid, the Vision's cab-forward design makes it very roomy inside. Although you'll have to pay extra for ABS on the base ESi model, dual airbags are standard.

The AutoStick, introduced last year, is an excellent feature and worth test driving. The 3.5-liter V6 is quite powerful; with the AutoStick, the Vision is enjoyable to drive. The base ESi and the up-level TSi are well-equipped, and the "touring" suspension on both provide a nice compromise between ride and handling. The TSi's optional "performance handling" suspension may make the ride a bit too firm. The Vision offers large-car comfort and safety in a mid-sized package.

The Ratings

	POOR	GOOD
COMPARATIVE RATING		
CRASH TEST		
SAFETY FEATURES		
FUEL ECONOMY		
PM COST		
REPAIR COST		
WARRANTY		
COMPLAINTS		
INSURANCE COST		

Safety

CRASH TEST	Very Good
AIRBAGS	Dual
ABS	4-wheel (optional)
DAY. RUNNING LIGHTS	None
BELT ADJUSTORS	None
BUILT-IN CHILD SEAT	Optional
INSURANCE INJURY CLAIMS	Low

General Information

WHERE MADE	Canada
YEAR OF PRODUCTION	Fifth
PARKING INDEX	Average
BUMPERS	Strong
THEFT RATING	Very Low
TWINS	Chrys. Concorde, Intrepid
DRIVE	Front

Specifications

FUEL ECONOMY (cty/hwy)	19/27	Poor
DRIVING RANGE (miles)	396	Average
SEATING	5	
LENGTH (inches)	201.6	Very Long
HEAD/LEG ROOM (in.)	38.4/42.4	Average
INTERIOR SPACE (cu. ft.)	105	Roomy
CARGO SPACE (cu. ft.)	17	Large

Specifications may vary.

Prices

Model	Retail	Mkup
Vision ESi	20,305	9%
Vision TSi	24,485	9%

Competition

	POOR	GOOD	Pg.
Eagle Vision			134
Chevrolet Lumina			121
Dodge Intrepid			131
Nissan Maxima			189
Toyota Avalon			214

The Aerostar was scheduled to cease production in 1994, with the introduction of the Windstar, but it has been carried over into 1997 buoyed by continued steady sales. However, the end is in sight as Ford announced that it will stop production after this year. The Aerostar only comes with a driver airbag and rear-wheel ABS.

The passenger van is actually called a wagon, while the cargo van is called a van. The wagon is available in rear-wheel drive regular- and extended-length, or 4WD extended-length. The 3-liter V6, standard on the rear-wheel drive models, is adequate. The 4-liter V6, standard on 4WD models and available on the rear-wheel-drive extended-length model, is slightly more powerful. Handling improves with 4WD, and ride is fairly good. Built-in child restraints are a noteworthy option, but not much else on the Aerostar is.

The Ratings

	POOR	GOOD
COMPARATIVE RATING	■	
CRASH TEST		■
SAFETY FEATURES		■
FUEL ECONOMY	■	
PM COST		■
REPAIR COST		
WARRANTY	■	
COMPLAINTS		■
INSURANCE COST		■

Safety

CRASH TEST	Average
AIRBAGS	Driver
ABS	2-wheel
DAY. RUNNING LIGHTS	None
BELT ADJUSTORS	None
BUILT-IN CHILD SEAT	Optional
INSURANCE INJURY CLAIMS	Average (4WD = Low)

General Information

WHERE MADE	U.S.
YEAR OF PRODUCTION	Thirteenth
PARKING INDEX	Hard
BUMPERS	Weak
THEFT RATING	Very Low
TWINS	
DRIVE	Rear/All

Specifications

FUEL ECONOMY (cty/hwy)	17/23	Poor
DRIVING RANGE (miles)	399	Average
SEATING	7	
LENGTH (inches)	174.9	Short
HEAD/LEG ROOM (in.)	39.4/41.3	Average
INTERIOR SPACE (cu. ft.)		
CARGO SPACE (cu. ft.)	133	Large

Specifications may vary.

Prices

Model	Retail	Mkup
Aerostar XLT	18,405	11%
Aerostar XLT Ext.	21,170	11%
Aerostar XLT Ext. Awd	24,180	11%

Competition

	POOR	GOOD	Pg.
Ford Aerostar	■		135
Chevrolet Astro		■	118
Dodge Caravan		■	130
Ford Windstar	■		144
Toyota Previa		■	219

This Kia-built car has suffered from slumped sales in recent years. A replacement is due in 2000, but Ford may not wait that long to stop production of this version. The options list is quite short, which keeps the price down. Dual airbags are standard and ABS is optional.

The 1.3-liter, 4-cylinder has as much power as its competition—but don't be fooled, acceleration is not very quick, though its small size and light weight does help. The Aspire's fuel economy is good, but still falls behind the Geo Metro. You can choose between manual or automatic transmissions, but, with the automatic, you will lose fuel efficiency. You can choose between a 2-, 4- or 5-door hatchback, but adults will be uncomfortable in the back no matter which you choose. Repair costs are high as is insurance. As gas misers go, you'd do better with a Suzuki Swift.

The Ratings

	POOR ... GOOD
COMPARATIVE RATING	▢▢■▢▢▢▢▢▢
CRASH TEST	▢▢▢▢▢■▢▢▢
SAFETY FEATURES	▢▢▢▢▢▢■▢▢
FUEL ECONOMY	▢▢▢▢▢▢▢■▢
PM COST	▢▢▢▢▢▢■▢▢
REPAIR COST	■▢▢▢▢▢▢▢▢
WARRANTY	▢■▢▢▢▢▢▢▢
COMPLAINTS	▢▢▢▢▢■▢▢▢
INSURANCE COST	■▢▢▢▢▢▢▢▢

Safety

CRASH TEST	Average
AIRBAGS	Dual
ABS	4-wheel (optional)
DAY. RUNNING LIGHTS	None
BELT ADJUSTORS	None
BUILT-IN CHILD SEAT	None
INSURANCE INJURY CLAIMS	Very High

General Information

WHERE MADE	Korea
YEAR OF PRODUCTION	Fourth
PARKING INDEX	Very Easy
BUMPERS	Strong
THEFT RATING	Very Low
TWINS	
DRIVE	Front

Specifications

FUEL ECONOMY (cty/hwy)	34/42	Very Good
DRIVING RANGE (miles)	370	Short
SEATING	5	
LENGTH (inches)	155.9	Very Short
HEAD/LEG ROOM (in.)	38.2/41.6	Cramped
INTERIOR SPACE (cu. ft.)	82	Cramped
CARGO SPACE (cu. ft.)	17	Large

Specifications may vary.

Prices

Model	Retail	Mkup
Aspire 3dr	9,530	7%
Aspire 5dr	10,160	7%

Competition

	POOR ... GOOD	Pg.
Ford Aspire	▢▢■▢▢▢▢▢	136
Dodge Neon	▢■▢▢▢▢▢▢	132
Geo Metro	▢▢■▢▢▢▢▢	146
Hyundai Accent	▢▢■▢▢▢▢▢	153
Suzuki Swift	▢▢▢▢▢▢■▢	213

A facelift for the Contour is due in 1998, yet the Ford Contour is still one of the best cars in Ford's lineup. The Contour, along with its twin the Mercury Mystique, are the American versions of Ford's new "world car," which is called the Mondeo in Europe. Filling the void left by the departure of the Tempo, Ford plans to market the Contour to a broader audience. Dual airbags are standard, but you'll have to pay extra for ABS.

The base GL is pretty plain. The mid-level LX is somewhat more plush. Both of these get a 2-liter engine that is only adequate. The sportier SE model comes with a much more powerful 2.5-liter V6 that is very quiet and peppy. A nice feature to both engines are the maintenance free 100,000 spark plugs. The handling with the SE's tighter sports suspension is outstanding.

The Ratings

	POOR ← → GOOD
COMPARATIVE RATING	(mark near poor)
CRASH TEST	(mark near good)
SAFETY FEATURES	(mark mid-good)
FUEL ECONOMY	(mark middle)
PM COST	(mark near good)
REPAIR COST	(mark near good)
WARRANTY	(mark near poor)
COMPLAINTS	(mark near poor)
INSURANCE COST	(mark left-mid)

Safety

CRASH TEST	Good
AIRBAGS	Dual
ABS	4-wheel (optional)
DAY. RUNNING LIGHTS	None
BELT ADJUSTORS	None
BUILT-IN CHILD SEAT	None
INSURANCE INJURY CLAIMS	Average

General Information

WHERE MADE	U.S./Mexico
YEAR OF PRODUCTION	Third
PARKING INDEX	Easy
BUMPERS	Strong
THEFT RATING	Very Low
TWINS	Mercury Mystique
DRIVE	Front

Specifications

FUEL ECONOMY (cty/hwy)	24/33	Average
DRIVING RANGE (miles)	392	Average
SEATING	5	
LENGTH (inches)	183.9	Average
HEAD/LEG ROOM (in.)	39.0/42.4	Average
INTERIOR SPACE (cu. ft.)	89	Cramped
CARGO SPACE (cu. ft.)	14	Average

Specifications may vary.

Prices

Model	Retail	Mkup
Contour Base	13,995	9%
Contour GL	14,820	9%
Contour LX	15,450	9%
Contour SE	17,150	9%

Competition

	POOR ← → GOOD	Pg.
Ford Contour	(mark near poor)	137
Buick Skylark	(mark near good)	113
Honda Accord	(mark left-mid)	148
Hyundai Sonata	(mark far poor)	155
VW Golf/Jetta	(mark near good)	221

Ford Crown Victoria

Ford is now the proud sole producer of large, rear-wheel drive cars, since General Motors dropped out last year. At one time Ford had thought about discontinuing the Crown Victoria and its twin, the Mercury Grand Marquis, but is now planning a facelift for 1998—so America's travelling living room is not about to die. Dual airbags are standard, but you inexplicably still have to pay extra for ABS.

The 4.6-liter V8 is powerful, but you have an option to choose an upgrade on the same engine which delivers 20 more horses with little decrease in fuel efficiency. The base-level model comes with plenty of equipment, but to get some of the more choice options, you have to move up to the LX. The Crown Victoria's standard suspension isn't as mushy-riding or awkward in cornering as some other big American sedans. Still, it benefits from the performance and handling package.

The Ratings

	POOR	GOOD
COMPARATIVE RATING		
CRASH TEST		
SAFETY FEATURES		
FUEL ECONOMY		
PM COST		
REPAIR COST		
WARRANTY		
COMPLAINTS		
INSURANCE COST		

Safety

CRASH TEST	Very Good
AIRBAGS	Dual
ABS	4-wheel (optional)
DAY. RUNNING LIGHTS	None
BELT ADJUSTORS	Standard
BUILT-IN CHILD SEAT	None
INSURANCE INJURY CLAIMS	Very Low

General Information

WHERE MADE	Canada
YEAR OF PRODUCTION	Sixth
PARKING INDEX	Hard
BUMPERS	Strong
THEFT RATING	Very Low
TWINS	Town Car, Gr. Marquis
DRIVE	Rear

Specifications

FUEL ECONOMY (cty/hwy)	17/25	Poor
DRIVING RANGE (miles)	400	Average
SEATING	6	
LENGTH (inches)	212.0	Very Long
HEAD/LEG ROOM (in.)	39.4/42.5	Roomy
INTERIOR SPACE (cu. ft.)	111	Very Roomy
CARGO SPACE (cu. ft.)	21	Very Large

Specifications may vary.

Prices

Model	Retail	Mkup
Crown Victoria	22,080	7%
Crown Victoria LX	23,800	7%

Competition

	POOR	GOOD	Pg.
FordCrown Victoria			138
Chrysler Concorde			126
Eagle Vision			134
Merc. Gr. Marquis			178
Toyota Avalon			214

Ford Escort

After a bold remake of the Taurus, Ford's next facelift went to the Escort. However, the all-new '97 Escort is a mere ripple—a smaller, less curvy version of the Taurus that could easily be mistaken for most other Saturn-like subcompacts. The 1997 Ford Escort is the last version to be based on the Mazda Protégé. The mom-and-pop of compacts, the Ford Escort comes standard with dual airbags and optional ABS.

A revamped engine make this car much more enjoyable to drive than previous versions. Room and comfort are all improved and a major difference will be in noticed in improved ride and less noise. The trunk is adequate, especially with the fold down rear seat. Seating for four is good, tight for three in the back. With a more contemporary look, the Escort remains a safe and economical choice.

The Ratings

	POOR ⟷ GOOD
COMPARATIVE RATING*	(no rating)
CRASH TEST	(no rating)
SAFETY FEATURES	▮ (high)
FUEL ECONOMY	▮ (high)
PM COST	▮ (high)
REPAIR COST	▮ (mid)
WARRANTY	▮ (low)
COMPLAINTS	▮ (mid)
INSURANCE COST	▮ (mid)

Safety

CRASH TEST	No government results
AIRBAGS	Dual
ABS	4-wheel (optional)
DAY. RUNNING LIGHTS	None
BELT ADJUSTORS	Standard
BUILT-IN CHILD SEAT	Optional
INSURANCE INJURY CLAIMS	

General Information

WHERE MADE	U.S. /Mexico
YEAR OF PRODUCTION	First
PARKING INDEX	Very Easy
BUMPERS	Strong
THEFT RATING	
TWINS	Mercury Tracer
DRIVE	Front

Specifications

FUEL ECONOMY (cty/hwy)	26/37	Good
DRIVING RANGE (miles)	394	Average
SEATING	5	
LENGTH (inches)	174.7	Short
HEAD/LEG ROOM (in.)	39.0/42.5	Average
INTERIOR SPACE (cu. ft.)	87	Cramped
CARGO SPACE (cu. ft.)	13	Small

Specifications may vary.

Prices

Model	Retail	Mkup
Escort	11,430	7%
Escort LX	12,210	7%
Escort LX Wagon	12,865	7%

Competition

	POOR ⟷ GOOD	Pg.
Ford Escort	(no rating)	139
Chevrolet Cavalier	▮ (mid)	120
Dodge Neon	▮ (low)	132
Nissan Sentra	▮ (high)	191
Toyota Tercel	▮ (mid)	220

*Due to the importance of crash tests, cars with no results as of publication date cannot be given an overall rating.

Ford Mustang

One of Ford's bread-and-butter cars, the 1997 Mustang is a popular sports/performance car with a fairly low price tag. The Mustang, totally redesigned in 1994, is not due for any significant changes until 1999. Coupes and convertibles are available in base, sporty GT or limited-production Cobra models. All models have dual airbags, but ABS, standard on the other models, will cost extra on base Mustangs.

A 3.8-liter V6, which is optional on the Ford Taurus, comes standard and should provide ample power for most drivers. However, you can choose between two new 4.6-liter V8 engines; they are smaller than the V8 engines of the past, but deliver the same amount of horses with smoother shifts. With steering and suspension improvements, handling should be better than on the older models. Expect high insurance bills.

The Ratings

	POOR	GOOD
COMPARATIVE RATING	■	
CRASH TEST		■
SAFETY FEATURES		■
FUEL ECONOMY		■
PM COST		■
REPAIR COST		■
WARRANTY	■	
COMPLAINTS		■
INSURANCE COST	■	

Safety

CRASH TEST	Good*
AIRBAGS	Dual
ABS	4-wheel (optional)
DAY. RUNNING LIGHTS	None
BELT ADJUSTORS	None
BUILT-IN CHILD SEAT	None
INSURANCE INJURY CLAIMS	Average

General Information

WHERE MADE	U.S.
YEAR OF PRODUCTION	Fourth
PARKING INDEX	Average
BUMPERS	Strong
THEFT RATING	Very High
TWINS	
DRIVE	Rear

Specifications

FUEL ECONOMY (cty/hwy)	20/30	Average
DRIVING RANGE (miles)	370	Short
SEATING	4	
LENGTH (inches)	181.5	Short
HEAD/LEG ROOM (in.)	38.2/42.5	Average
INTERIOR SPACE (cu. ft.)	83	Cramped
CARGO SPACE (cu. ft.)	11	Small

Specifications may vary.

Prices

Model	Retail	Mkup
Mustang	15,880	9%
Mustang GT	18,525	9%
Mustang Convertible	21,280	10%
Mustang GT Convertible	24,510	10%

Competition

	POOR	GOOD	Pg.
Ford Mustang	■		140
Chevrolet Camaro	■		119
Eagle Talon	■		133
Mitsubishi Eclipse	■		184
Pontiac Firebird	■		200

*Data given for coupe. Crash test for Convertible is Very Good; Overall rating is a 2.

Ford Probe

The Probe and its close relative, the Mazda MX-6, are due to go separate ways next year when Ford releases an all-new Probe, based on the Mercury Cougar. For 1997, the Probe and MX-6 carry on unchanged. Dual airbags are standard, but ABS, standard on the GT, costs extra on the base Probe.

The base model has a 2-liter 4-cylinder engine that is barely powerful enough. If you want more power, the GT, with its 2.5-liter V6, will cost another couple of thousand. One benefit of the GT is a firmer suspension that gives excellent handling. While the ride can be uncomfortable and noisy, you'll find the 5-speed is much more enjoyable than the primitive-feeling automatic. The controls are not what you would hope for. Like other sporty cars, the Probe is really a 2-seater with a back seat for occasional use only.

The Ratings

	POOR GOOD
COMPARATIVE RATING	▨
CRASH TEST	▨
SAFETY FEATURES	▨
FUEL ECONOMY	▨
PM COST	▨
REPAIR COST	▨
WARRANTY	▨
COMPLAINTS	▨
INSURANCE COST	▨

Safety

CRASH TEST	Very Good
AIRBAGS	Dual
ABS	4-wheel (optional)
DAY. RUNNING LIGHTS	None
BELT ADJUSTORS	None
BUILT-IN CHILD SEAT	None
INSURANCE INJURY CLAIMS	Average

General Information

WHERE MADE	U.S.
YEAR OF PRODUCTION	Fifth
PARKING INDEX	Easy
BUMPERS	Strong
THEFT RATING	Average
TWINS	Mazda MX-6
DRIVE	Front

Specifications

FUEL ECONOMY (cty/hwy)	26/33	Good
DRIVING RANGE (miles)	450	Long
SEATING	4	
LENGTH (inches)	178.7	Short
HEAD/LEG ROOM (in.)	37.8/43.1	Average
INTERIOR SPACE (cu. ft.)	80	Cramped
CARGO SPACE (cu. ft.)	19	Large

Specifications may vary.

Prices

Model	Retail	Mkup
Probe	14,680	9%
Probe GT	17,180	9%

Competition

	POOR GOOD	Pg.
Ford Probe	▨	141
Acura Integra	▨	101
Eagle Talon	▨	133
Mazda MX-6	▨	173
Mitsubishi Eclipse	▨	184

Ford Taurus

The Taurus led the way in revolutionizing car design in the mid-1980's and its current incarnation is no exception. Ford hoped its futuristic redesign of the Taurus would increase sales for its best-selling car even higher. But due to a higher price tag, and mixed reactions to the new look, sales will likely fall short of the Accord. A longer wheelbase make this car very spacious inside and oval-shaped headlights and dash give it a fresh, unique look. Choose from a base model, GL or LX trim levels. All are standard with dual airbags. ABS is optional.

A standard 3-liter V6 engine should provide ample power, although you can opt for the same sized engine with more horses. The SHO is due midyear and will come with many features that are optional on the base models as well as a 3.4-liter V8 which will really make the car move. The Taurus remains a fine choice.

The Ratings

	POOR — GOOD
COMPARATIVE RATING	▮ (high)
CRASH TEST	▮ (high)
SAFETY FEATURES	▮ (high)
FUEL ECONOMY	▮ (mid)
PM COST	▮ (mid-high)
REPAIR COST	▮ (mid)
WARRANTY	▮ (low)
COMPLAINTS	▮ (low-mid)
INSURANCE COST	▮ (high)

Safety

CRASH TEST	Very Good
AIRBAGS	Dual
ABS	4-wheel (optional)
DAY. RUNNING LIGHTS	Optional
BELT ADJUSTORS	Standard
BUILT-IN CHILD SEAT	Optional
INSURANCE INJURY CLAIMS	Average (Wgn.=Low)

General Information

WHERE MADE	U.S.
YEAR OF PRODUCTION	Second
PARKING INDEX	Average
BUMPERS	Strong
THEFT RATING	
TWINS	Mercury Sable
DRIVE	Front

Specifications

FUEL ECONOMY (cty/hwy)	20/28	Average
DRIVING RANGE (miles)	368	Short
SEATING	5/6	
LENGTH (inches)	197.5	Long
HEAD/LEG ROOM (in.)	39.2/42.2	Average
INTERIOR SPACE (cu. ft.)	102	Roomy
CARGO SPACE (cu. ft.)	16	Average

Specifications may vary.

Prices

Model	Retail	Mkup
Taurus G	18,545	9%
Taurus GL	19,535	10%
Taurus GL Wagon	20,745	10%
Taurus LX	22,160	10%
Taurus LX Wagon	23,265	10%

Competition

	POOR — GOOD	Pg.
Ford Taurus	▮ (high)	142
Honda Accord	▮ (low-mid)	148
Mazda 626	▮ (mid)	169
Nissan Maxima	▮ (low-mid)	189
VW Passat	▮ (high)	222

Ford Thunderbird

The Thunderbird, which shares a chassis with the Mercury Cougar and the Lincoln Mark VIII, received very few changes this year due to the cost of redesigning the new Escort. The Thunderbird is one of Ford's longest running name plates, having been around since 1955. There is only one trim level base (LX) and it comes nicely equipped with dual airbags and optional ABS.

The LX's standard 3.8-liter V6 is adequate for this fairly heavy car. If you like more performance, you can order the optional modular 4.6-liter V8. Gauges and controls are well-designed. Ride is comfortable, but the LX's handling isn't as crisp as it should be. This is one coupe with enough room for four, possibly five, plus luggage. This version of the Thunderbird should continue to sell well and compete nicely against rivals such as the Monte Carlo.

The Ratings

	POOR — GOOD
COMPARATIVE RATING	▮ (mid)
CRASH TEST	▮ (good)
SAFETY FEATURES	▮ (above mid)
FUEL ECONOMY	▮ (below mid)
PM COST	▮ (mid)
REPAIR COST	▮ (mid)
WARRANTY	▮ (poor)
COMPLAINTS	▮ (mid)
INSURANCE COST	▮ (good)

Safety

CRASH TEST	Very Good
AIRBAGS	Dual
ABS	4-wheel (optional)
DAY. RUNNING LIGHTS	None
BELT ADJUSTORS	None
BUILT-IN CHILD SEAT	None
INSURANCE INJURY CLAIMS	Average

General Information

WHERE MADE	U.S.
YEAR OF PRODUCTION	Ninth
PARKING INDEX	Average
BUMPERS	Strong
THEFT RATING	Average
TWINS	Lincoln Mark VIII, Merc. Cougar
DRIVE	Rear

Specifications

FUEL ECONOMY (cty/hwy)	18/26	Poor
DRIVING RANGE (miles)	378	Short
SEATING	5	
LENGTH (inches)	200.3	Long
HEAD/LEG ROOM (in.)	38.1/42.5	Average
INTERIOR SPACE (cu. ft.)	101	Roomy
CARGO SPACE (cu. ft.)	15	Average

Specifications may vary.

Prices

Model	Retail	Mkup
Thunderbird LX	18,395	9%

Competition

	POOR — GOOD	Pg.
Ford Thunderbird	▮ (mid)	143
Chev. Monte Carlo	▮ (poor)	123
Chrysler Sebring	▮ (mid)	128
Mazda MX-6	▮ (good)	173
Mercury Cougar	▮ (mid)	177

Ford Windstar

In the chase to catch the highly successful Chrysler minivans, Ford came close to developing a winning vehicle. Yet, the Windstar still falls a bit short. The Windstar is an exceptional performer in the governments crash tests; however, the lack of a second sliding side door has turned off many buyers. The Windstar offers great optional built-in child restraints; dual airbags and 4-wheel ABS are both standard.

The base GL comes standard with the same 3-liter V6 also available on the Aerostar and Ranger. A 3.8-liter V6 is optional on the GL and standard on the LX, which provides much more power. At over 200 inches, the Windstar has more interior room than a Grand Caravan, but not quite as much as a Toyota Previa. Even without the second sliding door, the Windstar is one of the top minivans on the market today.

The Ratings

	POOR	GOOD
COMPARATIVE RATING	■	
CRASH TEST *		■
SAFETY FEATURES		■
FUEL ECONOMY	■	
PM COST		■
REPAIR COST		■
WARRANTY	■	
COMPLAINTS	■	
INSURANCE COST	■	

Safety

CRASH TEST	Very Good
AIRBAGS	Dual
ABS	4-wheel
DAY. RUNNING LIGHTS	None
BELT ADJUSTORS	Standard
BUILT-IN CHILD SEAT	Optional
INSURANCE INJURY CLAIMS	Low

General Information

WHERE MADE	Canada
YEAR OF PRODUCTION	Third
PARKING INDEX	Hard
BUMPERS	Weak
THEFT RATING	Very Low
TWINS	
DRIVE	Front

Specifications

FUEL ECONOMY (cty/hwy)	17/25	Poor
DRIVING RANGE (miles)	400	Average
SEATING	7	
LENGTH (inches)	201.2	Very Long
HEAD/LEG ROOM (in.)	39.3/40.7	Cramped
INTERIOR SPACE (cu. ft.)		
CARGO SPACE (cu. ft.)	144	Large

Specifications may vary.

Prices

Model	Retail	Mkup
Windstar G	18,995	10%
Windstar GL	20,920	10%
Windstar LX	25,875	10%

Competition

	POOR	GOOD	Pg.
Ford Windstar	■		144
Chrysler T & C		■	129
Isuzu Oasis		■	160
Nissan Quest		■	190
Toyota Previa	■		219

*A version of this vehicle is scheduled to be tested later this year. Results are expected to be equal or better.

GM EV1

The fall of the gas guzzler begins with the introduction of GM's EV1, a sports coupe which will be available (unfortunately, for lease only) from Saturn dealers in parts of southern California and Arizona. This is not a glorified golf cart as it comes standard with dual airbags, traction control, ABS, daytime running lights and self-sealing tires with a tire pressure monitoring system.

The EV1 runs on lead-acid batteries, which take up to 8 hours to recharge and offer a driving range of 70-90 miles. Acceleration is good but drains the juice that much faster. The interior is sparsely designed and spacious. The typical engine rumbling is replaced by a high pitched whining of the electric motor during acceleration. The EV1, good for people with short commutes or quick trips, is a great start to a promising technology.

The Ratings

	POOR	GOOD
COMPARATIVE RATING*		
CRASH TEST		
SAFETY FEATURES	■	
FUEL ECONOMY		
PM COST		
REPAIR COST		
WARRANTY		
COMPLAINTS	■	
INSURANCE COST	■	

Safety

CRASH TEST	No government results
AIRBAGS	Dual
ABS	4-wheel
DAY. RUNNING LIGHTS	Standard
BELT ADJUSTORS	Standard
BUILT-IN CHILD SEAT	None
INSURANCE INJURY CLAIMS	

General Information

WHERE MADE	U.S.
YEAR OF PRODUCTION	First
PARKING INDEX	Very Easy
BUMPERS	Weak
THEFT RATING	
TWINS	
DRIVE	Front

Specifications

FUEL ECONOMY (cty/hwy)		
DRIVING RANGE (miles)	70-90	Very Short
SEATING	2	
LENGTH (inches)	193.0	Long
HEAD/LEG ROOM (in.)	38.7/42.4	Average
INTERIOR SPACE (cu. ft.)	50	Vry. Cramped
CARGO SPACE (cu. ft.)	11	Small

Specifications may vary.

Prices

Model	Retail	Mkup
Prices unavailable at press time.		
Espected range: $33-37,000		

Competition

	POOR	GOOD	Pg.
GM EV1			145
Dodge Neon	■		132
Geo Metro	■		146
Hyundai Accent	■		153
Suzuki Swift	■		213

*Due to the importance of crash tests, cars with no results as of publication date cannot be given an overall rating.

With the rising cost of gas, the Geo Metro is becoming more attractive to many buyers. Metro's hatchback coupe with a manual transmission boasts a fuel rating of 44/49 mpg. For 1997, you can choose between a hatchback coupe, which comes in a base and LSi trim level, or a roomier sedan, only available as an LSi. Daytime running lights and dual airbags are standard; ABS is optional.

The base coupe gets a 1-liter, 3-cylinder engine, which lacks power, but leads the industry in fuel efficiency. For '97, the LSi models now come standard with a 1.3-liter, 4-cylinder engine, which offers only 25 more hp. The sedan looks similar to a Prizm and is slightly roomier than a hatchback, though either one is cramped for interior space. However, high repair costs and insurance bills plague the Metro. Check out the Tercel or Swift first.

The Ratings

	POOR	GOOD
COMPARATIVE RATING	■	
CRASH TEST		■
SAFETY FEATURES		■
FUEL ECONOMY		■
PM COST		■
REPAIR COST	■	
WARRANTY	■	
COMPLAINTS	■	
INSURANCE COST	■	

Safety

CRASH TEST	Good
AIRBAGS	Dual
ABS	4-wheel (optional)
DAY. RUNNING LIGHTS	Standard
BELT ADJUSTORS	None
BUILT-IN CHILD SEAT	None
INSURANCE INJURY CLAIMS	

General Information

WHERE MADE	Canada/Japan
YEAR OF PRODUCTION	Third
PARKING INDEX	Very Easy
BUMPERS	Weak
THEFT RATING	
TWINS	Suzuki Swift
DRIVE	Front

Specifications

FUEL ECONOMY (cty/hwy)	44/49	Very Good
DRIVING RANGE (miles)	488	Very Long
SEATING	4	
LENGTH (inches)	149.4	Very Short
HEAD/LEG ROOM (in.)	39.1/42.5	Average
INTERIOR SPACE (cu. ft.)	82	Cramped
CARGO SPACE (cu. ft.)	10	Very Small

Specifications may vary.

Prices

Model	Retail	Mkup
Metro Coupe	8,580	6%
Metro LSi Coupe	9,180	7%
Metro LSi Sedan	9,850	7%

Competition

	POOR	GOOD	Pg.
Geo Metro	■		146
Dodge Neon	■		132
Ford Aspire	■		136
Suzuki Swift		■	213
Toyota Tercel		■	220

Geo Prizm

The Geo Prizm is the quiet sibling to Toyota's more popular Corolla. While less expensive than the Corolla, the Prizm only sells a third of Corolla's sales. You can only find the Prizm as a sedan in either base or LSi trim levels. Dual airbags are standard and ABS is optional.

The Prizm comes standard with a 1.6-liter, 4-cylinder engine, though the LSi offers an optional 1.8-liter 4-cylinder with slightly more power in exchange for slightly lower fuel economy. The handling and ride are good, especially now that power steering comes standard. Inside, the controls are logical and easy to use. Daytime running lamps are a great safety feature. Economical and well built, the Prizm seats four nicely with room for luggage. When it comes to getting value for your money, the Prizm is a great choice.

The Ratings

	POOR — GOOD
COMPARATIVE RATING	■ (high)
CRASH TEST	■ (high)
SAFETY FEATURES	■ (high)
FUEL ECONOMY	■ (high)
PM COST	■ (mid-low)
REPAIR COST	■ (low)
WARRANTY	■ (low)
COMPLAINTS	■ (high)
INSURANCE COST	■ (lowest)

Safety

CRASH TEST	Good
AIRBAGS	Dual
ABS	4-wheel (optional)
DAY. RUNNING LIGHTS	Standard
BELT ADJUSTORS	Standard
BUILT-IN CHILD SEAT	Optional
INSURANCE INJURY CLAIMS	High

General Information

WHERE MADE	Canada/Japan
YEAR OF PRODUCTION	Fifth
PARKING INDEX	Very Easy
BUMPERS	Weak
THEFT RATING	Very Low
TWINS	Toyota Corolla
DRIVE	Front

Specifications

FUEL ECONOMY (cty/hwy)	30/34	Good
DRIVING RANGE (miles)	422	Long
SEATING	5	
LENGTH (inches)	173.0	Short
HEAD/LEG ROOM (in.)	36.4/41.7	Vry. Cramped
INTERIOR SPACE (cu. ft.)	84	Cramped
CARGO SPACE (cu. ft.)	13	Small

Specifications may vary.

Prices

Model	Retail	Mkup
Prizm	12,840	8%
Prizm LSi	13,485	8%

Competition

	POOR — GOOD	Pg.
Geo Prizm	■ (high)	147
Honda Civic	■ (low)	149
Nissan Sentra	■ (high)	191
Subaru Impreza	■ (high)	209
Toyota Corolla	■ (high)	217

The Honda Accord recaptured the best-selling car status from its rival, the Ford Taurus, in 1996. The same is expected to happen in 1997 as both Ford and Honda have made very few changes to their models. Dual airbags are standard, but ABS is still optional.

Accords come in three body styles including coupes, sedans, and wagons, and each with four trim levels: base DX, mid-level LX, Special Edition, and up-level EX. The standard 4 cylinder engine is powerful enough, but the VTEC version found on the EX will probably suit you better. Both versions are pretty economical, even with the optional automatic transmission. Performance and handling are comparable to its competitors. The Accord's controls and gauges are excellent. Unfortunately, high repair costs and a lousy warranty prevents the Accord from being a top choice.

The Ratings

	POOR ——— GOOD
COMPARATIVE RATING	▪ (poor)
CRASH TEST*	▪ (good)
SAFETY FEATURES	▪ (mid)
FUEL ECONOMY	▪ (mid)
PM COST	▪ (poor)
REPAIR COST	▪ (poor)
WARRANTY	▪ (very poor)
COMPLAINTS	▪ (good)
INSURANCE COST	▪ (good)

Safety

CRASH TEST	Average
AIRBAGS	Dual
ABS	4-wheel (optional)
DAY. RUNNING LIGHTS	None
BELT ADJUSTORS	Std. (Sdn/Wgn Only)
BUILT-IN CHILD SEAT	None
INSURANCE INJURY CLAIMS	Avg. (Wgn. = Very Low)

General Information

WHERE MADE	U.S./Japan
YEAR OF PRODUCTION	Fourth
PARKING INDEX	Easy
BUMPERS	Strong
THEFT RATING	Very High (Wagon=Low)
TWINS	
DRIVE	Front

Specifications

FUEL ECONOMY (cty/hwy)	25/31	Average
DRIVING RANGE (miles)	476	Very Long
SEATING	5	
LENGTH (inches)	185.6	Average
HEAD/LEG ROOM (in.)	39.4/42.7	Roomy
INTERIOR SPACE (cu. ft.)	94	Average
CARGO SPACE (cu. ft.)	13	Small

Specifications may vary.

Prices

Model	Retail	Mkup
Accord DX Sedan	15,495	13%
Accord LX Coupe	18,385	13%
Accord LX Sedan	18,585	13%
Accord SE Coupe	20,495	13%
Accord SE Sedan	20,695	13%

Competition

	POOR ——— GOOD	Pg.
Honda Accord	▪ (poor)	148
Ford Taurus	▪ (good)	142
Mazda 626	▪ (mid)	169
Nissan Altima	▪ (good)	188
Olds Achieva	▪ (good)	193

*A version of this vehicle is scheduled to be tested later this year. Results are expected to be equal or better.

Honda Civic

Little has changed on the Civic for 1997 after a major rework last year. Little needed to be changed—the Civic remains the epitome of utility, style and value. As before, you can buy a coupe with trim levels DX, HX, and EX; a sedan with trim levels DX, LX and EX; or a hatchback with trim levels, CX or DX. Dual airbags are standard and ABS is standard on the EX sedan, but remains optional on all other models.

The base engine is a 1.6-liter 4-cylinder which delivers 106 hp, and you can upgrade to more powerful engines with 115 or 127 hp on higher trim levels. The ride is characterized by responsive handling and a smooth suspension. Interior space increased with last year's reworking, especially in back. With excellent crash tests results, the Civic is a dependable car.

The Ratings

	POOR	GOOD
COMPARATIVE RATING		
CRASH TEST		
SAFETY FEATURES		
FUEL ECONOMY		
PM COST		
REPAIR COST		
WARRANTY		
COMPLAINTS		
INSURANCE COST		

Safety

CRASH TEST	Very Good
AIRBAGS	Dual
ABS	4-wheel (optional)
DAY. RUNNING LIGHTS	None
BELT ADJUSTORS	Standard (Sdn. Only)
BUILT-IN CHILD SEAT	None
INSURANCE INJURY CLAIMS	Average

General Information

WHERE MADE	U.S./Canada/Japan
YEAR OF PRODUCTION	Second
PARKING INDEX	Very Easy
BUMPERS	Strong
THEFT RATING	
TWINS	
DRIVE	Front

Specifications

FUEL ECONOMY (cty/hwy)	29/35	Good
DRIVING RANGE (miles)	428	Long
SEATING	5	
LENGTH (inches)	175.1	Short
HEAD/LEG ROOM (in.)	39.8/42.7	Roomy
INTERIOR SPACE (cu. ft.)	90	Average
CARGO SPACE (cu. ft.)	12	Small

Specifications may vary.

Prices

Model	Retail	Mkup
Civic CX 3dr	10,945	10%
Civic DX 3dr	12,195	10%
Civic DX 2dr	12,675	10%
Civic DX 4dr	13,030	10%
Civic LX 4dr	15,045	10%

Competition

	POOR	GOOD	Pg.
Honda Civic			149
Geo Prizm			147
Hyundai Accent			153
Nissan Sentra			191
Toyota Corolla			217

There have been many rumors that the del Sol was going to be discontinued for 1997, but Honda has decided to carry it over one more year. Dual airbags are standard and, new for this year, Honda is offering optional ABS.

You can choose 102 HP (S), 120 HP (Si), or 160 HP (VTEC) versions of the same 4-cylinder engine. The 5-speed shifts smoothly; the automatic is acceptable for those who don't like to shift. Gas mileage is particularly good on the del Sol S. Handling is decent on the S, better on the Si, very good on the VTEC. The ride itself isn't bad. The del Sol has no rear seat so be sure you have enough room inside before you plunk down your money. The top panel is easily removable, although you'll have even less cargo space after you stow it. Controls are well designed.

The Ratings

	POOR GOOD
COMPARATIVE RATING*	(blank)
CRASH TEST	(blank)
SAFETY FEATURES	■ (6th)
FUEL ECONOMY	■ (6th)
PM COST	■ (2nd)
REPAIR COST	■ (4th)
WARRANTY	■ (1st)
COMPLAINTS	■ (3rd)
INSURANCE COST	■ (1st)

Safety

CRASH TEST	No government results
AIRBAGS	Dual
ABS	4-wheel (optional)
DAY. RUNNING LIGHTS	None
BELT ADJUSTORS	None
BUILT-IN CHILD SEAT	None
INSURANCE INJURY CLAIMS	Average

General Information

WHERE MADE	Japan
YEAR OF PRODUCTION	Fifth
PARKING INDEX	Very Easy
BUMPERS	Strong
THEFT RATING	Very High
TWINS	
DRIVE	Front

Specifications

FUEL ECONOMY (cty/hwy)	28/35	Good
DRIVING RANGE (miles)	428	Long
SEATING	2	
LENGTH (inches)	157.7	Very Short
HEAD/LEG ROOM (in.)	37.5/40.3	Vry. Cramped
INTERIOR SPACE (cu. ft.)	Not Available	
CARGO SPACE (cu. ft.)	11	Small

Specifications may vary.

Prices

Model	Retail	Mkup
del Sol S	15,475	14%
del Sol Si	17,695	14%
del Sol VTEC	19,995	14%

Competition

	POOR GOOD	Pg.
Honda del Sol	(blank)	150
Acura Integra	■ (2nd)	101
Ford Probe	■ (5th)	141
Mazda Miata	■ (4th)	170
Mitsubishi Eclipse	■ (2nd)	184

*Due to the importance of crash tests, cars with no results as of publication date cannot be given an overall rating.

Honda Odyssey

This front-wheel drive vehicle is different than most other minivans in many respects. It is lower and narrower than other minivans, making it easier to maneuver. While most minivans have only one sliding door, the Odyssey sports two sedan-type doors for access to the rear seats. Dual airbags and ABS are standard. The Odyssey meets 1997 passenger car side impact standards.

Honda is rumored to be introducing a V6 on the Odyssey for next year's model, but for now, it gets the same 2.2-liter 4-cylinder engine found on the Accord. The middle bench seat doesn't come out, and the rear seat, which cleverly folds into the floor of the cargo bay, doesn't quite become flush with the floor, making the loading surface uneven. As a result, cargo space is not quite as generous as the competition. A fine crash test performer, the Odyssey is worth looking at.

The Ratings

	POOR GOOD
COMPARATIVE RATING	
CRASH TEST	
SAFETY FEATURES	
FUEL ECONOMY	
PM COST	
REPAIR COST	
WARRANTY	
COMPLAINTS	
INSURANCE COST	

Safety

CRASH TEST	Good
AIRBAGS	Dual
ABS	4-wheel
DAY. RUNNING LIGHTS	None
BELT ADJUSTORS	Standard
BUILT-IN CHILD SEAT	None
INSURANCE INJURY CLAIMS	

General Information

WHERE MADE	Japan/U.S.
YEAR OF PRODUCTION	Third
PARKING INDEX	Average
BUMPERS	Strong
THEFT RATING	
TWINS	Isuzu Oasis
DRIVE	Front

Specifications

FUEL ECONOMY (cty/hwy)	21/26	Average
DRIVING RANGE (miles)	396	Average
SEATING	7	
LENGTH (inches)	187.2	Average
HEAD/LEG ROOM (in.)	40.1/40.7	Average
INTERIOR SPACE (cu. ft.)		
CARGO SPACE (cu. ft.)	103	Average

Specifications may vary.

Prices

Model	Retail	Mkup
Odyssey	23,560	13%

Competition

	POOR GOOD	Pg.
Honda Odyssey		151
Dodge Caravan		130
Mazda MPV		172
Mercury Villager		182
Nissan Quest		190

Honda Prelude

There is change in the air for the 1997 Honda Prelude. Honda is designing the new Prelude to be a mix between luxury and performance with a more conservative look than in years past. Dual airbags and ABS are standard.

The only engine expected to be sold with the new Prelude will be a 2.2-liter 4-cylinder engine which will be capable of producing 190 hp, which is plenty to power this compact car. Expect the ride to be firm, yet comfortable and provide the driver and passengers with the feel of a sports car. Controls are expected to be more conventional for '97 and a larger trunk will make traveling more comfortable. Prices for the new Prelude are estimated to start in the low to mid-20's, so it certainly will be out of reach for many.

The Ratings

	POOR		GOOD
COMPARATIVE RATING *			
CRASH TEST			
SAFETY FEATURES		■	
FUEL ECONOMY			
PM COST	■		
REPAIR COST	■		
WARRANTY	■		
COMPLAINTS		■	
INSURANCE COST		■	

Safety

CRASH TEST	No government results
AIRBAGS	Dual
ABS	4-wheel
DAY. RUNNING LIGHTS	None
BELT ADJUSTORS	None
BUILT-IN CHILD SEAT	None
INSURANCE INJURY CLAIMS	

General Information

WHERE MADE	Japan
YEAR OF PRODUCTION	First
PARKING INDEX	Easy
BUMPERS	Strong
THEFT RATING	
TWINS	
DRIVE	Front

Specifications

FUEL ECONOMY (cty/hwy)	22/26	Average
DRIVING RANGE (miles)	366	Short
SEATING	4	
LENGTH (inches)	178.0	Short
HEAD/LEG ROOM (in.)	37.9/43.0	Average
INTERIOR SPACE (cu. ft.)	80	Cramped
CARGO SPACE (cu. ft.)	8	Very Small

Specifications may vary.

Prices**

Model	Retail	Mkup
Prelude S Coupe	19,760	13%
Prelude Si Coupe	22,430	13%
Prelude VTEC Coupe	25,620	13%
Prelude SE Coupe	23,650	13%

Competition

	POOR		GOOD	Pg.
Honda Prelude				152
Acura Integra	■			101
Eagle Talon	■			133
Mazda MX-6		■		173
Mitsubishi Eclipse	■			184

**1997 prices not available at press time. Prices based on 1996 data.

*Due to the importance of crash tests, cars with no results as of publication date cannot be given an overall rating.

Hyundai Accent

Available in 3- or 4-door coupes and sedans, the Accent is the smallest Hyundai and the only Hyundai for '97 without major changes. The front-wheel drive Accent is much improved over its predecessor, the Hyundai Excel, and it should give competitors a few worries. The Accent comes with dual airbags and ABS is available.

The 1.5-liter 4-cylinder engine that comes on all Accents is adequate for this light car and is fuel efficient. Although front seat occupants will be comfortable, passengers in the rear will feel cramped; choose the 4-door for more room. The Accent is just as powerful as the Toyota Tercel, but it's not quite as fuel efficient or as roomy as the Geo Metro and Suzuki Swift. Not outstanding in any one category, the Accent is a decent subcompact which offers a little bit of everything.

The Ratings

	POOR → GOOD
COMPARATIVE RATING	▪ (low)
CRASH TEST	▪ (mid)
SAFETY FEATURES	▪ (mid-high)
FUEL ECONOMY	▪ (mid-high)
PM COST	▪ (high)
REPAIR COST	▪ (high)
WARRANTY	▪ (low-mid)
COMPLAINTS	▪ (low-mid)
INSURANCE COST	▪ (poor)

Safety

CRASH TEST	Average
AIRBAGS	Dual
ABS	4-wheel (optional)
DAY. RUNNING LIGHTS	None
BELT ADJUSTORS	Standard
BUILT-IN CHILD SEAT	None
INSURANCE INJURY CLAIMS	

General Information

WHERE MADE	Korea
YEAR OF PRODUCTION	Third
PARKING INDEX	Very Easy
BUMPERS	Strong
THEFT RATING	
TWINS	
DRIVE	Front

Specifications

FUEL ECONOMY (cty/hwy)	28/37	Good
DRIVING RANGE (miles)	381	Average
SEATING	5	
LENGTH (inches)	162.1	Very Short
HEAD/LEG ROOM (in.)	38.7/42.6	Average
INTERIOR SPACE (cu. ft.)	88	Cramped
CARGO SPACE (cu. ft.)	13	Small

Specifications may vary.

Prices

Model	Retail	Mkup
Accent Coupe L	8,599	10%
Accent Coupe GS Man.	9,399	10%
Accent Sedan GL	9,799	10%
Accent Coupe GS Auto.	10,154	10%

Competition

	POOR → GOOD	Pg.
Hyundai Accent	▪ (low)	153
Chevrolet Cavalier	▪ (mid)	120
Dodge Neon	▪ (low)	132
Nissan Sentra	▪ (high)	191
Subaru Impreza	▪ (high)	209

Hyundai markets the Elantra as a high-level subcompact and, for 1997, it lives up to this distinction. Ride and comfort are good in this small car and, with refined insulation, it should be relatively quiet. You will find standard dual airbags which should help improve the average crash test rating it received last year. Unfortunately, you still have to pay extra for ABS.

The only engine offered will be a 1.8-liter 4 cylinder, not especially powerful but good enough to move this subcompact. The front seats are comfortable, but adults will feel cramped in the back. Handling has improved in '97 with sturdier front and rear subframes. Available in both a sedan and wagon, the Elantra comes with plenty of equipment packages to choose from. Of course, the low prices are what you expect from Hyundai and the Elantra is no exception.

The Ratings

	POOR GOOD
COMPARATIVE RATING	▪
CRASH TEST	▪
SAFETY FEATURES	▪
FUEL ECONOMY	▪
PM COST	▪
REPAIR COST	▪
WARRANTY	▪
COMPLAINTS	▪
INSURANCE COST	▪

Safety

CRASH TEST	Average
AIRBAGS	Dual
ABS	4-wheel (optional)
DAY. RUNNING LIGHTS	None
BELT ADJUSTORS	Standard
BUILT-IN CHILD SEAT	None
INSURANCE INJURY CLAIMS	Very High

General Information

WHERE MADE	Korea
YEAR OF PRODUCTION	Second
PARKING INDEX	Very Easy
BUMPERS	Strong
THEFT RATING	
TWINS	
DRIVE	Front

Specifications

FUEL ECONOMY (cty/hwy)	24/32	Average
DRIVING RANGE (miles)	392	Average
SEATING	5	
LENGTH (inches)	174.0	Short
HEAD/LEG ROOM (in.)	38.6/43.2	Roomy
INTERIOR SPACE (cu. ft.)	93	Average
CARGO SPACE (cu. ft.)	12	Small

Specifications may vary.

Prices

Model	Retail	Mkup
Elantra	11,099	11%
Elantra Wagon	11,899	11%
Elantra GLS	12,549	11%
Elantra GLS Wagon	13,999	11%

Competition

	POOR GOOD	Pg.
Hyundai Elantra	▪	154
Dodge Neon	▪	132
Honda Civic	▪	149
Nissan Sentra	▪	191
Toyota Tercel	▪	220

Hyundai Sonata

Refined both inside and out, the Sonata delivers more to the consumer than is expected. The Sonata, all-new in 1995, receives new front and rear panels for '97. The wheelbase on the Sonata is slightly longer than most other intermediate cars, resulting in a little more leg room inside. A refined interior helps make the ride more comfortable. ABS will cost extra, but dual airbags are standard.

The base comes with an adequately powered 2-liter engine. The 3-liter that is standard on the GLS gives more horsepower. With added insulation, the Sonata should do a good job at keeping the road noise down. The Sonata's low sticker price makes it very attractive. There is plenty of interior space, but not much room for luggage. Interestingly, over 85% of the Sonata is recyclable and no harmful CFCs were used in the manufacturing process.

The Ratings

	POOR — GOOD
COMPARATIVE RATING	■
CRASH TEST *	■
SAFETY FEATURES	■
FUEL ECONOMY	■
PM COST	■
REPAIR COST	■
WARRANTY	■
COMPLAINTS	■
INSURANCE COST	■

Safety

CRASH TEST	Average
AIRBAGS	Dual
ABS	4-wheel (optional)
DAY. RUNNING LIGHTS	None
BELT ADJUSTORS	Standard
BUILT-IN CHILD SEAT	None
INSURANCE INJURY CLAIMS	

General Information

WHERE MADE	Korea
YEAR OF PRODUCTION	Third
PARKING INDEX	Easy
BUMPERS	Strong
THEFT RATING	Low
TWINS	
DRIVE	Front

Specifications

FUEL ECONOMY (cty/hwy)	21/28	Average
DRIVING RANGE (miles)	413	Average
SEATING	5	
LENGTH (inches)	185.0	Average
HEAD/LEG ROOM (in.)	38.5/43.3	Roomy
INTERIOR SPACE (cu. ft.)	101	Roomy
CARGO SPACE (cu. ft.)	13	Small

Specifications may vary.

Prices

Model	Retail	Mkup
Sonata	14,749	12%
Sonata GL	16,349	12%
Sonata GL V6	17,349	12%
Sonata GLS	18,549	12%

Competition

	POOR — GOOD	Pg.
Hyundai Sonata	■	155
Ford Contour	■	137
Mercury Mystique	■	179
Olds Cut. Supreme	■	196
VW Golf/Jetta	■	221

*A version of this vehicle is scheduled to be tested later this year. Results are expected to be equal or better.

Hyundai Tiburon

Hyundai's newest car, based on the Elantra, closely resembles the exterior styling of the Toyota Celica and the interior designs of the Mitsubishi Eclipse and Ford Probe. This is no surprise since the Tiburon is Hyundai's challenge to more established coupes like the Celica and Probe. Dual airbags are standard features, but you pay extra for ABS.

Powering this all-new coupe will be a pair of engines, a 1.8-liter and a 2.0-liter which produce 130 and 138 horsepower, respectively. Hyundai held nothing back in designing the Tiburon—the suspension is rumored to have been tuned by engineers at Porsche. Expect the ride to be good on smooth roads; get onto something bumpy and you won't have much fun. The controls are well placed and easy to read. Price will help sell this car, too—the base starts around $13,000.

The Ratings

	POOR	GOOD
COMPARATIVE RATING*		
CRASH TEST		
SAFETY FEATURES		███
FUEL ECONOMY	██	
PM COST		██
REPAIR COST		██
WARRANTY	██	
COMPLAINTS	██	
INSURANCE COST	██	

Safety

CRASH TEST	No government results
AIRBAGS	Dual
ABS	4-wheel (optional)
DAY. RUNNING LIGHTS	None
BELT ADJUSTORS	Standard
BUILT-IN CHILD SEAT	None
INSURANCE INJURY CLAIMS	

General Information

WHERE MADE	Korea
YEAR OF PRODUCTION	First
PARKING INDEX	Very Easy
BUMPERS	Strong
THEFT RATING	
TWINS	
DRIVE	Front

Specifications

FUEL ECONOMY (cty/hwy)	22/30	Average
DRIVING RANGE (miles)	363	Short
SEATING	5	
LENGTH (inches)	170.9	Very Short
HEAD/LEG ROOM (in.)	38.0/43.1	Average
INTERIOR SPACE (cu. ft.)	80	Cramped
CARGO SPACE (cu. ft.)	13	Small

Specifications may vary.

Prices

Model	Retail	Mkup
Tiburon	13,499	10%
Tiburon FX	14,899	10%

Competition

	POOR	GOOD	Pg.
Hyundai Tiburon			156
Chevrolet Cavalier		██	120
Honda Civic	██		149
Hyundai Elantra	██		154
Nissan Sentra		██	191

*Due to the importance of crash tests, cars with no results as of publication date cannot be given an overall rating.

Infiniti I30

Large

The Ratings

	POOR → GOOD
COMPARATIVE RATING	above average
CRASH TEST	average
SAFETY FEATURES	good
FUEL ECONOMY	below average
PM COST	average
REPAIR COST	poor
WARRANTY	very good
COMPLAINTS	below average
INSURANCE COST	below average

Basically a fully-loaded Nissan Maxima, the I30 is the second cheapest Infiniti that you can buy. It sells for just a bit more than the G20, just a bit less than the J30, with the Q45 topping them all. The I30, a mid-sized luxury car, offers a comfortable ride and is geared to performance. As you would expect, dual airbags and 4-wheel ABS are standard.

Like the Maxima, the I30 is powered by a 3.0-liter V6 engine, which is powerful enough to please most people. Fuel economy for this heavy car will be slightly lower than the Maxima, but still competitive with other mid-sized luxury cars. With a very rigid body shell, driver and passengers will move in comfort; the controls and gauges are easy to read and use. The numerous options are expensive so choose carefully. If you can live without the name-plate, consider a Maxima.

Safety

CRASH TEST	Average
AIRBAGS	Dual
ABS	4-wheel
DAY. RUNNING LIGHTS	None
BELT ADJUSTORS	Standard
BUILT-IN CHILD SEAT	None
INSURANCE INJURY CLAIMS	

General Information

WHERE MADE	Japan
YEAR OF PRODUCTION	Second
PARKING INDEX	Easy
BUMPERS	Strong
THEFT RATING	
TWINS	Nissan Maxima
DRIVE	Front

Specifications

FUEL ECONOMY (cty/hwy)	21/28	Average
DRIVING RANGE (miles)	463	Very Long
SEATING	5	
LENGTH (inches)	189.6	Average
HEAD/LEG ROOM (in.)	40.1/43.9	Very Roomy
INTERIOR SPACE (cu. ft.)	100	Roomy
CARGO SPACE (cu. ft.)	14	Average

Specifications may vary.

Prices

Model	Retail	Mkup
I30 Standard	28,800	12%
I30 Leather	29,900	12%
I30 Touring	31,500	12%

Competition

	POOR → GOOD	Pg.
Infiniti I30	above average	157
Audi A6	very good	105
BMW 3-Series	below average	106
Mazda Millenia	average	171
Oldsmobile Aurora	below average	194

157

Infiniti J30

The J30, which looks like a Jaguar, changes little for 1997 with the most significant changes being additional color choices. The fluid style of the car is a nice break from the traditional low front/high rear styling that is seen on many larger cars today. All models feature dual airbags and ABS.

The 3-liter V6 is more than powerful enough and provides average fuel economy for a car this size. Ride is smooth on most roads, but handling isn't as responsive as the Jaguar styling suggests. The touring package, sold as the J30t, comes with firmer springs, 4-wheel steering, a spoiler on the trunk and a price tag that's $2,000 higher. The J30 focuses on luxurious accommodation for two up-front and adults in the rear seat will not be comfortable. Instruments and controls are very nice, but trunk space is tight.

The Ratings

	POOR → GOOD
COMPARATIVE RATING	■ (near good)
CRASH TEST	■ (mid)
SAFETY FEATURES	■ (mid-high)
FUEL ECONOMY	■ (poor)
PM COST	■ (mid-high)
REPAIR COST	■ (poor)
WARRANTY	■ (good)
COMPLAINTS	■ (good)
INSURANCE COST	■ (low)

Safety

CRASH TEST	Good
AIRBAGS	Dual
ABS	4-wheel
DAY. RUNNING LIGHTS	None
BELT ADJUSTORS	Standard
BUILT-IN CHILD SEAT	None
INSURANCE INJURY CLAIMS	Average

General Information

WHERE MADE	Japan
YEAR OF PRODUCTION	Fifth
PARKING INDEX	Average
BUMPERS	Strong
THEFT RATING	Very High
TWINS	
DRIVE	Rear

Specifications

FUEL ECONOMY (cty/hwy)	18/23	Poor
DRIVING RANGE (miles)	399	Average
SEATING	5	
LENGTH (inches)	191.3	Long
HEAD/LEG ROOM (in.)	37.7/41.3	Vry. Cramped
INTERIOR SPACE (cu. ft.)	87	Cramped
CARGO SPACE (cu. ft.)	10	Very Small

Specifications may vary.

Prices

Model	Retail	Mkup
J30 Luxury Sports Sedan	35,750	13%

Competition

	POOR → GOOD	Pg.
Infiniti J30	■ (good)	158
Audi A6	■ (good)	105
Lexus GS300	■ (mid-high)	163
Mazda Millenia	■ (mid)	171
Oldsmobile Aurora	■ (poor)	194

Infiniti Q45

This is the second generation for the Q45 and Infiniti is hoping that this version does better than the first. The Q45 first debuted in 1989 with a very unusual ad campaign and an equally unusually styled car. Since then, Infiniti has toned the Q45 down and, today, it resembles a conservative large-luxury sedan. Performance is still the strong point of the Q45 and dual airbags and 4-wheel ABS lead the list of safety features.

Tipping the scales at 3,900 pounds, Infiniti needed to find an engine powerful enough to move the Q45. They found it in a 4.1 liter V8 which produces over 260 horsepower. Not a bad find. Plushness and comfort are what you would expect from the top of the luxury line and ride will be as smooth as silk, though not bouncy or floaty like other large cars. This new conservative luxury sedan is among the best.

The Ratings

	POOR ... GOOD
COMPARATIVE RATING*	
CRASH TEST	
SAFETY FEATURES	
FUEL ECONOMY	
PM COST	
REPAIR COST	
WARRANTY	
COMPLAINTS	
INSURANCE COST	

Safety

CRASH TEST	No government results
AIRBAGS	Dual
ABS	4-wheel
DAY. RUNNING LIGHTS	None
BELT ADJUSTORS	Standard
BUILT-IN CHILD SEAT	None
INSURANCE INJURY CLAIMS	

General Information

WHERE MADE	Japan
YEAR OF PRODUCTION	First
PARKING INDEX	Average
BUMPERS	Strong
THEFT RATING	
TWINS	
DRIVE	Rear

Specifications

FUEL ECONOMY (cty/hwy)	18/24	Poor
DRIVING RANGE (miles)	443	Long
SEATING	5	
LENGTH (inches)	199.2	Long
HEAD/LEG ROOM (in.)	37.6/43.6	Average
INTERIOR SPACE (cu. ft.)	97	Average
CARGO SPACE (cu. ft.)	13	Small

Specifications may vary.

Prices

Model	Retail	Mkup
Q45	47,900	19%
Q45 T	49,900	19%

Competition

	POOR ... GOOD	Pg.
Infiniti Q45		159
Acura TL		103
Cadillac Seville		117
Infiniti J30		158
Lexus GS300		163

*Due to the importance of crash tests, cars with no results as of publication date cannot be given an overall rating.

Isuzu Oasis

The first minivan for Isuzu is not really Isuzu's creation, but Honda's. Just as Honda sells Isuzu's Rodeo as the Passport, Isuzu now sells Honda's Odyssey as the Oasis. Like the Odyssey, the Oasis is designed to be more like a car than a minivan. With a wide stance and low ground clearance, the Oasis drives much like a car and also has conventional doors instead of a sliding door like the rest of its minivan competition. Dual airbags and ABS are standard. Photo is from '96.

The power comes from a 2.2-liter 4-cylinder engine which is only adequate, but unfortunately, there are no other engine choices. The middle seat in the Oasis does not come out, and the rear seat cleverly folds into the floor, but not quite flush, making the loading surface uneven. As a result, cargo space is not as generous as the competition, but head and leg room are competitive.

The Ratings

	POOR GOOD
COMPARATIVE RATING	■ (center)
CRASH TEST	■ (good side)
SAFETY FEATURES	■ (good side)
FUEL ECONOMY	■ (center)
PM COST	■ (poor side)
REPAIR COST	■ (poor side)
WARRANTY	■ (good side)
COMPLAINTS	■ (center)
INSURANCE COST	■ (center)

Safety

CRASH TEST	Good
AIRBAGS	Dual
ABS	4-wheel
DAY. RUNNING LIGHTS	None
BELT ADJUSTORS	Standard
BUILT-IN CHILD SEAT	None
INSURANCE INJURY CLAIMS	

General Information

WHERE MADE	Japan
YEAR OF PRODUCTION	Second
PARKING INDEX	Average
BUMPERS	Strong
THEFT RATING	
TWINS	Honda Odyssey
DRIVE	Front

Specifications

FUEL ECONOMY (cty/hwy)	21/26	Average
DRIVING RANGE (miles)	396	Average
SEATING	7	
LENGTH (inches)	187.2	Average
HEAD/LEG ROOM (in.)	40.1/40.7	Average
INTERIOR SPACE (cu. ft.)		
CARGO SPACE (cu. ft.)	46	Very Small

Specifications may vary.

Prices**

Model	Retail	Mkup
Oasis S	23,495	10%
Oasis LS	25,990	10%

Competition

	POOR GOOD	Pg.
Isuzu Oasis	■ (center)	160
Ford Windstar	■ (poor side)	144
Mazda MPV	■ (poor side)	172
Nissan Quest	■ (good side)	190
Plymouth Voyager	■ (center)	198

**1997 prices not available at press time. Prices based on 1996 data.

Kia Sephia

Kia, the Korean manufacturer that has been making models for Ford, is the first new manufacturer in the U.S. in several years. The Kia Sephia (it rhymes) first came out in 1994 and enters 1997 with only minor changes. The Sephia comes standard with dual airbags and optional ABS. Photo is from 1996.

To power this car, Kia has equipped the Sephia with an impressive 1.8-liter, 4-cylinder engine which can produce 122 hp. The Sephia comes in several trim levels: RS, LS, and GS — but unfortunately, it is only available in one body style, a sedan, unlike the Sephia's competitors. The styling is similar to the old Mazda 323, which should not be too surprising, as Mazda is part-owner of Kia. The Sephia could be a major player in the small sedan market, especially with its attractive price tag.

The Ratings

	POOR ⟷ GOOD
COMPARATIVE RATING *	(no rating)
CRASH TEST	(no rating)
SAFETY FEATURES	▣ (above average)
FUEL ECONOMY	▣ (above average)
PM COST	▣ (above average)
REPAIR COST	▣ (below average)
WARRANTY	▣ (average)
COMPLAINTS	▣ (below average)
INSURANCE COST	▣ (poor)

Safety

CRASH TEST	No government results
AIRBAGS	Dual
ABS	4-wheel (optional)
DAY. RUNNING LIGHTS	None
BELT ADJUSTORS	Standard
BUILT-IN CHILD SEAT	None
INSURANCE INJURY CLAIMS	

General Information

WHERE MADE	Korea/Japan
YEAR OF PRODUCTION	Fourth
PARKING INDEX	Very Easy
BUMPERS	Weak
THEFT RATING	Very Low
TWINS	
DRIVE	Front

Specifications

FUEL ECONOMY (cty/hwy)	28/34	Good
DRIVING RANGE (miles)	394	Average
SEATING	5	
LENGTH (inches)	171.7	Very Short
HEAD/LEG ROOM (in.)	38.2/42.9	Average
INTERIOR SPACE (cu. ft.)	93	Average
CARGO SPACE (cu. ft.)	11	Small

Specifications may vary.

Prices**

Model	Retail	Mkup
Sephia	9,495	11%

Competition

	POOR ⟷ GOOD	Pg.
Kia Sephia	(no rating)	161
Dodge Neon	▣ (poor)	132
Geo Prizm	▣ (good)	147
Hyundai Elantra	▣ (below average)	154
Nissan Sentra	▣ (good)	191

**1997 prices not available at press time. Prices based on 1996 data.

*Due to the importance of crash tests, cars with no results as of publication date cannot be given an overall rating.

Lexus ES300

Built on the same platform as the Toyota Camry, this top seller for Lexus enters 1997 with a slightly new look and a refined interior. The ES300 is able to reduce costs by using the same basic body style as the mass-produced Camry, thus keeping prices low and sales high—a winning combination. The changes for '97 are not readily apparent, but you will appreciate the increase in interior room. Dual airbags and 4-wheel ABS are standard.

The standard engine for the ES300 is the optional engine on the Camry, a 3.0 liter V6 which produces 200 horsepower. Head and leg room have increased, making the cabin more comfortable. Noise and vibration are kept to a minimum and handling is responsive. Unlike the Camry, the ES does not have a fold-down rear seat. The ES300 is a solid, affordable luxury sedan.

The Ratings

	POOR	GOOD
COMPARATIVE RATING*		
CRASH TEST		
SAFETY FEATURES		
FUEL ECONOMY		
PM COST		
REPAIR COST		
WARRANTY		
COMPLAINTS		
INSURANCE COST		

Safety

CRASH TEST	No government results
AIRBAGS	Dual
ABS	4-wheel
DAY. RUNNING LIGHTS	None
BELT ADJUSTORS	Standard
BUILT-IN CHILD SEAT	None
INSURANCE INJURY CLAIMS	

General Information

WHERE MADE	Japan/U.S.
YEAR OF PRODUCTION	First
PARKING INDEX	Average
BUMPERS	Strong
THEFT RATING	
TWINS	Toyota Camry
DRIVE	Front

Specifications

FUEL ECONOMY (cty/hwy)	19/26	Poor
DRIVING RANGE (miles)	407	Average
SEATING	5	
LENGTH (inches)	190.2	Average
HEAD/LEG ROOM (in.)	38.0/43.5	Average
INTERIOR SPACE (cu. ft.)	92	Average
CARGO SPACE (cu. ft.)	13	Small

Specifications may vary.

Prices

Model	Retail	Mkup
ES300	30,395	18%

Competition

	POOR	GOOD	Pg.
Lexus ES300			162
BMW 3-Series			106
Infiniti J30			158
Saab 9000			206
Volvo 850			223

*Due to the importance of crash tests, cars with no results as of publication date cannot be given an overall rating.

Lexus GS300

The GS300 has not changed since it was introduced in 1993, but the styling is by no means outdated. The GS300 bridges the nearly $20,000 gap between the entry-level ES300 and the luxurious LS400. It has done this nicely and become a popular luxury car. As can be expected, dual airbags and ABS are standard.

The GS300 is powered by a gas-guzzling 3-liter, 6-cylinder engine that will provide more than enough power for any driver. The 5-speed automatic transmission was redesigned last year and it makes driving the GS300 more enjoyable. The GS300 emphasizes a smooth, silent ride for two front-seat passengers; rear-seat occupants will be cramped. You can find less expensive cars with the GS300's luxurious feel—consider the BMW 3-Series, or save even more money and look at a Bonneville, Volvo 850 or Taurus SHO.

The Ratings

	POOR ... GOOD
COMPARATIVE RATING	
CRASH TEST	
SAFETY FEATURES	
FUEL ECONOMY	
PM COST	
REPAIR COST	
WARRANTY	
COMPLAINTS	
INSURANCE COST	

Safety

CRASH TEST	Average
AIRBAGS	Dual
ABS	4-wheel
DAY. RUNNING LIGHTS	None
BELT ADJUSTORS	Standard
BUILT-IN CHILD SEAT	None
INSURANCE INJURY CLAIMS	Average

General Information

WHERE MADE	Japan
YEAR OF PRODUCTION	Fourth
PARKING INDEX	Average
BUMPERS	Strong
THEFT RATING	Very High
TWINS	
DRIVE	Rear

Specifications

FUEL ECONOMY (cty/hwy)	18/24	Poor
DRIVING RANGE (miles)	422	Long
SEATING	5	
LENGTH (inches)	194.9	Long
HEAD/LEG ROOM (in.)	38.3/44.0	Roomy
INTERIOR SPACE (cu. ft.)	97	Average
CARGO SPACE (cu. ft.)	13	Small

Specifications may vary.

Prices

Model	Retail	Mkup
GS300	46,195	17%

Competition

	POOR ... GOOD	Pg.
Lexus GS300		163
Audi A6		105
BMW 3-Series		106
Merc.-Bz C-Class		175
Volvo 850		223

The LS400, Lexus's flagship sedan, has an important addition for 1997—side airbags for both the driver and front passenger. These new side airbags teamed with the previously standard dual airbags and 4-wheel ABS make the LS400 one of the safest cars on the road.

The engine that powers this large car is a 4.0-liter V8, helping make the LS400 one of the quickest luxury cars around. Fuel economy in the city, though certainly not great, is surprising for a car in this size class. You'll find a very smooth ride and an extremely roomy rear seat. But, trunk space is rather small when compared to other large cars. With all its standard features and its powerful engine, the LS400 is worth the money; that is, if you can afford it. If you can't, don't despair—you can easily find what you're looking for in something less expensive.

The Ratings

	POOR → GOOD
COMPARATIVE RATING*	(no rating)
CRASH TEST	(no rating)
SAFETY FEATURES	good
FUEL ECONOMY	poor
PM COST	good
REPAIR COST	poor
WARRANTY	mid
COMPLAINTS	good
INSURANCE COST	good

Safety

CRASH TEST	No government results
AIRBAGS	Dual
ABS	4-wheel
DAY. RUNNING LIGHTS	None
BELT ADJUSTORS	Standard
BUILT-IN CHILD SEAT	None
INSURANCE INJURY CLAIMS	

General Information

WHERE MADE	Japan
YEAR OF PRODUCTION	Third
PARKING INDEX	Easy
BUMPERS	Weak
THEFT RATING	
TWINS	
DRIVE	Rear

Specifications

FUEL ECONOMY (cty/hwy)	19/25	Poor
DRIVING RANGE (miles)	495	Very Long
SEATING	5	
LENGTH (inches)	196.7	Long
HEAD/LEG ROOM (in.)	38.9/43.7	Roomy
INTERIOR SPACE (cu. ft.)	102	Roomy
CARGO SPACE (cu. ft.)	14	Average

Specifications may vary.

Prices

Model	Retail	Mkup
LS400	53,395	19%

Competition

	POOR → GOOD	Pg.
Lexus LS400	(no rating)	164
Acura TL	poor	103
Cadillac Seville	good	117
Infiniti J30	good	158
Lincoln Town Car	good	168

*Due to the importance of crash tests, cars with no results as of publication date cannot be given an overall rating.

Lexus SC300/400

These two luxuriously-equipped coupes differ only in standard engines and luxury appointments; many items standard on the more expensive SC400 will cost extra on the SC300. Other than subtle front- and rear-end styling updates, both models receive few changes for 1997. The new styling updates give the SC a more muscular appearance. All SC models have dual airbags and ABS.

The SC300 shares a powerful 3-liter 6-cylinder engine with the GS300 and Toyota Supra. For about $11,000 more, you can step up to the SC400, with the 4-liter V8, from the big Lexus LS400. Be sure to get traction control. Handling is excellent, and ride is comfortably firm. The front seats are close to ideal for people of the right size, but check them out before you buy. Back seat is for kids only, and the trunk is skimpy. The instrument panel and controls are well designed.

The Ratings

	POOR GOOD
COMPARATIVE RATING*	
CRASH TEST	
SAFETY FEATURES	
FUEL ECONOMY	
PM COST	
REPAIR COST	
WARRANTY	
COMPLAINTS	
INSURANCE COST	

Safety

CRASH TEST	No government results
AIRBAGS	Dual
ABS	4-wheel
DAY. RUNNING LIGHTS	None
BELT ADJUSTORS	None
BUILT-IN CHILD SEAT	None
INSURANCE INJURY CLAIMS	Low

General Information

WHERE MADE	Japan
YEAR OF PRODUCTION	Sixth
PARKING INDEX	Average
BUMPERS	Weak
THEFT RATING	Very High
TWINS	
DRIVE	Rear

Specifications

FUEL ECONOMY (cty/hwy)	18/24	Poor
DRIVING RANGE (miles)	412	Average
SEATING	4	
LENGTH (inches)	192.5	Long
HEAD/LEG ROOM (in.)	38.3/44.1	Roomy
INTERIOR SPACE (cu. ft.)	85	Cramped
CARGO SPACE (cu. ft.)	9	Very Small

Specifications may vary.

Prices

Model	Retail	Mkup
SC300	39,900	15%
SC400	50,800	15%

Competition

	POOR GOOD	Pg.
Lexus SC300/400		165
Infiniti J30		158
Mercury Cougar		177
Saab 900		205
Volvo 850		223

*Due to the importance of crash tests, cars with no results as of publication date cannot be given an overall rating.

Lincoln Continental

This big front wheel drive car enters 1997 with an uncertain future and few changes since its 1995 overhaul. Ford has scheduled a facelift for the 1998 model; however, what the Continental will become at the turn of the century is still unknown. Dual airbags and ABS are standard.

As you would expect, it takes a large engine to move such a heavy car (almost 2 tons) and that's why Ford installed the huge 4.6-liter V8 engine. It does a good job in accelerating; but, as you would expect with such a large car and such a large engine, fuel economy is poor. Most anything you'll want comes standard, including a computer that stores each driver's seat position and radio stations. Heated seats and traction control are among the few options. There will be plenty of room for five passengers and their luggage.

The Ratings

	POOR	GOOD
COMPARATIVE RATING*		
CRASH TEST		
SAFETY FEATURES		
FUEL ECONOMY		
PM COST		
REPAIR COST		
WARRANTY		
COMPLAINTS		
INSURANCE COST		

Safety

CRASH TEST	No government results
AIRBAGS	Dual
ABS	4-wheel
DAY. RUNNING LIGHTS	None
BELT ADJUSTORS	Standard
BUILT-IN CHILD SEAT	None
INSURANCE INJURY CLAIMS	

General Information

WHERE MADE	U.S.
YEAR OF PRODUCTION	Third
PARKING INDEX	Hard
BUMPERS	Strong
THEFT RATING	
TWINS	
DRIVE	Front

Specifications

FUEL ECONOMY (cty/hwy)	17/25	Poor
DRIVING RANGE (miles)	356	Short
SEATING	5/6	
LENGTH (inches)	206.3	Very Long
HEAD/LEG ROOM (in.)	39.0/41.9	Average
INTERIOR SPACE (cu. ft.)	102	Roomy
CARGO SPACE (cu. ft.)	18	Large

Specifications may vary.

Prices

Model	Retail	Mkup
Continental	37,950	11%

Competition

	POOR	GOOD	Pg.
Lincoln Continental			166
Acura TL			103
Cadillac Seville			117
Mazda Millenia			171
Merc.-Bz C-Class			175

*Due to the importance of crash tests, cars with no results as of publication date cannot be given an overall rating.

Lincoln Mark VIII

The Mark VIII is based on the same chassis as the Mercury Cougar and Ford Thunderbird; however, unlike its twins, the Mark VIII did not receive a facelift last year. Instead, the Mark VIII receives a facelift for 1997 which should help increase Lincoln's dropping sales. The '97 Mark VIII has distinctive styling, inside and out, and a slightly better ride than its twins. Dual airbags and ABS are standard, and traction control is optional.

This two-ton car comes in only one well-equipped version, though you can add about $4,000 worth of options to the sticker price. The modular 4.6-liter V8 engine is smooth and quite powerful. The ride is outstanding on smooth roads. There's room for four, but the rear seat is tight. The Thunderbird SC may be a better buy if you can live without the Lincoln name and distinctive style.

The Ratings

	POOR → GOOD
COMPARATIVE RATING	Good
CRASH TEST	Good
SAFETY FEATURES	Above Average
FUEL ECONOMY	Poor
PM COST	Above Average
REPAIR COST	Below Average
WARRANTY	Average
COMPLAINTS	Average
INSURANCE COST	Good

Safety

CRASH TEST	Very Good
AIRBAGS	Dual
ABS	4-wheel
DAY. RUNNING LIGHTS	None
BELT ADJUSTORS	None
BUILT-IN CHILD SEAT	None
INSURANCE INJURY CLAIMS	Very Low

General Information

WHERE MADE	U.S.
YEAR OF PRODUCTION	Fifth
PARKING INDEX	Average
BUMPERS	Strong
THEFT RATING	Very High
TWINS	Ford T-bird, Merc. Cougar
DRIVE	Rear

Specifications

FUEL ECONOMY (cty/hwy)	18/26	Poor
DRIVING RANGE (miles)	378	Short
SEATING	5	
LENGTH (inches)	207.3	Very Long
HEAD/LEG ROOM (in.)	38.1/42.6	Average
INTERIOR SPACE (cu. ft.)	102	Roomy
CARGO SPACE (cu. ft.)	14	Average

Specifications may vary.

Prices

Model	Retail	Mkup
Mark VIII	37,950	11%
Mark VIII LSC	39,550	11%

Competition

	POOR → GOOD	Pg.
Lincoln Mark VIII	Good	167
Infiniti J30	Good	158
Mercury Cougar	Average	177
Saab 9000	Average	206
Volvo 850	Good	223

Lincoln Town Car

The Town Car, which shares the Ford Crown Victoria/Mercury Grand Marquis chassis, is the largest of the three Lincoln cars. One of the few large American-made, rear wheel drive cars, the Town Car's very well-equipped. Optional extras include heated outside mirrors with position memory tied into the seat position memory buttons, as well as traction control. Dual airbags and ABS are standard on all models.

Typical of American luxury cars, the Town Car's ride is smooth and quiet, and not for speedy corners or sudden maneuvers. The 4.6-liter V8 is smooth, responsive and fairly fuel-efficient for its class. These big cars truly provide room for six and an immense trunk. Seats are comfortable and noise levels are very low. The Town Car is a good, large luxury car.

The Ratings

	POOR	GOOD
COMPARATIVE RATING		■
CRASH TEST		■
SAFETY FEATURES		■
FUEL ECONOMY	■	
PM COST		■
REPAIR COST		■
WARRANTY		■
COMPLAINTS		■
INSURANCE COST	■	

Safety

CRASH TEST	Very Good
AIRBAGS	Dual
ABS	4-wheel
DAY. RUNNING LIGHTS	None
BELT ADJUSTORS	Standard
BUILT-IN CHILD SEAT	None
INSURANCE INJURY CLAIMS	Very Low

General Information

WHERE MADE	U.S.
YEAR OF PRODUCTION	Eighth
PARKING INDEX	Very Hard
BUMPERS	Strong
THEFT RATING	Very High
TWINS	Cr. Victoria, Gr. Marquis
DRIVE	Rear

Specifications

FUEL ECONOMY (cty/hwy)	17/25	Poor
DRIVING RANGE (miles)	400	Average
SEATING	6	
LENGTH (inches)	218.9	Very Long
HEAD/LEG ROOM (in.)	39.1/42.6	Roomy
INTERIOR SPACE (cu. ft.)	116	Very Roomy
CARGO SPACE (cu. ft.)	22	Very Large

Specifications may vary.

Prices

Model	Retail	Mkup
Town Car	37,950	13%
Town Car Signature	40,310	13%
Town Car Cartier	43,870	13%

Competition

	POOR	GOOD	Pg.
Lincoln Town Car		■	168
Cadillac Seville		■	117
Chrysler LHS	■		127
Mazda Millenia		■	171
Merc. Gr. Marquis		■	178

Mazda has positioned the 626 to be an alternative for the Accord/Camry buyers and, over the past few years, it has done pretty well. The 626 is built on the same assembly line as the MX-6 and the Probe, though it is more of a sedan than a sports car. Dual airbags are standard, but you'll have to pay extra for ABS.

Like most Japanese mid-sized cars, the base 626 has plenty of standard equipment. The base 2-liter, 4-cylinder engine is adequate and reasonably economical. For more power, consider the 2.5-liter V6 available on the LX and ES; this engine, however, requires premium fuel and gets worse mileage. Room, comfort and trunk space are adequate for four. With more room up front, slightly better crash test results and a smaller price tag than most of the competitors, the 626 does fairly well against the popular competition.

The Ratings

	POOR — GOOD
COMPARATIVE RATING	▮ (below middle)
CRASH TEST	▮ (good side)
SAFETY FEATURES	▮ (good side)
FUEL ECONOMY	▮ (good side)
PM COST	▮ (middle)
REPAIR COST	▮ (good side)
WARRANTY	▮ (poor side)
COMPLAINTS	▮ (middle)
INSURANCE COST	▮ (poor end)

Safety

CRASH TEST	Good
AIRBAGS	Dual
ABS	4-wheel (optional)
DAY. RUNNING LIGHTS	None
BELT ADJUSTORS	Standard
BUILT-IN CHILD SEAT	None
INSURANCE INJURY CLAIMS	Average

General Information

WHERE MADE	U.S./Japan
YEAR OF PRODUCTION	Fifth
PARKING INDEX	Easy
BUMPERS	Strong
THEFT RATING	Very Low
TWINS	
DRIVE	Front

Specifications

FUEL ECONOMY (cty/hwy)	26/34	Good
DRIVING RANGE (miles)	477	Very Long
SEATING	5	
LENGTH (inches)	184.4	Average
HEAD/LEG ROOM (in.)	39.2/43.5	Roomy
INTERIOR SPACE (cu. ft.)	97	Average
CARGO SPACE (cu. ft.)	14	Average

Specifications may vary.

Prices**

Model	Retail	Mkup
626 DX	15,495	9%
626 LX	17,695	12%
626 LX-V6	19,895	14%
626 ES	22,795	15%

Competition

	POOR — GOOD	Pg.
Mazda 626	▮ (below middle)	169
Buick Skylark	▮ (good side)	113
Ford Taurus	▮ (good side)	142
Honda Accord	▮ (poor side)	148
Nissan Altima	▮ (middle)	188

**1997 prices not available at press time. Prices based on 1996 data.

Mazda Miata

The Miata has been around for nine years, and there is no sign that this small sporty car will cease production anytime soon. It enters 1997 with only minor changes in models that are nearly identical to those sold in 1989. The big difference is that dual airbags are now standard and ABS is an expensive option.

The 1.8-liter, 4-cylinder powering this small car provides enough acceleration for most drivers. Brakes are good, even better with ABS. Controls and displays are sensibly designed. Fuel economy is just average and could be much better with only 2,200 pounds to haul. You won't get a soft, quiet ride, a spacious interior, or much of a trunk in a Miata, but you aren't be buying it for any of those reasons either. You'll get crisp, responsive handling, a peppy engine, and a real "top down" car.

The Ratings

	POOR — GOOD
COMPARATIVE RATING	■ (mid)
CRASH TEST	■ (mid)
SAFETY FEATURES	■ (high)
FUEL ECONOMY	■ (mid)
PM COST	■ (mid)
REPAIR COST	■ (mid)
WARRANTY	■ (low)
COMPLAINTS	■ (high)
INSURANCE COST	■ (mid)

Safety

CRASH TEST	Average
AIRBAGS	Dual
ABS	4-wheel (optional)
DAY. RUNNING LIGHTS	None
BELT ADJUSTORS	None
BUILT-IN CHILD SEAT	None
INSURANCE INJURY CLAIMS	Average

General Information

WHERE MADE	Japan
YEAR OF PRODUCTION	Eighth
PARKING INDEX	Very Easy
BUMPERS	Weak
THEFT RATING	Average
TWINS	
DRIVE	Rear

Specifications

FUEL ECONOMY (cty/hwy)	23/29	Average
DRIVING RANGE (miles)	330	Very Short
SEATING	2	
LENGTH (inches)	155.4	Very Short
HEAD/LEG ROOM (in.)	37.1/42.7	Cramped
INTERIOR SPACE (cu. ft.)	Not Available	
CARGO SPACE (cu. ft.)	4	Very Small

Specifications may vary.

Prices**

Model	Retail	Mkup
Miata MX-5	18,450	10%

Competition

	POOR — GOOD	Pg.
Mazda Miata	■ (mid)	170
Acura Integra	■ (low)	101
Eagle Talon	■ (very low)	133
Ford Probe	■ (high)	141
Mitsubishi Eclipse	■ (low)	184

**1997 prices not available at press time. Prices based on 1996 data.

Mazda Millenia

Mazda has turned its full attention to the Millenia this year after discontinuing the 929. It is hoping that the Millenia will pick up lost 929 sales and take sales away from its competition in the premium sedan market. Slight exterior and interior changes were made for 1997. Dual airbags and ABS are standard.

The standard 2.5-liter V6 found on the base model is more than adequate; however, the Millenia S comes with the more powerful and responsive "Miller-cycle," a supercharged version of the same engine. The base engine runs on regular fuel, while the S version requires premium fuel which will increase your operating costs. This front wheel drive sedan is slightly smaller than the old 929, though it still should be quite comfortable for 4 passengers, 5 in a pinch. The Millenia competes well in the luxury market.

The Ratings

	POOR — GOOD
COMPARATIVE RATING	
CRASH TEST	
SAFETY FEATURES	
FUEL ECONOMY	
PM COST	
REPAIR COST	
WARRANTY	
COMPLAINTS	
INSURANCE COST	

Safety

CRASH TEST	Very Good
AIRBAGS	Dual
ABS	4-wheel
DAY. RUNNING LIGHTS	None
BELT ADJUSTORS	Standard
BUILT-IN CHILD SEAT	None
INSURANCE INJURY CLAIMS	Average

General Information

WHERE MADE	Japan
YEAR OF PRODUCTION	Third
PARKING INDEX	Average
BUMPERS	Strong
THEFT RATING	High
TWINS	
DRIVE	Front

Specifications

FUEL ECONOMY (cty/hwy)	20/28	Average
DRIVING RANGE (miles)	432	Long
SEATING	5	
LENGTH (inches)	189.8	Average
HEAD/LEG ROOM (in.)	39.3/43.3	Roomy
INTERIOR SPACE (cu. ft.)	94	Average
CARGO SPACE (cu. ft.)	13	Small

Specifications may vary.

Prices**

Model	Retail	Mkup
Millenia	27,995	10%
Millenia w/Leather	31,995	10%
Millenia S	35,955	10%

Competition

	POOR — GOOD	Pg.
Mazda Millenia		171
BMW 3-Series		106
Merc.-Bz C-Class		175
Oldsmobile Aurora		194
Volvo 850		223

**1997 prices not available at press time. Prices based on 1996 data.

Mazda MPV

The Mazda MPV, which was unchanged for seven years, finally received an overhaul for 1996 and enters 1997 with a new lineup. What used to be the base level DX model has been discontinued, so there are now only two trim levels, the LX and EX. Dual airbags and 4-wheel ABS are standard.

There are plenty of options to choose from, among which are the choice of four captain's chairs or a bench seat which will raise the seating to eight. Fuel economy is poor; it gets even worse if you choose the optional 4-wheel drive over the standard rear-wheel drive. Brakes, handling and ride are inferior to most minivans. Like the Honda minivan, the MPV comes with swing-out sedan style side doors. Its lack of size and poor gas mileage makes the MPV a weak entry in a competitive minivan market.

The Ratings

	POOR — GOOD
COMPARATIVE RATING	▪ (below middle)
CRASH TEST	▪ (good)
SAFETY FEATURES	▪ (above middle)
FUEL ECONOMY	▪ (poor)
PM COST	▪ (middle)
REPAIR COST	▪ (below middle)
WARRANTY	▪ (middle)
COMPLAINTS	▪ (middle)
INSURANCE COST	▪ (middle)

Safety

CRASH TEST	Very Good
AIRBAGS	Dual
ABS	4-wheel
DAY. RUNNING LIGHTS	None
BELT ADJUSTORS	None
BUILT-IN CHILD SEAT	None
INSURANCE INJURY CLAIMS	Average

General Information

WHERE MADE	Japan
YEAR OF PRODUCTION	Ninth
PARKING INDEX	Easy
BUMPERS	Weak
THEFT RATING	High
TWINS	
DRIVE	Rear/All

Specifications

FUEL ECONOMY (cty/hwy)	16/21	Poor
DRIVING RANGE (miles)	372	Short
SEATING	7/8	
LENGTH (inches)	183.5	Average
HEAD/LEG ROOM (in.)	40.0/40.4	Cramped
INTERIOR SPACE (cu. ft.)		
CARGO SPACE (cu. ft.)	38	Very Small

Specifications may vary.

Prices **

Model	Retail	Mkup
MPV DX 2WD	21,795	10%
MPV LX 2WD	22,595	10%
MPV ES 2WD	24,995	10%
MPV LX 4WD	25,595	10%
MPV ES 4WD	27,895	10%

Competition

	POOR — GOOD	Pg.
Mazda MPV	▪ (below middle)	172
Chrysler T & C	▪ (middle)	129
Ford Windstar	▪ (poor)	144
Honda Odyssey	▪ (good)	151
Nissan Quest	▪ (middle)	190

**1997 prices not available at press time. Prices based on 1996 data.

Mazda MX-6

The MX-6, which shares a chassis with the Mazda 626 and Ford Probe, enters 1997 with a new role: to pick up some of the lost sales from the discontinued RX-7. That will be a very large challenge for the MX-6. The MX-6 approaches the size of the 626, though it really only seats two comfortably like the Probe. Dual airbags are standard; ABS is optional.

The base model has a long list of standard features and a 2-liter 4-cylinder engine. The up-level LS comes with a 2.5-liter V6 that is more powerful, though fuel economy suffers in comparison. Avoid the unpleasant, rough-shifting optional automatic transmission that the MX-6 shares with the 626. Driving position and front seat comfort are as good as the best sporty cars. The MX-6 is a top choice for 1997.

The Ratings

	POOR — GOOD
COMPARATIVE RATING	
CRASH TEST	
SAFETY FEATURES	
FUEL ECONOMY	
PM COST	
REPAIR COST	
WARRANTY	
COMPLAINTS	
INSURANCE COST	

Safety

CRASH TEST	Very Good
AIRBAGS	Dual
ABS	4-wheel (optional)
DAY. RUNNING LIGHTS	None
BELT ADJUSTORS	None
BUILT-IN CHILD SEAT	None
INSURANCE INJURY CLAIMS	Average

General Information

WHERE MADE	U.S./Japan
YEAR OF PRODUCTION	Fifth
PARKING INDEX	Easy
BUMPERS	Weak
THEFT RATING	Average
TWINS	Ford Probe
DRIVE	Front

Specifications

FUEL ECONOMY (cty/hwy)	26/34	Good
DRIVING RANGE (miles)	465	Very Long
SEATING	4	
LENGTH (inches)	181.5	Short
HEAD/LEG ROOM (in.)	38.1/44.0	Roomy
INTERIOR SPACE (cu. ft.)	79	Vry. Cramped
CARGO SPACE (cu. ft.)	12	Small

Specifications may vary.

Prices**

Model	Retail	Mkup
MX-6	19,795	10%
MX-6 LS	23,095	10%
MX-6 M	25,795	10%

Competition

	POOR — GOOD	Pg.
Mazda MX-6		173
Acura Integra		101
Eagle Talon		133
Ford Probe		141
Mitsubishi Eclipse		184

**1997 prices not available at press time. Prices based on 1996 data.

Mazda Protégé

The Protégé offers more room inside than you might expect from a subcompact car which has helped it become a popular subcompact. The Protégé was the replacement for the 323 and its larger size has produced a better riding car. Dual airbags are standard, and ABS can be found on higher models.

The Protégé comes only in sedan with three trim levels designed to meet individual needs. DX and LX models come standard with a 1.5-liter 4-cylinder engine that is relatively weak, although quite fuel efficient. The up-level ES comes with a 1.8-liter engine—more powerful, but less efficient. The Protégé is worth checking out in a crowded and tough subcompact market with the Honda Civic, and Nissan Sentra and also with its American competitors, the Dodge Neon and Chevrolet Cavalier.

The Ratings

	POOR	GOOD
COMPARATIVE RATING*		
CRASH TEST		
SAFETY FEATURES		
FUEL ECONOMY		
PM COST		
REPAIR COST		
WARRANTY		
COMPLAINTS		
INSURANCE COST		

Safety

CRASH TEST	No government results
AIRBAGS	Dual
ABS	4-wheel (optional)
DAY. RUNNING LIGHTS	None
BELT ADJUSTORS	Standard
BUILT-IN CHILD SEAT	None
INSURANCE INJURY CLAIMS	Very High

General Information

WHERE MADE	Japan
YEAR OF PRODUCTION	Third
PARKING INDEX	Very Easy
BUMPERS	Weak
THEFT RATING	Very Low
TWINS	
DRIVE	Front

Specifications

FUEL ECONOMY (cty/hwy)	30/37	Good
DRIVING RANGE (miles)	493	Very Long
SEATING	5	
LENGTH (inches)	174.8	Short
HEAD/LEG ROOM (in.)	39.2/42.2	Average
INTERIOR SPACE (cu. ft.)	95	Average
CARGO SPACE (cu. ft.)	13	Small

Specifications may vary.

Prices**

Model	Retail	Mkup
Protege DX	11,695	10%
Protege LX	13,095	11%
Protege ES	14,695	11%

Competition

	POOR	GOOD	Pg.
Mazda Protege			174
Geo Prizm			147
Honda Civic			149
Nissan Sentra			191
Toyota Tercel			220

**1997 prices not available at press time. Prices based on 1996 data.

174

*Due to the importance of crash tests, cars with no results as of publication date cannot be given an overall rating.

The Cougar could well be in its final year of production; Ford may use the Cougar as part of a joint venture with Mazda in 1998, based on the Contour/Mystique platform. However, for 1997, the Cougar carries on unchanged. Dual airbags are standard, but you'll have to pay extra for ABS.

The Cougar comes in one model, the XR7, which has just about everything you need. Engine choices are a 3.8-liter V6 and a 4.6-liter V8 with much more power. The Cougar's long wheelbase leads to a smooth ride and handling is average for a car this large. There are no optional suspensions to give you a more high-performance ride. Inside, there's room for four and plenty of luggage space. If you can live without the extras and the nameplate, the cheaper Thunderbird may be the way to go.

The Ratings

	POOR ··· GOOD
COMPARATIVE RATING	▓ (above average)
CRASH TEST	▓ (very good)
SAFETY FEATURES	▓ (good)
FUEL ECONOMY	▓ (below average)
PM COST	▓ (average)
REPAIR COST	▓ (below average)
WARRANTY	▓ (poor)
COMPLAINTS	▓ (poor)
INSURANCE COST	▓ (good)

Safety

CRASH TEST	Very Good
AIRBAGS	Dual
ABS	4-wheel (optional)
DAY. RUNNING LIGHTS	None
BELT ADJUSTORS	None
BUILT-IN CHILD SEAT	None
INSURANCE INJURY CLAIMS	Average

General Information

WHERE MADE	U.S.
YEAR OF PRODUCTION	Ninth
PARKING INDEX	Average
BUMPERS	Strong
THEFT RATING	Low
TWINS	Ford T-bird, Linc. Mark VIII
DRIVE	Rear

Specifications

FUEL ECONOMY (cty/hwy)	18/26	Poor
DRIVING RANGE (miles)	378	Short
SEATING	5	
LENGTH (inches)	199.9	Long
HEAD/LEG ROOM (in.)	38.1/42.5	Average
INTERIOR SPACE (cu. ft.)	102	Roomy
CARGO SPACE (cu. ft.)	15	Average

Specifications may vary.

Prices

Model	Retail	Mkup
Cougar XR7	18,340	9%

Competition

	POOR ··· GOOD	Pg.
Mercury Cougar	▓	177
Chev. Monte Carlo	▓	123
Chrysler Sebring	▓	128
Ford Thunderbird	▓	143
Mazda MX-6	▓	173

Based on the same chassis as the Ford Crown Victoria and the Lincoln Town Car, the Grand Marquis, a rear wheel drive car, gets a new life for 1997. While there are no major changes, the Grand Marquis and its twins are now one of a kind as GM discontinued its large rear wheel drive cars last year. The Grand Marquis comes in two versions and the less expensive GS is quite well equipped. No matter which you get, you'll have to pay extra for ABS; dual airbags are standard.

The 4.6-liter V8 is responsive and powerful, but has predictably poor gas mileage for a car this size. While the Grand Marquis isn't quite as difficult to handle as some other big American sedans, it will benefit from the performance and handling option which includes a firmer suspension and 20 more hp. There's plenty of room for six and their luggage.

The Ratings

	POOR → GOOD
COMPARATIVE RATING	■ (middle)
CRASH TEST	■ (good)
SAFETY FEATURES	■ (above middle)
FUEL ECONOMY	■ (poor)
PM COST	■ (above middle)
REPAIR COST	■ (above middle)
WARRANTY	■ (poor)
COMPLAINTS	■ (below middle)
INSURANCE COST	■ (good)

Safety

CRASH TEST	Very Good
AIRBAGS	Dual
ABS	4-wheel (optional)
DAY. RUNNING LIGHTS	None
BELT ADJUSTORS	Standard
BUILT-IN CHILD SEAT	None
INSURANCE INJURY CLAIMS	Very Low

General Information

WHERE MADE	U.S./Canada
YEAR OF PRODUCTION	Sixth
PARKING INDEX	Hard
BUMPERS	Strong
THEFT RATING	Low
TWINS	Cr. Victoria, Town Car
DRIVE	Rear

Specifications

FUEL ECONOMY (cty/hwy)	17/25	Poor
DRIVING RANGE (miles)	400	Average
SEATING	6	
LENGTH (inches)	211.8	Very Long
HEAD/LEG ROOM (in.)	39.4/42.5	Roomy
INTERIOR SPACE (cu. ft.)	109	Roomy
CARGO SPACE (cu. ft.)	21	Very Large

Specifications may vary.

Prices

Model	Retail	Mkup
Grand Marquis GS	23,100	7%
Grand Marquis LS	24,520	7%

Competition

	POOR → GOOD	Pg.
Merc. Gr. Marquis	■ (middle)	178
Chrysler Concorde	■ (below middle)	126
Ford Crown Victoria	■ (below middle)	138
Pontiac Bonneville	■ (above middle)	199
Toyota Avalon	■ (poor)	214

Mercury Mystique

The Mystique is part of the "world" car that Ford is selling as the Mondeo in European markets. Teamed with the Ford Contour here in the U.S., the Mystique has been attracting many buyers because of its ride and solid mid-size car features. Styling is contemporary yet conservative. Dual airbags are standard, but you'll have to pay extra for ABS and traction control.

The Mystique is about 6 inches longer than its predecessor, the Topaz, and front seat passengers are the biggest beneficiaries of the extra room. Both the base GS and the up-level LS come standard with a 2-liter engine that is only adequate. A more powerful 2.5-liter V6 with a tighter suspension system is optional. An average choice if you're looking for a small, inexpensive car—however, if you can live without the nameplate, consider the Contour.

The Ratings

	POOR	GOOD
COMPARATIVE RATING	■	
CRASH TEST		■
SAFETY FEATURES		■
FUEL ECONOMY		■
PM COST		■
REPAIR COST		■
WARRANTY	■	
COMPLAINTS	■	
INSURANCE COST		■

Safety

CRASH TEST	Good
AIRBAGS	Dual
ABS	4-wheel (optional)
DAY. RUNNING LIGHTS	None
BELT ADJUSTORS	Standard
BUILT-IN CHILD SEAT	None
INSURANCE INJURY CLAIMS	Average

General Information

WHERE MADE	U.S./Mexico
YEAR OF PRODUCTION	Third
PARKING INDEX	Easy
BUMPERS	Strong
THEFT RATING	Very Low
TWINS	Ford Contour
DRIVE	Front

Specifications

FUEL ECONOMY (cty/hwy)	24/33	Average
DRIVING RANGE (miles)	392	Average
SEATING	5	
LENGTH (inches)	183.5	Average
HEAD/LEG ROOM (in.)	39.0/42.4	Average
INTERIOR SPACE (cu. ft.)	89	Cramped
CARGO SPACE (cu. ft.)	14	Average

Specifications may vary.

Prices

Model	Retail	Mkup
Mystique	14,495	9%
Mystique GS	15,310	9%
Mystique LS	16,685	9%

Competition

	POOR	GOOD	Pg.
Mercury Mystique	■		179
Buick Skylark		■	113
Honda Accord	■		148
Hyundai Sonata	■		155
VW Golf/Jetta		■	221

Mercury Sable

This twin of the popular Ford Taurus has received few changes for 1997 after its complete remake in 1996. The Sable does not sell nearly as well as the Taurus, but it is geared to a different buyer. Because the Sable is designed to be the luxury line of the Taurus, it has much more standard features. Dual airbags are standard and ABS is optional.

Like its headlights, the interior is shaped in an ovoid figure which allows for easy-to-use controls and dash. The standard engine, a 3-liter V6, is quite powerful and delivers decent gas millage. For more power and slightly lower gas mileage, you can choose a more powerful version of the same engine. A stiff structure improves handling over the past Sables. There is plenty of room for 4 adults and you can even squeeze in 5 or 6 if needed. The Sable is a 'Best Bet' for 1997.

The Ratings

	POOR		GOOD
COMPARATIVE RATING			
CRASH TEST			
SAFETY FEATURES			
FUEL ECONOMY			
PM COST			
REPAIR COST			
WARRANTY			
COMPLAINTS			
INSURANCE COST			

Safety

CRASH TEST	Very Good
AIRBAGS	Dual
ABS	4-wheel (optional)
DAY. RUNNING LIGHTS	None
BELT ADJUSTORS	Standard
BUILT-IN CHILD SEAT	Optional
INSURANCE INJURY CLAIMS	Avg. (Wgn.=Very Low)

General Information

WHERE MADE	U.S.
YEAR OF PRODUCTION	Second
PARKING INDEX	Average
BUMPERS	Strong
THEFT RATING	
TWINS	Ford Taurus
DRIVE	Front

Specifications

FUEL ECONOMY (cty/hwy)	20/28	Average
DRIVING RANGE (miles)	368	Short
SEATING	5/6	
LENGTH (inches)	199.7	Long
HEAD/LEG ROOM (in.)	39.4/42.2	Average
INTERIOR SPACE (cu. ft.)	103	Roomy
CARGO SPACE (cu. ft.)	16	Average

Specifications may vary.

Prices

Model	Retail	Mkup
Sable GS	20,045	9%
Sable GS Wagon	20,045	9%
Sable LS	22,630	9%
Sable LS Wagon	22,630	9%

Competition

	POOR	GOOD	Pg.
Mercury Sable			180
Honda Accord			148
Mazda 626			169
Nissan Maxima			189
Pontiac Grand Am			201

Mercury Tracer

After six years, Mercury decided it was time for a change and, along with the Ford Escort, the new Tracer was born. This new version is much rounder, promises to be a better seller and, more importantly, a better vehicle than the past versions. Like other Mercury's, the Tracer is aimed at a higher class of car buyer unlike its Ford twin. The Tracer comes with standard dual airbags, however, and ABS is only optional.

The engine for the 1997 model has been refined and should produce quick accelerations and smooth shifts. As is expected in a small car, fuel economy should be good. Ride is comfortable, but don't expect a bump free drive. Noise levels are good under average acceleration, anything more than average and you may have to turn up the radio. Let's hope it performs well in the government crash tests.

The Ratings

	POOR — GOOD
COMPARATIVE RATING*	
CRASH TEST	
SAFETY FEATURES	
FUEL ECONOMY	
PM COST	
REPAIR COST	
WARRANTY	
COMPLAINTS	
INSURANCE COST	

Safety

CRASH TEST	No government results
AIRBAGS	Dual
ABS	4-wheel (optional)
DAY. RUNNING LIGHTS	None
BELT ADJUSTORS	Standard
BUILT-IN CHILD SEAT	Optional
INSURANCE INJURY CLAIMS	

General Information

WHERE MADE	U.S.
YEAR OF PRODUCTION	First
PARKING INDEX	Very Easy
BUMPERS	Strong
THEFT RATING	
TWINS	Ford Escort
DRIVE	Front

Specifications

FUEL ECONOMY (cty/hwy)	28/37	Good
DRIVING RANGE (miles)	394	Average
SEATING	5	
LENGTH (inches)	174.7	Short
HEAD/LEG ROOM (in.)	39.0/42.5	Average
INTERIOR SPACE (cu. ft.)	87	Cramped
CARGO SPACE (cu. ft.)	13	Small

Specifications may vary.

Prices

Model	Retail	Mkup
Tracer GS	11,560	8%
Tracer LS	12,385	8%
Tracer Wagon	13,020	8%

Competition

	POOR — GOOD	Pg.
Mercury Tracer		181
Chevrolet Cavalier		120
Dodge Neon		132
Nissan Sentra		191
Toyota Tercel		220

*Due to the importance of crash tests, cars with no results as of publication date cannot be given an overall rating.

Mercury Villager

In an effort to catch the popular Dodge Caravan and Plymouth Voyager, the Mercury Villager will add a powered fourth door this year. The Villager minivan, a near-twin of the Nissan Quest, is more like a tall car than a minivan. It is available in three trim levels: base GS, luxury LS, and sport-luxury Nautica. The Villager's resemblance to the Dodge Caravan is no coincidence; Mercury is trying to emulate Chrysler's minivan success. ABS and dual airbags are standard.

The 3-liter V6, with automatic overdrive, is acceptably responsive. Go for the towing package if you'll be hauling anything at all. The ride is a bit soft, very much like a regular passenger car's, with standard suspension. Handling is competent, but can be firmed up with the optional handling package. The integrated child seats are excellent options.

The Ratings

	POOR	GOOD
COMPARATIVE RATING		
CRASH TEST		
SAFETY FEATURES		
FUEL ECONOMY		
PM COST		
REPAIR COST		
WARRANTY		
COMPLAINTS		
INSURANCE COST		

Safety

CRASH TEST	Good
AIRBAGS	Dual
ABS	4-wheel
DAY. RUNNING LIGHTS	None
BELT ADJUSTORS	Standard
BUILT-IN CHILD SEAT	Optional
INSURANCE INJURY CLAIMS	Very Low

General Information

WHERE MADE	U.S.
YEAR OF PRODUCTION	Fifth
PARKING INDEX	Average
BUMPERS	Weak
THEFT RATING	Very Low
TWINS	Nissan Quest
DRIVE	Front

Specifications

FUEL ECONOMY (cty/hwy)	17/23	Poor
DRIVING RANGE (miles)	400	Average
SEATING	7	
LENGTH (inches)	190.2	Average
HEAD/LEG ROOM (in.)	39.4/39.9	Cramped
INTERIOR SPACE (cu. ft.)		
CARGO SPACE (cu. ft.)	126	Average

Specifications may vary.

Prices

Model	Retail	Mkup
Villager GS	20,795	10%
Villager LS	25,665	10%
Villager Nautica	27,495	10%

Competition

	POOR	GOOD	Pg.
Mercury Villager			182
Chevrolet Astro			118
Dodge Caravan			130
Honda Odyssey			151
Nissan Quest			190

Mitsubishi Diamante

To bolster sluggish sales during the past few years, Mitsubishi redesigned the Diamante for 1997. The new Diamante sports a new exterior and refined interior, making it a formidable challenger in the "near luxury" sedan market. Wheelbase remains the same, but the length is extended giving more room inside for passengers. Dual airbags are standard and ABS is optional.

Powering this new Diamante is a refined 3.5-liter V6, which is good enough for this mid-size sedan. As with past Diamante's, the ride should be smooth and comfortable. Two great safety features are an optional fold-down child safety seat and a standard 3-point seatbelt for the middle back seat. There are two trim levels, the base ES and up-level LS. With its redesign, the new Diamante should sell better than past versions.

The Ratings

	POOR — GOOD
COMPARATIVE RATING*	□□□□□□□□□□
CRASH TEST	□□□□□□□□□□
SAFETY FEATURES	□□□□□□□■□□
FUEL ECONOMY	□□□■□□□□□□
PM COST	□■□□□□□□□□
REPAIR COST	□■□□□□□□□□
WARRANTY	□□□□■□□□□□
COMPLAINTS	□□□□□■□□□□
INSURANCE COST	□□□□□□□□□□

Safety

CRASH TEST	No government results
AIRBAGS	Dual
ABS	4-wheel (optional)
DAY. RUNNING LIGHTS	None
BELT ADJUSTORS	Standard
BUILT-IN CHILD SEAT	Optional
INSURANCE INJURY CLAIMS	

General Information

WHERE MADE	Australia/Japan
YEAR OF PRODUCTION	First
PARKING INDEX	Average
BUMPERS	Weak
THEFT RATING	
TWINS	
DRIVE	Front

Specifications

FUEL ECONOMY (cty/hwy)	18/26	Poor
DRIVING RANGE (miles)	399	Average
SEATING	5	
LENGTH (inches)	194.1	Long
HEAD/LEG ROOM (in.)	39.4/44.3	Very Roomy
INTERIOR SPACE (cu. ft.)	101	Roomy
CARGO SPACE (cu. ft.)	14	Average

Specifications may vary.

Prices

Model	Retail	Mkup
Diamante LS	29,990	20%

Competition

	POOR — GOOD	Pg.
Mitsu. Diamante	□□□□□□□□□□	183
Dodge Intrepid	□□□□□□■□□□	131
Nissan Maxima	□□■□□□□□□□	189
Pontiac Bonneville	□□□□□□□□■□	199
Toyota Avalon	□□□■□□□□□□	214

*Due to the importance of crash tests, cars with no results as of publication date cannot be given an overall rating.

Mitsubishi Eclipse

As a twin of the Eagle Talon, a sedan brother of the Mitsubishi Galant, and the coupe cousin of the Chrysler Sebring and Dodge Avenger, the Mitsubishi Eclipse tries to stand on its own. It enters 1997 with no major additions from its recent redesign in 1995. Dual airbags are standard, but you'll have to pay extra for ABS.

The RS is the stripped-down base model and the GS has a few more bells and whistles, some of which are optional. Both of those models get the standard 2-liter engine, which may not be powerful enough for sports enthusiasts. The up-level GS-T and GSX both get a turbo version that pumps out 50% more power, and the GSX comes with all-wheel drive. The Eclipse does have a back seat, but it's not really meant for adults. With all this extra power, expect high insurance bills.

The Ratings

	POOR	GOOD
COMPARATIVE RATING	■	
CRASH TEST		■
SAFETY FEATURES		■
FUEL ECONOMY		■
PM COST		■
REPAIR COST		■
WARRANTY		■
COMPLAINTS	■	
INSURANCE COST	■	

Safety

CRASH TEST	Good
AIRBAGS	Dual
ABS	4-wheel (optional)
DAY. RUNNING LIGHTS	None
BELT ADJUSTORS	Standard
BUILT-IN CHILD SEAT	None
INSURANCE INJURY CLAIMS	Very High

General Information

WHERE MADE	U.S./Japan
YEAR OF PRODUCTION	Third
PARKING INDEX	Easy
BUMPERS	Weak
THEFT RATING	High
TWINS	Eagle Talon
DRIVE	Front/All

Specifications

FUEL ECONOMY (cty/hwy)	23/31	Average
DRIVING RANGE (miles)	439	Long
SEATING	4	
LENGTH (inches)	172.2	Very Short
HEAD/LEG ROOM (in.)	37.9/43.3	Average
INTERIOR SPACE (cu. ft.)	79	Vry. Cramped
CARGO SPACE (cu. ft.)	15	Average

Specifications may vary.

Prices

Model	Retail	Mkup
Eclipse	13,830	15%

Competition

	POOR	GOOD	Pg.
Mitsubishi Eclipse	■		184
Acura Integra	■		101
Eagle Talon	■		133
Ford Probe		■	141
Mazda MX-6		■	173

Mitsubishi Galant

The Galant, Mitsubishi's #1 seller, competes in a very crowded size class against the likes of the Honda Accord and Toyota Camry. A new lineup for 1997 includes the addition of three trim levels, each with specific product features. Dual airbags have greatly improved results in the government's crash test program. ABS will cost you extra.

The base DE, mid-level ES, and up-level LS all come with the same 2.4-liter 4-cylinder engine, which is powerful but gets only average mileage. An optional 2.5-liter V6 engine has more power, but will sacrifice even more fuel efficiency. The Galant's ride is on the firm side. Handling is okay, typical of mid-size Japanese sedans. The Galant's rear seat is somewhat uncomfortable, though the front seat's head and leg room is generous. The price of the Galant helps it to hold its ground against the more popular competition.

The Ratings

	POOR GOOD
COMPARATIVE RATING*	
CRASH TEST	
SAFETY FEATURES	
FUEL ECONOMY	
PM COST	
REPAIR COST	
WARRANTY	
COMPLAINTS	
INSURANCE COST	

Safety

CRASH TEST	No government results
AIRBAGS	Dual
ABS	4-wheel (optional)
DAY. RUNNING LIGHTS	None
BELT ADJUSTORS	Standard
BUILT-IN CHILD SEAT	None
INSURANCE INJURY CLAIMS	High

General Information

WHERE MADE	U.S./Japan
YEAR OF PRODUCTION	Fourth
PARKING INDEX	Easy
BUMPERS	Weak
THEFT RATING	High
TWINS	Chrys. Sebring, Avenger
DRIVE	Front

Specifications

FUEL ECONOMY (cty/hwy)	23/30	Average
DRIVING RANGE (miles)	439	Long
SEATING	5	
LENGTH (inches)	187.6	Average
HEAD/LEG ROOM (in.)	39.4/43.3	Roomy
INTERIOR SPACE (cu. ft.)	96	Average
CARGO SPACE (cu. ft.)	12	Small

Specifications may vary.

Prices

Model	Retail	Mkup
Galant	15,420	12%

Competition

	POOR GOOD	Pg.
Mitsubishi Galant		185
Buick Skylark		113
Honda Accord		148
Mercury Sable		180
Oldsmobile Achieva		193

*Due to the importance of crash tests, cars with no results as of publication date cannot be given an overall rating.

Mitsubishi Mirage

The smallest offering from Mitsubishi, the Mirage, enters 1997 with a new look. The new Mirage comes in sedan and coupe models with two trim levels. This year's car is longer and taller giving passengers more room inside which should make the ride much more comfortable. All Mirages have dual airbags, but ABS is optional.

The 1.5-liter 4-cylinder engine that comes with the base model Mirage DE is not very powerful, though you'll be pleased with its fuel economy. The 1.8-liter engine on the LS coupes and sedans is much more powerful, but gas mileage suffers dramatically. The Mirage handles crisply, and the interior is fairly comfortable for four people. Ride is decent. Attractively styled, the Mirage still remains competitive with the Toyota Paseo and Saturn SC.

The Ratings

	POOR → GOOD
COMPARATIVE RATING*	(no rating)
CRASH TEST	(no rating)
SAFETY FEATURES	●●●○○○○○
FUEL ECONOMY	●●●●●●●○
PM COST	●○○○○○○○
REPAIR COST	●●●○○○○○
WARRANTY	●●●●○○○○
COMPLAINTS	●●●○○○○○
INSURANCE COST	●●○○○○○○

Safety

CRASH TEST	No government results
AIRBAGS	Dual
ABS	4-wheel (optional)
DAY. RUNNING LIGHTS	None
BELT ADJUSTORS	Standard
BUILT-IN CHILD SEAT	None
INSURANCE INJURY CLAIMS	

General Information

WHERE MADE	Japan
YEAR OF PRODUCTION	First
PARKING INDEX	Very Easy
BUMPERS	Weak
THEFT RATING	
TWINS	
DRIVE	Front

Specifications

FUEL ECONOMY (cty/hwy)	33/40	Very Good
DRIVING RANGE (miles)	475	Very Long
SEATING	5	
LENGTH (inches)	173.6	Short
HEAD/LEG ROOM (in.)	39.8/43.0	Roomy
INTERIOR SPACE (cu. ft.)	91	Average
CARGO SPACE (cu. ft.)	11	Small

Specifications may vary.

Prices

Model	Retail	Mkup
Mirage Coupe	10,400	9%
Mirage Sedan	12,090	9%

Competition

	POOR → GOOD	Pg.
Mitsubishi Mirage	(no rating)	186
Chevrolet Cavalier	●●●●○○○○	120
Geo Prizm	●●●●●●○○	147
Nissan Sentra	●●●●●●○○	191
Toyota Tercel	●●●○○○○○	220

*Due to the importance of crash tests, cars with no results as of publication date cannot be given an overall rating.

Nissan 240SX

New exterior and interior refinements can be found on the 1997 240SX. The 240SX is less of a sports car than a luxury vehicle and it looks more like a Lexus than a Camaro. These new refinements are designed to give this rear wheel drive car more of a sports car feel. Dual airbags are standard, but you'll have to pay extra for ABS.

The 2.4-liter 4-cylinder engine is adequate, but won't please performance-seekers; unfortunately, you do not have another engine choice. The 240 comes in three trim levels: base, SE, or a new LE which will include leather seats. An improved interior should make the 240 more comfortable to ride in, however, adults in the rear seats will still not be comfortable. The ride is smooth and the handling is good due to the wide stance of the car. You can do better with other vehicles.

The Ratings

	POOR	GOOD
COMPARATIVE RATING	■	
CRASH TEST		■
SAFETY FEATURES		■
FUEL ECONOMY		■
PM COST		■
REPAIR COST		■
WARRANTY		■
COMPLAINTS	■	
INSURANCE COST	■	

Safety

CRASH TEST	Average
AIRBAGS	Dual
ABS	4-wheel (optional)
DAY. RUNNING LIGHTS	None
BELT ADJUSTORS	None
BUILT-IN CHILD SEAT	None
INSURANCE INJURY CLAIMS	Very High

General Information

WHERE MADE	Japan
YEAR OF PRODUCTION	Third
PARKING INDEX	Very Easy
BUMPERS	Strong
THEFT RATING	Very High
TWINS	
DRIVE	Rear

Specifications

FUEL ECONOMY (cty/hwy)	22/28	Average
DRIVING RANGE (miles)	413	Average
SEATING	4	
LENGTH (inches)	177.2	Short
HEAD/LEG ROOM (in.)	38.3/42.6	Average
INTERIOR SPACE (cu. ft.)	71	Vry. Cramped
CARGO SPACE (cu. ft.)	9	Very Small

Specifications may vary.

Prices

Model	Retail	Mkup
240SX	18,359	12%
240SX SE	21,999	12%
240SX LE	24,449	12%

Competition

	POOR	GOOD	Pg.
Nissan 240SX	■		187
Acura Integra	■		101
Eagle Talon	■		133
Ford Probe		■	141
Mazda MX-6		■	173

Nissan Altima

Nissan's best-selling model has changed little since its introduction in 1993, and Nissan has little reason to change anything—the Altima is an outstanding competitor in a crowded intermediate sizeclass. The Altima's styling mimics the Infiniti J30, though it comes with a much smaller price tag. Dual airbags are standard, but you'll have to pay extra for ABS. Unfortunately, on the base XE and mid-level GXE, you'll have to buy expensive option packages before you can order ABS.

The 2.4-liter 4-cylinder engine is powerful enough, though you'll by no means feel like you're in a performance car. Fuel economy is pretty good. Handling is good, though the ride can be a bit on the rough side. Gauges and controls are easy to use. You have your pick of four trim levels (XE, GXE, SE and GLE) and options are plentiful, so shop carefully.

The Ratings

	POOR	GOOD
COMPARATIVE RATING		
CRASH TEST		
SAFETY FEATURES		
FUEL ECONOMY		
PM COST		
REPAIR COST		
WARRANTY		
COMPLAINTS		
INSURANCE COST		

Safety

CRASH TEST	Average
AIRBAGS	Dual
ABS	4-wheel (optional)
DAY. RUNNING LIGHTS	None
BELT ADJUSTORS	Standard
BUILT-IN CHILD SEAT	None
INSURANCE INJURY CLAIMS	High

General Information

WHERE MADE	Japan/U.S.
YEAR OF PRODUCTION	Fifth
PARKING INDEX	Average
BUMPERS	Strong
THEFT RATING	Average
TWINS	
DRIVE	Front

Specifications

FUEL ECONOMY (cty/hwy)	24/30	Average
DRIVING RANGE (miles)	413	Average
SEATING	5	
LENGTH (inches)	180.5	Short
HEAD/LEG ROOM (in.)	39.3/42.6	Roomy
INTERIOR SPACE (cu. ft.)	94	Average
CARGO SPACE (cu. ft.)	14	Average

Specifications may vary.

Prices

Model	Retail	Mkup
Altima XE	15,849	11%
Altima GXE	17,399	11%
Altima SE	19,699	11%
Altima GLE	20,899	11%

Competition

	POOR	GOOD	Pg.
Nissan Altima			188
Ford Taurus			142
Honda Accord			148
Mazda 626			169
Pontiac Grand Am			201

Nissan Maxima

The flagship of Nissan's model line, the Maxima has been a solid seller and shows no signs of slipping. New for 1997 are an updated interior and exterior styling, which makes this car even more attractive and comfortable. Dual airbags are standard, and you'll have to pay extra for ABS, which is not available on the manual transmission GXE.

The 3-liter V6 is very powerful and quite fuel efficient. The GXE and GLE trim levels come standard with an automatic transmission, while the SE comes with a five speed manual. The large wheelbase increases interior room, making the front seats quite comfortable and improving the ride. But handling is mediocre. The rear seats will be comfortable for most adults. You'll have the typical Nissan variety of trim levels and option packages, so shop carefully.

The Ratings

	POOR → GOOD
COMPARATIVE RATING	▮ (2)
CRASH TEST	▮ (6)
SAFETY FEATURES	▮ (6)
FUEL ECONOMY	▮ (4)
PM COST	▮ (6)
REPAIR COST	▮ (1)
WARRANTY	▮ (3)
COMPLAINTS	▮ (6)
INSURANCE COST	▮ (4)

Safety

CRASH TEST	Average
AIRBAGS	Dual
ABS	4-wheel (optional)
DAY. RUNNING LIGHTS	None
BELT ADJUSTORS	Standard
BUILT-IN CHILD SEAT	None
INSURANCE INJURY CLAIMS	Average

General Information

WHERE MADE	Japan
YEAR OF PRODUCTION	Third
PARKING INDEX	Easy
BUMPERS	Strong
THEFT RATING	Very High
TWINS	Infiniti I30
DRIVE	Front

Specifications

FUEL ECONOMY (cty/hwy)	22/27	Average
DRIVING RANGE (miles)	444	Long
SEATING	5	
LENGTH (inches)	187.7	Average
HEAD/LEG ROOM (in.)	40.1/43.9	Very Roomy
INTERIOR SPACE (cu. ft.)	100	Roomy
CARGO SPACE (cu. ft.)	15	Average

Specifications may vary.

Prices

Model	Retail	Mkup
Maxima GXE	21,499	10%
Maxima SE	23,299	12%
Maxima GLE	26,899	12%

Competition

	POOR → GOOD	Pg.
Nissan Maxima	▮ (2)	189
Audi A4	▮ (9)	104
Eagle Vision	▮ (6)	134
Ford Taurus	▮ (8)	142
Honda Accord	▮ (3)	148

Nissan Quest

With the Quest and its look-alike twin, the Villager, Nissan and Mercury have tried to catch up with Chrysler's successful minivans. They've been successful on many fronts with standard safety features like dual airbags. With ABS, they may well catch up. The Quest also meets 1997 side impact standards for passenger cars.

The only available engine is a 3-liter V6, but acceleration and power are good with poor fuel economy. You'll find the ride and handling are good by minivan standards. On the interior, seating is comfortable and the Quest offers integrated child safety seats which are great options for parents. With Nissan's flexible seating system, you are able to arrange the seating to suit most any purpose. The Quest has been the best-selling import minivan since 1993 and it should continue to do well in 1997.

The Ratings

	POOR			GOOD
COMPARATIVE RATING				
CRASH TEST				
SAFETY FEATURES				
FUEL ECONOMY				
PM COST				
REPAIR COST				
WARRANTY				
COMPLAINTS				
INSURANCE COST				

Safety

CRASH TEST	Good
AIRBAGS	Dual
ABS	4-wheel
DAY. RUNNING LIGHTS	None
BELT ADJUSTORS	Standard
BUILT-IN CHILD SEAT	Optional
INSURANCE INJURY CLAIMS	Average

General Information

WHERE MADE	Japan/U.S.
YEAR OF PRODUCTION	Fifth
PARKING INDEX	Hard
BUMPERS	Weak
THEFT RATING	Very Low
TWINS	Mercury Villager
DRIVE	Front

Specifications

FUEL ECONOMY (cty/hwy)	17/23	Poor
DRIVING RANGE (miles)	400	Average
SEATING	7	
LENGTH (inches)	189.9	Average
HEAD/LEG ROOM (in.)	39.5/39.9	Cramped
INTERIOR SPACE (cu. ft.)		
CARGO SPACE (cu. ft.)	125	Average

Specifications may vary.

Prices

Model	Retail	Mkup
Quest XE	21,249	12%
Quest GXE	26,049	12%

Competition

	POOR	GOOD	Pg.
Nissan Quest			190
Dodge Caravan			130
Ford Windstar			144
Isuzu Oasis			160
Toyota Previa			219

Nissan Sentra

Since introducing an all-new, slightly enlarged Sentra late in 1995, Nissan has given its competitors headaches. The Sentra's rounded and contemporary styling is attracting many subcompact buyers. Nissan dropped the two-door version from the Sentra nameplate to compete solely with the sedan versions of the Civic, Tercel, Saturn and Neon. The two-door version became the 200SX. The Sentra has dual airbags and optional ABS.

The 1.6-liter, 4-cylinder engine is only adequate, but gets good gas mileage. There are no other engine choices, only a choice of a manual or automatic transmission. The Sentra handles and rides better than its predecessors and is good, basic transportation. With dual airbags and contemporary looks, the Sentra is one of this year's best.

The Ratings

	POOR ··· GOOD
COMPARATIVE RATING	▮ (near good)
CRASH TEST	▮ (good side)
SAFETY FEATURES	▮ (good side)
FUEL ECONOMY	▮ (middle)
PM COST	▮ (middle)
REPAIR COST	▮ (middle)
WARRANTY	▮ (poor side)
COMPLAINTS	▮ (good side)
INSURANCE COST	▮ (poor end)

Safety

CRASH TEST	Good
AIRBAGS	Dual
ABS	4-wheel (optional)
DAY. RUNNING LIGHTS	None
BELT ADJUSTORS	Standard
BUILT-IN CHILD SEAT	None
INSURANCE INJURY CLAIMS	Very High

General Information

WHERE MADE	Japan/U.S.
YEAR OF PRODUCTION	Third
PARKING INDEX	Very Easy
BUMPERS	Strong
THEFT RATING	Very Low
TWINS	
DRIVE	Front

Specifications

FUEL ECONOMY (cty/hwy)	29/39	Good
DRIVING RANGE (miles)	436	Long
SEATING	5	
LENGTH (inches)	170.1	Very Short
HEAD/LEG ROOM (in.)	39.1/42.3	Average
INTERIOR SPACE (cu. ft.)	87	Cramped
CARGO SPACE (cu. ft.)	10	Very Small

Specifications may vary.

Prices

Model	Retail	Mkup
Sentra	11,499	5%
Sentra XE	13,649	7%
Sentra GXE	14,799	7%
Sentra GLE	15,649	10%

Competition

	POOR ··· GOOD	Pg.
Nissan Sentra	▮ (near good)	191
Chevrolet Cavalier	▮ (middle)	120
Honda Civic	▮ (poor-middle)	149
Pontiac Sunfire	▮ (near good)	203
Toyota Tercel	▮ (middle)	220

Oldsmobile 88

This twin of the Buick LeSabre and Pontiac Bonneville is Oldsmobile's entry into the plush mid-sized car market. The 88 used to come in three trim levels, but now only two, base and LS, as the LSS trim level becomes its own line (but don't be fooled, it's still based on the 88). Dual airbags and ABS are standard.

The 88's 3.8-liter V6, connected to an automatic overdrive, delivers plenty of smooth power. You no longer have another engine choice as in years past, but this one should do well. The 88's suspension favors a too-soft ride at the expense of handling. However, the optional touring suspension and speed-sensitive steering renders good handling and a comfortable ride. The LSS is slightly smaller and aimed at the import car buyer. New interior trim for '97 helps make this a very good choice in the large size class.

The Ratings

	POOR → GOOD
COMPARATIVE RATING	▮ (near good)
CRASH TEST *	▮ (middle)
SAFETY FEATURES	▮ (above middle)
FUEL ECONOMY	▮ (middle)
PM COST	▮ (middle)
REPAIR COST	▮ (middle)
WARRANTY	▮ (poor side)
COMPLAINTS	▮ (good side)
INSURANCE COST	▮ (good end)

Safety

CRASH TEST	Good
AIRBAGS	Dual
ABS	4-wheel
DAY. RUNNING LIGHTS	Standard
BELT ADJUSTORS	Standard
BUILT-IN CHILD SEAT	None
INSURANCE INJURY CLAIMS	Very Low

General Information

WHERE MADE	U.S.
YEAR OF PRODUCTION	Sixth
PARKING INDEX	Hard
BUMPERS	Strong
THEFT RATING	Very Low
TWINS	Buick LeSabre, Pont. B'ville
DRIVE	Front

Specifications

FUEL ECONOMY (cty/hwy)	19/29	Average
DRIVING RANGE (miles)	414	Average
SEATING	5	
LENGTH (inches)	200.4	Long
HEAD/LEG ROOM (in.)	38.7/42.5	Average
INTERIOR SPACE (cu. ft.)	106	Roomy
CARGO SPACE (cu. ft.)	18	Large

Specifications may vary.

Prices

Model	Retail	Mkup
88	23,100	7%
88 LS	24,400	7%

Competition

	POOR → GOOD	Pg.
Oldsmobile 88	▮ (good side)	192
Ford Taurus	▮ (good side)	142
Mazda 626	▮ (middle)	169
Nissan Altima	▮ (good side)	188
Pontiac Grand Am	▮ (good side)	201

*A version of this vehicle is scheduled to be tested later this year. Results are expected to be equal or better.

Oldsmobile Achieva

First introduced in 1992, this compact is the smallest Oldsmobile and is styled much more conservatively than its twins, the Buick Skylark and Pontiac Grand Am. Oldsmobile has simplified its lineup for 1997 by offering only two trim levels, series 1 and series 2. This solid car comes with dual airbags and 4-wheel ABS is standard.

The Achieva is nearly as large as some mid-size cars, but you'll find its back seat cramped for adults. The new standard 2.4-liter 4-cylinder engine is adequate, and the optional 3.1-liter V6 only gives you five more horsepower. At least you don't lose much in fuel economy. Speed-sensitive steering is standard, and the suspension is firm. Considering the cost of a well-equipped Achieva, you will be hard pressed to find a cheaper, better vehicle. The Achieva is a best bet for 1997.

The Ratings

	POOR — GOOD
COMPARATIVE RATING	
CRASH TEST *	
SAFETY FEATURES	
FUEL ECONOMY	
PM COST	
REPAIR COST	
WARRANTY	
COMPLAINTS	
INSURANCE COST	

Safety

CRASH TEST	Good
AIRBAGS	Dual
ABS	4-wheel
DAY. RUNNING LIGHTS	Standard
BELT ADJUSTORS	Standard
BUILT-IN CHILD SEAT	None
INSURANCE INJURY CLAIMS	Average

General Information

WHERE MADE	U.S.
YEAR OF PRODUCTION	Sixth
PARKING INDEX	Easy
BUMPERS	Strong
THEFT RATING	Very Low
TWINS	Buick Skylark, Pont. Gr. Am
DRIVE	Front

Specifications

FUEL ECONOMY (cty/hwy)	23/33	Average
DRIVING RANGE (miles)	395	Average
SEATING	5	
LENGTH (inches)	187.9	Average
HEAD/LEG ROOM (in.)	37.8/43.1	Average
INTERIOR SPACE (cu. ft.)	88	Cramped
CARGO SPACE (cu. ft.)	14	Average

Specifications may vary.

Prices

Model	Retail	Mkup
Achieva SL Sedan Series1	15,750	7%
Achieva SC Coupe Series 1	15,950	7%
Achieva SL Sedan Series 2	17,300	7%
Achieva SC Coupe Series 2	17,500	7%

Competition

	POOR — GOOD	Pg.
Oldsmobile Achieva		193
Buick Skylark		113
Ford Taurus		142
Honda Accord		148
Pontiac Grand Am		201

*A version of this vehicle is scheduled to be tested later this year. Results are expected to be equal or better.

Oldsmobile Aurora

Olds is counting on the Aurora to bring it into the 21st century. So far, so good. First introduced in 1995, the Aurora enters 1997 with only minor changes, the most notable of which is a new right side outside mirror which tilts down to improve visibility when backing up. Dual airbags, ABS, traction control, speed-variable power steering, and a host of other items are standard.

The Aurora benefits greatly from a very rigid structure and rides well for a car its size. However, the car wallows in turns like many large cars. The 4-liter V8 is more powerful than most any of its competitors, and its fuel economy, though not notable by any means, holds its own with the competition. Room for five is more than spacious, though not quite as generous as some of the larger domestic cars, and it's priced lower than the smaller imports it targets.

The Ratings

	POOR	GOOD
COMPARATIVE RATING	▮	
CRASH TEST	▮	
SAFETY FEATURES		▮
FUEL ECONOMY	▮	
PM COST		▮
REPAIR COST	▮	
WARRANTY		▮
COMPLAINTS	▮	
INSURANCE COST		▮

Safety

CRASH TEST	Average
AIRBAGS	Dual
ABS	4-wheel
DAY. RUNNING LIGHTS	Standard
BELT ADJUSTORS	None
BUILT-IN CHILD SEAT	None
INSURANCE INJURY CLAIMS	Very Low

General Information

WHERE MADE	U.S.
YEAR OF PRODUCTION	Third
PARKING INDEX	Hard
BUMPERS	Strong
THEFT RATING	Very Low
TWINS	Buick Park Ave., Buick Riviera
DRIVE	Front

Specifications

FUEL ECONOMY (cty/hwy)	17/26	Poor
DRIVING RANGE (miles)	400	Average
SEATING	5/6	
LENGTH (inches)	205.4	Very Long
HEAD/LEG ROOM (in.)	38.4/42.6	Average
INTERIOR SPACE (cu. ft.)	102	Roomy
CARGO SPACE (cu. ft.)	16	Average

Specifications may vary.

Prices

Model	Retail	Mkup
Aurora	35,735	8%

Competition

	POOR	GOOD	Pg.
Oldsmobile Aurora	▮		194
Audi A6		▮	105
Chrysler LHS	▮		127
Nissan Maxima	▮		189
Volvo 850		▮	223

Oldsmobile Cutlass

Where has Oldsmobile focused its attention for 1997? The answer is the new Cutlass. After fifteen years with the same model, Oldsmobile decided it was time to make big changes and the new Cutlass is a vast improvement. It now has sleeker lines and an improved interior. The best part about the new Cutlass is that dual airbags are finally available, which means the end of the dreaded door-mounted belts.

Powering the new Cutlass will be an improved 3.1 liter V6 engine which should provide good, smooth power. A refined suspension should make the ride more enjoyable and the noise levels should be acceptable. Because of an increased wheelbase, passengers will have more head and leg room, making the refined interior very comfortable. Overall, this should be a very competitive car.

The Ratings

	POOR ... GOOD
COMPARATIVE RATING*	
CRASH TEST	
SAFETY FEATURES	▮ (high)
FUEL ECONOMY	▮ (mid)
PM COST	▮ (mid)
REPAIR COST	▮ (mid)
WARRANTY	▮ (low)
COMPLAINTS	▮ (mid)
INSURANCE COST	▮ (low-mid)

Safety

CRASH TEST	No government results
AIRBAGS	Dual
ABS	4-wheel (optional)
DAY. RUNNING LIGHTS	Standard
BELT ADJUSTORS	Standard
BUILT-IN CHILD SEAT	None
INSURANCE INJURY CLAIMS	

General Information

WHERE MADE	U.S.
YEAR OF PRODUCTION	First
PARKING INDEX	Average
BUMPERS	Weak
THEFT RATING	
TWINS	Chevrolet Malibu
DRIVE	Front

Specifications

FUEL ECONOMY (cty/hwy)	20/29	Average
DRIVING RANGE (miles)	350	Short
SEATING	5	
LENGTH (inches)	192.0	Long
HEAD/LEG ROOM (in.)	39.4/42.2	Average
INTERIOR SPACE (cu. ft.)	98	Average
CARGO SPACE (cu. ft.)	16	Average

Specifications may vary.

Prices**

Model	Retail	Mkup
Cutlass SL Sedan I	14,455	5%
Cutlass SL Sedan II	16,455	7%
Cutlass SL Wagon	17,455	7%

Competition

	POOR ... GOOD	Pg.
Olds Cutlass		195
Ford Taurus	▮ (high)	142
Honda Accord	▮ (low)	148
Mazda 626	▮ (mid)	169
Pontiac Grand Am	▮ (high)	201

**1997 prices not available at press time. Prices based on 1996 data.

*Due to the importance of crash tests, cars with no results as of publication date cannot be given an overall rating.

195

Oldsmobile Cutlass Supreme

Name recognition is one factor that helps to sell this car; the name Cutlass has been around since 1954 and the Cutlass Supreme has been in production since 1967. The Cutlass Supreme is available in both a coupe and sedan version and seats five or six. Dual airbags and speed sensitive steering are standard; ABS is optional.

The sedan models handle fairly well and have a ride better suited to smooth roads. However, a new sport coupe design should improve the coupe's handling and ride. All Cutlass Supremes have an automatic overdrive transmission, which helps both acceleration and gas mileage. The 3.1-liter V6 is adequate, and unlike past years, there is no longer an optional engine. Comfort and noise levels inside are good. This is a good solid choice with low complaints and insurance costs.

The Ratings

	POOR	GOOD
COMPARATIVE RATING		▮
CRASH TEST	▮	
SAFETY FEATURES		▮
FUEL ECONOMY	▮	
PM COST	▮	
REPAIR COST	▮	
WARRANTY	▮	
COMPLAINTS		▮
INSURANCE COST		▮

Safety

CRASH TEST	Average
AIRBAGS	Dual
ABS	4-wheel (optional)
DAY. RUNNING LIGHTS	Standard
BELT ADJUSTORS	Standard (Sdn. Only)
BUILT-IN CHILD SEAT	None
INSURANCE INJURY CLAIMS	Very Low (Coupe=Avg.)

General Information

WHERE MADE	U.S.
YEAR OF PRODUCTION	Tenth
PARKING INDEX	Average
BUMPERS	Strong
THEFT RATING	
TWINS	
DRIVE	Front

Specifications

FUEL ECONOMY (cty/hwy)	17/26	Poor
DRIVING RANGE (miles)	342	Short
SEATING	5/6	
LENGTH (inches)	193.7	Long
HEAD/LEG ROOM (in.)	38.7/42.4	Average
INTERIOR SPACE (cu. ft.)	101	Roomy
CARGO SPACE (cu. ft.)	16	Average

Specifications may vary.

Prices

Model	Retail	Mkup
Cutlass Supreme Coupe 1	19,500	7%
Cutlass Supreme Sedan 1	19,500	7%
Cutlass Supreme Coupe 2	20,400	7%
Cutlass Supreme Sedan 2	20,400	7%
Cutlass Supreme Coupe 3	21,300	7%

Competition

	POOR	GOOD	Pg.
Olds Cut. Supreme		▮	196
Ford Contour	▮		137
Hyundai Sonata	▮		155
Mercury Mystique	▮		179
VW Golf/Jetta		▮	221

Oldsmobile Silhouette

This completely redesigned and re-engineered minivan is sure to attract some buyers away from Chrysler's minivan. In years past, the Silhouette has only been an average minivan; however, with a new exterior and interior style (which resembles the Chrsyler products) and the addition of a fourth door, the Silhouette has become a very attractive choice. Standard for '97 are dual airbags and 4-wheel ABS.

There are three models available for 1997: the base, GL and GLS. Each comes with an increasingly higher level of standard equipment. This new minivan is powered by a 3.4 liter V6 which should provide good acceleration. There are many different seating arrangements and there are plenty of cup holders. A new comfort feature is a mini-cargo holder between the front seats which should keep small things from sliding around.

The Ratings

	POOR ⟷ GOOD
COMPARATIVE RATING *	(blank)
CRASH TEST	(blank)
SAFETY FEATURES	▓ (high)
FUEL ECONOMY	▓ (low)
PM COST	▓ (high)
REPAIR COST	▓ (high)
WARRANTY	▓ (low)
COMPLAINTS	▓ (mid)
INSURANCE COST	▓ (mid)

Safety

CRASH TEST	No government results
AIRBAGS	Dual
ABS	4-wheel
DAY. RUNNING LIGHTS	Standard
BELT ADJUSTORS	None
BUILT-IN CHILD SEAT	Optional (two)
INSURANCE INJURY CLAIMS	

General Information

WHERE MADE	U.S.
YEAR OF PRODUCTION	First
PARKING INDEX	Average
BUMPERS	Weak
THEFT RATING	
TWINS	Chev. Venture, Pont. Tr. Sport
DRIVE	Front

Specifications

FUEL ECONOMY (cty/hwy)	18/25	Poor
DRIVING RANGE (miles)	420	Long
SEATING	7	
LENGTH (inches)	187.4	Average
HEAD/LEG ROOM (in.)	39.9/39.9	Cramped
INTERIOR SPACE (cu. ft.)		
CARGO SPACE (cu. ft.)	127	Average

Specifications may vary.

Prices

Model	Retail	Mkup
Silhouette 3dr	22,245	11%
Silhouette 3dr Extended	23,075	11%
Silhouette GL 3dr Extended	24,595	11%
Silhouette GL 4dr Extended	25,145	11%
Silhouette GLS 3dr Extended	26,255	11%

Competition

	POOR ⟷ GOOD	Pg.
Olds Silhouette	(blank)	197
Dodge Caravan	▓ (mid)	130
Ford Windstar	▓ (low)	144
Honda Odyssey	▓ (high)	151
Nissan Quest	▓ (mid)	190

*Due to the importance of crash tests, cars with no results as of publication date cannot be given an overall rating.

Plymouth Voyager

The Voyager, along with the other Chrysler minivans, is leading the pack in sales in a highly competitive minivan market. Safety features include standard dual airbags and a structure that meets 1997 government side impact standards for passenger cars. A new standard ABS system for '97 has lowered pedal feedback which should help increase its performance.

When choosing among the options, you get to choose between four engines: an inadequate 2.5-liter 4-cylinder, an adequate 3-liter V6, or the more powerful 3.3-liter or 3.8-liter V6s. All except the 3.8-liter are equally efficient. Since Grand Voyagers have a longer wheelbase and a body with more room, the 3.3-liter is worth the extra money. Handling improves with the heavy duty suspension, and the ride remains good. The built-in child restraints are an excellent option.

The Ratings

	POOR ‖ ‖ GOOD
COMPARATIVE RATING	(mid)
CRASH TEST *	(mid)
SAFETY FEATURES	(good)
FUEL ECONOMY	(poor)
PM COST	(good)
REPAIR COST	(good)
WARRANTY	(poor)
COMPLAINTS	(mid)
INSURANCE COST	(good)

Safety

CRASH TEST	Average
AIRBAGS	Dual
ABS	4-wheel
DAY. RUNNING LIGHTS	None
BELT ADJUSTORS	Standard
BUILT-IN CHILD SEAT	Optional (two)
INSURANCE INJURY CLAIMS	Low

General Information

WHERE MADE	U.S./Austria/Canada
YEAR OF PRODUCTION	Second
PARKING INDEX	Average
BUMPERS	Strong
THEFT RATING	
TWINS	Dodge Caravan
DRIVE	Front

Specifications

FUEL ECONOMY (cty/hwy)	20/25	Poor
DRIVING RANGE (miles)	440	Long
SEATING	7	
LENGTH (inches)	186.3	Average
HEAD/LEG ROOM (in.)	39.8/41.2	Average
INTERIOR SPACE (cu. ft.)		
CARGO SPACE (cu. ft.)	143	Large

Specifications may vary.

Prices

Model	Retail	Mkup
Voyager	17,235	10%
Voyager SE	19,925	10%
Grand Voyager	18,580	10%
Grand Voyager SE	20,755	10%

Competition

	POOR ‖ ‖ GOOD	Pg.
Plymouth Voyager	(mid)	198
Ford Windstar	(poor)	144
Honda Odyssey	(good)	151
Mazda MPV	(poor-mid)	172
Nissan Quest	(mid)	190

*A version of this vehicle is scheduled to be tested later this year. Results are expected to be equal or better.

Pontiac Bonneville

If you like options, the Bonneville, GM's sportiest large sedan, may be the car for you. The base model is the SE, and the SSE is the up-level version. The SLE is a sporty package available on the SE. Traction control is available on the SSE, and a supercharged engine is offered on both the SE and SSE. Dual airbags and ABS are standard; daytime running lamps are a great standard safety feature.

You can easily spend over $25,000 for a Bonneville, so shop wisely. Stick to the base SE with the performance and handling package. The base 3.8-liter V6 is powerful enough; the optional, supercharged V6 only adds a little more power and more repair complexity. Interior room and trunk space is good; the driver's visibility could be better. The Bonneville is good competition to the Japanese luxury sports sedans.

The Ratings

	POOR — GOOD
COMPARATIVE RATING	■ (good side)
CRASH TEST*	■
SAFETY FEATURES	■
FUEL ECONOMY	■
PM COST	■
REPAIR COST	■
WARRANTY	■ (poor side)
COMPLAINTS	■
INSURANCE COST	■

Safety

CRASH TEST	Good
AIRBAGS	Dual
ABS	4-wheel
DAY. RUNNING LIGHTS	Standard
BELT ADJUSTORS	Standard
BUILT-IN CHILD SEAT	None
INSURANCE INJURY CLAIMS	Very Low

General Information

WHERE MADE	U.S.
YEAR OF PRODUCTION	Sixth
PARKING INDEX	Hard
BUMPERS	Strong
THEFT RATING	Very Low
TWINS	Buick LeSabre, Olds 88
DRIVE	Front

Specifications

FUEL ECONOMY (cty/hwy)	19/28	Poor
DRIVING RANGE (miles)	396	Average
SEATING	5/6	
LENGTH (inches)	200.5	Long
HEAD/LEG ROOM (in.)	39.2/42.6	Roomy
INTERIOR SPACE (cu. ft.)	110	Very Roomy
CARGO SPACE (cu. ft.)	18	Large

Specifications may vary.

Prices

Model	Retail	Mkup
Bonneville	22,719	10%

Competition

	POOR — GOOD	Pg.
Pontiac Bonneville	■	199
Chrysler Concorde	■	126
Mazda Millenia	■	171
Nissan Maxima	■	189
Volvo 850	■	223

*A version of this vehicle is scheduled to be tested later this year. Results are expected to be equal or better.

Pontiac Firebird

Like its twin, the Camaro, the Firebird has been a mainstay in the American sports car market for many years and its looks and styling have helped make it one of the best selling sports cars around. New for '97 is a center console with dual power outlets which is a very nice feature. The Firebird has always been a strong performer in the crash tests and it comes with dual airbags and optional 4-wheel ABS.

The standard 3.8 liter V6 should offer good power and acceleration. The Firebird added a new trim level last year, the RS, to complement the coupe, convertible and Trans Am versions. The Trans Am comes standard with a 5.7-Liter V8 that is more powerful and only slightly less economical than the standard engine. The ride is firm and the handling is good. Room inside is good for the driver and front seat passenger.

The Ratings

	POOR	GOOD
COMPARATIVE RATING		
CRASH TEST		
SAFETY FEATURES		
FUEL ECONOMY		
PM COST		
REPAIR COST		
WARRANTY		
COMPLAINTS		
INSURANCE COST		

Safety

CRASH TEST	Very Good
AIRBAGS	Dual
ABS	4-wheel (optional)
DAY. RUNNING LIGHTS	Standard
BELT ADJUSTORS	None
BUILT-IN CHILD SEAT	None
INSURANCE INJURY CLAIMS	Average

General Information

WHERE MADE	Canada
YEAR OF PRODUCTION	Fifth
PARKING INDEX	Average
BUMPERS	Strong
THEFT RATING	Average
TWINS	Chevrolet Camaro
DRIVE	Rear

Specifications

FUEL ECONOMY (cty/hwy)	19/30	Average
DRIVING RANGE (miles)	357	Short
SEATING	4	
LENGTH (inches)	195.6	Long
HEAD/LEG ROOM (in.)	37.2/43.0	Cramped
INTERIOR SPACE (cu. ft.)	84	Cramped
CARGO SPACE (cu. ft.)	13	Small

Specifications may vary.

Prices

Model	Retail	Mkup
Firebird	17,649	9%

Competition

	POOR	GOOD	Pg.
Pontiac Firebird			200
Chevrolet Camaro			119
Eagle Talon			133
Ford Mustang			140
Mitsubishi Eclipse			184

Pontiac Grand Am

After receiving a face lift in '96, Pontiac's best-seller receives very few changes for 1997. The most notable change is the addition of air conditioning to the standard equipment list, a feature that many cars in its size-class don't offer as standard. Dual airbags and daytime running lamps are standard and you can find adjustable safety belts which should improve comfort.

The standard 2.4-liter Twin Cam engine makes the Grand Am quite fun to drive, though fuel economy is lousy. There are plenty of options including 2 trim levels: SE coupe and sedan and GT coupe and sedan. Seating is tight when you have three adults in the back seat; two should be comfortable. Ride is good and the Grand Am handles well. Interior noise is acceptable and driver vision is good. The Grand Am competes well with such cars as the Nissan Altima.

The Ratings

	POOR → GOOD
COMPARATIVE RATING	(rating: good)
CRASH TEST *	(rating: good)
SAFETY FEATURES	(rating: good)
FUEL ECONOMY	(rating: below average)
PM COST	(rating: above average)
REPAIR COST	(rating: above average)
WARRANTY	(rating: poor)
COMPLAINTS	(rating: good)
INSURANCE COST	(rating: below average)

Safety

CRASH TEST	Good
AIRBAGS	Dual
ABS	4-wheel (optional)
DAY. RUNNING LIGHTS	Standard
BELT ADJUSTORS	Standard
BUILT-IN CHILD SEAT	None
INSURANCE INJURY CLAIMS	Average

General Information

WHERE MADE	U.S.
YEAR OF PRODUCTION	Sixth
PARKING INDEX	Easy
BUMPERS	Strong
THEFT RATING	Very Low
TWINS	Buick Skylark, Olds Achieva
DRIVE	Front

Specifications

FUEL ECONOMY (cty/hwy)	23/33	Average
DRIVING RANGE (miles)	395	Average
SEATING	5	
LENGTH (inches)	186.9	Average
HEAD/LEG ROOM (in.)	37.8/43.1	Average
INTERIOR SPACE (cu. ft.)	89	Cramped
CARGO SPACE (cu. ft.)	13	Small

Specifications may vary.

Prices

Model	Retail	Mkup
Grand Am	15,159	9%

Competition

	POOR → GOOD	Pg.
Pontiac Grand Am	(rating)	201
Ford Taurus	(rating)	142
Honda Accord	(rating)	148
Mazda 626	(rating)	169
VW Passat	(rating)	222

*A version of this vehicle is scheduled to be tested later this year. Results are expected to be equal or better.

Pontiac Grand Prix

There are plenty of new features on this year's Grand Prix, but the most obvious is the exterior. Pontiac has developed a wide track stance and a low roof line to produce a unique and exciting car. The exterior lines are flowing and they are nicely complemented by new front and rear fascias. Inside, a new driver control cockpit should improve comfort. The Grand Prix comes with dual airbags and 4-wheel ABS.

The Grand Prix is available in both coupe and sedan body styles with your choice of two trim levels, the base SE or the up-level GT. The standard 195 horsepower 3.8 liter V6 engine should deliver more than enough power for this car, though you can choose a supercharged version of the same engine and get 45 more horses. The Grand Prix is worth, at least, a test drive.

The Ratings

	POOR — GOOD
COMPARATIVE RATING*	(no rating)
CRASH TEST	(no rating)
SAFETY FEATURES	Good
FUEL ECONOMY	Below average
PM COST	Average
REPAIR COST	Average
WARRANTY	Poor
COMPLAINTS	Average
INSURANCE COST	Average

Safety

CRASH TEST	No government results
AIRBAGS	Dual
ABS	4-wheel
DAY. RUNNING LIGHTS	Standard
BELT ADJUSTORS	None
BUILT-IN CHILD SEAT	Optional
INSURANCE INJURY CLAIMS	

General Information

WHERE MADE	U.S.
YEAR OF PRODUCTION	First
PARKING INDEX	Average
BUMPERS	Strong
THEFT RATING	
TWINS	Buick Century
DRIVE	Front

Specifications

FUEL ECONOMY (cty/hwy)	20/29	Average
DRIVING RANGE (miles)	414	Average
SEATING	5	
LENGTH (inches)	196.5	Long
HEAD/LEG ROOM (in.)	38.3/42.4	Average
INTERIOR SPACE (cu. ft.)	99	Average
CARGO SPACE (cu. ft.)	16	Average

Specifications may vary.

Prices

Model	Retail	Mkup
Grand Prix	18,579	9%

Competition

	POOR — GOOD	Pg.
Pontiac Grand Prix	(no rating)	202
Honda Accord		148
Hyundai Sonata		155
Mercury Mystique		179
Olds Cut. Supreme		196

*Due to the importance of crash tests, cars with no results as of publication date cannot be given an overall rating.

Pontiac Sunfire

The Sunfire, twin of the Cavalier, is a good seller with attractive styling and a fun-to-drive feeling. The coupes, and especially the convertibles, have borrowed heavily from the Firebird's design, and this helps in catering to young drivers looking for an affordable, sporty car. Dual airbags and ABS are standard. Standard daytime running lamps and optional traction control are great features.

The SE coupe, sedan and convertible come standard with a 2.2-liter engine that is only adequate. The GT coupe has a 2.4-liter dual cam engine with 25% more power. Ride is good on smooth roads, a little bumpy on anything else. Noise level is better than most competitors. Attractive styling, adequate performance and generous front seat room make the Sunfire a strong choice among inexpensive sports cars.

The Ratings

	POOR → GOOD
COMPARATIVE RATING	■ (good side)
CRASH TEST*	■ (middle)
SAFETY FEATURES	■ (good side)
FUEL ECONOMY	■ (good side)
PM COST	■ (good side)
REPAIR COST	■ (middle)
WARRANTY	■ (poor side)
COMPLAINTS	■ (good side)
INSURANCE COST	■ (middle)

Safety

CRASH TEST	Average
AIRBAGS	Dual
ABS	4-wheel
DAY. RUNNING LIGHTS	Standard
BELT ADJUSTORS	Standard (Sdn. Only)
BUILT-IN CHILD SEAT	None
INSURANCE INJURY CLAIMS	High

General Information

WHERE MADE	U.S.
YEAR OF PRODUCTION	Third
PARKING INDEX	Average
BUMPERS	Strong
THEFT RATING	
TWINS	Chevrolet Cavalier
DRIVE	Front

Specifications

FUEL ECONOMY (cty/hwy)	25/37	Good
DRIVING RANGE (miles)	441	Long
SEATING	5	
LENGTH (inches)	181.7	Short
HEAD/LEG ROOM (in.)	38.9/42.1	Average
INTERIOR SPACE (cu. ft.)	92	Average
CARGO SPACE (cu. ft.)	13	Small

Specifications may vary.

Prices

Model	Retail	Mkup
Sunfire	12,559	8%

Competition

	POOR → GOOD	Pg.
Pontiac Sunfire	■ (good side)	203
Dodge Neon	■ (poor side)	132
Honda Civic	■ (middle)	149
Nissan Sentra	■ (good side)	191
Toyota Tercel	■ (middle)	220

*A version of this vehicle is scheduled to be tested later this year. Results are expected to be equal or better.

Pontiac Trans Sport

In GM's constant pursuit to win over customers from the Chrysler minivans, it has introduced a totally re-designed version of the Trans Sport for 1997. The Trans Sport, twin of the Chevrolet Venture and Oldsmobile Silhouette, has a redesigned exterior and an improved interior. Seats are now easier to move and, like the Chryslers, the Trans Sport has a driver's side sliding door. Standard for 1997 are dual airbags and 4-wheel ABS.

The Trans Sport comes in three versions: regular length with one sliding door, extended length with one sliding door, or extended length with two sliding doors. There are also five seating arrangements with a total capacity of eight. The standard engine is a 3.4 liter V6 which should proved ample power. Many comfort features are available including 17 cup holders!

The Ratings

	POOR	GOOD
COMPARATIVE RATING*		
CRASH TEST		
SAFETY FEATURES		■
FUEL ECONOMY	■	
PM COST		■
REPAIR COST		■
WARRANTY	■	
COMPLAINTS		■
INSURANCE COST		■

Safety

CRASH TEST	No government results
AIRBAGS	Dual
ABS	4-wheel
DAY. RUNNING LIGHTS	Standard
BELT ADJUSTORS	None
BUILT-IN CHILD SEAT	Optional (two)
INSURANCE INJURY CLAIMS	

General Information

WHERE MADE	U.S.
YEAR OF PRODUCTION	First
PARKING INDEX	Average
BUMPERS	Strong
THEFT RATING	
TWINS	Chev. Venture, Silhouette
DRIVE	Front

Specifications

FUEL ECONOMY (cty/hwy)	18/25	Poor
DRIVING RANGE (miles)	420	Long
SEATING	7/8	
LENGTH (inches)	187.3	Average
HEAD/LEG ROOM (in.)	39.9/39.9	Cramped
INTERIOR SPACE (cu. ft.)		
CARGO SPACE (cu. ft.)	127	Average

Specifications may vary.

Prices

Model	Retail	Mkup
Trans Sport 2dr	21,049	11%
Trans Sport 3dr Extended	22,009	11%
Trans Sport 4dr Extended	23,939	11%

Competition

	POOR	GOOD	Pg.
Pont. Trans Sport			204
Dodge Caravan	■		130
Ford Windstar	■		144
Nissan Quest		■	190
Toyota Previa	■		219

*Due to the importance of crash tests, cars with no results as of publication date cannot be given an overall rating.

Saab 900

The 900, Saab's best-selling car, enters 1997 with only minor changes after a relatively successful 1996. Changes are planned for 1998 which include a widening of the car's track to increase interior room. Dual airbags and ABS are standard, as are daytime running lights.

The 900 S comes with an adequate 2.3-liter 4-cylinder engine, but the SE sedan and convertible come with a more powerful 2.5-liter V6. If you want even more power, choose the turbocharged version of the 4-cylinder available on the SE coupe and convertible. The 900 has room for four, plus plenty of luggage, though adults will be cramped in the rear of the convertible. Handling is responsive, and controls are designed well and easy to use. A dealer-installed integrated child safety seat is an excellent option. The 900 is a fine example of Saab's engineering.

The Ratings

	POOR → GOOD
COMPARATIVE RATING	▣ (middle)
CRASH TEST	▣ (good)
SAFETY FEATURES	▣ (good)
FUEL ECONOMY	▣ (middle-low)
PM COST	▣ (good)
REPAIR COST	▣ (poor)
WARRANTY	▣ (middle-good)
COMPLAINTS	▣ (poor)
INSURANCE COST	▣ (poor)

Safety

CRASH TEST	Good
AIRBAGS	Dual
ABS	4-wheel
DAY. RUNNING LIGHTS	Standard
BELT ADJUSTORS	Standard
BUILT-IN CHILD SEAT	Optional
INSURANCE INJURY CLAIMS	Very Low

General Information

WHERE MADE	Sweden/Germany
YEAR OF PRODUCTION	Fourth
PARKING INDEX	Easy
BUMPERS	Strong
THEFT RATING	Very Low
TWINS	
DRIVE	Front

Specifications

FUEL ECONOMY (cty/hwy)	21/29	Average
DRIVING RANGE (miles)	432	Long
SEATING	5	
LENGTH (inches)	182.6	Short
HEAD/LEG ROOM (in.)	39.3/42.3	Average
INTERIOR SPACE (cu. ft.)	92	Average
CARGO SPACE (cu. ft.)	24	Very Large

Specifications may vary.

Prices

Model	Retail	Mkup
900 S 3dr	24,995	12%
900 S 5dr	25,995	12%
900 SE 3dr	29,995	12%
900 SE 5dr	30,995	12%
900 S 2dr Convertible	24,995	12%

Competition

	POOR → GOOD	Pg.
Saab 900	▣ (middle)	205
Audi A6	▣ (good)	105
BMW 3-Series	▣ (low-middle)	106
Mazda Millenia	▣ (middle-good)	171
Volvo 850	▣ (poor)	223

While most Americans shy away from hatchbacks, Saab is one auto maker that continues to have success with its 5-door hatchback model, the 9000. A strong performer in the government crash test program, the 9000 comes with dual airbags and ABS as standard.

The 9000 comes in only three trim levels, the CS, CSE and Aero, all of which are hatchbacks. With three engine choices, you will find the right amount of power, but the 2.4-liter base engine is a great choice. Interior room is spacious and comfortable. Standard daytime running lights help make it easier to see and contribute greatly to car safety. Luggage space is generous, and controls and instruments are easy to use. Ride is comfortable for both driver and passengers. Most Saab owners have only praise for their cars.

The Ratings

	POOR → GOOD
COMPARATIVE RATING	▐ (high)
CRASH TEST	▐ (high)
SAFETY FEATURES	▐ (high)
FUEL ECONOMY	▐ (mid)
PM COST	▐ (high)
REPAIR COST	▐ (poor)
WARRANTY	▐ (mid-high)
COMPLAINTS	▐ (low-mid)
INSURANCE COST	▐ (mid)

Safety

CRASH TEST	Good
AIRBAGS	Dual
ABS	4-wheel
DAY. RUNNING LIGHTS	Standard
BELT ADJUSTORS	Standard
BUILT-IN CHILD SEAT	Optional
INSURANCE INJURY CLAIMS	Low

General Information

WHERE MADE	Sweden/Germay
YEAR OF PRODUCTION	Twelfth
PARKING INDEX	Easy
BUMPERS	Strong
THEFT RATING	Very Low
TWINS	
DRIVE	Front

Specifications

FUEL ECONOMY (cty/hwy)	20/29	Average
DRIVING RANGE (miles)	400	Average
SEATING	5	
LENGTH (inches)	187.4	Average
HEAD/LEG ROOM (in.)	38.6/41.7	Cramped
INTERIOR SPACE (cu. ft.)	99	Average
CARGO SPACE (cu. ft.)	24	Very Large

Specifications may vary.

Prices

Model	Retail	Mkup
9000 CS	31,695	13%
9000 CSE 2.3	31,695	13%
9000 CSE 3.0	40,495	13%
9000 Aero	41,495	13%

Competition

	POOR → GOOD	Pg.
Saab 9000	▐ (mid-high)	206
Audi A6	▐ (high)	105
Infiniti I30	▐ (mid-high)	157
Mazda Millenia	▐ (mid)	171
Pontiac Bonneville	▐ (mid-high)	199

Saturn SC

Unlike its sibling, the SL/SW, the SC was not all new last year. Instead, Saturn held off on the revision a year to concentrate on the promotion of the SL/SW. Now it's the SC's turn and Saturn presents a new, sleeker looking coupe for 1997. The SC has a new exterior which includes a new deck lid and a slightly different headlight configuration which includes standard daytime running lights. Other safety features include standard dual airbags and optional ABS.

On the interior, the SC looks much like the SL/SW. New inside trim and freshened controls increase comfort. The SC is powered by a 1.9 liter 4-cylinder engine that delivers 100 horsepower, not tops in this competitive market. Ride should be fairly smooth, though less so on rough roads. Noise levels inside have been reduced.

The Ratings

	POOR GOOD
COMPARATIVE RATING*	
CRASH TEST	
SAFETY FEATURES	
FUEL ECONOMY	
PM COST	
REPAIR COST	
WARRANTY	
COMPLAINTS	
INSURANCE COST	

Safety

CRASH TEST	No government results
AIRBAGS	Dual
ABS	4-wheel (optional)
DAY. RUNNING LIGHTS	Standard
BELT ADJUSTORS	Standard
BUILT-IN CHILD SEAT	None
INSURANCE INJURY CLAIMS	

General Information

WHERE MADE	U.S.
YEAR OF PRODUCTION	First
PARKING INDEX	Easy
BUMPERS	Strong
THEFT RATING	
TWINS	
DRIVE	Front

Specifications

FUEL ECONOMY (cty/hwy)	28/40	Good
DRIVING RANGE (miles)	403	Average
SEATING	5	
LENGTH (inches)	180.0	Short
HEAD/LEG ROOM (in.)	38.5/42.6	Average
INTERIOR SPACE (cu. ft.)	77	Vry. Cramped
CARGO SPACE (cu. ft.)	11	Small

Specifications may vary.

Prices

Model	Retail	Mkup
SC1	12,495	15%
SC2	13,695	15%

Competition

	POOR GOOD	Pg.
Saturn SC		207
Chevrolet Cavalier		120
Dodge Neon		132
Geo Prizm		147
Nissan Sentra		191

*Due to the importance of crash tests, cars with no results as of publication date cannot be given an overall rating.

Both the SL (sedan) and the SW (wagon) were all-new for 1996, so this year's models receive very few changes. Last year's design brought a higher roofline and new safety features like standard daytime running lamps. The SL and SW come with standard dual airbags and optional ABS.

The dual over-head cam engine available on the SL and the SW is more powerful than the base 4-cylinder model and only reduces fuel efficiency slightly. The raised roofline adds headroom which makes the sedan and wagon more comfortable, although the back seat is still tight for adults. The ride is good on smooth roads. Gauges and controls are well placed and easy to use. The noise level is not the best available in this crowed compact market. This economically priced vehicle competes nicely with the Dodge Neon and Chevy Cavalier.

The Ratings

	POOR → GOOD
COMPARATIVE RATING*	(no rating)
CRASH TEST	(no rating)
SAFETY FEATURES	▓ (good)
FUEL ECONOMY	▓ (good)
PM COST	▓ (poor)
REPAIR COST	▓ (good)
WARRANTY	▓ (below average)
COMPLAINTS	▓ (average)
INSURANCE COST	▓ (good)

Safety

CRASH TEST	No government results
AIRBAGS	Dual
ABS	4-wheel (optional)
DAY. RUNNING LIGHTS	Standard
BELT ADJUSTORS	Standard
BUILT-IN CHILD SEAT	None
INSURANCE INJURY CLAIMS	Average (SW=Low)

General Information

WHERE MADE	U.S.
YEAR OF PRODUCTION	Second
PARKING INDEX	Easy
BUMPERS	Strong
THEFT RATING	
TWINS	
DRIVE	Front

Specifications

FUEL ECONOMY (cty/hwy)	28/40	Good
DRIVING RANGE (miles)	403	Average
SEATING	5	
LENGTH (inches)	176.9	Short
HEAD/LEG ROOM (in.)	39.3/42.5	Roomy
INTERIOR SPACE (cu. ft.)	77	Vry. Cramped
CARGO SPACE (cu. ft.)	11	Small

Specifications may vary.

Prices

Model	Retail	Mkup
SL	10,595	15%
SL1	11,595	15%
SL2	12,495	15%
SW1	12,195	15%
SW2	13,095	15%

Competition

	POOR → GOOD	Pg.
Saturn SL/SW	(no rating)	208
Chevrolet Cavalier	▓ (average)	120
Honda Civic	▓ (below average)	149
Nissan Sentra	▓ (good)	191
Toyota Corolla	▓ (above average)	217

*Due to the importance of crash tests, cars with no results as of publication date cannot be given an overall rating.

Subaru Impreza

The Impreza, which replaced the Loyale in 1995, is the smallest of the three Subaru cars. The sedan and coupe come in base, L or LX, and the wagon comes in L, LX or Outback. For 1997, the Impreza receives a facelift which includes a new front bumper, grille and hood. Standard on the Impreza are dual airbags; ABS is optional.

Base models are front-wheel drive, LX models are all-wheel drive, and L and Outback can be either. There are as many engines to choose from as there are trim levels. The base model's engine is a 1.8-liter 4-cylinder, though a more powerful 2.2-liter 4-cylinder is standard on the LX and optional on the L and Outback. The LX is easily the best with its rear stabilizer bar; it out handles the cheaper models. Front seats are comfortable; the back seat is the typical subcompact squeeze, and trunk space is small.

The Ratings

	POOR	GOOD
COMPARATIVE RATING		
CRASH TEST		
SAFETY FEATURES		
FUEL ECONOMY		
PM COST		
REPAIR COST		
WARRANTY		
COMPLAINTS		
INSURANCE COST		

Safety

CRASH TEST	Good
AIRBAGS	Dual
ABS	4-wheel (optional)
DAY. RUNNING LIGHTS	None
BELT ADJUSTORS	Std. (Sdn/Wgn Only)
BUILT-IN CHILD SEAT	None
INSURANCE INJURY CLAIMS	Average

General Information

WHERE MADE	Japan
YEAR OF PRODUCTION	Fifth
PARKING INDEX	Very Easy
BUMPERS	Strong
THEFT RATING	Very Low
TWINS	
DRIVE	Front/All

Specifications

FUEL ECONOMY (cty/hwy)	23/30	Average
DRIVING RANGE (miles)	330	Very Short
SEATING	5	
LENGTH (inches)	172.2	Very Short
HEAD/LEG ROOM (in.)	39.2/43.1	Roomy
INTERIOR SPACE (cu. ft.)	84	Cramped
CARGO SPACE (cu. ft.)	11	Small

Specifications may vary.

Prices

Model	Retail	Mkup
Impreza	13,795	8%

Competition

	POOR	GOOD	Pg.
Subaru Impreza			209
Dodge Neon			132
Honda Civic			149
Nissan Sentra			191
Pontiac Sunfire			203

Subaru Legacy

There are seven Legacy models to choose from for 1997, each of which have new exterior changes and slightly modified interiors. The fresh styling the Legacy received in 1995 has helped make this car a good seller and it should continue that way for a number of years. ABS and dual airbags are standard across the board.

You have two engines to choose from: a 2.2-liter 4-cylinder or a 2.5-liter 4-cylinder with 30 more horses. Both engines will deliver decent gas mileage. The base model is front-wheel drive, while the LSi models are all-wheel drive; the Outback model comes in either. New this year is a GT model aimed at sportier buyers. Traction control is available for the front-wheel drive vehicles and is a very good option. Ride and comfort are both good. Changes to the front grill and bumper help improve the looks.

The Ratings

	POOR	GOOD
COMPARATIVE RATING		
CRASH TEST		
SAFETY FEATURES		
FUEL ECONOMY		
PM COST		
REPAIR COST		
WARRANTY		
COMPLAINTS		
INSURANCE COST		

Safety

CRASH TEST	Very Good
AIRBAGS	Dual
ABS	4-wheel
DAY. RUNNING LIGHTS	None
BELT ADJUSTORS	Standard
BUILT-IN CHILD SEAT	None
INSURANCE INJURY CLAIMS	Low

General Information

WHERE MADE	U.S./Japan
YEAR OF PRODUCTION	Third
PARKING INDEX	Easy
BUMPERS	Strong
THEFT RATING	Very Low
TWINS	
DRIVE	Front/All

Specifications

FUEL ECONOMY (cty/hwy)	23/30	Average
DRIVING RANGE (miles)	398	Average
SEATING	5	
LENGTH (inches)	180.9	Short
HEAD/LEG ROOM (in.)	38.9/43.3	Roomy
INTERIOR SPACE (cu. ft.)	92	Average
CARGO SPACE (cu. ft.)	13	Small

Specifications may vary.

Prices

Model	Retail	Mkup
Legacy	16,895	10%

Competition

	POOR GOOD	Pg.
Subaru Legacy		210
Ford Taurus		142
Honda Accord		148
Nissan Altima		188
Olds Achieva		193

Subaru SVX

The SVX, the sportiest and most expensive Subaru, receives a new grille for 97, just like its siblings, the Impreza and Legacy. Its styling is noted by an unusual stripe along the windows, as it tries to be both a luxury and a sport coupe all in one. Dual airbags are standard, and new this year, 4-wheel ABS is standard also.

The SVX is powered by a 3.3-liter 6-cylinder engine linked to an automatic transmission, resulting in adequate power and poor fuel economy. The base L comes in front- or all-wheel drive, or choose the up-level LSi in AWD. Room inside is spacious for the driver and front passenger; the rear seat is not too useful. You will find that the trunk space in the SVX is also very small. Oddly enough, only part of the strange side windows roll down. You may do better with a Chevy Camaro or Honda Prelude.

The Ratings

	POOR — GOOD
COMPARATIVE RATING *	
CRASH TEST	
SAFETY FEATURES	■ (high)
FUEL ECONOMY	■ (low)
PM COST	■ (high)
REPAIR COST	■ (low)
WARRANTY	■ (low)
COMPLAINTS	■ (high)
INSURANCE COST	■ (mid)

Safety

CRASH TEST	No government results
AIRBAGS	Dual
ABS	4-wheel
DAY. RUNNING LIGHTS	None
BELT ADJUSTORS	None
BUILT-IN CHILD SEAT	None
INSURANCE INJURY CLAIMS	

General Information

WHERE MADE	Japan
YEAR OF PRODUCTION	Sixth
PARKING INDEX	Easy
BUMPERS	Strong
THEFT RATING	
TWINS	
DRIVE	Front/All

Specifications

FUEL ECONOMY (cty/hwy)	17/24	Poor
DRIVING RANGE (miles)	370	Short
SEATING	4	
LENGTH (inches)	182.1	Short
HEAD/LEG ROOM (in.)	38.0/43.5	Average
INTERIOR SPACE (cu. ft.)	85	Cramped
CARGO SPACE (cu. ft.)	8	Very Small

Specifications may vary.

Prices

Model	Retail	Mkup
SVX	30,625	10%

Competition

	POOR — GOOD	Pg.
Subaru SVX		211
Chevrolet Camaro	■	119
Ford Mustang	■	140
Nissan 240SX	■	187
Pontiac Firebird	■	200

*Due to the importance of crash tests, cars with no results as of publication date cannot be given an overall rating.

Suzuki Esteem

The Esteem, the larger of Suzuki's two cars, is their first entry into the crowded compact-sedan market. It comes standard with dual airbags and optional ABS. Daytime running lamps are standard.

You can choose between the base model or the upgrade GLX, though both come with the same engine. The standard 1.6-liter 4-cylinder engine offers poor power and little excitement, though you will get 31 miles to the gallon in the city. The interior promises to be tight as the car is nearly 20 inches shorter than the small Ford Contour; trunk space will not be any better. Noise levels should be comfortable inside. Suzuki claims that "you get what you pay for" and they're right. While its price may be enticing, you can definitely get more for your money elsewhere. Look at a Chevy Cavalier or Nissan Sentra.

The Ratings

	POOR ··· GOOD
COMPARATIVE RATING *	
CRASH TEST	
SAFETY FEATURES	
FUEL ECONOMY	
PM COST	
REPAIR COST	
WARRANTY	
COMPLAINTS	
INSURANCE COST	

Safety

CRASH TEST	No government results
AIRBAGS	Dual
ABS	4-wheel (optional)
DAY. RUNNING LIGHTS	Standard
BELT ADJUSTORS	Standard
BUILT-IN CHILD SEAT	None
INSURANCE INJURY CLAIMS	

General Information

WHERE MADE	Canada
YEAR OF PRODUCTION	Second
PARKING INDEX	Very Easy
BUMPERS	Weak
THEFT RATING	
TWINS	
DRIVE	Front

Specifications

FUEL ECONOMY (cty/hwy)	31/37	Good
DRIVING RANGE (miles)	446	Long
SEATING	5	
LENGTH (inches)	165.2	Very Short
HEAD/LEG ROOM (in.)	39.1/42.3	Average
INTERIOR SPACE (cu. ft.)	86	Cramped
CARGO SPACE (cu. ft.)	12	Small

Specifications may vary.

Prices**

Model	Retail	Mkup
Esteem GL Manual	11,599	10%
Esteem GL Auto	12,599	10%
Esteem GLX Manual	12,899	10%
Esteem GLX Auto	13,899	10%

Competition

	POOR ··· GOOD	Pg.
Suzuki Esteem		212
Dodge Neon		132
Geo Metro		146
Hyundai Accent		153
Nissan Sentra		191

**1997 prices not available at press time. Prices based on 1996 data.

212

*Due to the importance of crash tests, cars with no results as of publication date cannot be given an overall rating.

Suzuki Swift

The Swift, along with its twin the Geo Metro, are two of the smallest cars on the road today. As you might expect, their small size helps provide excellent gas mileage. But, don't expect much room inside. Dual airbags are standard and those awful door-mounted belts are gone. ABS is optional.

The Swift offers a fairly puny 1.3-liter 4-cylinder engine. But the fuel economy of all other cars pales in comparison to the Swift. However, efficiency suffers dramatically at the hands of the optional automatic transmission, so stick to the standard 5-speed. Room for two is tight; the rear seat is really for kids only. Handling is quick and precise, but crosswinds and large trucks can pose a problem. The starting price is about $9,000 and you can get many options. This is true basic transportation, and a good choice.

The Ratings

	POOR GOOD
COMPARATIVE RATING	▮ (good side)
CRASH TEST	▮ (good side)
SAFETY FEATURES	▮ (good side)
FUEL ECONOMY	▮ (good side)
PM COST	▮ (middle)
REPAIR COST	▮ (poor side)
WARRANTY	▮ (poor side)
COMPLAINTS	▮ (good side)
INSURANCE COST	▮ (poor side)

Safety

CRASH TEST	Good
AIRBAGS	Dual
ABS	4-wheel (optional)
DAY. RUNNING LIGHTS	Standard
BELT ADJUSTORS	None
BUILT-IN CHILD SEAT	None
INSURANCE INJURY CLAIMS	

General Information

WHERE MADE	Japan
YEAR OF PRODUCTION	Third
PARKING INDEX	Very Easy
BUMPERS	Weak
THEFT RATING	
TWINS	Geo Metro
DRIVE	Front

Specifications

FUEL ECONOMY (cty/hwy)	39/43	Very Good
DRIVING RANGE (miles)	435	Long
SEATING	4	
LENGTH (inches)	149.4	Very Short
HEAD/LEG ROOM (in.)	39.1/42.5	Average
INTERIOR SPACE (cu. ft.)	81	Cramped
CARGO SPACE (cu. ft.)	8	Very Small

Specifications may vary.

Prices**

Model	Retail	Mkup
Swift Base	8,699	9%

Competition

	POOR GOOD	Pg.
Suzuki Swift	▮ (good side)	213
Ford Aspire	▮ (poor side)	136
Geo Metro	▮ (poor side)	146
Hyundai Accent	▮ (poor side)	153
Toyota Tercel	▮ (middle)	220

**1997 prices not available at press time. Prices based on 1996 data.

213

Toyota Avalon

The Toyota Avalon, a model built exclusively in Kentucky, is a stretched version of Toyota's flagship, the Camry. With more interior room and a higher price tag than the Camry, the Avalon is more upscale in design, competing with the Mercury Sable. Dual airbags are standard as is ABS.

The Avalon's extra length makes the ride a bit smoother, but it hardly weighs more than the Camry, so the handling is just as responsive. The Avalon comes in two trim levels, base XL and deluxe XLS, both with the same powerful 3-liter V6 and automatic transmission. Fuel economy is merely average. Although the Avalon is a foot longer than the Dodge Intrepid, interior space on the two vehicles is comparable. Five adults will be comfortable, but don't count on fitting three adults comfortably on the front bench seat.

The Ratings

	POOR ⟷ GOOD
COMPARATIVE RATING	▪ (left-center)
CRASH TEST	▪ (good)
SAFETY FEATURES	▪ (good)
FUEL ECONOMY	▪ (center)
PM COST	▪ (left)
REPAIR COST	▪ (left)
WARRANTY	▪ (poor)
COMPLAINTS	▪ (center-right)
INSURANCE COST	▪ (center)

Safety

CRASH TEST	Very Good
AIRBAGS	Dual
ABS	4-wheel
DAY. RUNNING LIGHTS	None
BELT ADJUSTORS	Standard
BUILT-IN CHILD SEAT	None
INSURANCE INJURY CLAIMS	Average

General Information

WHERE MADE	U.S.
YEAR OF PRODUCTION	Third
PARKING INDEX	Average
BUMPERS	Weak
THEFT RATING	Very Low
TWINS	
DRIVE	Front

Specifications

FUEL ECONOMY (cty/hwy)	21/31	Average
DRIVING RANGE (miles)	444	Long
SEATING	5/6	
LENGTH (inches)	190.2	Average
HEAD/LEG ROOM (in.)	39.1/44.1	Very Roomy
INTERIOR SPACE (cu. ft.)	106	Roomy
CARGO SPACE (cu. ft.)	15	Average

Specifications may vary.

Prices

Model	Retail	Mkup
Avalon XL Bucket Seats	23,958	14%
Avalon XL Bench Seats	24,778	14%
Avalon XLS	27,468	14%

Competition

	POOR ⟷ GOOD	Pg.
Toyota Avalon	▪ (left-center)	214
Chrysler Concorde	▪ (center)	126
Chrysler LHS	▪ (center)	127
Ford Crown Victoria	▪ (center-right)	138
Nissan Maxima	▪ (center-right)	189

Toyota Camry

Toyota is touting the all-new 1997 Camry as quieter, lighter and more powerful than 1996's version. The new Camry should continue to attract buyers with its increased interior room and better ride, thanks to a stretched chassis. You have your choice between three trim levels: CE, LE and XLE and there are many option packages. Dual airbags are standard and 4-wheel ABS is optional.

The Camry CE comes standard with a 2.2 liter 4-cylinder engine which produces 133 horsepower. You can opt for a more powerful V6 engine with a slight loss in fuel economy. Just as in years past, handling should be crisp and responsive. Controls are well designed and easy to use and the interior is comfortable for both driver and passengers. The '97 Camry should continue Toyota's tradition of good, dependable cars.

The Ratings

	POOR ⟶ GOOD
COMPARATIVE RATING*	(no rating)
CRASH TEST	(no rating)
SAFETY FEATURES	▮ (high)
FUEL ECONOMY	▮ (mid-high)
PM COST	▮ (low)
REPAIR COST	▮ (low)
WARRANTY	▮ (low)
COMPLAINTS	▮ (mid)
INSURANCE COST	▮ (mid)

Safety

CRASH TEST	No government results
AIRBAGS	Dual
ABS	4-wheel (optional)
DAY. RUNNING LIGHTS	None
BELT ADJUSTORS	Standard
BUILT-IN CHILD SEAT	Optional
INSURANCE INJURY CLAIMS	

General Information

WHERE MADE	U.S./Japan
YEAR OF PRODUCTION	First
PARKING INDEX	Easy
BUMPERS	Weak
THEFT RATING	
TWINS	Lexus ES300
DRIVE	Front

Specifications

FUEL ECONOMY (cty/hwy)	23/31	Average
DRIVING RANGE (miles)	481	Very Long
SEATING	5	
LENGTH (inches)	188.5	Average
HEAD/LEG ROOM (in.)	38.6/43.5	Roomy
INTERIOR SPACE (cu. ft.)	97	Average
CARGO SPACE (cu. ft.)	14	Average

Specifications may vary.

Prices

Model	Retail	Mkup
Camry CE 4dr	16,818	10%
Camry CE V-6 4dr	19,668	10%
Camry LE 4dr	20,288	10%
Camry XLE 4dr	22,228	10%
Camry LE V-6 4dr	22,588	10%

Competition

	POOR ⟶ GOOD	Pg.
Toyota Camry	(no rating)	215
Ford Taurus	▮ (high)	142
Honda Accord	▮ (low)	148
Mazda 626	▮ (mid)	169
Pontiac Bonneville	▮ (mid-high)	199

*Due to the importance of crash tests, cars with no results as of publication date cannot be given an overall rating.

Toyota Celica

The Celica is Toyota's mid-priced sports coupe between the cheaper Paseo and the more expensive Supra. Trying to pick up the lost sales from the discontinued MR2, the Celica has no major changes this year. You can choose between a hatchback, a coupe or a convertible. Dual airbags are standard and four-wheel ABS is optional.

The base model ST gets a 1.8-liter 4-cylinder engine that's meek for a supposed performance car, although fuel economy is pretty good. The up-level GT coupe and convertible get a slightly more powerful 2.2-liter 4-cylinder engine that's not quite as economical. The standard suspension handles well, but the sport suspension available on the GT is even better. Ride is decent. The dashboard is functional and intelligently laid out. The interior has room for two; the rear seat seems to be an afterthought.

The Ratings

	POOR → GOOD
COMPARATIVE RATING*	(no rating)
CRASH TEST	(no rating)
SAFETY FEATURES	7
FUEL ECONOMY	8
PM COST	2
REPAIR COST	3
WARRANTY	1
COMPLAINTS	8
INSURANCE COST	1

Safety

CRASH TEST	No government results
AIRBAGS	Dual
ABS	4-wheel (optional)
DAY. RUNNING LIGHTS	None
BELT ADJUSTORS	None
BUILT-IN CHILD SEAT	None
INSURANCE INJURY CLAIMS	Average

General Information

WHERE MADE	Japan
YEAR OF PRODUCTION	Fourth
PARKING INDEX	Very Easy
BUMPERS	Strong
THEFT RATING	Average
TWINS	
DRIVE	Front

Specifications

FUEL ECONOMY (cty/hwy)	29/35	Good
DRIVING RANGE (miles)	509	Very Long
SEATING	4	
LENGTH (inches)	174.2	Short
HEAD/LEG ROOM (in.)	34.3/43.1	Vry. Cramped
INTERIOR SPACE (cu. ft.)	77	Vry. Cramped
CARGO SPACE (cu. ft.)	16	Average

Specifications may vary.

Prices

Model	Retail	Mkup
Celica ST	17,548	15%
Celica ST Hatchback	17,908	15%
Celica GT Hatchback	20,598	15%
Celica GT Convertible	24,798	15%

Competition

	POOR → GOOD	Pg.
Toyota Celica		216
Acura Integra	2	101
Eagle Talon	1	133
Ford Probe	7	141
Mazda MX-6	8	173

*Due to the importance of crash tests, cars with no results as of publication date cannot be given an overall rating.

Toyota Corolla

The Corolla can cost up to two thousand dollars more than its twin, the Geo Prizm, but three times as many people buy it because of Toyota's reputation for quality (despite the fact that the two cars roll off the same assembly line in California). Unlike Prizms, Corollas come in wagons as well as sedans. Little has changed for the Corolla. Dual airbags are standard, and ABS is optional.

The 1.6-liter base engine is average, producing only 100 hp; the optional 1.8-liter 4-cylinder adds a touch more power with only a slight loss in fuel efficiency. The Corolla can transport four people in moderate comfort with room for luggage. Handling and ride are good, and the controls are logical and easy to use. Styling and lines are clean and contemporary and there is a slight change in the door panels for '97. This is a solid choice, but a bit overpriced, considering the Prizm.

The Ratings

	POOR — GOOD
COMPARATIVE RATING	
CRASH TEST	
SAFETY FEATURES	
FUEL ECONOMY	
PM COST	
REPAIR COST	
WARRANTY	
COMPLAINTS	
INSURANCE COST	

Safety

CRASH TEST	Good
AIRBAGS	Dual
ABS	4-wheel (optional)
DAY. RUNNING LIGHTS	None
BELT ADJUSTORS	Standard
BUILT-IN CHILD SEAT	Optional
INSURANCE INJURY CLAIMS	Vry.High (Wgn.=Avg.)

General Information

WHERE MADE	U.S./Canada
YEAR OF PRODUCTION	Fifth
PARKING INDEX	Very Easy
BUMPERS	Weak
THEFT RATING	Average (2dr=Very Low)
TWINS	Geo Prizm
DRIVE	Front

Specifications

FUEL ECONOMY (cty/hwy)	31/35	Good
DRIVING RANGE (miles)	422	Long
SEATING	5	
LENGTH (inches)	172.0	Very Short
HEAD/LEG ROOM (in.)	38.8/42.4	Average
INTERIOR SPACE (cu. ft.)	86	Cramped
CARGO SPACE (cu. ft.)	13	Small

Specifications may vary.

Prices

Model	Retail	Mkup
Corolla	13,418	10%
Corolla Deluxe	14,608	10%
Corolla CE	15,063	12%

Competition

	POOR — GOOD	Pg.
Toyota Corolla		217
Chevrolet Cavalier		120
Geo Prizm		147
Honda Civic		149
Nissan Sentra		191

The Paseo is basically a Tercel, trying to be a sports car. New for 1997, Toyota adds a convertible version which will be partially assembled in both the US and Japan. The Paseo comes standard with dual airbags and ABS is optional.

The 1.5-liter, 4-cylinder engine cranks out only 93 horsepower, not exactly what you want in a sports car. Both the standard manual and optional automatic transmissions are fairly fuel efficient. If you're tall, you won't fit inside comfortably and forget about the rear seat. The ride is smooth on good roads, but the handling doesn't match up with the sporty looks. Expect a noisy ride. There are plenty of options to choose from which can really push up the price. You'll find more performance and a better value with the Neon Sport or Saturn SC.

The Ratings

	POOR　　　　　　GOOD
COMPARATIVE RATING*	□□□□□□□□□□
CRASH TEST	□□□□□□□□□□
SAFETY FEATURES	□□□□■□□□□□
FUEL ECONOMY	□□□□□□□□■□
PM COST	□□■□□□□□□□
REPAIR COST	□□□□□■□□□□
WARRANTY	□■□□□□□□□□
COMPLAINTS	□□□□□□□□□■
INSURANCE COST	■□□□□□□□□□

Safety

CRASH TEST	No government results
AIRBAGS	Dual
ABS	4-wheel (optional)
DAY. RUNNING LIGHTS	None
BELT ADJUSTORS	None
BUILT-IN CHILD SEAT	None
INSURANCE INJURY CLAIMS	Very High

General Information

WHERE MADE	Japan/U.S.
YEAR OF PRODUCTION	Seventh
PARKING INDEX	Very Easy
BUMPERS	Weak
THEFT RATING	Very Low
TWINS	
DRIVE	Front

Specifications

FUEL ECONOMY (cty/hwy)	31/37	Good
DRIVING RANGE (miles)	393	Average
SEATING	4	
LENGTH (inches)	163.6	Very Short
HEAD/LEG ROOM (in.)	37.8/41.1	Vry. Cramped
INTERIOR SPACE (cu. ft.)	74	Vry. Cramped
CARGO SPACE (cu. ft.)	8	Very Small

Specifications may vary.

Prices

Model	Retail	Mkup
Paseo	13,628	12%
Paseo Convertible	17,148	12%

Competition

	POOR　　　GOOD	Pg.
Toyota Paseo	□□□□□□□□□□	218
Chevrolet Cavalier	□□□□□□■□□□	120
Dodge Neon	□■□□□□□□□□	132
Hyundai Accent	□□□■□□□□□□	153
Suzuki Swift	□□□□□□□■□□	213

*Due to the importance of crash tests, cars with no results as of publication date cannot be given an overall rating.

Toyota Previa

The Previa has plenty of interior room, but has not been able to compete with the Chrysler minivans the past few years. It comes in two trim levels, DX or LE and is available in both two or four wheel drive. Dual airbags are standard, and ABS is optional on all models.

All Previa's seat seven people and have one of the largest interiors in the industry. The standard, and only engine, is a 2.4-liter supercharged engine which is adept at carrying this big vehicle. Handling and ride are about the best you can get in a minivan, especially if you buy an All-Trac version. The interior is comfortable and cargo space is even greater than in the Chrysler "Grand" models. The Previa is a solid minivan—but, in a market with Chrysler's pace-setting minivans and GM's newly redesigned minivans, being "solid" may not be enough.

The Ratings

	POOR GOOD
COMPARATIVE RATING	
CRASH TEST	
SAFETY FEATURES	
FUEL ECONOMY	
PM COST	
REPAIR COST	
WARRANTY	
COMPLAINTS	
INSURANCE COST	

Safety

CRASH TEST	Average
AIRBAGS	Dual
ABS	4-wheel (optional)
DAY. RUNNING LIGHTS	None
BELT ADJUSTORS	Standard
BUILT-IN CHILD SEAT	None
INSURANCE INJURY CLAIMS	Avg. (4WD=Very Low)

General Information

WHERE MADE	Japan
YEAR OF PRODUCTION	Seventh
PARKING INDEX	Average
BUMPERS	Weak
THEFT RATING	Average
TWINS	
DRIVE	Rear/All

Specifications

FUEL ECONOMY (cty/hwy)	18/22	Poor
DRIVING RANGE (miles)	376	Short
SEATING	7	
LENGTH (inches)	187.0	Average
HEAD/LEG ROOM (in.)	39.4/40.1	Cramped
INTERIOR SPACE (cu. ft.)		
CARGO SPACE (cu. ft.)	158	Large

Specifications may vary.

Prices

Model	Retail	Mkup
Previa Deluxe 2wd	25,228	14%
Previa LE 2wd	29,858	14%
Previa Deluxe 4wd	28,838	14%
Previa LE 4wd	33,258	14%

Competition

	POOR GOOD	Pg.
Toyota Previa		219
Ford Windstar		144
Isuzu Oasis		160
Mazda MPV		172
Plymouth Voyager		198

Toyota Tercel

The Tercel is Toyota's cheapest model, but the available options can quickly increase the price tag. Changes for '97 include an update interior fabric and trim panels. Larger wheels help in handling and ride. Dual airbags are standard on the Tercel, though you'll still have to pay extra for ABS.

The 1.5-liter, 4-cylinder engine does a decent job at powering the vehicle, but it only offers 93 horsepower. What you lose in power, you gain in fuel efficiency, but only with the manual transmission. You can choose standard or DX trim levels in two- or four-door models. Interior room is not as large as other vehicles in its size class and it is rather noisy inside during hard accelerations. Look for the mid-year release of a sportier Tercel (seemingly redundant, with the Tercel-based Paseo). A sound, economical choice.

The Ratings

	POOR	GOOD
COMPARATIVE RATING		
CRASH TEST		
SAFETY FEATURES		
FUEL ECONOMY		
PM COST		
REPAIR COST		
WARRANTY		
COMPLAINTS		
INSURANCE COST		

Safety

CRASH TEST	Average
AIRBAGS	Dual
ABS	4-wheel (optional)
DAY. RUNNING LIGHTS	None
BELT ADJUSTORS	Standard (Sdn. Only)
BUILT-IN CHILD SEAT	None
INSURANCE INJURY CLAIMS	Very High

General Information

WHERE MADE	Japan
YEAR OF PRODUCTION	Third
PARKING INDEX	Very Easy
BUMPERS	Weak
THEFT RATING	Very Low
TWINS	
DRIVE	Front

Specifications

FUEL ECONOMY (cty/hwy)	32/39	Good
DRIVING RANGE (miles)	417	Long
SEATING	5	
LENGTH (inches)	161.8	Very Short
HEAD/LEG ROOM (in.)	38.6/41.2	Cramped
INTERIOR SPACE (cu. ft.)	81	Cramped
CARGO SPACE (cu. ft.)	9	Very Small

Specifications may vary.

Prices

Model	Retail	Mkup
Tercel CE 2dr	11,068	8%
Tercel CE Deluxe 4dr	12,528	8%

Competition

	POOR	GOOD	Pg.
Toyota Tercel			220
Chevrolet Cavalier			120
Dodge Neon			132
Honda Civic			149
Nissan Sentra			191

VW makes several cars on the Golf/Jetta platform. There is the Golf, the sportier Golf Sport, the GTI VR6, the Jetta GL, the mid-level Jetta GLS, the up-level Jetta GLX, and the convertible Cabrio. New trim levels for '97 include the Golf TDI, or turbo direct engine, and the Jetta GT. They vary in character, but all have the same basic specifications and components. Dual airbags are standard, ABS is available. Photo is from 1996.

The Golf and Jetta offer a 2-liter 4-cylinder engine or a 2.8-liter V6, though the Cabrio comes only with a more fuel efficient 3-cylinder. All models come with 5-speed manual or automatic overdrive, and a 10-year/100,000 mile power train warranty. For '97, the 2.0 liter engine has been modified to reduce engine noise, making the interior more comfortable. Handling is responsive, and the seats are comfortable.

The Ratings

	POOR → GOOD
COMPARATIVE RATING	Good
CRASH TEST*	Below Average
SAFETY FEATURES	Average
FUEL ECONOMY	Very Good
PM COST	Average
REPAIR COST	Average
WARRANTY	Good
COMPLAINTS	Poor
INSURANCE COST	Average

Safety

CRASH TEST	Average
AIRBAGS	Dual
ABS	4-wheel (optional)
DAY. RUNNING LIGHTS	Standard
BELT ADJUSTORS	Standard
BUILT-IN CHILD SEAT	None
INSURANCE INJURY CLAIMS	High

General Information

WHERE MADE	Mexico/Germany
YEAR OF PRODUCTION	Fourth
PARKING INDEX	Very Easy
BUMPERS	Weak
THEFT RATING	Very Low
TWINS	
DRIVE	Front

Specifications

FUEL ECONOMY (cty/hwy)	40/49	Very Good
DRIVING RANGE (miles)	624	Very Long
SEATING	5	
LENGTH (inches)	173.4	Short
HEAD/LEG ROOM (in.)	39.2/42.3	Average
INTERIOR SPACE (cu. ft.)	88	Cramped
CARGO SPACE (cu. ft.)	15	Average

Specifications may vary.

Prices

Model	Retail	Mkup
Golf GL	13,470	8%
Golf GTI	16,320	8%
Jetta GL	14,570	10%
Jetta GT	14,965	10%
Jetta GLS	16,920	10%

Competition

	POOR → GOOD	Pg.
VW Golf/Jetta	Good	221
Ford Contour	Below Average	137
Hyundai Sonata	Poor	155
Olds Cut. Supreme	Good	196
Nissan Altima	Good	188

*A version of this vehicle is scheduled to be tested later this year. Results are expected to be equal or better.

Volkswagen Passat

The Passat, VW's plushiest and largest model, has a few trim lines, though not nearly as many as its sibling, the Golf/Jetta. One trim level, TDI (Turbo Direct Injection) was new last year and helps attract performance buyers. Dual airbags are standard, as is traction control. ABS is optional. Photo is from '96.

The Passat has the same potent 2.8-liter V6 as the Golf/Jetta GTI, with 5-speed manual or automatic transmission, and a 10-year/100,000 mile power train warranty. The TDI comes with a 2-liter turbocharged diesel engine, the same found in the Golf/Jetta TDI. Acceleration is impressive. The Passat is rigid, and handling is responsive with a firm, sometimes uncomfortable, ride. From the outside, the car looks about the size of the Camry, but its interior room resembles a larger car as seats are roomy enough for four and well designed for long trips.

The Ratings

	POOR ⟶ GOOD
COMPARATIVE RATING	▮ (good)
CRASH TEST	▮ (mid)
SAFETY FEATURES	▮ (mid-good)
FUEL ECONOMY	▮ (good)
PM COST	▮ (good)
REPAIR COST	▮ (poor)
WARRANTY	▮ (mid-good)
COMPLAINTS	▮ (mid)
INSURANCE COST	▮ (poor)

Safety

CRASH TEST	Good
AIRBAGS	Dual
ABS	4-wheel (optional)
DAY. RUNNING LIGHTS	Standard
BELT ADJUSTORS	Standard
BUILT-IN CHILD SEAT	None
INSURANCE INJURY CLAIMS	

General Information

WHERE MADE	Germany
YEAR OF PRODUCTION	Eighth
PARKING INDEX	Easy
BUMPERS	Weak
THEFT RATING	Very High
TWINS	
DRIVE	Front

Specifications

FUEL ECONOMY (cty/hwy)	38/47	Very Good
DRIVING RANGE (miles)	777	Very Long
SEATING	5	
LENGTH (inches)	181.5	Short
HEAD/LEG ROOM (in.)	39.3/45.1	Very Roomy
INTERIOR SPACE (cu. ft.)	99	Average
CARGO SPACE (cu. ft.)	14	Average

Specifications may vary.

Prices

Model	Retail	Mkup
Passat TDI	19,430	11%
Passat TDI Wagon	19,860	11%
Passat GLX	21,890	11%
Passat GLX Wagon	22,320	11%

Competition

	POOR ⟶ GOOD	Pg.
VW Passat	▮ (good)	222
Honda Accord	▮ (poor)	148
Mercury Sable	▮ (mid-good)	180
Nissan Altima	▮ (mid-good)	188
Saab 900	▮ (mid)	205

Volvo 850

The Ratings

	POOR GOOD
COMPARATIVE RATING	□□□□□□□■□
CRASH TEST	□□□□□□■□□
SAFETY FEATURES	□□□□□□□■□
FUEL ECONOMY	□□□□■□□□□
PM COST	■□□□□□□□□
REPAIR COST	□□□□■□□□□
WARRANTY	□□□□□□□■□
COMPLAINTS	□□□□■□□□□
INSURANCE COST	□□□□□□□□■

What is the safest car on the road? If you said, the Volvo 850, you may be right. Safety is high priority to Volvo—the 850 comes standard with dual airbags, daytime running lights and ABS. An integrated child booster seat is available on the 850R. Side-impact airbags are also available. Volvo's best-selling car, the 850 comes in four version, each with two trim levels; needless to say, you have many options to choose from .

This is the first front-wheel drive vehicle Volvo sold in the U.S. The 5-cylinder engine is powerful, but not extremely smooth. The 850 is biased more toward cornering ability than comfort in ride. Inside, the 850 accommodates four people comfortably, though five is a squeeze. Traction control is available and highly recommended. Trunk space is generous. With good crash tests, the 850 should definitely be considered.

Safety

CRASH TEST	Good
AIRBAGS	Dual
ABS	4-wheel
DAY. RUNNING LIGHTS	Standard
BELT ADJUSTORS	Standard
BUILT-IN CHILD SEAT	Optional (Wgn.=Std.)
INSURANCE INJURY CLAIMS	Very Low

General Information

WHERE MADE	Sweden/Belgium
YEAR OF PRODUCTION	Fifth
PARKING INDEX	Easy
BUMPERS	Weak
THEFT RATING	Very Low
TWINS	
DRIVE	Front

Specifications

FUEL ECONOMY (cty/hwy)	20/29	Average
DRIVING RANGE (miles)	444	Long
SEATING	5	
LENGTH (inches)	183.5	Average
HEAD/LEG ROOM (in.)	39.1/41.4	Average
INTERIOR SPACE (cu. ft.)	98	Average
CARGO SPACE (cu. ft.)	14	Average

Specifications may vary.

Prices

Model	Retail	Mkup
854 O	26,710	9%
854 A	27,685	9%
854 GTO	28,040	9%
855 0	28,010	9%
855 A	28,985	9%

Competition

	POOR GOOD	Pg.
Volvo 850	□□□□□□□■□	223
Audi A6	□□□□□□□■□	105
BMW 3-Series	□□□■□□□□□	106
Mazda Millenia	□□□□□■□□□	171
Saab 900	□□□□□■□□□	205

The 960 is the only model being sold in the 900 Series; the 940 was discontinued last year. Volvo's top-level model is relatively unchanged for 1997. Leading the industry in safety, the Volvo 960 has standard side-impact airbags. Along with these new airbags, the 960 also comes standard with daytime running lamps, dual airbags and ABS.

The 960's independent rear suspension provides excellent ride and better-than-average handling, though the smaller Volvo 850 is more maneuverable. The 960 will be slower and less fuel efficient than the 850. Comfort and room for four are exceptional, but the rear center seat should be saved for children; you'll find a fold-out child booster seat, standard in wagons and optional in sedans. Luggage space on the sedan is average, even more on the wagon. A nicely designed car and a good buy.

The Ratings

	POOR ————— GOOD
COMPARATIVE RATING*	(no rating)
CRASH TEST	(no rating)
SAFETY FEATURES	Good
FUEL ECONOMY	Poor-Average
PM COST	Poor
REPAIR COST	Average
WARRANTY	Good
COMPLAINTS	Good
INSURANCE COST	Poor-Average

Safety

CRASH TEST	No government results
AIRBAGS	Dual
ABS	4-wheel
DAY. RUNNING LIGHTS	Standard
BELT ADJUSTORS	Standard
BUILT-IN CHILD SEAT	Optional (Wgn.=Std.)
INSURANCE INJURY CLAIMS	Low (Wgn. = Very Low)

General Information

WHERE MADE	Sweden
YEAR OF PRODUCTION	Seventh
PARKING INDEX	Very Easy
BUMPERS	Weak
THEFT RATING	Low (Wagon=Very Low)
TWINS	
DRIVE	Front

Specifications

FUEL ECONOMY (cty/hwy)	18/26	Poor
DRIVING RANGE (miles)	426	Long
SEATING	5	
LENGTH (inches)	191.8	Long
HEAD/LEG ROOM (in.)	37.4/41.0	Vry. Cramped
INTERIOR SPACE (cu. ft.)	91	Average
CARGO SPACE (cu. ft.)	16	Average

Specifications may vary.

Prices

Model	Retail	Mkup
964	24,300	8%
965	35,850	8%

Competition

	POOR ————— GOOD	Pg.
Volvo 900 Series	(low)	224
Audi A6	Good	105
BMW 3-Series	Poor-Average	106
Infiniti I30	Good	157
Saab 9000	Good	206

*Due to the importance of crash tests, cars with no results as of publication date cannot be given an overall rating.